Cult, Religion, and Pilgrimage

Archaeological Investigations at the Neolithic and Bronze Age Monument Complex of Thornborough, North Yorkshire

Cult, Religion, and Pilgrimage

Archaeological Investigations at the Neolithic and Bronze Age Monument Complex of Thornborough, North Yorkshire

Jan Harding

with contributions by

Lindsay Allason-Jones, Arnold Aspinall[†], Alan Biggins, Ed Dennison, Sarah Groves, Benjamin Johnson, Robert Johnston, Eva Laurie, Peter Makey, Simon Mays, Roger Martlew, Joshua Pollard, Armin Schmidt, Kristian Strutt, and Blaise Vyner

CBA Research Report 174
Council for British Archaeology
2013

Published in 2013 by the Council for British Archaeology
St Mary's House, 66 Bootham, York, YO30 7BZ

A catalogue record for this book is available from the British Library
ISBN 978-1-902771-97-7

DOI: 10.11141/RR174

Typeset by Archétype Informatique, www.archetype-it.com
Printed and bound by Henry Ling Ltd

The publisher acknowledges with gratitude a generous grant from English Heritage towards the cost of
publication

Front cover: Aerial view of the Thornborough henges, looking north (© English Heritage)
Back cover: Excavation underway on the double pit alignment, 1999 (© English Heritage)

Contents

Digital Appendices

(these can be found on the Archaeology Data Service (ADS) website, reference DOI: 10.5284/1020064)

List of figures

Figures in Digital Appendices

List of tables

Tables in Digital Appendices

List of contributors

Lindsay Allason-Jones BA MLitt FSA FSA(Scot)
FMA FRSA
School of History, Classics and Archaeology
Newcastle University
Newcastle upon Tyne
NE1 7RU

Arnold Aspinall†
Formerly Honorary Professor
Department of Archaeological Sciences
University of Bradford
Bradford
BD7 1DP

J Alan Biggins TD MA MSc PhD MRSC MIBiol
FSA FSA(Scot)
Director of Timescape Surveys and Marie Curie
Research Fellow
Northumbria
Main Road
Dinnington
Newcastle upon Tyne
NE13 7JW

Ed Dennison BSc MA
Ed Dennison Archaeological Services Ltd
18 Springdale Way
Beverley
East Yorkshire
HU17 8NU

Sarah Groves BA MSc PhD
Durham University
Department of Archaeology
South Road
Durham
DH1 3LE

Jan Harding BA PhD
School of History, Classics and Archaeology
Newcastle University
Newcastle upon Tyne
NE1 7RU

Benjamin Johnson BA MA
Archaeological Research Services Ltd
Angel House
Bakewell
Derbyshire
DE45 1HB

Robert Johnston BA MA PhD
Department of Archaeology
University of Sheffield
Northgate House
West Street
Sheffield
S1 4ET

Eva Laurie BA PhD
Department of Archaeology
University of York
The King's Manor
York
YO1 7EP

Peter Makey HND BA
Bridge House
17 Bridge Street
Driffield
East Yorkshire
YO25 6DA

Simon Mays BSc MSc PhD
Investigation and Analysis Division
English Heritage
Portsmouth
PO4 9LD

Roger Martlew PhD FSA
Yorkshire Dales Landscape Research Trust
Chapel Beck
Kettlewell
Skipton
BD23 5RL

Joshua Pollard BA PhD FSA
Faculty of Humanities
University of Southampton
Avenue Campus
Highfield
Southampton
SO17 1BF

Armin Schmidt Dipl.-Phys. Dr. rer. nat.
Department of Archaeological Sciences
University of Bradford
Bradford
BD7 1DP

Kristian Strutt BA
Experimental Officer
Faculty of Humanities
University of Southampton
Avenue Campus
Highfield
Southampton
SO17 1BF

Blaise Vyner BA
Director of Blaise Vyner Consultancy
16 College Square
Stokesley
Middlesbrough
TS9 5DL

Acknowledgements

None of the work described in this volume would have been possible without the generous financial support of a number of institutions. The Arts and Humanities Research Board, the British Academy, English Heritage, Reading University, Newcastle University, the Prehistoric Society, the Robert Kiln Charitable Trust, and the Society of Antiquaries of London funded the Vale of Mowbray Neolithic Landscape Project between 1994 and 1998. The Aggregates Levy Sustainability Fund, disbursed by English Heritage, provided a grant for the additional work in 2003–04. The excavation of the double pit alignment in 1998–99 was generously funded by Robert Staveley of Lightwater Holdings plc and its radiocarbon dates provided courtesy of an Oxford Radiocarbon Accelerator Dating Service (ORADS) grant and by further financial support from both CBA Yorkshire and the Yorkshire Archaeological Society Prehistory Research Section.

The fieldwork was supported by farmers and local landowners who provided both access and practical assistance. Particular thanks go to Robert Staveley of Lightwater Holdings plc, Mr Robinson of Howgrave Hall Farm, Mrs D Benson of Chapel Hill Farm, Mr A Almack of Ladybridge Farm, Mr P Almack of Hill House Farm, and Mr C Bourne-Arton of The Lodge, West Tanfield. Many local villagers, particularly Dick Lonsdale of Nosterfield, offered support and a helping hand when it was most needed.

A large number of students from Reading University, Newcastle University, and other European Higher Education institutions, along with volunteers from across Britain, participated in the fieldwork. Their hard work and good humour made the fieldwork both rewarding and enjoyable. They were led by a supervisory team whose dedication and patience should be acknowledged. Special thanks are due to Richard Chatterton, Hannah Lynch, and Leigh Pollinger. Jonathan Shipley and Richard Smalley ably assisted with the ALSF-funded geophysical surveys completed in 2003.

The projects benefited from the expertise of a number of specialists, especially Dr H Cockburn, then of the BBC series *Time Flyers*, Dr A Cooper of the British Geological Survey, Harry Kenwood and Raimonda Usai of the Environmental Archaeology Unit at the University of York, and Robert Shiel of Newcastle University. Frances Healy completed the flint reports for the ALSF project and offered tremendous assistance afterwards. John Ette and Keith Emerick of English Heritage provided both assistance and support throughout. A larger number of people freely provided information, unpublished reports, and ideas. Acknowledgements are due to Peter Almack, Katherine Baxter (Leeds City Museums and Galleries), Doreen Benson, Neil Campling (then of North Yorkshire County Council), Timothy Champion (Southampton University), the late Richard Hall (York Archaeological Trust), Philip de Jersey (Guernsey Museum and Galleries), Lindsay Jones (National Monuments Record), Graham Lee (North York Moors National Park), Jodie Lewis (University College Worcester), Dick Lonsdale (Friends of Thornborough), Roy Loveday, Terry Manby, Stephen Moorhouse, Stuart Needham (then of The British Museum), Mike Sanders (Friends of Thornborough), Mark Sampson, Stephen Sayer, Heather Sebire (then of Guernsey Museum and Galleries, now of English Heritage), Brian Sheen (Roseland Observatory), Greg Speed (Northern Archaeological Associates), Steve Timms (Mike Griffiths and Associates), and Peter Yates (Friends of Thornborough).

The volume was funded by a publication grant from English Heritage. During its long gestation it benefited enormously from the advice of Jonathan Last and Marcus Jecock of English Heritage. The volume's illustrations were completed with consummate skill by Marie-Claire Ferguson, whose patience and understanding will never be forgotten. Its content was improved greatly by the insightful comments of the anonymous referees.

To all the above we express our warmest thanks.

Summary

This volume describes the results of two university field projects at the Neolithic and Bronze Age monument complex of Thornborough in North Yorkshire. This complex is focused around three large henge monuments which all survive as upstanding earthworks; a variety of other monuments are situated in the surrounding landscape. The *Vale of Mowbray Neolithic Landscape Project* (1994–99) and *Aggregates Levy Sustainability Fund Project* (2002–04) undertook geophysical prospection, topographic survey, and excavation at the central and southern henges, two round barrows, an oval enclosure, double pit alignment, and pit cluster. A large part of its landscape was fieldwalked and some of its lithic scatters test-pitted. Collectively, the evidence demonstrates the long and intricate story of Thornborough's remarkable growth from a relatively modest monument complex into what can be described as a regionally important 'sacred landscape' for later Neolithic communities.

General interpretive themes are considered first. The building of three giant henges, and another three nearby, suggests different intentions, motivations, and strategies to other monument complexes. These can be grasped only by acknowledging that Thornborough was a place of intense religiosity – and then by understanding how sacred architecture speaks to people and acts on social reality. A 'double mediation' between monument and worshipper is essential to interpretation. This is followed by an account of how biographies of knowledge about Thornborough have developed in the recent era. Whilst this sacred landscape is likely to have held special significance during the medieval period, the following centuries saw its alienation from local people through landscape reorganisation, and from prehistorians through neglect. Previous archaeological investigations and other sources of information are considered fully.

The monuments and broader patterns of activity across the immediate landscape are then described. The results of fieldwalking suggest repeated activity in the later Mesolithic and earlier Neolithic on higher ground near to wetland and forest resources. A triple-ditched round barrow, built and remodelled in the second quarter of the 4th millennium BC, may have been a 'founder monument'. Excarnated human body parts were deposited here. Thornborough's role was then transformed through the construction of the cursus. Built across the plateau, away from ancestral places, it brought into being a greater level of order and alignment, changing the way people moved around and experienced this landscape. New relationships and identities were created through building the earthwork and its inner features. The cursus was succeeded by the erection of three henges whose positioning suggests a carefully planned vision, or sacred geometry, was at play. They represent a major escalation in monumentality and their layout, chronology, and relationships with the surrounding landscape are more complex than hitherto thought. Impressive architecture and the regionalisation of their setting were employed to ensure that experience was highly choreographed. Sacredness was enlivened by restricting occupation to the landscape's fringes, where a mosaic of specialised flint knapping, short-term settlement, and other activities emerged. These patterns continued into the Bronze Age, with at least ten round barrows clustering around the axis of the henges. An impressive timber alignment was constructed alongside the southern henge for accessing the monumentalised plateau, or what was now a place of the ancestors and distant dead.

The volume concludes with a discussion of Thornborough's regional significance. Strategically sited on an important routeway between people's homeworlds it became a place where exchange and interaction could freely occur. The circulation of Cumbrian polished stone axes and Yorkshire flint was especially important to its role. That the majority of collected lithics comprised coastal till flint suggests that many visitors came from eastern Yorkshire. People were also drawn here by the landscape's natural character, and more specifically, by the prevalence of water and gypsum. Thornborough developed into a supralocal 'cult centre' with its own beliefs, practices, and spiritual associations, drawing on and exploiting celestial phenomena. It was most likely a place of pilgrimage only occasionally visited.

Résumé

Ce volume rend compte des résultats de deux projets universitaires entrepris dans le complexe monumental de Thornborough dans le nord du Yorkshire datant du Néolithique et de l'âge du Bronze. Le complexe s'agence autour de trois grands monuments circulaires (*henges* en anglais) encore conservés comme ouvrages de terre; on trouve également une série d'autres monuments aux alentours. Les projets dénommés *Vale of Mowbray Neolithic Landscape Project* (1994–99) et *Aggregates Levy Sustainability Fund Project* (2002–04) eurent pour objet des campagnes de prospections géophysiques, de relevés topographiques et de fouilles entreprises sur deux *henges* au centre et au sud, deux tumulus circulaires, une enceinte ovale, un double alignement de fosses et une concentration de fosses. Ces campagnes furent accompagnées d'une prospection en surface de la majeure partie de cette zone et de sondages sur certaines concentrations de matériel lithique. La somme de ces recherches documente une histoire longue et complexe et démontre que Thornborough s'est développé à partir d'un complexe monumental relativement modeste pour devenir un 'espace sacré' important pour les communautés du Néolithique Final de la région.

Notre ouvrage considère en premier lieu certains grands thèmes d'interprétation. La mise en place de trois énormes monuments de type *henge* et d'un autre à proximité indique des intentions, des motivations et des stratégies qui se démarquent par rapport à d'autres complexes monumentaux. On reconnaîtra que Thornborough est un lieu de ferveur spirituelle intense – et on appréciera à quel point l'architecture sacrée affecte les communautés et influence leur réalité sociale. Une 'double médiation' entre monuments et pratiquants d'une religion s'avère essentielle pour l'interprétation. Suit un exposé des différentes idées que l'on s'est faites sur Thornborough au cours des époques récentes. Le paysage sacré de Thornborough garda une importance spéciale au Moyen Age mais durant les siècles suivants les communautés locales en ont été éloignées à travers des réaménagements du territoire, puis par négligence de la part des préhistoriens. On trouvera dans cette section un traitement complet des interventions archéologiques plus anciennes et d'autres sources d'information.

Les monuments et la configuration des diverses activités dans le paysage à proximité immédiate sont décrits ensuite. Les résultats des prospections pédestres indiquent que la zone élevée, proche de zones humides et de forêts, a été occupée de façon répétée pendant le Mésolithique et le début du Néolithique. Un tumulus circulaire cerné de trois fossés concentriques, érigé et remanié pendant le second quart du 4ème millénaire avant J.C. est peut-être le 'monument fondateur' où des éléments de corps humains dépouillés de leur chair ont été retrouvés. Thornborough s'est ensuite transformé par la construction d'un *cursus* (enclos long) aménagé sur le plateau en dehors des lieux ancestraux ; la construction de ces ouvrages de terre et de ses structures internes a créé de nouveaux rapports d'identité en établissant plus d'ordre et de direction et en modifiant la façon de se mouvoir dans ce paysage et de le percevoir. Au *cursus* succédèrent trois monuments circulaires (*henges*) dont l'agencement suggère qu'une vision précise, voire une 'géométrie sacrée', était envisagée. Ils représentent un changement d'échelle marqué au niveau de leur monumentalité et de leur disposition; leur appartenance chronologique et leur rapport avec le paysage s'avèrent plus complexes que prévu. Une architecture visant à impressionner et un rattachement au milieu régional servaient à favoriser une expérience hautement orchestrée. L'aspect sacré du paysage était rehaussé en limitant l'occupation aux confins du territoire, où des ateliers spécialisés de taille de silex, des sites d'habitat éphémères et d'autres signes d'activité on été retrouvés. Ce schéma sera respecté à l'âge du Bronze, comme l'indiquent au moins dix tumuli concentrés sur l'axe des *henges*. Un important alignement de poteaux de bois fut construit le long du monument circulaire sud pour accéder au plateau sacré, qui était alors devenu un lieu réservé aux ancêtres ou aux morts distants.

Une discussion de la portée de Thornborough au niveau régional conclut le volume. Par sa position stratégique sur d'importants axes de communications entre sites d'habitat, le site devint un lieu d'échange et d'interaction libre, jouant un rôle particulièrement notable dans la circulation de haches de pierre polies issues de la région de Cumbria et de silex provenant du Yorkshire. La fréquentation du site par des communautés venant de l'est du Yorkshire est suggérée par le fait que la majorité du matériel lithique provienne de la côte est. Le caractère du paysage naturel, plus précisément la prévalence de l'eau et du gypse, était également un attrait. Thornborough s'est transformé en 'lieu de culte' à l'échelle supra-locale, avec ses propres croyances, rites et associations spirituelles inspirées par des phénomènes célestes. Il est fort probable que ce lieu de pèlerinage ait été fréquenté seulement occasionnellement.

Zusammenfassung

Dieser Band berichtet über zwei wissenschaftliche Forschungsprojekte, die auf dem neolithischen und bronzezeitlichen monumentalen Komplex von Thornborough (North Yorkshire) durchgeführt worden sind. Die Anlage ist rund um drei, als Erdwerk erhaltene, große kreisförmige *henge* Denkmäler konzentriert; mehrere andere Denkmäler sind auch in der umliegenden Landschaft zu finden. Im Rahmen der sogenannten *Vale of Mowbray Neolithic Landscape Project* (1994–99) und *Aggregates Levy Sustainability Fund Project* (2002–04) Projekten wurden geophysikalische Prospektionen, topografische Vermessungen und Ausgrabungen im Bereich der zentralen und südlichen *henge* Denkmäler sowie die Ausgrabungen von zwei Hügelgräbern, einer ovalen Grabanlage, einer doppelten geradlinigen Reihe von Gruben und einer Gruppe von Gruben unternommen. Ein großer Teil dieser Landschaft wurde durch Oberflächenbegehungen untersucht und einige Konzentrationen von Steinartefakten und Abschlägen wurden durch Sondagen geprüft. Zusammengenommen zeigen die Daten, dass Thronborough sich allmählich aus eimem relativ bescheidenen Monumentkomplex zu einer für die spätneolithischen Gemeinschaften der Gegend sehr bedeutende „Sakrallandschaft" entwickelt hat.

Der Band fängt mit einer Untersuchung von generellen Themen der Interpretation an. Die Errichtung von drei riesigen *henges*, sowie von drei anderen in der unmittelbaren Umgebung, deutet auf Zwecke, Motivierungen und Strategien, die sich von anderen Monumentkomplexen unterscheiden. Man kann das am Besten verstehen, wenn man anerkennt, dass Thornborough einen Ort von höchster Heiligkeit darstellt – und wenn man die Art, wie die Sakralarchitektur auf Gemeinschaften und ihre soziale Wirklichkeit wirkt, in Betracht zieht. Eine „doppelte Vermittlung" zwischen Denkmal und Verehrer ist dabei tätig. Es folgt dann eine Schilderung der verschiedenen Deutungen von Thornborough, die sich in den letzten Zeiten entwickelt haben. Während die Sakrallandschaft von Thornborough im Mittelalter weiter bedeutend blieb, wurde die Bevölkerung der folgenden Jahrhunderte durch Umgestaltung der Landschaft und durch Vernachlässigung seitens der Prähistoriker davon entfremdet. Frühere Untersuchungen und andere Informationsquellen werden hier vollständig behandelt.

Es folgt dann eine Beschreibung der Denkmäler und weiterer Belege der Tätigkeit in der unmittelbaren Umgebung des Komplexes. Die Ergebnisse der Oberflächenbegehungen belegen, dass das höhere Gelände in der Nähe von Feuchtgebieten und Wäldern im Spätmesolithikum und Frühneolithikum wiederholt besucht wurde. Ein Hügelgrab mit drei konzentrischen Gräben, der in der zweiten Hälfte des 4. Jahrtausends v. Chr. errichtet und umgestaltet wurde, ist wahrscheinlich ein „Gründermonument". Entfleischte menschliche Körperteile wurden dort niedergelegt. Mit der Errichtung eines *cursus* (lange Anlage) nahm Thornborough eine neue Rolle an. Die Lage des *cursus*, der eine Hochebene durchquert und weit von Ahnenstätten entfernt ist, gab den Anlass für mehr Ordnung und Ausrichtung und veränderte die Weise, wie man sich in dieser Landschaft bewegte und sie erlebte. Durch die Errichtung von Erdwerken und ihrer inneren Ausstattung wurden neue Beziehungen und Identitäten geschaffen. Die drei *henge* Anlagen folgten den *cursus*; ihre Lage deutet auf eine sorgfältig geplante Vorstellung oder sozusagen eine Sakralgeometrie. Diese großen Anlagen stellen eine erhebliche Steigerung der Monumentalität dar, und ihre Ausführung, chronologische Zugehörigkeit sowie ihr Zusammenhang mit der Umgebung haben sich als komplexer als bislang erwartet sein konnte erwiesen. Eindrucksvolle Architektur und die regionale Gliederung des Gebietes wurden so angewendet, dass es ein höchst choreografiertes Erlebnis erzeugte. Die Heiligkeit des Ortes wurde durch eine Beschränkung der Besiedlung auf das Randgebiet erhöht; dort entwickelte sich ein Mosaik von spezialisierten Silex Werkstätten, kurzfristigen Siedlungen und weiteren Aktivitäten. Diese Belegung dauerte bis in die Bronzezeit, mit mindestens zehn Grabhügeln in der Nähe der Axis der *henges*. Eine monumentale Aufrichtung von Pfosten wurde entlang der südlichen *henge* Anlage errichtet. Diese Einrichtung leitete die Verehrer in die Richtung der Hochebene, die inzwischen eine Ahnenstätte oder einen den fernen Gestorbenen gewidmeten Ort geworden ist.

Der Band schließt mit einer Auswertung der regionalen Bedeutung von Thornborough. Seine strategische Lage an einem wichtigen Weg zwischen den Wohngebieten verschiedener Gemeinschaften besagt, dass Thornborough sich zu einem Ort wo Austausch und andere Kontakte frei stattfanden entwickelte. Dabei spielte die Verteilung von geschliffenen Steinäxten aus Cumbria und Silex aus Yorkshire eine ganz besondere Rolle. Bedeutend ist es, dass der größte Teil der Silexfundsammlung aus Silex von der östlichen Yorkshire Küste bestand, was wahrscheinlich auf Besuchern aus dieser Gegend hinweist. Der Charakter der Landschaft lockte die Menschen auch an, namentlich, weil diese Landschaft wasser- und gipsreich war. Thornborough entwickelte sich zu einer supra-lokalen „Kultstätte" mit ihrer eigenen Glauben, Bräuche und geistigen Verbindungen, die sich auf himmlischen Phänomenen stützen. Sehr wahrscheinlich handelte es sich um eine nur selten besuchte Pilgerstätte.

Preface

This volume is based on the results of two field projects at the long-neglected Neolithic and Bronze Age monument complex of Thornborough in North Yorkshire. It brings together the events and sources that have contributed to our knowledge of Thornborough (Chapter 2) with a description of the monuments themselves and their topographic setting (Chapter 3). There then follows a detailed account of excavations at the monuments (Chapter 4) and of survey, surface collection, and test-pitting across the wider landscape (Chapter 5). These chapters are supplemented by five digital appendices (D1–5) hosted by the Archaeology Data Service, including all the survey reports, the specialist artefact studies, and an account of the radiocarbon dating evidence. The level of detail contained within the volume and digital appendices will hopefully satisfy those with an appetite for data.

From the outset an attempt is made to develop a context for these results and accommodate those who want to read an interpretive account without the trouble of working through the entire volume. The resulting narrative is sub-divided into sections which hopefully build logically on one another and are easily located. It starts with a discussion of the general motivations and intentions of monument building and their likely religious poignancy (Chapter 1). Many of these themes are returned to at the end of Chapter 4, where the excavated evidence is employed to consider the sequence of monument construction at Thornborough and what this tells us about the priorities of their builders and worshippers (4.9). In the following chapter the focus moves to the wider landscape, and more specifically, to its development and the experience of those creating and using it during the Mesolithic, Neolithic, and Bronze Age (5.4 and 5.5). The narrative is broadened yet further in Chapter 6 which discusses the wider region, Thornborough's distinctive role within it, the beliefs of people, and the symbolic properties of the universe they inhabited. Those who are interested first and foremost in a storyline can read these sections before deciding whether to explore other parts of the volume.

The volume is the work of many – as is acknowledged where appropriate. Sections without named authors were written by Jan Harding, the director of the two field projects, and the volume's co-ordinator.

The calibrated radiocarbon date ranges used throughout are those for 95% confidence.

1 Interpreting monument complexes

1.1 Introduction

The Thornborough landscape, in North Yorkshire, is known, first and foremost, for its three massive henges (Fig 1.1). Collectively they represent one of the largest earthmoving episodes ever undertaken in later Neolithic Britain, yet their history is best characterised by neglect. There was some antiquarian interest, and surveys were completed in the 19th century (2.3), but their connection with the better-known enclosures of Avebury and Stonehenge went largely unexplored, even by Thomas Kendrick and Christopher Hawkes who first coined the term 'henge' (1932, chapter vii). Their failure to mention Thornborough no doubt reflected its lack of excavation, and it was not until 1952 that this was rectified, by Nicholas Thomas who had just completed the excavation of the Big Rings henge at Dorchester-on-Thames in Oxfordshire (Whittle *et al* 1992, 184–93). Both he and his co-director, Richard Atkinson, were keen to find parallels elsewhere, and whilst the latter famously went on to excavate Stonehenge, Thomas headed north to what his sponsor, the Yorkshire Archaeological Society, described as 'one of the most important monuments of its kind in Europe' (Strickland and Bunnett nd). Like the Dorchester henge, those at Thornborough were enclosed by double-ditches and closely associated with an earlier cursus.

It is regrettable that Thornborough subsequently failed to attract the attention of others. Regardless of mention in gazetteers (Crawford 1927, 8; Clark 1936, 50–1; Atkinson *et al* 1951, 102–3), a small-scale salvage excavation along the terminal of the accompanying cursus (Vatcher 1960), and a great deal of aerial photography (2.4), the landscape passed largely into national obscurity, rarely getting a mention in published overviews of the British Neolithic. It is not cited in either the first or second edition of Stuart Piggott's *Neolithic Cultures of the British Isles* (1954; 1970), although he was aware of its existence (Piggott and Piggott 1939, 140). Some 30 years later, in Richard Bradley's equally important *The Social Foundations of Prehistoric Britain*, the complex, and the three nearby henges of Nunwick, Hutton Moor, and Cana Barn (Fig 1.2B), failed to

Fig 1.1 Looking east at the three Thornborough henges in June 2011 (NMR 28175-015). (© English Heritage)

1

register as one of his later Neolithic 'core areas' (1984, 41, fig 3.2). It would be unfair to chastise these writers, for little was known about these giant enclosures. The henges' obscurity largely reflected their location, sited as they were a long way from Wessex and Orkney, areas traditionally favoured by Neolithic specialists, in an often ignored part of the British Isles. Whereas these better-known landscapes became the foci for research projects and large-scale rescue excavation, the low-lying vales between the Pennines and Hambledon Hills, where Thornborough is found, were largely forgotten, despite the considerable destruction being wrought around and at the monuments by mineral extraction (2.4). Even the uplands of the Yorkshire Dales, Moors, and Wolds became better known, largely through the efforts of local amateur archaeologists organising fieldwalking, excavation, and the publication of regional syntheses (eg Manby 1988a; Manby and Turnbull 1986; Spratt 1982; Spratt and Burgess 1985; Pierpoint 1980; Vyner 1995; White 1997).

This volume goes some way to remedy the oversight. It reports on the first systematic investigation of Thornborough since the 1950s. The scale of this study – which combines the *Vale of Mowbray Neolithic Landscape Project* (VMNLP) (1994–99) and a project funded by the Aggregates Levy Sustainability Fund (2002–04) – went beyond the earlier investigations, and indeed, many comparative studies elsewhere, employing a range of field techniques over a ten-year period (see Chapter 2). Survey and excavation was conducted at the henges and other nearby Neolithic and Bronze Age monuments, providing a sometimes detailed account of their construction and use (see Chapters 3 and 4). This is complemented by evidence about the landscape's occupation during these periods, derived from fieldwalking and test-pitting (see Chapter 5). Together this body of information demonstrates the long and intricate story of Thornborough's remarkable growth from a relatively modest 4th-millennium monument complex into what can be described as a regional 'hub' for later Neolithic communities (see Chapter 6). Its development has broader implications for Neolithic and Bronze Age studies, and indeed, is best understood alongside a more general consideration of monumental 'sacred landscapes'. This chapter will explore the interpretive problems and social implications of complexes like Thornborough.

1.2 Monuments as socio-political narratives

The Thornborough henges are located on a broad shelf of Permian limestone and marl between the Vale of Mowbray to the east and the Pennine hills to the west (Fig 1.2). Their setting is topographically distinct to adjoining areas, being built across a largely flat and narrow fluvio-glacial plateau (SE 285 795), known locally as Thornborough Moor, and bounded to the south and south-west by the River Ure and its terrace deposits, to the west and north-

west by a Lower Magnesian Limestone ridge, to the north by a shallow basin, and to the east by knolls and ridges of till (3.2). The three double-entranced henges, each sited 0.55km apart on a north-west to south-east alignment, dominate this narrow plateau. Such a layout is highly unusual or even unique, and these are the fifth largest monuments of their kind in the British Isles, each of their banks and double ditches some 240m across. They do not, however, occur alone, for the plateau is also home to a cursus and triple-ditched round barrow, known to be earlier than the henges, and at least ten round barrows and a double pit alignment, thought to be later (3.3). Collectively, they form a distinctive complex (Fig 1.2C) with a chronology of more than 2000 years, and its more-or-less exclusive association with the plateau suggests an important and integral relationship between these built places and local topography. The henges were especially carefully positioned, with the central site built on the existing cursus (Fig 1.3).

Similar clusters are known elsewhere, such as in the Thames Valley and the river corridors of the Midlands to cite two of the better-researched areas, and most are spaced less than 10km apart, or within comfortable walking distance of each other. During the earlier and middle Neolithic they consisted of two or three long barrows, or, more rarely, a pair of causewayed enclosures, but usually incorporated a cursus along with a range of 4th-millennium burial sites, enclosures, and ring-ditches (Allen *et al* 2004, fig 9.1; Barclay and Hey 1999; Barclay *et al* 2003; Gibson and Loveday 1989; Harding and Healy 2007; Last 1999; Lewis and Welsh 2004; Loveday 1989; 1999; Malim 1999; Pryor *et al* 1985). They are currently thought to be rarer in northern England, being virtually unknown from large parts of the region including the North-West and Northumberland, yet their establishment has been documented across parts of Yorkshire, albeit with small numbers of contemporary sites. In addition to Thornborough, an impressive cursus is known at Scorton, near to Catterick in North Yorkshire, although it is far from clear whether this now quarried-out site was associated with other earlier and middle Neolithic monuments (Topping 1982), and most spectacularly, at Rudston, in East Yorkshire, where no fewer than five such monuments are found, converging on a bend in the Gypsey Race, along with rectilinear enclosures and long barrows (Dymond 1966; Manby *et al* 2003, fig 17; Riley 1988, 91, fig 5.1; Stoertz 1997, figs 11:1 and 32). These clusters attest to the use of favoured locations whose significance was repeatedly renewed by monument building, perhaps as concentrated embodiments of group history and sacred belief, even as 'ritual landscapes' (Thorpe 1984, 58) or places which symbolise newly emerging political structures (Harding 1995, 124). Their association with rivers or streams makes sense if these natural features acted as territorial markers, the monuments 'juxtaposed for reasons of competition or the sanctioning of social interaction' (Loveday 1989, 71).

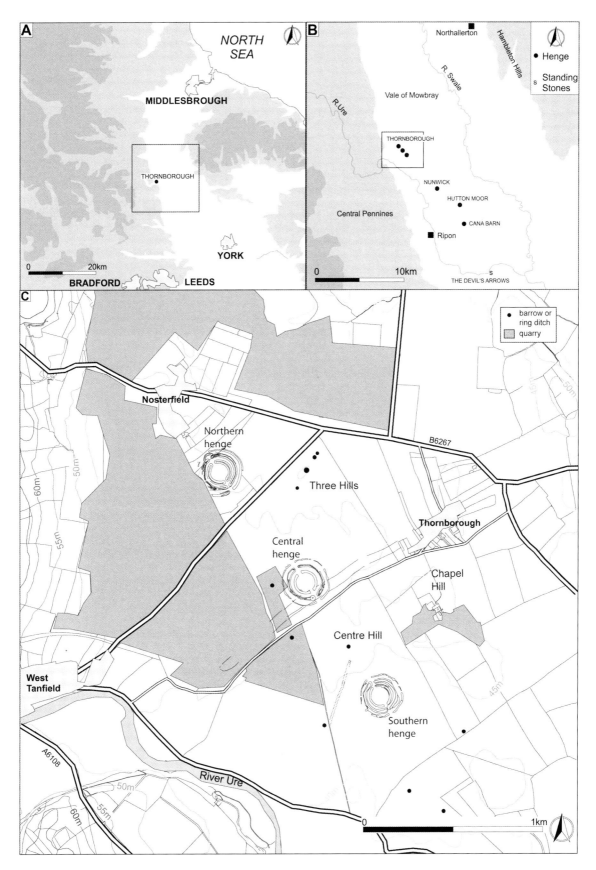

Fig 1.2 Location of Thornborough. © Crown Copyright / database right 2013. An Ordnance Survey / EDINA supplied service

Fig 1.3   Central henge and cursus in August 1952 (CUCAP AGG28). (Copyright reserved Cambridge University Collection of Aerial Photography)

Many 4th-millennium complexes served as centres for ritual and ceremony during the later Neolithic and earlier Bronze Age. More usually associated are hengiforms, ring-ditches, and pit circles (Bradley and Chambers 1988; Gibson and Loveday 1989; Last 1999; Loveday 1989; Malim 1999; Whittle *et al* 1992), but there are rarer instances where a large henge was also built, as at Dorchester-on-Thames in Oxfordshire, and Maxey in Cambridgeshire (Atkinson *et al* 1951; Loveday 1999; Pryor *et al* 1985; Whittle *et al* 1992). These two examples offer the closest parallels to Thornborough, for at both an impressive 3rd-millennium enclosure was sited over or immediately next to an earlier cursus. The four henges built within 1.5km of the cursuses at Stonehenge, in Wiltshire, may demonstrate a similar concern with the past (Cleal *et al* 1995; Richards 1990). Complexes also underwent change around the turn of the 3rd and 2nd millennia with the construction of round barrows (Barclay *et al* 2003; Gibson and Loveday 1989, 43; Last 1999; Loveday 1989, 71–2; Loveday 1999, 49, table 5.1; Malim 1999; Pryor *et al* 1985, fig 15; Stoertz 1997, fig 11.1), their distribution often gravitating strongly towards these earlier landscapes, as best demonstrated across Wessex (Braithwaite 1984, fig 1; Fleming 1971). The number of new monuments clustered together differs greatly, from the 474 barrows built within 4km of Stonehenge (Richards 1990, table 1), to just a handful of sites, suggesting that a complex's size and prominence in previous centuries did not always determine the extent of monument construction during the later Neolithic and early Bronze Age. The complexity and local variability of what was built where is also suggested by barrow cemeteries avoiding earlier complexes altogether, as is the case in the Thames Valley (Barclay *et al* 2003, 239–40).

These complexes represent the long-term ebb and flow of monument building, and, as such, 'offer a kind of narrative that is as close as prehistorians can come to writing a political history' (Bradley 1993, 98). This is implicit to the argument that Neolithic Wessex was characterised by the development of centralised social polities, or more specifically chiefdoms, where wealth and power were concentrated in the hands of a few, and large monuments served as symbolic and ideological 'central places' (Renfrew 1973; Earle 1991). The origins of these societies were in the earlier Neolithic, with causewayed enclosures acting as meeting-places for nascent polities, and by the later Neolithic we see the appearance of fully blown stratification, each chiefdom undertaking its own large-scale communal building project, like that at Stonehenge or Knowlton and Mount Pleasant in Dorset. These impressive henges were centres for the social, religious, and economic life of each of the chiefdoms, but according to Timothy Earle, 'created a sacred space set off for ceremonies that fundamentally separated the rulers from the ruled and identified their legitimacy with universal forces outside the world accessible to commoners' (1991, 96). As such, they contrast with the smaller henges which were arenas for local ceremonies (Earle 1991, 91). Variations in monument size, and the amount of labour invested in their construction, is therefore indicative of a hierarchy of ceremonial centres across each territorial unit – the Neolithic equivalent of the different roles undertaken in more recent times by parish churches and cathedrals, and by town halls and the seat of central government. The transportation and erection of the Stonehenge bluestones is taken to represent the development of a confederation, the five Wessex chiefdoms coalescing into one greater polity (Renfrew 1973, 552).

The existence of such well-organised and unified social entities, which are often seen to compete with and emulate one another, has become unconsciously embedded within our view of later Neolithic society over the past 30 years, partly because of our own familiarity with centralised societies, but also because of the unfortunate tendency to look no further than Wessex, or indeed Orkney where Renfrew (1979, 217–18; 2000) envisaged a similar, if less hierarchical, social togetherness. Whether or not we agree with the use of the chiefdom model, and John Barrett (1994, 158–64) has dismissed it

as problematic and inappropriate, it has proved difficult to think about the more impressive monuments without also assuming that the large-scale participation demanded by their building was linked to social centralisation (a notable exception would be Whittle 1997a, 146ff). They may have been communal endeavours serving a widespread population, but this is seen as an intrinsically political process, the mobilisation of large amounts of labour and other resources legitimising and reinforcing pre-existing social elites, or perhaps as is more likely, creating them in the first place (Barrett 1994, 27–9; Bradley 1985; Richards 2004). Hence, the distribution and scale of henges and other broadly contemporary monuments equates directly to the socio-political realities of their builders and descendants, as explored by John Barnatt (1989, chapter 5) in his sophisticated and geographically wide-ranging discussion of the later Neolithic and early Bronze Age. He argues that networks of regularly spaced and architecturally similar henges and stone circles are recognisable across parts of Britain. In some regions, including the low-lying vales of Yorkshire and their surrounding uplands, these networks indicate hierarchical spatial patterns where the monuments 'functioned differently in the sense that they relate to varying levels of organisation within regional communities, ranging from monuments for local use by individual farming units, to regional centres which may have been gathering places for the majority of factions within a region' (*ibid*, 166). Here, large and small monuments alike map the organisational building-blocks of society, and, in the case of the Wessex chalkland and its surrounding areas, indicate that each later Neolithic 'central place' was associated with equal-sized territories of about 500–700km^2 (*ibid*, 208–9).

Such an approach is not, however, without its problems, as illustrated by Thornborough and the surrounding vales and uplands of Yorkshire. The henges of this region are distributed as either widely spaced single sites or clustered to form one of the densest concentrations in the British Isles (Fig 1.4). Whilst this could partly reflect the incomplete nature of the archaeological record, it also highlights some meaningful patterns. It is surely significant that half of the known monuments are located along a 12km stretch of the River Ure. The concentration of six massive henges near the cathedral town of Ripon, including those at Thornborough, testify to the importance of this particular area during the later Neolithic, forming what John Barnatt described as an 'inter-regional centre'. As he notes, 'evidence for such centres is absent elsewhere in Britain. Even in Wessex the largest Late Neolithic henges are regularly spaced' (*ibid*, 188). This is perhaps too many closely spaced sites for each to be interpreted as the central-place of a powerful social grouping – currently it takes only around an hour to walk from complex to complex – and such an explanation fails to account for the identical size and appearance of these sites, or indeed, an apparent absence of earlier

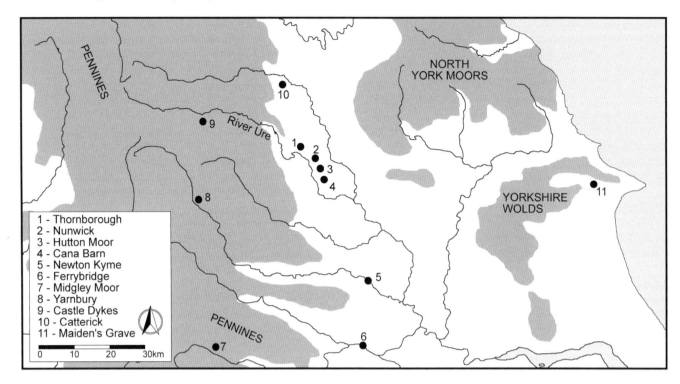

Fig 1.4   The henge monuments of Yorkshire

monuments at all except the Thornborough complex. Alternative interpretations appear necessary, like that proposed by Roy Loveday (1998), who saw these henges as possibly located along, or at the end of, a ritual path or 'pilgrims' routeway'. Later Neolithic social centralisation may also fail to fit the rest of the region. Despite the intensity of archaeological fieldwork across the Yorkshire Wolds there is as yet only one definite henge, the site of Maiden's Grave alongside the Rudston 'D' cursus (McInnes 1964), in an area of relatively high population during the later Neolithic, an absence Thorpe and Richards (1984, 70–3) ascribe to an alternative emphasis on burial sites and a 'prestige goods economy'. There are a number of other possible henges, but all are small in size (Manby *et al* 2003, 73; Stoertz 1997, 30–3; see also Powlesland 2003, 285–6). To the other side of the Yorkshire vales, in the eastern central Pennines, are the albeit modest henges of Castle Dykes, Yarnbury, and possibly Midgley Moor (Dymond 1965; Harding and Lee 1987, 306–7, 317–18; Howcroft 2011, 88, fig 4), yet this area is presumed to have been more sparsely populated than the Wolds.

Why does the basic spatial pattern of modular and repetitive 'central places' (see also Renfrew 1977, 102–5) begin to break down when considered for Yorkshire and other areas like Cumbria, where the only known henges are the two large neighbouring enclosures of Mayburgh and King Arthur's Round Table (Topping 1992; see also Cowell 2000, 119–20; McCarthy 2000, 134)? At the heart of the mismatch is the assumption that later Neolithic society must *always* be characterised by centrally controlled, territorially bounded, and politically competitive

social units, for to accept their existence in Wessex, in itself problematic, is not to imply their presence elsewhere. Alternative forms of social organisation must be considered, and given John Barrett's (1994, 161–2) criticism of Renfrew for letting the contemporary world strongly prejudice his reconstruction of prehistoric society, these should perhaps be 'dedicated to preserving the radical differences which exist between states and non-state systems', including the absence of 'extensive and authoritative power which was also the site of personal power' (*ibid*, 163). Less emphasis, in other words, should be placed on fixed notions of group exclusivity and incorporation, with an uncomplicated and continuous association between political entities, ceremonial centres, and power. There may have been no absolute criteria for belonging to an individual social group and no constant sense of identity, but a more fluid network of social relationships which changed across time and space. This is not to deny a link between henges and the expression of social identity or power, but to accept that there may have been a mosaic of differently configured social entities in Neolithic Britain, each employing varying strategies to inscribe notions of distinction, commonality, and integration (see Thomas 1996, 178–81). This alternative view of social organisation moves us away from a single fit-all model for monument complexes, and rather, places the accent on the specific *tensions, intentions, and motivations* of local and regional systems.

The opportunities and challenges of this approach are highlighted by simple variations amongst monuments and the development of complexes.

Henges are frequently of small size and often appear to have fallen rapidly out of use or been deliberately backfilled soon after digging (Clare 1987, 298), suggesting that the act of construction was of more significance than their continued use (Bradley 1993, 98). These smaller sites could be regarded as ceremonial foci for local communities, but this says little about their exact role and meaning. Their size and short history may be better understood if seen as meeting the immediate and very specific needs of a community, built, perhaps, in response to a crisis or to celebrate a single event. Crucially, these motivations could have varied greatly from henge to henge, whilst their significance need not have lasted longer than a few days. In contrast are the larger henges whose construction involved grand amounts of communal labour, and which may cluster together (Harding and Lee 1987, 43–4). They may possess a more lengthy history, including episodes of maintenance, modification, and even transformation (Bradley 1993, 98); as noted, they are often regarded as central-places for the reaffirmation of a wider communal identity. Yet if their construction and use did involve large-scale participation, this in no way means they must have been the product of a single centralised social grouping, or have been 'conceived as an entity, a plan in the mind of some autocratic chief' (Barrett 1994, 13). Neither does it imply they were arenas for ritualised competition and social dominance which invariably led to greater social differentiation (Richards 2004, 111). Instead, they could be the outcome of inter-group festivals, whose impact on the long-term centralisation of power was negligible, or the product of occasional, expedient, and unfinished projects whose motivations and outcomes varied so widely as to have affected society in many different and conflicting ways (Barrett 1994, 13–24).

Of specific interest in relation to Thornborough may be the tensions, intentions, and motivations behind those very much rarer instances where a large henge is directly associated with an earlier ceremonial focus. As mentioned, examples are few and far between, but include the monument complexes of Dorchester-on-Thames, where the double-ditched Big Rings henge was built alongside a cursus of impressive length (Bradley and Chambers 1988; Loveday 1999; Whittle *et al* 1992), and Maxey, where an ovate-shaped henge, with a narrow ditch and entrance, was sited over an earlier cursus (Pryor *et al* 1985). The close spatial relationship between these 4th- and 3rd-millennia sites certainly differs from the general pattern whereby henges are usually located some distance from cursuses (Harding 1995, 128–31), and the distinctiveness of both Dorchester and Maxey is reiterated by the unusual design and size of each henge, and the cluster of other later Neolithic sites, which, as Loveday (1999, 51–2) notes, extend or run parallel to the alignment of the cursus. These complexes form a very select group where later monument building indicates continued and active respect (Loveday 1999, 52; see also

Loveday 2006, 146–9, 152), and Barclay *et al* (2003, 242) consider Dorchester to have become of supralocal or regional importance by the later Neolithic. These complexes could therefore be seen as central-places for societies which had achieved long-term stability, and hence a high degree of centralisation, but Richard Bradley (1993, 100–2) has proposed a different explanation which focuses on the values implicit to each of these complexes. He considers the very deliberate siting of the henges as attempts to subvert the meaning of the earlier sites. To him this represents the radical reinterpretation of an established monument complex – and perhaps also the affiliations and relationships between people – rather than any social continuity between past and present. As such, the reasons for their siting were not necessarily linked to the emergence of a more centralised society, or indeed, to any changes in socio-political organisation.

There may, then, have been a range of potential reasons for the development of a monument complex like Thornborough. One necessary consideration is whether it resulted from bursts or pulses of activity, in which a number of structural foci were created and used concurrently, or whether it was an ongoing project, with only a single monument in use at any one time. The question is all the more important because these processes reflect contrasting social dynamics. If the development of monument complexes resulted from large-scale bursts of activity, in which complementary or alternative places were constructed, then it may indeed represent the creation of a 'central place', perhaps for the articulation of new social identities and alliances during periods of insecurity or rapid change. If it resulted from successive small-scale episodes of construction, or the creation over the long-term of individual foci for ritual and ceremony, then the monuments need represent no more than the cumulative labour of a single social group, as its members inscribed their own unique biography or identity into the landscape. Moreover, it needs to be asked if its development reflects a continuity of tradition, the conscious commemoration of an earlier set of meanings using the architectural repertoire of the time, and if so, whether this suggests an unchanging political history or one which embraced change through continuity. Alternatively, the monuments could indicate the invention of tradition, or what has been described as the effective reworking and transformation of earlier places in a conscious attempt to legitimise a new social order (Bradley 1987a, 3–4). These, then, are crucial questions, but as the general literature on monumentality demonstrates, the motivations and implications of the construction and use of monuments are likely to have been more complex than simply the articulation of power or the materialisation of a socio-political narrative. These issues require greater consideration if we are to understand the tensions, intentions, and motivations behind individual complexes.

1.3   Monuments as sacred architecture

The emphasis placed by Renfrew and others on the link between larger henges and the development of social polities is unsurprising given that much of the general literature on monumentality concerns the massive ceremonial mounds, pyramids, and enclosures built by highly centralised groups like Polynesian chiefdoms or the early Egyptian, Aegean, Mesopotamian, and Mesoamerican states. These often complex and sophisticated sites leave little doubt as to their important role in establishing and maintaining hierarchies for they contain 'a simple message about the central control of people's labor in the construction of a cultural landscape' (Earle 1997, 144). Their logic as built expressions of social power is undeniable, for as Bruce Trigger (1990) argues, they represent the conspicuous reversal of the 'principle of least effort' which he sees as governing much of social life. It is their monumentality, in other words, that makes them different from other symbolic representations and potentially controllable by social elites. Such symbols of power appear to have been especially important during the emergence of new socio-political institutions (Bradley 1985, 4–7; Cherry 1978; Trigger 1990, 127–8; see also Adler and Wilshusen 1990, 140–1; Richards 1999), as in Hawaii where the biggest heiau, or stone-built ceremonial enclosures, were constructed early in the formation of chiefdoms (Earle 1997, 177–9; Kirch 1990, 218). Once built, monuments are subject to ownership, transference, and inheritance, becoming capital investments in the long-term stability of social elites; and they are often conceived as ongoing projects, so that 'inasmuch as there remains a population to be taxed, the monuments will continue to grow in size or increase in number' (Earle 1997, 157). Even among the less-centralised Mapuche of south-central Chile, building a cultural landscape with mounds and ritual fields created the stage for ceremonial cycles central to the emergence and persistence of a chiefly elite (Dillehay 1990). Chiefs and their lineages owned these sites and directed the ceremonies that institutionalised and materialised their social world. Monuments therefore serve as a solid foundation upon which lasting institutions were constructed, and could even effectively represent power long after a social system has disappeared.

It must not be forgotten, however, that monuments, irrespective of whether they were the product of a centralised society or not, serve to express and recreate ideology. This is not to say that they did not possess specific functions, such as being used for socio-political administration or as defended refuges, but that normally it was these sites, and indeed their immediate landscapes, where beliefs were most fully represented, articulated, and negotiated. In most traditional societies this means that they were loci for spiritual power or energy – places where 'the air is thick with *religion*' (Jones 2000a, xi, my italics) – and one of the basic ways this is expressed is by asserting that a monument is where a god, or some

numinous power, manifests itself, either by descending from the sky to take up residence or through the entire site being an earthly manifestation of a deity or spirit (Jones 2000b, 71). There is, then, much more to monuments than simply the expression of power, as Renfrew himself has acknowledged (1994; 2000, 15). Of course, the tie between religious meanings and socio-political authority can be especially tight. Leaders, time and again, have owned, controlled, and manipulated the materialisation of sacred ideology to express power; and the size of some monuments makes them ideal places to disseminate elitist propaganda, their enormity facilitating large-scale gatherings and inducing a helpful sense of admiration or respect amongst the attendees about their physical surroundings and its designers (Jones 2000b, chapter 19). Those who built and congregated within these places, however, were not worshipping dupes unable to see beyond such self-glorifying pretension, and religion is never the preserve of an elite minority. Rather, the sacred inspired and motivated people, often in ways unintended or unforeseen by 'big men', chiefs, or kings. It could even invoke a sense of revulsion, exclusion, and resentment about a dominant ideology, or could be a means of suspending, undermining, or overriding the status quo, as with the Sikh and Baha'i temples in India, which were a direct challenge to the institutionalised inequality of the Hindu caste system (*ibid*, 137–8). Thus, there can be noticeable differences between the sometimes esoteric and technical top-down apprehensions of social elites and the more popular bottom-up apprehensions of the faithful or not-so-faithful.

There is also an intimacy to *religious experience*, so that the architects and builders of monuments 'almost immediately lose control of the significances and meanings of their projects. And consequently, as devotees ... use, reflect upon, and "play with" the built structures in their environment, they endlessly disrupt old meanings and awaken fresh ones' (Jones 2000a, 22). People's age, sex, background, and expectations influence tremendously the ways in which these places were interpreted or understood, and sites of relatively large size, with impressive and permanent architecture, were especially susceptible to alternative readings. In particular, vested interests and cults are known to have strongly determined people's attitudes, but sacred places could be understood in different ways by the same person, depending, for instance, on whether they were experiencing the monument on their own or with other people, whether they were actually within the monument or experiencing it at a distance, or when in their life, and the life of the monument, the experience was happening. There is never one 'correct' interpretation of what these places represent for this is fluid, situational, and transient; hence, they serve both to create and transform social order. The difficulty of grasping such specificity, variability, and changeability contributes towards archaeological accounts usually avoiding any discussion of religion, focusing more normally on the materiality of specific rituals (Insoll 2004a, 3–4). Ritual is obviously important, for it must not be forgotten that meaning resides exclusively neither in the monuments themselves nor in the mind of the human subject experiencing them, but rather in the interactive negotiation, often articulated via rites, which subsumes both monument and beholder (Jones 2000a, xxviii, 41). This is, nevertheless, to 'use an element to describe the whole' (Insoll 2004a, 3), producing interpretations which ignore the fact that ritual, however defined, operates within a 'thick' context of which religion is a vital part, and that this wider interconnectivity is the means by which the ritual practices themselves and their meanings are generated (Insoll 2004b, 66–76; but see Bell 1992). It is also to dehumanise the past, for sacred experience is closely connected to an altered mental state, or emotional catharsis, whose appreciation goes beyond the materiality of ritual and ceremony (for introductory discussions see Lambek 2000, part III; Lewis-Williams and Pearce 2005, 26–8, 33–59).

Given this failure to engage with the theme of religion, it is unsurprising that so little is known about the spiritual mindset, specific beliefs, and sacred experiences of the Neolithic and Bronze Age. Generally, there have been two very different approaches to these subjects. The first is essentially deductive, assuming the existence of key structuring principles which pervaded all aspects of social life, but which remained largely unchanged by practice and the generation of meaning. Perhaps the best example of such a top-down approach is Ian Hodder's (1990) *The Domestication of Europe*, a book which heroically attempts to identify the 'structural logic' of belief and practice. Religion is not mentioned by name, and the spiritual experiences of those who actually generated this structural logic go unexplored, but the account's principal limitation is its monotheism, or put more accurately, its assumption that religion can be reduced to a simple set of shared abstract principles. Similar problems are evident with other attempts to impose a structural logic on the archaeological evidence, such as *Inside the Neolithic Mind* (Lewis-Williams and Pearce 2005), which, to its credit, places religion centre-stage, but which reduces spirituality to rule-governed human neurology. These studies, and others beside, consider materiality as purely symbolic, with monuments and their associated rituals operating principally to generate neatly bound cosmological categories. They greatly simplify what would have been a much more complex relationship between belief and practice, and, at the same time, fail to 'engage with the aspect of the intangible, the numinous element of belief which extends beyond a functional conceptual framework' (Insoll 2004b, 78). By contrast, other accounts provide specific and detailed studies of the materiality of ritual, and as such, consider the sacred from the bottom-up (eg Barrett 1994; Parker Pearson and Ramilisonina 1998; Watson 2001). This is certainly a wholly appropriate and rewarding

level of analysis, and has generated sophisticated interpretations of individual sites whilst highlighting the possible importance of ancestry and shamanism. Nevertheless, these studies are limited by a failure to consider specific evidence as part of the broader range of human existence. Ritual is taken as a distinct and autonomous aspect of social life, generating meaning which is both pragmatic and spontaneous, instead of embedded within differing contexts and an encompassing religiosity. This is again to simplify the sacred, reducing it to single elements, like ancestry, which are seen as meaningful only within specific spheres of life.

The untapped significance of religious experience for Neolithic and Bronze Age studies comes sharply into focus if we consider how monuments operate or speak to people and act on social reality. The effective negotiation of sacredness – which crucially, includes personal self-reflection by the beholder – has been described as a 'double mediation' by Lindsay Jones (2000a, 60ff). Monuments will allure the congregation, or engage them in 'conversation', producing familiarity and assurance by appealing to people's shared values and traditions. However, this encouragement is akin to a kind of surrender or acquiescence allowing the beholder to suspend disbelief and feed on the religious nourishment offered by these places. It is during this second stage of the 'double mediation' that the congregation's views will be disrupted or challenged, for only by experiencing bewilderment and disorientation can people learn something new about their cosmology and thereby achieve spiritual renewal. Aspects of life previously concealed or taken for granted would be exposed, unmasked, or demystified, allowing the beholder to break free of their normal worldly limits and confront the strangeness permeating their universe. The process of allurement draws upon conventionalised tastes and pre-understandings, generating what Catherine Bell (1992, 80ff) describes as a socially acceptable 'sense of ritual', but if this was nuanced by the worshipper's sociocultural background, it is through the conscious deliberation of disruption and renewal that religious experience becomes deeply subjective and almost inseparable from a person's history, needs, hopes, desires, and fears. This, then, is the means by which people achieve mental transcendence of the here-and-now and enter into a dialogue about divinity, world creation, human purpose, and occasionally, specific socio-political questions (Jones 2000a, 90). They develop understandings of both the sacred and the social order which often differ from the intention of the monument's designers, and, in some instances, 'the same religiocivic performance that was intended to breed conformity and loyalty … backfires, engendering resentment rather than respect, perhaps even serving to incite rebellion against the very powers that orchestrated it' (*ibid*, 94).

This 'double mediation' has direct consequences for studying sacred landscapes like Thornborough. For monuments to communicate sacredness effectively they must possess elements of conservatism and familiarity to allure the congregation. This was described by Jones as the 'front half' of sacred architecture. At the same time, however, these physical characteristics are counterpoised by elements of originality and novelty – or alterity, defined by van der Guchte (1999), in his study of pre-Hispanic Andean landscapes, as features characterised by irregularity or difference – which serve to confront and surprise the beholder, even to encourage fresh revalorisation of the structures themselves. Without this 'back half', the architecture fails to stimulate, becoming boring, predictable and uneventful (Jones 2000a, 88–9). These simple mechanics are directly relevant to the study of Neolithic and Bronze Age monuments. Without understanding the basic principles which structured the conversation between the architecture and the beholder it is impossible to grasp why monuments were built in the way that they were, the sorts of meanings they generated, and the religious experiences that people had with these places: in short, it is to rob them of everything that defined their very existence. Furthermore, to ignore these fundamental properties prevents an understanding of how sacred places developed through time. The specific monument categories recognised by prehistorians, like later Neolithic henges, are often presented as largely unchanging symbols of their age, so that each of our chronological sub-divisions is represented by its own discrete form of architectural expression. Yet, a 'double mediation' implies that the physical characteristics of individual monument types, along with their relationship with the beholder, possessed a far more dynamic history, each act of construction incorporating elements which incited new ways of seeing the world. The monuments and religious experiences of any one of our eras is therefore far from fixed and timeless, each varying, often significantly, as they are temporally and spatially reproduced. If the relationships between broadly contemporary monument types have been considered (eg Braithwaite 1984; Thorpe and Richards 1984), we have failed to grasp the potential links between chronologically extended inventiveness or experimentation in specific forms of sacred architecture and variation, alteration, or transformation in people's outlook and their societies. In short, we have ignored the fact that the very building of individual monuments embodied change.

One of the common ways in which traditional cultures achieve allurement is by physically replicating their cosmos or universe. Such acts of architectural design – described by Mircea Eliade, the well-known historian of religion, as *imago mundi* – allow the builder and beholder to find, both literally and metaphorically, their place in the world (Jones 2000b, 26ff). The relationship between the specific layout of Neolithic and Bronze Age monuments and this religious act of orientation has been discussed, most notably for henges (Bradley 1998, chapters 7–8; Harding 2003, chapter 2; Richards 1996), but what has not been so readily grasped is that this is virtually always the beginning, rather than the

summation, of an architectural event's significance (Jones 2000b, 44–6). Microscopic representations work primarily to capture the interest of a congregation by engendering trust and assurance, thereby opening people to the kind of receptivity needed for the subsequent transactions of meaning and transformative experiences. What follows can take many different forms, for there can 'be a wide variety of different kinds of sacred sites, with quite different forms and functions, within one culture' (Hubert 1994, 11). It often involves interaction with supernatural beings and forces, with monuments being the places where these make themselves visible or accessible to human devotees (Jones 2000b, chapter 17). It could involve the reliving of mythical and miraculous episodes, the monuments not just commemorating these events, but actually allowing those present to participate in their happening (*ibid*, 115). Or the emphasis may be on an individual personage or animal, often to create tangible prototypes or practical guides for ethical conduct (*ibid*, 116–18). Monuments could also be used to honour, memorialise, and even embody the dead, something which does not necessarily rely on the placement or display of actual bodily remains (*ibid*, chapter 20). Finally, religious acts need not just be concerned with the 'who' and 'what' of cosmology, for sacred places could also focus on the 'where' by simply marking or connecting people with a place of mythical importance (*ibid*, 118). Monuments therefore embody an extensive range of religious concerns, with some sites considered more sacred than others, a potential diversity which Neolithic and Bronze Age studies have been slow to understand, but which nonetheless may relate to some of the variations mentioned earlier.

Nor can we assume that individual sites possessed only one of these roles. Whilst sacred places can be rather specialised facilities, notably amongst centralised communities like the Polynesian chiefdoms of Tonga and Hawaii, others are characterised by more generalised and wide-ranging usage, especially where a sacred place is used for temporary or even permanent habitation (Kirch 1990; see also Adler and Wilshusen 1990). Examples include the 'monumental' Amazonian long houses which served as temples for a range of initiation, fertility, and ancestral rites (Århem 1998). The simple U-shaped ceremonial fields of the Mapuche in south-central Chile consisted of dwelling huts and an altar, and were used during large public events 'to propitiate ancestors, to worship gods and celestial beings, to maintain and recruit marriage and trade alliances, and, in past times, to pray for, or celebrate, victory in battle' (Dillehay 1990, 227). Permanently occupied and more physically complex are the monumental stone-walled kaya of the Mijikenda of Kenya, each serving as 'a residential, political, burial and religious centre', being used for, amongst other things, initiation and fertility ceremonies, the exorcism of evil spirits, and praying for rain during long periods of drought, food during famine, and peace or victory during war (Mutoro 1994, 134–7). These examples highlight the problem with assigning single roles to specific sites, but also the interpretive possibilities when thinking through the differences in the size and architecture of specific monument types. There has been some discussion about the extent to which Neolithic and Bronze Age monuments were themselves used in either specialised or generalised ways, particularly in relation to causewayed enclosures (Drewett 1977, 222–6; Oswald *et al* 2001, chapter 7; Whittle and Pollard 1999), but much more could be done, especially for the later Neolithic. Following Adler and Wilshusen's (1990, 143) discussion of Hopi kivas, it may be there was a continuum of places with increasingly dedicated roles. Varying degrees of specialisation could equate with greater or lesser sacredness. It is even possible that some sites were operating simultaneously at several different levels, perhaps serving very different audiences.

Differing roles would have been embedded in practice, and although the latter has come to the fore in recent approaches to Neolithic and Bronze Age monuments, its implicit religious significance is all too often obscured by interpretive generality. The well-intentioned use of terms like 'structured deposition' and 'ritual practice', regularly used over the last twenty years to explain many of the archaeological remains associated with these sites, has served to distance these deposits from their original religiosity by becoming insipid catch-all labels for acts which once reeked of intimacy and sacred significance. The disparity between many of our archaeological narratives and the lived experience of sacred architecture is illustrated by the importance that historians of religion and anthropologists attach to *propitiation*, an attitude on the part of the beholder which

> touches upon a whole nexus of loosely interrelated forms of ritual practice: from offering and oblation to petitioning sacrifices and fertility rites; healing, cleansing, and exorcism; worship, supplication, thanksgiving, and expressions of gratitude; atonement, pleas for forgiveness, expiation, and vindication; and thus exercises of penance, fasting, flagellation, or other forms of self-mortification (Jones 2000b, 238; see also chapter 23).

These practices are acted out in different ways, overlapping with the roles mentioned above, and can be understood at either an individual or a communal level. They are nonetheless united by an attempt to appease, assuage, make peace with, or otherwise strategically negotiate with, the spirits and gods (for present-day examples see Abungu 1994; Mumah 1994; Radimilahy 1994; Wandibba 1994). Of course, there are considerable difficulties with identifying many of these practices archaeologically, but it is striking nonetheless that propitiation is rarely discussed, despite the very making, moving, rebuilding, and destroying of sacred architecture being themselves tasks of offertory or propitiatory significance. The shortcoming is all the more surprising

given the complexity and richness of the cultural residues found at many monuments – and, for that matter, within many contemporary pits – and is symptomatic of a failure to embed the remains in their proper religious context.

These key themes in the study of Neolithic and Bronze Age monuments will reappear in following chapters. Whilst these sites can indeed offer the prehistorian a kind of socio-political history, and be understood as strategies by which human relations were regulated and negotiated, these narratives were nonetheless steeped in deep-rooted spiritual concerns. If we are to understand the specific tensions, intentions, and motivations of local and regional systems we need to focus on the intricate religious mechanisms which produced the wide-ranging gamut of Neolithic and Bronze Age monuments through space and time. The same issues apply to sacred landscapes, especially since they often assume significance over and above the building, use, and abandonment of their constituent monuments. As time passes, these foci can become emblematic, physically contracting or expanding, diversifying or simplifying, as a result of factors like demographic expansion or fragmentation, internal and external friction or conflict, and political marriage. Integral to all these factors, however, was a place's sacredness. This was not an abstract force which stretched arbitrarily across a landscape, creating meaning from its earth, wood, stone and water, but rather was something generated by, and firmly embedded within, people's spiritual and emotional view of the world; and if shared myths and the worship of the supernatural potentially invoke a sense of loyalty or collective belonging, they can also generate difference, intrigue, disagreement, even revulsion. As such, the biography of a sacred landscape was far from predetermined or overwhelmingly associated with the creation of socio-political unity. These were also *contested places* or localities for division, fragmentation, and social tension.

1.4 Conclusion

The Thornborough henges are therefore much more than fixed symbols of power, and this complex cannot be understood simply as the physical manifestation of socio-political history. This is not to deny that impressive monuments like them could be potent expressions of centralised power or identity, but rather to emphasise how their architecture only meant something as part of broader human experience. However overtly monuments symbolised the control of labour, this message is likely to have been short-lived, open to spontaneous reinterpretation, and may have even led to rebellion against the status quo. To see them as 'central places' for social polities is, at best, an agenda with which only a minority is likely to have been originally engaged. Neither can we assume these sites possessed just one or two meanings, for their interpretation and use would have been dynamic, multi-faceted, and dependent on the backgrounds of those assembled. Their situational and contingent character has a further implication. As we endeavour to move beyond generalised models and investigate the specific meanings and roles associated with individual monuments, we must also accept that our narratives of individual sites and complexes will never decipher the entirety of their meaning, however systematic and thoughtful the study (for a fuller discussion see Jones 2000a, 44–58). Inevitably, many of the different ways in which these places were read by their builders and users will escape us. The following account, which is only able to hint at possible meanings, is no exception, and those engaging with this text will create their own interpretations which will differ, to varying degrees, with my own. This inexorable superabundance of meaning must be accepted at the outset. To do otherwise is to suggest it is somehow possible to capture the totality of the landscape's significance.

There is another reason for the above discussion. If Thornborough is to be understood as part of a more explicit and rounded view of monumentality, this, most crucially, must focus on the relationship between its built places and religion, for 'Rightly understood, sacred architecture represents, in a distilled and crystallised form, the religious experience of humankind, on both a communal and an individual scale' (Sullivan 2000, xi). This is not to imply that by studying Thornborough we can somehow grasp the complete religious system of those who used this landscape, for in reality we are investigating a small and incomplete part of what would have largely been a metaphysical sacred universe; nor is it to insist that religion is not in itself a problematic notion, for it is, and anthropologists especially have highlighted the intricate and convoluted implications of its various definitions (for an introduction see Bowie 2000, 21–8; Lambek 2000, part I and references therein). But it is to consider the concept of religion – by which I mean a belief in gods, spirits, ancestors, and a supernatural realm of existence to explain, order, and make sense of human experience – as preferable to those of 'ritual' or 'ceremony', used so liberally in Neolithic and Bronze Age studies. Religion not only provides the 'thick' context in which much of traditional social life is embedded, but, as a concept, serves to communicate the intimacy and emotional potency so essential to sacred experience (see Insoll 2004b, chapter 4). The term therefore appears

unapologetically in the title of this volume, for first and foremost, Thornborough was a place where the air was thick with religion, and consequently, can be understood best by exploring its sacredness or spiritual power. Whilst it is not necessary to empathise with Neolithic and Bronze Age faith, it is necessary to emphasise the important role of spirituality amongst most societies (Insoll 2004b, 21–2). In this respect, the hundreds of people who now congregate yearly within the henges to celebrate Beltane represent a welcome and long-overdue reminder of the site's broader role.

Religion also provides a context for the non-monumental aspects of human behaviour across a sacred landscape, for they were also used for habitation, for the making of objects, and for the exchange of items, information, and even perhaps people. The building and using of monuments more generally are often closely associated with settlement or large-scale festivals during which a diverse variety of activities, and on occasions sites, were occupied (eg see Adler and Wilshusen 1990; Dillehay 1990, 227–8; Kirch 1991, 137). This is certainly the case at Thornborough, for the worked flint found regularly in its ploughsoil relates to activities undertaken outside the monuments as people periodically gathered here. This aspect of Neolithic and Bronze Age sacred landscapes has not been explored as fully as the evidence will allow, although there are useful discussions for a small number of complexes (Barrett *et al* 1991; Bradley 2000b; Cleal *et al* 1995; Harding and Healy 2007; Hey 1997; Richards 2005; Richards 1990; Waddington 1999). The following will hopefully highlight the extent to which an understanding of monumentality can be greatly enhanced by the study of associated settlement patterns, the latter actually serving to bring to prominence the architecture and significance of these sites. Crucially, though, this evidence should not be considered as unconnected to religion. The sacred not only explains why people were drawn to Thornborough in the first place, but also contributed to the manner in which this wider landscape was occupied during their stays. It is as though the sacredness of the henges stretched across the surrounding area, akin to a weakening gravitation field, determining where it was appropriate to complete certain tasks. Thornborough, then, was not just a place of ritual and ceremony, but also a location for everyday activity, and this too was embedded in people's religion.

2 Creating narratives

2.1 Introduction

This chapter introduces the key events and sources which have contributed to our knowledge of the Thornborough monument complex, including the written evidence of the medieval period, the enclosure maps and antiquarianism of the 18th and 19th centuries, the archaeology of the early 20th century, and the larger-scale investigations of the late 20th and early 21st centuries (Table 2.1 lists all known investigations by antiquaries and archaeologists). What follows, however, is more than simple background to the subsequent chapters, for the evidence is no objective body of data, but a number of value-loaded, subjective, often ambiguous, and sometimes contradictory *narratives* shaped by the actions, attitudes, priorities, and practical realities of their creators. It is therefore necessary to regard each and every one of these as socially mediated, and wherever possible critically interrogate their background, motivations, methods, potentials, and limitations. They were also affected by the landscape itself. The physical nature of a place and its history of land use play an obvious role in the preservation of the archaeological resource, and these factors will, to varying degrees, determine the aims and objectives of the investigators and their investigations. For this reason, reference will be made to some of the broader themes in the landscape's historic development, especially enclosure and large-scale quarrying, and their role in the creation of narratives.

Table 2.1 Investigations at Thornborough

Date	Investigated by	Activity	Source
1774	?	'a survey'	Pennant 1804
18th century	John Mowbray?	Henge survey	1776 Enclosure Map
1816	'Copy of a plan made in 1816'	Henge and barrow survey	This volume
19th century	Ordnance Survey	Henge survey	First Edition Ordnance Survey map
19th century	John Walbran	Henge survey	Hall 2005
1864	Revd W C Lukis	Barrow excavations at 'Centre Hill' and 'Three Hills Field'	Lukis 1870b
1952	Nicholas Thomas	Excavation of cursus, central henge, and northern henge	Thomas 1955
1952	Leslie Grinsell	Barrow survey	Thomas 1955
1958	Faith Vatcher, Ministry of Works	Salvage excavation of cursus	Vatcher 1960
1990	Bradford Archaeological Science Service	Evaluation of Bellflask Farm	Cheetham and Clarke nd
1991–92	Mike Griffiths and Associates	Evaluation of Nosterfield Quarry	Copp and Toop 2005
1992	Roger Martlew, University of Leeds	Geophysical prospection at southern henge	This volume
199?	North Yorkshire County Council	Salvage excavation of two pits near northern henge	North Yorkshire Historic Environment Record
1994–95	Ed Dennison Archaeological Services	Survey of northern henge	This volume
1994–99	Jan Harding, Reading and Newcastle University	Vale of Mowbray Neolithic Landscape Project	This volume
1995–2008	Mike Griffiths and Associates	Watching brief of Nosterfield Quarry	Dickson and Hopkinson 2011
2003–04	Jan Harding, Newcastle University	Aggregate Levy Sustainability Fund Project	This volume
2003–04	Mike Griffiths and Associates	Evaluation of Ladybridge Farm	Garner-Lahire *et al* 2005

Each section of this chapter refers to different types of evidence and highlights the relationships that may have once existed between the monuments and the communities which inhabited this landscape over the last thousand years. The account starts with the earliest maps, place names, and folklore (2.2), a narrative yet to be complemented by the detailed investigation of its contemporary archaeology. The written evidence has been used recently to understand Thornborough's medieval and post-medieval landscape, and whilst this is not of direct concern here, the henges' possible significance during the Middle Ages deserves mention. This narrative hints at the attitudes of those living here, and could indicate the direct and communal appropriation of the past by those making daily use of local places and spaces. In the 19th century, by contrast, the available maps indicate the physical disconnection of the henges from local communities through the increasing demarcation of private ownership (2.3). At the same time, these sites become archaeological objects for study. What was created was a narrative of 'outsiders' as the earthworks no longer had sustained relationships with the contemporary rural population regularly using this landscape, and antiquaries saw them as belonging to a distant past, either as the temporary camps of foreign invaders or as religious monuments of a prehistoric date. From the 1950s Thornborough was recognised to be of regional importance and many aerial photographic sorties were flown over the henges (2.4). This resulted in new evidence, but as mentioned in the previous chapter, the full implications of the complex were rarely ever grasped by the wider community of Neolithic and Bronze Age scholars. The henges remained unconnected to developing national research agendas, and indeed, to the contemporary communities living across this diverse and increasingly wrecked landscape.

This biography of knowledge ends with the fieldwork presented in this volume (2.5) and ongoing controversies about the landscape's future (2.6). It was not until the 1990s that Thornborough's detachment from the broader research themes of Neolithic and Bronze Age studies began to be addressed. At the time there was growing interest in regional variation, the landscape setting of monuments, and the importance of understanding material remains through the three-dimensional real world experience of its creators and users. These concerns provided the framework for the inception and development of the fieldwork and interpretations presented here: it was believed that Thornborough's remarkable archaeology could take our knowledge and understanding in new directions. An attempt was also made to disseminate to the general public what was known about this landscape's archaeology at a time when there was a growing local, regional, and national debate about its future. It therefore seems wholly appropriate to conclude with the current dispute about further quarrying at Thornborough and the conflicting claims being made by the local community, landowners, planners and elected councillors, and a multi-national company. The outcome was a strongly contested narrative firmly grounded in the area's archaeology and the aspirations of those living nearby.

2.2   Early documentation, place-name evidence, and folklore

The earliest written evidence – most notably, the Domesday Book of 1086, 12th-century charters, and 18th-century enclosure maps – provide valuable insights into Thornborough's medieval and post-medieval landscapes (for a recent study see Moorhouse 2004; also Roe 2003, 18–28; Dickson and Hopkinson 2011, 46–53). Stephen Moorhouse (2004) employs the documentary evidence to demonstrate that the three henges, and the plateau on which they are located, were part of a well-used and strategically organised medieval landscape of 'townships' or 'vills', each of these 'small rural cells' with their own settlements and composite open-field systems (for an introduction see Moorhouse 2003, 191; Muir 1997, 104–5). The villages of Upsland and West Tanfield, to the east and west of Thornborough Moor respectively (Fig 2.1), are both mentioned in the Domesday Book and were probably occupied prior to the Norman invasion, the former developing into a high-status moated site which survives today, the latter growing considerably in the post-Conquest centuries, becoming an important manorial centre for the Marmion family. The neighbouring village of East Tanfield, on the lower gravel terrace about 0.5km to the south of the southern henge (Fig 2.1), is also mentioned as a manor in the Domesday Book, and was occupied until the eviction of its inhabitants in the early 16th century. The hollow-way, building plots, and tofts of this splendidly preserved but largely uninvestigated deserted medieval village can still be seen (Moorhouse 2003, fig 46). Settlements are known to have existed at Nosterfield and Thornborough (or Thorn*brough* as Moorhouse believes it was originally known) by at least the 13th century. Despite the scarcity of recorded archaeology, there is every reason to surmise that extensive arable cultivation and grazing was undertaken in the vicinity of each of these locations, and indeed, the infilling of the inner ditches of both the central and southern henges between the 12th and 15th centuries (N Thomas 1955; 4.5.2 and 4.6.3) may attest to this. Early enclosure maps suggest there were few areas not used agriculturally by the late 18th century, hardly surprising given the well-draining quality of the area's soils.

The location of known villages and field systems demonstrates that the henges played a major role in the development of this landscape (Moorhouse 2004, 19, see also fig 4). The siting of township boundaries could suggest a conscious effort to ensure that the three separate townships of Nosterfield, Thornborough, and East Tanfield each contained a henge,

Fig 2.1   Place-names mentioned in Chapter 2. © Crown Copyright/database right 2013. An Ordnance Survey/EDINA supplied service

a division currently undated, but which could have conceivably been established during the Anglo-Saxon period or even earlier (Muir 1997, 105). The reasons for allocating the henges in such a manner may 'reflect a need to provide local communities with access to different types of land and resources' (Atkins Heritage 2005, 45). The earthworks would have certainly been of use to farmers. Moorhouse notes how Nosterfield means 'the sheepfold field' and it is possible that the sheepfold, or what can more accurately be described as an early medieval sheep farm, was 'within the ideally suited northern henge which lay in Nosterfield township' (2004, 25). At the same time, the place name of Thornborough, whose second element derives from the Old Norse 'Berg', means 'thorn hill', and it seems likely that the 'hill' refers to either the banks of the central henge, which could have provided a ready-made enclosure for the Marmion family farm known to have been located at the village (Moorhouse 2004, 26), or to Chapel Hill immediately to the south of the village. The central henge would have been

easily accessible, located as close as it was to the track between West Tanfield and Thornborough. More direct archaeological evidence for the reuse of these monuments comes from the southern henge, where excavations found predominantly 13th- and 14th-century medieval pottery in the top of its inner ditch (4.6.3).

All three earthworks may therefore have been used practically, but we could go further and suggest that the occupants of this medieval landscape were purposefully creating their own mythology, perhaps to demonstrate the ancestry of townships, and thereby legitimate their very existence. Prehistoric monuments were used as meeting places, ceremonial centres or even as high-status settlements or palaces during the early medieval period (Bradley 1987a; 1993, chapter 6). A greater number of sites, including some henges, were places of burial in the 1st millennium AD (eg Barclay 1983, 145, 188; 1999, 37; Harding 1981, 93, 101; Piggott 1948, 100; Scull and Harding 1990; Williams 1998), and Howe Hill, a prominent local landmark a few kilometres to the north-east of Thornborough which happened to look like a large long barrow, had been 'reused' for the interment of four inhumations (Lukis 1870a; see also Hall 2003, 178). At least some of these could be seen as very deliberate manipulations of the past, often made at a time of intense socio-political rivalry or conflict. Nor was the reuse of prehistoric earth-works confined to the early medieval period, for the practice clearly continued in the following centuries, as illustrated, for example, by the Norman church within the central Knowlton henge, Dorset (Grinsell 1976, 109, see also 16–20, 50–3). The later exploitation of the massive Thornborough enclosures may have been a similarly deliberate act of assimilation, even an invention of tradition by which new rules or practices about the landscape's organisation were presented as simple continuities from the past. One can only speculate whether the same motivations were behind the 'Supposed site of a chapel', shown on the First Edition Ordnance Survey map of 1856 as located on the south-western side of *Chapel* Hill, at one of the few locations which overlook all three henges (Fig 2.1). References to the past may even have occurred in the Roman period, as illustrated perhaps by the deposition of a 1st-century brooch in the inner ditch of the southern henge (4.6.3).

Another possible insight into the medieval role of the henges is provided by an unlikely source. A C Thomas, in Appendix III of the report on the excavations of 1952 (see 2.4), reported on the folklore associated with these monuments, and recalls that a villager, 'a fairly intelligent quarry foreman of about 50', had commented on how the central henge

> was known as the 'charging-ground' and had been used as such by either the Romans or the Saxons … The protagonists, mounted on horseback either for tilting or for single combat, had entered at the two opposing entrances, and had hurtled to their mutual encounter at the centre. Cheering spectators had thronged the banks, isolated from the combatants by the inner ditch, which was filled with water (1955, 443).

It would clearly be a mistake to attach too much importance to the anecdote, yet this admirably simple explanation clearly has older origins, for Thomas Pennant, writing in an entry dated 30 August 1774 (1804, 48–51), cites the *Saxo Grammaticus* and suggests the same, labelling the henges 'Danish Tilting Circles'. That this may be what Thomas calls a 'true folk-tradition' is suggested by similar 17th- and 18th-century accounts of King Arthur's Round Table, the smaller double-entranced henge near Penrith on the other side of the Pennines, which envisage an identical role (see N Thomas 1955, 443–4). With this in mind, it is of interest that some of the glazed medieval pottery discovered by excavations within the southern henge are identified as imports from further afield in Yorkshire (D4.1.3), highlighting the intriguing possibility that the site was reused as a medieval fair or for some other form of large-scale rural gathering by the area's different townships,

including perhaps the spectacle of jousting. The earthworks would have certainly provided an ideal arena and the medieval use of prehistoric sites for fairs, races, and other assemblies is well-documented (Grinsell 1976, 52). Also of interest in this regard is the southern henge's proximity to the boundary between the townships of Thornborough and Nosterfield to the north and West Tanfield and East Tanfield to the west and south respectively (Moorhouse 2004, fig 4). The views of the 'fairly intelligent quarry foreman' cannot therefore be so easily dismissed.

This evidence, limited though it is, hints at a close relationship between the henges and the people who occupied and exploited the surrounding landscape. The same can surely be concluded for this landscape's most prominent natural feature. A C Thomas notes the River Ure's close physical relationship with the Thornborough henges, and that between other water courses and double-entranced monuments, and reflects on the consistent importance of rivers in British folklore. They were considered 'both ancient and sinister, and the idea that a river is a divine or semi-divine entity, claiming human lives at intervals, has been perpetuated in some cases to the present day' (A C Thomas 1955, 444). A legend associated with the Ure at Middleham, some 15km upstream of Thornborough, sees the river as infested 'with a horrid kelpie or waterhorse who rises from the stream at evening and ramps along the meadows searching for prey, and it is imagined that the kelpie claims at least one human victim annually' (*ibid*). As someone who has been trapped on the wrong side of the River Ure when it abruptly and violently broke its banks, this link with folklore and death is unsurprising, and seems especially pertinent given that the name Ure or Yore has been attributed to the Celtic 'isura' meaning 'holy one' (Ekwall 1928, 427). Others have explored this link with water, noting its importance elsewhere around Thornborough, as with the swampy area known to have existed to the north around the course of Ings Goit during the medieval period (Roe 2003, 22–3), or with the springs in and around the village of Well (Fig 2.1), where an important medieval estate and large Roman villa complex were sited (Moorhouse 2004, 30–1). Water, one of nature's most powerful phenomena, was a constant feature of this landscape and a beneficiary of deeply held convictions, especially at Well where some of the springs have Christian names of great antiquity. Springs and swampy areas are also known near to the Hutton Moor henge (Moorhouse 2004, 30; Roe 2003, 23).

It is difficult to draw many firm conclusions from these written sources, but they are nonetheless intriguing, and offer historic parallels to many possible Neolithic practices and beliefs (see Chapter 6). They suggest the manner in which the landscape, and especially its henges, was a social resource for those living there. The documentary evidence populates these places with people who, during the Middle Ages, were making use, socially, materially, and spiritually, of the world around them, and by doing so, contributing to its biography. This is most apparent through the folklore, which mirrors people's fears, religiosity, and social interaction. It seems that communities and groups may have come together within the henges for their mutual benefaction. This narrative, however, is associated with another, for the sources hint at the landscape's alienation from the agency which contributed towards its very creation: as Moorhouse states, the concept of township 'strikes at the heart of communal sharing in the exploiting of the landscape', and these divisions 'formed the basic framework for the judicial and fiscal structure, and are the fundamental building block of the manorial system, monastic estates and the medieval parish' (2004, 20). Hence, the experience of Thornborough's landscape was intrinsically linked to social fragmentation, division, and eventually ownership. There are, then, at least two competing narratives, one principally concerned with people's experiences, the other with the control of these experiences through land-use rights. The latter was connected to enclosure, and especially the transfer to private ownership of land previously subject to communal rights, which in following centuries resulted in the reorganisation of both landscape and social relationships.

2.3   Enclosure and antiquarianism

At Thornborough, as elsewhere, the 15th, 16th, and 17th centuries saw some families 'creating their own small farming empires by extracting their lands from the semi-communal pool of resources'(Muir 1997, 212). The occupants of East Tanfield village were evicted in the early 16th century in advance of enclosure (*ibid*, 165), and areas labelled 'old inclosure' on a 1796 Enclosure Map by John Mowbray, the appointed commissioner, suggest earlier demarcation to the north-east of West Tanfield along the road which led to Thornborough Common (Roe 2003, fig 5), an area for communal grazing and other shared land-use presumably utilised during the medieval period by the townships of Nosterfield and Thornborough. By 1792 a significant part of this landscape had been enclosed. A map of that year, illustrating the Lordships of East and West Tanfield (North Yorkshire County Records Office 10 MIC 1930/38–49 ZJX 10/6), depicts an irregular patchwork of small fields to the west of the northern and central henges, including some based upon medieval strip fields, whilst to the south of the West Tanfield to Thornborough road are fields whose more regular grid-like appearance is characteristic of parliamentary enclosure in the latter half of the 18th century. Further change followed shortly: Jefferys' map of Yorkshire (North Yorkshire County Records Office ZDU: Busby Hall Archive), published in 1771 and 1772, clearly shows the northern henge within the then unenclosed and unploughed Thornborough Common, but on the 1796 map by Mowbray (North Yorkshire County Records Office QDD(1) 42 MIC 1541/350) much of the latter was divided, what was

left being separated into Tanfield Common, Nosterfield Common, and Thornborough Moor (Dickson and Hopkinson 2011, fig 19), presumably for use by the named settlements. It also depicts the enclosure of the open fields around the central henge to the north of the Thornborough road. The division of common land appears to have been complete by the 1840s; the First Edition Ordnance Survey map of 1856 shows all three henges within an enclosed landscape with the northern henge covered in woodland.

Enclosure and cartography were part of 'a changing technology of power' by which property was redefined (Bender 1998, 108). They also provide possible insights into how the landscape's reorganisation altered people's perceptions of the three henges. Unlike earlier centuries, when the earthworks are likely to have been an integral part of communal activity and farming, they may now have lost their specific roles, and, as a consequence, become less connected to the daily lives and identities of local communities. Their abandonment as sheep farms and the location for fairs most likely pre-dates the 1790s, and could be some centuries earlier. It was the enclosure of common land, its division amongst various landowners, and the planting of trees on the northern henge, however, which saw the monuments' complete integration into a system of property and arable agriculture, a fact recorded in the Diary of Charles Fothergill, who upon visiting on 24 August 1805, recorded that these sites were 'now chiefly enclosed and is arable land of a good quality: the platforms of most if not all the encampments themselves are ploughed and produce corn' (Romney 1984, 92). This would surely have distanced the monuments from the comings and goings of many, especially since reorganisation also saw road building across the newly enclosed common, including the construction of Green Lane connecting the West Tanfield to Thornborough road with the village of Nosterfield, an act which probably damaged or destroyed part of the northern henge's outer ditch. Local villagers were undoubtedly still aware of the monuments, but most likely experienced these places less and less as part of their daily working lives. There would have been a decreasing number of villagers with an intimate knowledge of these sites, their principal connection to the earthworks now being through folklore and other oral traditions.

These monuments became disconnected from the everyday in another way. Roger Gale, editing his father's commentary on the Antonine Itinerary, was the first to regard them within a historical perspective, as relics of a distant past, describing all three as the 'summer camps of the Romans' (1709, 13). Likewise, Jefferys' map of 1771 and 1772 referred to them as 'Roman Camps', and as already noted, they were considered by Pennant to be 'Danish Tilting Circles'. These classifications are not repeated in their entirety by subsequent cartographers, but the maps produced in 1792, 1796, and 1856 label each of these sites, or just the northern and central henges, as a 'Camp', whilst an estate map of 1804 describes the

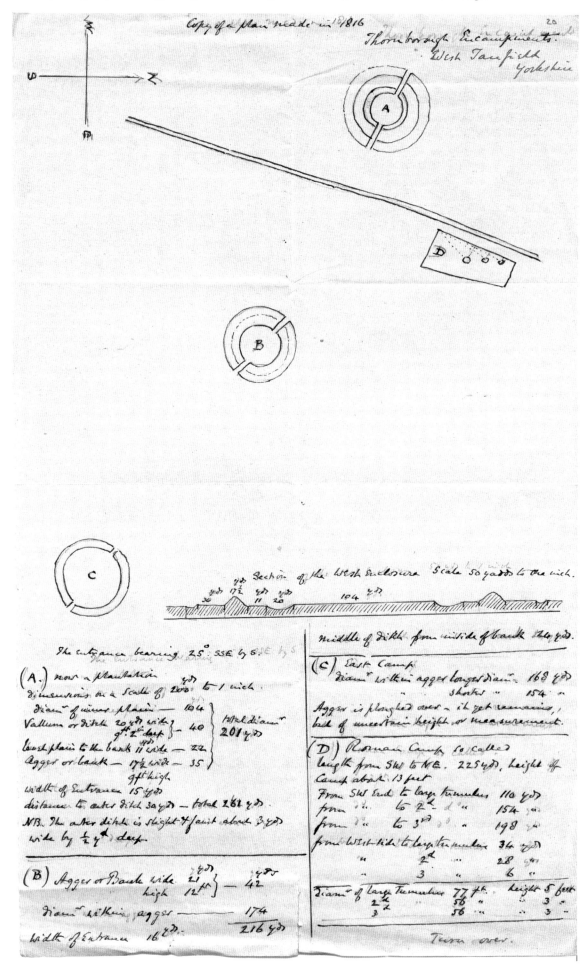

central henge as 'Castle Hill'. A perceived antiquity and martial role is explicit to these descriptors. The same was concluded by Charles Fothergill upon his visit to these 'ancient encampments' (Romney 1984, 92). Somewhat ambiguously, he refers to 'a Roman station on this moor', but continues 'Whether or not these Camps are Danish and have some connection with the etymology of Tanfield or Thanefield perhaps remains to be proved'. A similar interpretation was proposed in a more detailed, but anonymous, entry to Volume II of the *History and Topography of the City of York and the North Riding of Yorkshire* published in 1859 (quoted in its entirety in Hall 2005, 1–2). After a brief description of these 'three enormous entrenchments', which 'certainly have the appearance of defensive works', they are ascribed 'with some degree of probability' as the works of the Danes. These interpretations create a new narrative. If medieval communities appropriated the henges as belonging to a *present* past, they now became something more dim and distant, a relic of invasion and warfare a thousand or more years earlier. If this further severed their connection with local communities, then their enclosure perhaps appeared incidental and legitimate, at least to the landowners.

The great antiquary William Stukeley must have passed close to Thornborough during his northern tour in 1725 (see Piggott 1950, 77–8). His guide was Roger Gale, whose family seat was at nearby Scruton and who had dug at the Devil's Arrows in 1709 (Burl 1991, 10). Gale was aware of the henges, but as mentioned, considered them of Roman origin. Stukeley would surely have challenged their classification as 'camps' or arenas for combat had he seen the sites, but it fell to John Richard Walbran of Ripon to put the record straight, over a hundred years later (Hall 2005). From the fifth edition of *The Pictorial Guide to Ripon and Harrogate*, published in 1851, he refers to the 'temples' of Thornborough, which, along with that at Hutton Moor (and Cana Barn from the sixth edition of 1856/57), demonstrate that 'the immediate vicinity of Ripon was regarded with particular interest and veneration; since one

of the tribes of the Brigantian Celts had chosen it as their station for the dispensation of justice and the celebration of religious rites; in fact, had made it the seat of their government' (quoted in Hall 2005, 3). He continues by noting how at Hutton Moor 'the antiquity and purpose of that place, as a temple for the performance of Druidical rites, is satisfactorily ascertained by the existence of at least eight large Celtic Barrows in its immediate vicinity'. Walbran's explanation, which included a comparison with Avebury and Stonehenge, represents an insightful 19th-century commentary. Subsequent writers were more cautious. The Revd W C Lukis, who from 1862 until his death in 1892 was Rector of Wath, a parish immediately to the south-east of the Thornborough complex, briefly mentions the henges in an account of his barrow excavations, stating they were not defensive earthworks, but were rather

> constructed for pacific reasons, either for permanent cattle pens … or for places of religious assembly, or for the exhibition of periodical games. It must be noted that the entrances to each enclosure are opposite to one another, and have all the same orientation, suggesting the idea that a continuous roadway passed through all of them (Lukis 1870b, 118–19).

He reasoned that they may be earlier than the '"Centre Hill" Tumulus, which lies exactly in the line of this supposed roadway, and that their use must have been long discontinued' (*ibid*, 119).

This literature was connected to the first fieldwork. Maps until the 1790s had simply, albeit quite accurately, marked the circumference of the henges. Pennant (1804, 48) mentions 'a survey' in 1774, but nothing else is known about this. John Mowbray's Enclosure Map of 1796 records the inner ditch and bank at both the northern and central henges, even if it fails to discern the outer lip of the ditch at the more denuded central henge. More useful surveys followed in the 19th century. The earliest was less than twenty years later than Mowbray's according to a hitherto unpublished foolscap 'Copy of a plan made

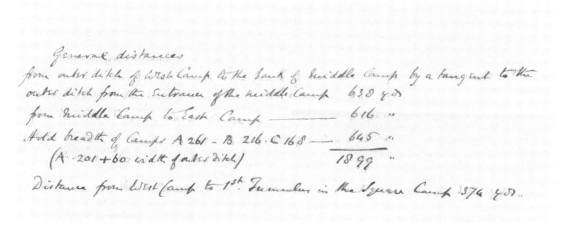

*Fig 2.2   Front (*opposite*) and back of a 'Copy of a Plan made in 1816' (Lukis Archive GMAG 7633.20).
Reproduced courtesy of Guernsey Museums and Art Gallery*

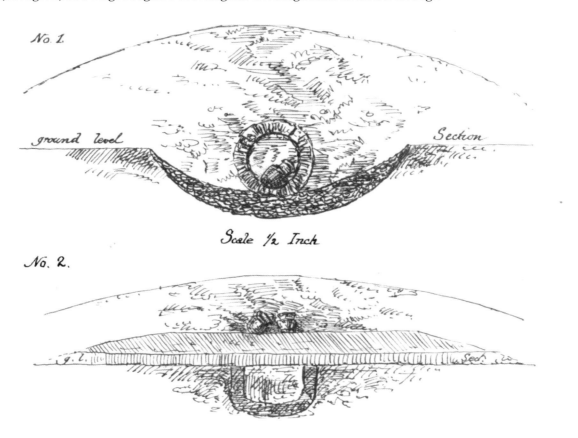

Fig 2.3   Lukis's sections of Centre Hill Tumulus (No. 1) and Tumulus No. 3 in Three Hills Field (No. 2) (1870b, plate V)

in 1816' (Fig 2.2), located by Heather Sebire in the Lukis Archive at Guernsey Museum and Art Gallery (GMAG 7633.20). This copy of an unknown original was made by Lukis, presumably whilst Rector of Wath, and includes a cross-section of the northern henge, or what is described as 'the West Enclosure', along with detailed measurements of all three henges. It also records the round barrows at 'Three Hills' as a 'Roman Camp so called'. This is the first detailed plan, although it contains some obvious inaccuracies and omissions. The inner and outer ditches of the northern henge, along with its intervening bank, are depicted, and mention is made of the covering plantation (Fig 2.2, A). At the central and southern henges (Fig 2.2, B and C respectively), by contrast, there is no record of an outer ditch, despite partly surviving as an earthwork at the former, and there are no measurements for the southern henge bank. The drawing's cardinal points are extremely approximate and the entrances of the central henge are misaligned.

More accurate plans were produced for the 1856 First Edition Ordnance Survey map, at a scale of 1:10,560 (6 inches to 1 mile), providing an excellent depiction of the state of all three henges and also showing many of the known barrows as upstanding earthworks. The late Richard Hall (2005, 6–9) also recently discovered plans and cross-sections in one of Walbran's undated notebooks. These drawings, three of which are annotated with measurements,

are of unnamed sites with the exception of one of the cross-sections, titled 'Section of Circular Earth Work at Thornborough near Tanfield' (*ibid*, fig 5). It fails to show the outer ditches.

Unsurprisingly, the earliest excavations were of barrows. Walbran dug two such sites near the Hutton Moor henge in 1846, finding cremated human bone and flint arrowheads (*ibid*, 9–14), but it was not until 1864 that Lukis excavated the first at Thornborough, subsequently published to what at the time was a high standard. He opened four round barrows here – the one between the southern and central henges known as 'Centre Hill', and three in 'Three Hills Field' (see Fig 1.2, C for their location and Fig 2.3 for two recorded sections) – and another three upon Melmerby Common, near to the Hutton Moor and Cana Barn henges (Lukis 1870b). The results provide valuable information about local funerary practice and the earthworks. The Three Hills barrows produced unassociated cremations, or in the case of the most northerly site (Fig 2.3, No. 2), a 'coarse jar filled with calcined bones' accompanied by 'chipped flints, some of which had been exposed to great heat', a 'second smaller jar', and a circular clay-lined pit, with charcoal and a few small fragments of burnt human bone, in which, according to the excavator, the bodies were fired before being transferred to the jar (Lukis 1870b, 120). Lukis believed the burnt human bone belonged to an adult and child. The excavated barrows on Melmerby Common produced similar evidence, including one with 'two large coarse jars', containing burnt bone, and at another, 'a small curiously formed cup, ornamented with minute lines' at the bottom of a cremation pit (*ibid*, 121). Lukis concluded that cremation was the favoured local funerary practice during the 'pre-Roman period', but that the Centre Hill barrow (Fig 2.3, No. 1) was very different. Here the body of the deceased, consisting of small fragments of unburnt bone, had been 'placed in a wood coffin, probably the hollowed trunk of a tree, the remains of which, reduced to dust, were very discernible' (Lukis 1870b, 119). A 'rudely ornamented jar … on its side, empty … and a chipped flint implement' (*ibid*, 119) had apparently been placed in the coffin. He also discovered in ploughed fields near to Wath and on Hutton Moor, where the henge of that name is located, 'certain small flint implements', stone 'hammers' allegedly employed in the manufacture of these tools, and 'rubbers, for pounding grain and wild fruits for food' (*ibid*, 116).

Hence, the 19th century witnessed the first detailed description of Thornborough's sites and objects along with an appreciation of their antiquity, religiosity, and wider socio-political implications. Some of what was said echoes present-day themes in the study of henges, the Victorians doing much more than simply regarding them as ancient curiosities. There was another way in which an altogether new view of Thornborough was being created. If enclosure and its mapping were part of a discourse of power by which property was redefined, then similar relationships emerged between antiquaries and the relics of the past. Theirs was a narrative of the educated elite, and as such, largely unconnected to the daily working routines and identities of local communities. They clearly appreciated their wider social responsibilities, for publications like Walbran's repeatedly reprinted *The Pictorial Guide to Ripon and Harrogate* highlight an admirable effort to reach a wider audience. Yet at Thornborough other changes were at work. As mentioned, the henges were now used for the growing of crops, and with rapid enclosure and the ploughing of common land it is easy to imagine these sites as no longer intrinsic to local identity and belonging; some may have even seen the earthworks as an obstacle to 'improving' the organisation of land. They had become physically and socially marginal to all except the antiquary, who had, in turn, exacerbated this alienation by providing the henges with a historical perspective and purpose well beyond the memory and folklore of villagers. This is not to chastise the likes of Walbran and Lukis, but to contextualise their actions and understand how they contributed towards a newly emerging narrative which 'pickles the past, negates the present, and excludes very large numbers of people from the story' (Bender 1998, 6). What had once been places of the living had now become places of the long dead.

Central to these developments was a concern with *looking at* a landscape as opposed to *being in* a landscape. Enclosure and its mapping had its origins in the landholding rights of the medieval period, but from the 16th century was also part of an emerging 'politics of vision' in which culture dominated nature, and which, through painting, literature, and the landscaping of large estates, saw a new way of looking which placed the viewer outside of that being depicted, an alienation closely connected to land becoming a commodity (Cosgrove 1984; Olwig 1984). Antiquarianism was intellectually linked to these developments, for those involved gazed from the outside at a distant past, and created their own technology for observing, objectively recording, and controlling this past. Lukis himself touches upon the requirements of this new way of looking in his account of barrow-digging at Thornborough and Melmerby Common. It contains an admirable exploration of burial practice, and the implications for understanding society, but he is nonetheless unwilling to discuss what he cannot prove with evidence, a constraint acknowledged by having 'abstained from any attempt to assign a date to these grave-hills' (Lukis 1870b, 124). He continues by stating that 'The object of barrow openers should not be mere gratification of curiosity, nor the accumulation of ancient works of art. A museum of antiquities is comparatively worthless if the history of the discovery of each particular specimen is not accurately known and recorded' (*ibid*, 124–5). These are sentiments to which every modern fieldworker would subscribe, but demonstrate what was to become the priority of a scientific archaeology – the methods and techniques for the detached and objective recording of a place or object in an attempt to reveal its truth (Thomas 1993).

2.4 The archaeology of a 20th-century mixed economic landscape

There are similarities between the narrative of the 20th century and that of the previous hundred years. This is certainly the case with land use, Thornborough's extensive Grade 2 farmland and rich mineral resources the subject of continuing intensive economic exploitation. Enclosure boundaries depicted on the First Edition Ordnance Survey map of 1856 were to dominate the organisation of land until the late 1960s, but between then and the 1980s many hedgerows were destroyed to create larger fields, especially on the plateau around the northern and central henges. Intensive agricultural methods, including deep ploughing, the mechanical de-stoning of certain fields near the northern henge (Steve Timms, pers comm), and potato farming, were also practised during this period. Mineral extraction was another means by which land became a commodity to be controlled and exploited. There were pre-19th-century limestone workings less than 1km to the west of Nosterfield (Roe 2003), and 19th- and early 20th-century Ordnance Survey maps show

Fig 2.4   The central henge in July 1976 (DNR 983/13). (© English Heritage, Derrick Riley Collection)

small gravel or marl pits to the south-west of the henges and on or near to Chapel Hill, but from the 1950s there was a dramatic increase in the size of quarried areas. Large-scale extraction of sand and gravel occurred immediately to the west and south-west of the central henge in 1952–55, 1969, 1972–75, and 1978, to the west of the northern henge in 1973, and most recently, from 1995, with ongoing quarrying to the north of Nosterfield (Fig 2.1). Unlike earlier quarries, these were disconnected from the control and needs of the local community.

The response of the archaeological community was piecemeal and largely unrelated to the destruction. The single most important contribution was by aerial photography. Many sorties were flown by J K St Joseph of the Cambridge University Committee for Aerial Photography (CUCAP) between 1945 and 1979, by Derek Riley (DNR) between 1972 and 1976, and the Air Photo Unit of the National Monument Records (NMR) between 1991 and 2002 (see Deegan 2005, 5–7). Also worthy of note are early photographs dating to the 1930s and 1945 by O G S Crawford. This work was part of a growing national awareness of the importance and precarious nature of archaeology in Britain's river gravels (Fulford and Nichols 1992; RCHME 1960), and usually focused on the henges and the surrounding plateau, providing a more complete record of these monuments. Importantly, it highlighted 'the contrast between the regular finished appearance of the inner ditch and the irregular and discontinuous outer ditch', the latter's variable width and additional causeways suggesting it 'served mainly as a quarry to provide material for the bank additional to that obtained

from the inner ditch' (St Joseph 1980, 133; Fig 2.4). Aerial photography also led to the discovery of new monuments. The parallel side-ditches of the cursus, which continued under the central henge, were first identified in 1951 (CUCAP GU68–71), and its rounded western terminal recorded in 1955 (CUCAP RG7; Fig 2.5). Aerial photography during the drought of 1976 detected two rows of pits stretching for 350m on a north-north-east to south-south-west axis immediately to the west of the southern henge (St Joseph 1977; CUCAP BTY27–29, 31, 33–34, 37). At its northern end were two groups of nine closely set and narrow parallel trenches at right-angles to the pit rows (Fig 2.6). What looked like a further pair of pits, near the Centre Hill barrow excavated by Lukis, were some 80m to the north-east of the alignment's northern end, and a ring-ditch was discovered near the alignment's southern end (CUCAP BZG84, CAL54, CDK21–26, CQJ16–18; Fig 2.7).

Excavation complemented these discoveries. In 1927–28 'several hundred very small fragments' of cremated human bone, a possible chip of ochre, and five 'cremation pebbles' were found, by means unknown, at a barrow 'between the 2 Thornborough Rings' which must be Centre Hill (Leeds Museum Accession Records and finds labels, courtesy of Katherine Baxter). Nicholas Thomas undertook fieldwork in 1952 with sponsorship from the Yorkshire Archaeological Society, the Society of Antiquaries of London, and the Prehistoric Society. Two slot trenches were dug across the south-west inner ditch terminal of the central henge, another into the inside edge of the adjacent bank, and a further two where the northern cursus ditch ran under the western henge bank (N Thomas 1955, fig 2). Thomas also cleaned and recorded sections of the cursus ditch exposed in the working face of the quarry to the west (Fig 2.1). The cursus was found to be a modest earthwork with a ditch 2–3m wide and 0.6–1m deep (*ibid*, 429–32); sections suggested accompanying outer banks. By contrast, the henge earthworks were impressive. The inner ditch of the central henge was nearly 18m across and over 2m deep, and along with an outer ditch, provided spoil for a massive bank possibly constructed by piling heaps of earth and gravel which were then joined together and smoothed off (*ibid*, 432–3). Remarkably, a large quantity of what was identified as gypsum was found mixed throughout the lower bank deposits, raising the possibility that the earthwork had originally been coated in the material (*ibid*, 441–2; see also Cornwall 1953). A small test pit near the centre of the site revealed nothing of interest, and at the northern henge 'two small sounding pits' were dug into the bottom of its inner ditch, producing information very similar to that from the central henge (N Thomas 1955, 433–4).

The results were employed to tackle the chronology of the complex. The only prehistoric finds were a sherd of indeterminate pottery from the cursus ditch and a few pieces of worked flint and chert from the central henge (N Thomas 1955, 437–8), but fortunately, the soil analysis was informative (*ibid*,

Fig 2.5 The western cursus terminal in July 1955 (CUCAP RG7). (Copyright reserved Cambridge University Collection of Aerial Photography)

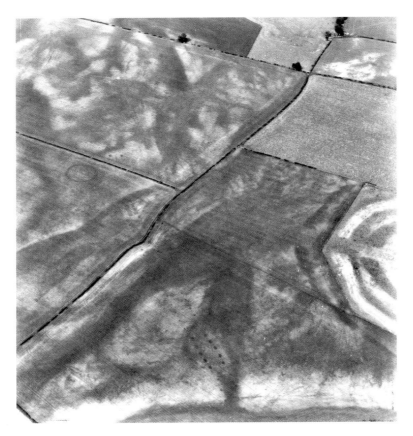

Fig 2.6 The northern half of the double pit alignment in July 1975 (CUCAP BTY28). 'Centre Hill' barrow and two adjacent cropmarks are clearly visible. (Copyright reserved Cambridge University Collection of Aerial Photography)

Fig 2.7   The double pit alignment in July 1984 (CUCAP CQJ18). The ring-ditch near the southern end of the alignment is visible towards the middle bottom of the photograph immediately to the left of the track. (Copyright reserved Cambridge University Collection of Aerial Photography)

432–3). The construction of the two monuments was separated by a significant period of time, the cursus ditch becoming filled, then supporting a turf-line, before the henge bank had been built. Climatic evidence was employed to support this interpretation, the primary fill of the cursus ditch, along with a buried surface sealed beneath the henge bank, indicating relatively close woodland typical of the 'Atlantic or Pre-Bronze Age climatic phase', in contrast to the basal henge ditch deposits which were characteristic of a dry and open environment. A similar difference had been observed between the cursus and henge at Dorchester-on-Thames, the latter 'attributed with certainty to the people who brought the Beakers and earliest metal tools to Britain' (*ibid*, 436). If this strongly intimated the chronological horizon to which the Thornborough henges belonged, then the contents of the associated round barrows – which were listed in an appendix by Leslie Grinsell, recording, amongst other things, their national grid reference and surviving dimensions – were also seen to indicate their date. After a brief discussion of these and other nearby barrows, it was concluded that the henges at Thornborough, along with those at Hutton Moor and Cana Barn, were 'in use at a period just subsequent to

the Beaker/early Food Vessel stage, and that their makers belonged to the full Early Bronze Age. They must be broadly contemporary with the final phase of building at Stonehenge' (*ibid*, 436–7).

The report offers a broader context for Thornborough. Previously, the Yorkshire Archaeological Society, in an urgent attempt to raise funds for Thomas's forthcoming excavations, had written to its members stating that 'It cannot be stressed too strongly that any light thrown on this, one of the most important monuments of its kind in Europe, will be of inestimable value to the study of Prehistory in general, and that of Yorkshire in particular' (Strickland and Bunnett nd). So it proved. Echoing an earlier statement that these 'were clearly ceremonial meeting-places of a plentiful population' (Elgee and Elgee 1933, 78; see also Raistrick 1929, 365), Thomas noted how these 'religious sites' indicated 'a population of some considerable size' towards the end of the Neolithic (1955, 437). The area's distinctiveness was also seen as being indicated by the wide berm separating the ditch and bank of each of the Thornborough henges, in contrast to Big Rings at Dorchester-on-Thames (*ibid*, 436–7). Despite this, they were regarded as copies of southern henges, perhaps the product of 'Yorkshire chiefs and their families who must have journeyed down the Jurassic Way, across Oxfordshire (past the Big Rings perhaps) to Wiltshire, on a pilgrimage to Stonehenge' (*ibid*, 436). The significance of movement and interaction was repeated a few years later by D P Dymond in his 1963 excavation report of the nearby Nunwick henge. He suggested that the concentration of monuments in the Ripon area was due to their location 'on a natural route-way from west to east, from Ireland and the Pennines to eastern Yorkshire' (1963, 103). Dymond also commented on the possible 'sanctity of rivers', although he attached the rider that 'such intangible and cerebral notions are not the stuff of archaeology'. Thomas similarly emphasised the link with rivers when some years later he wrote of a 'line of sacred sites extending … along the course of the Ure' (1976, 244).

More excavation soon followed. Topsoil stripping in advance of gravel extraction to the west of the central henge revealed a substantial length of the cursus, and under difficult salvage conditions in January 1958, Faith Vatcher (1960), on behalf of the Ministry of Works, excavated the monument's western terminal and flanking ditches. The side ditches were 43m apart, 2.1–2.7m wide, and 0.6–0.9m deep. The terminal consisted of a broadly curving ditch broken by two gaps, one towards its centre, the other where it meets the northern flanking ditch. There was a further causeway along the latter and the opposing section of the southern side-ditch may have been refilled to create another. The results were comparable to those of Thomas's excavation, except that the ditch was accompanied by an inner rather than outer bank. Soil analysis of a dark humic layer within the ditches similarly suggested a 'deciduous forest environment with plentiful drifted leaves' (Vatcher 1960, 171), and whilst no finds were recovered, this layer was taken to indicate a date during 'the later Neolithic or the time of transition from Neolithic to Bronze Age' (Cornwall in Vatcher 1960, 181). Later in 1958, during the further cutting back of the quarry face, a cist of five limestone slabs was uncovered by an excavator driver approximately 4.5m inside the monument along its central axis (Vatcher 1960, 181–2). It contained a crouched inhumation facing south-east whose head was pointing to the terminal. Vatcher also took the opportunity, when returning to Thornborough, to chase the cursus cropmark eastwards beyond the henge until 'the first cottage in Thornborough' (*ibid*, 173), establishing the monument's total known length as 1.2km.

By contrast to Vatcher's timely intervention, extensive sand and gravel extraction in the late 1960s and 1970s was undertaken without any archaeological mitigation. The archaeology went unrecorded during quarrying at the northern henge. The western edge of its bank and outer ditch is likely to have already been damaged by the construction of Green Lane in the late 18th century, but in the early 1970s extensive mineral extraction on the other side of this road destroyed an estimated 16m of the henge's outer ditch (Fig 2.1). At the same time, an L-shaped quarry immediately to the west of the central henge resulted in the destruction of about 4m of the monument's outer ditch, an estimated 80m length of the cursus, and a probable round barrow. Immediately on the other side of the West Tanfield to Thornborough road another round barrow, whose locality was recorded by Grinsell to be 'N.E. of Thornborough Crossing', was also destroyed by quarrying (N Thomas 1955, appendix II). That there was no archaeological intervention in advance of the destruction of known monuments is deeply regrettable, and made worse by the quarrying-out of almost the entire western half of the landscape (Fig 2.1). Elsewhere, cursus terminals are a focus for other monuments, some earlier and some later (Barrett *et al* 1991, 47, 49; Loveday 1985, 116, 121–2, table 5.2), and the area around the western end of the site at Thornborough could have added significantly to what is currently known about the complex had it escaped destruction.

Quarrying was matched by other acts of destruction. Unfortunately, the bank of the central henge was 'badly mutilated for road-building', and 'This robbing was accentuated during the Second World War when shelters were erected for storing shells' (N Thomas 1955, 427). Oblique aerial photographs taken in April 1945 (CUCAP B20–22) do show a single shelter, presumably holding munitions, on the inside of the north-eastern bank terminal. This novel reuse of the monument was completely in keeping for the area at the time: an ordnance factory was located just 6km to the south-east near the village of Melmerby and RAF vertical photographs taken in 1946 show munitions stacked and covered by tarpaulin alongside many local roadsides. The factory and these temporary stores were all strategically sited close to the former Leeds and Thirsk Railway which ran past the southern henge. Aerial photographs of the central henge taken a little later also show what looks like large rectilinear mounds or excavation trenches across the inner ditch on its eastern side – just one in July 1954 (CUCAP OW69–70), but a year later a further two were photographed (CUCAP RG17). There are no other records of what was being undertaken here and it left no detectable traces of disturbance. Cultivation also played a significant role in the destruction of the monuments. Thomas (1955, 427) notes how 'Heath and scrub covered the central circle until it recently came under cultivation', and the inner area of the monument was exploited for arable farming until 1993, when the farmer went bankrupt. Ploughing dug into the outer edge of its bank. The southern henge suffered even more and its inner area was under cultivation when Thomas (*ibid*, 427) conducted his fieldwork. Part of its inner area was allegedly bulldozed in the 1960s (Neil Campling, pers comm), and again, the plough encroached upon and seriously damaged the outer limits of its bank.

The narrative of the 20th century is therefore characterised by neglect – and not only in terms of the landscape's physical destruction. It would be wrong to say that Thornborough's archaeology became totally disconnected from local communities during the 20th century, for people did visit the henges, with villagers from Nosterfield frequently walking their dogs, or undertaking less innocent activities, on the northernmost site. And the general public, especially farmers and those with metal-detectors, were responsible for the discovery of stray finds from the area, including four polished stone axes, complementing the single flint specimen apparently found in 1827 within the 'Danish Camp on Thornbro Moor', or what is presumably the central or southern henge (Thomas 1963, 14), a perforated macehead and axe hammer, a middle Bronze Age palstave, and a later Bronze Age socketed spearhead. Yet despite these recreational visits and occasional discoveries, there was no public right of access to the henges. For the few who did explore the monuments nothing explained what they saw before them, or described the discoveries of antiquaries and archaeologists. Local alienation and frustration was evident amongst many of the villagers who visited the excavations between 1994 and 1999. Some had never been to 'The Rings' before or realised they were archaeological sites, and when asked, were more likely to say they had been built by Druids, or were the remains of settlements and stockades, than realise they were Neolithic monuments. Despite this, the overwhelming majority had an appetite to know more and wanted the henges to become part of their local identity.

It was not only local villagers who were alienated from these remains. The more detailed and comprehensive record which developed during the 20th century largely failed to stimulate a wider interest amongst Neolithic and Bronze Age specialists in spite of an increasing awareness of monument complexes nationally. The site's existence was widely reported during the first half of the 20th century, being included in early gazetteers of henges (Crawford 1927, 8; Clark 1936, 31, 50–1; Atkinson *et al* 1951, 102–3), but its importance remained unexplored in general discussions of the period. It is perhaps understandable that Thornborough gets no mention in Gordon Childe's (1940) *Prehistoric Communities of the British Isles*, or the first edition of Jacquetta and Christopher Hawkes's *Prehistoric Britain* (1944), for Thomas's fieldwork was still some years away, but its omission from the first two editions of Stuart Piggott's *Neolithic Cultures of the British Isles* (1954, 1970) is more puzzling. It was also absent from Richard Atkinson's popular but detailed book on Stonehenge and Neolithic and Bronze Age society, even though he mentions other henges of the 'Secondary Neolithic Cultures' and 'Beaker Cultures' (1956, 151–8), including some from northern England and Scotland. It seems that Thornborough's remarkable landscape was failing to attract the attention of those playing leading roles in developing Neolithic and Bronze Age research agendas, a failure which was to cast a long shadow over its future.

2.5 Research agendas and projects 1994–2004

Thornborough's marginalisation no doubt reflected a combination of factors, including the damage already wreaked by quarrying and farming, and the whereabouts, interests, and loyalties of amateur and professional archaeologists. A central issue was its location on the fringe of a low-lying landscape better known for its Roman and medieval archaeology than for its prehistory. By the 1950s a conspicuous bias had been established towards those areas perceived to possess nationally important Neolithic evidence, in the wake of impressive excavation results across the southern chalkland and the archipelago of Orkney (eg Atkinson 1956; Childe 1930; 1931; Curwen 1934; 1937; Piggott 1962; Smith 1965). These two very different regions were now the empirical cornerstones of Neolithic studies and were to continue as such for decades to come. Interpretations of the period failed to consider the evidence from Thornborough and the other henges along the Ure, despite the creation of archaeology departments at a number of nearby universities. Whilst a growing interest in the archaeology of Britain's river gravels had attracted fieldworkers like Thomas to the complex, it was nonetheless the case that the Yorkshire vales, a major river catchment with England's greatest expanse of gravel (RCHME 1960, fig 1), was punching well below its prehistoric weight when compared to other regions. If this suggests a largely southern bias to our interpretations, then in Yorkshire itself an eastern bias in fieldwork and evidence had become established during the 19th and 20th centuries, the attention of antiquaries and archaeologists alike falling more regularly on the Yorkshire Wolds, and to a lesser extent the North York Moors, than on the lowlands to the west (for an overview see Manby 1988a; Manby *et al* 2003).

Regional variation was eventually to become an issue for Neolithic studies (Bradley and Gardiner 1984, 2). The 1980s and early 1990s saw the publication of a large body of geographically specific and detailed studies, based largely on monument construction and use, for different parts of the Wessex and Sussex chalkland, the Upper Thames Valley, the English Midlands and East Anglia, the Peak District, and Orkney. They consistently demonstrated 'that there is no "typical" monument sequence, nor is there one "typical" complex of monuments in Britain' (Harding 1991, 146; see also 1995), and a similar emphasis on variation was suggested by regionally manufactured styles of earlier Neolithic pottery (Bradley 1984, 34, 38). If it was apparent that there were fundamental differences between regionally based communities, however, these were more difficult to grasp in relation to England north of the Humber Wash, or what at the time was described as 'a rather uncomfortable No Man's Land' between the uplands to the north and lowlands to the south (Barker 1981, 1). The area as a whole was not well investigated, existing studies focusing on eastern Yorkshire (Manby 1988a; Manby and Turnbull 1986; Spratt 1982; 1993; Spratt and Burgess 1985; Pierpoint 1980; Vyner 1995), the Milfield Plain in Northumberland (Harding 1981; Miket 1976; 1985), and Weardale in Co. Durham (Young 1987). At the same time, many of its distinctive traits, such as the apparent absence of causewayed enclosures in areas with significant numbers of long barrows (Harding 1997a, 281–3; but see Waddington 2001; Oswald *et al* 2001, 80–9), were under-valued and under-researched.

Regional variation provides the backdrop to my interest in Thornborough. The limited amount of fieldwork at the complex – and the three nearby henges of Nunwick, Hutton Moor, and Cana Barn – meant little could be said about the dynamic of monument building and use here, and they failed to qualify as a later Neolithic 'core area' in Richard Bradley's watershed publication, *The Social Foundations of Prehistoric Britain* (1984, 41, fig 3.2). Nevertheless, they had the *potential* to add greatly to the growing debate about regional variability. Henges are perhaps the most standardised and widely distributed of all Neolithic monument types (Harding 2003, chapter 2; Harding and Lee 1987, figs 23–4), and those along the Ure form a neatly defined group more-or-less unique in terms of their size, their double-ditched and two-entranced layout, and their nearness to each other (Burl 1969; Harding 1995, 131–2; 1997a, 288, fig 4). Regional distinctiveness was complemented by intriguing similarities with two other complexes. As already mentioned (1.2), the closest parallels to Thornborough were the monumental foci at Dorchester-on-Thames and Maxey, and all three differed to other complexes across their regions, possessing morphologically unusual henges placed on or next to a lengthy cursus with convex terminals (Harding 1991, 147–9; see also 1995, 127–31). The investigation of Thornborough was an opportunity to explore the relationship between regionally distinctive trajectories and inter-regional processes like the adoption of a widely recognised monument type and the creation of major centres of religious worship which stood apart from other complexes.

Thornborough could shed light on another major theme of Neolithic and Bronze Age research during the 1980s and 1990s. Prehistorians had begun to talk of 'ritual landscapes' (Richards 1984; Thorpe 1984, 58; Thorpe and Richards 1984, 75, 77; see also Richards 1990, chapter 10) or 'sacred geography' (Harding and Lee 1987, 62), and regional studies provided valuable insights into how monuments and settlements once related to each other. The organisation of the landscape was now seen as part of an overarching world-view where religion and subsistence were closely linked elements of daily life (Bradley and Chambers 1988, 272–3; Harding 1991, 146–7). Again, however, there was a geographical bias in favour of southern England. It was not known if the Thornborough complex and its immediate

hinterland was unassociated with contemporary occupation, as at Maxey (Pryor *et al* 1985, 232–3, 301; but see French and Pryor 2005, 164–70), or if it did exist, whether it was in any way special or different, as was the case near the Dorset Cursus (Barrett *et al* 1991, chapter 3) or the Durrington Walls complex (Richards 1990, 267–71). The detailed study of its landscape by surface collection could address these issues, and was seen as especially important given that the large size of the henges, and their siting in a region known to have possessed strategically important routeways and relatively large populations during historic periods, suggested extensive occupation during the Neolithic and Bronze Age. In addition, Thornborough's location on the edge of a low-lying landscape, flanked immediately to the west by the Pennines and 15km to the east by the Hambleton Hills, offered an opportunity to examine and understand better the lowland-upland relationship (eg Fox 1932; Evans *et al* 1975; Limbrey and Evans 1978; Bradley 1992a).

The result was the *Vale of Mowbray Neolithic Landscape Project* (VMNLP). Envisaged originally as an investigation of all six henges along the Ure, this was soon seen as unrealistic, the project focusing instead on Thornborough. It aimed to characterise monument building and the sequence of construction here. The irregular and segmentary appearance of the outer henge ditches was reminiscent of the circuits of later causewayed enclosures and early henges (Fig 2.4), and therefore possibly earlier than the inner earthworks (see Harding 2003, chapter 1). Exploring them was an important objective. Related to this was the broader issue of whether the henges were the product of a single burst of intensive construction or whether they developed more intermittently as people added to the complex. The project would also consider the relationship between the monuments and wider patterns of activity through intensive investigation. As shown in Figure 2.8, a 4km by 3km study area, centred on the henges (SE2677 to SE3282), was selected for fieldwalking. It encompassed the fluvioglacial plateau across which the larger monuments were built, and the different topographic zones of its immediate hinterland, including the lower river terrace to the south, the limestone escarpment to the west, and the knolls and ridges of till to the east. Roads and natural features marked its boundary.

Between 1994 and 1998 the VMNLP was funded by the Arts and Humanities Research Board, the British Academy, English Heritage, Reading University, Newcastle University, the Prehistoric Society, the Robert Kiln Charitable Trust, and the Society of Antiquaries of London. In five seasons of summer fieldwork the following was completed: a topographic survey of the southern and central henges and their immediate hinterland; geophysical prospection at the southern henge, the double pit alignment, an oval enclosure identified from an aerial photograph immediately to the south of Thornborough village and thought to be of earlier Neolithic date,

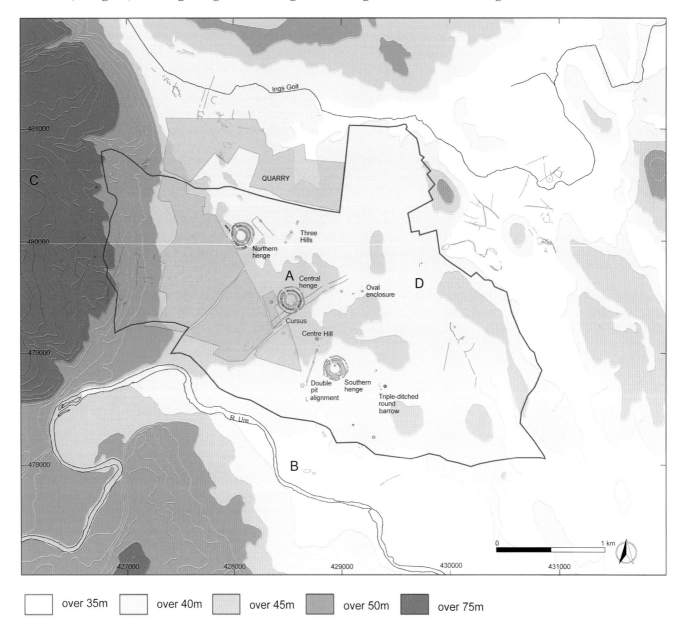

	over 35m		over 40m		over 45m		over 50m		over 75m

Fig 2.8   The topography of the VMNLP and ALSF Project study area: A, fluvio-glacial plateau; B, lower river terrace; C, limestone escarpment; D, plateau and till deposits. © Crown Copyright / database right 2013. An Ordnance Survey / EDINA supplied service

and a possible new cursus alongside the northern henge with a squared-off terminal, also identified by aerial photography; the small-scale excavation of the double pit alignment, the oval enclosure, and the southern and central henges; and widespaced surface collection across about 180ha of the study area (Fig 2.9). The VMNLP was complemented in 1998 and 1999 by the large-scale excavation of the double pit alignment, funded by Robert Staveley, the landowner of the central and southern henges, as part of a new management regime for the henges (2.6). The results of all this work are fully presented in this volume. Completed at broadly the same time as the VMNLP was an earthwork survey of the northern henge by Ed Dennison Archaeologi-

cal Services; a geophysical survey of the southern henge and double pit alignment by Arnold Aspinall and Roger Martlew of Bradford and Leeds Universities respectively; and the 'Prospection in Alluvial Environments Project', which considered the geomorphology and early Holocene Environments of the Yorkshire Ouse basin (Howard *et al* 2000; see also Howard and Macklin 1999). The work by Aspinall, Dennison, and Martlew can be found in Chapter 3 and D1.

The subsequent launch of the Aggregates Levy Sustainability Fund (ALSF) offered an opportunity for further investigations. The resulting ALSF project, disbursed through English Heritage and including a single season of fieldwork in the

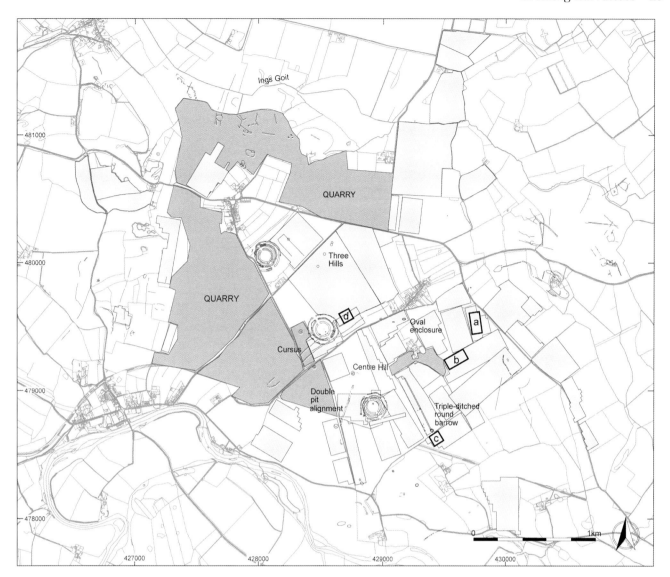

Fig 2.9 VMNLP and ALSF Project surface collection including the four intensively investigated lithic scatters of 'high' (a), 'medium' (b and c) and 'low' (d) density. © Crown Copyright/database right 2013. An Ordnance Survey/EDINA supplied service

summer of 2003, reflected the priorities of the Aggregates Levy itself. The emphasis was on providing additional information about the survival and preservation of the prehistoric archaeology, including the current condition of a number of monuments unexplored by the VMNLP, which could then be used by others to create a much-needed strategy for their long-term conservation and management. Topographical survey and geophysical prospection was completed at the Three Hills barrows, the Centre Hill barrow, and a triple-ditched round barrow (Fig 2.9). This was followed by the small-scale excavation of the triple-ditched round barrow, along with some nearby pits, and one of the Three Hills barrows, sites which the non-intrusive investigation had suggested were the 'best' and 'worst' preserved barrows respectively. The interiors of the central and southern henges were also recorded by geophysical prospection. Moreover, there remained large parts of the landscape where surface col-

lection was yet to be completed, and nothing was known about the relationship between the surface lithic scatters, discovered by the VMNLP, and any associated sub-surface archaeology. A further 129 hectares were fieldwalked and there was the intensive investigation – by geophysical prospection, total surface collection, and test-pitting – of four known lithic scatters of 'high', 'medium', and 'low' density to evaluate their buried potential (Fig 2.9). Results are fully presented here and occasional reference will be made to two other ALSF projects: the 'Thornborough Henges Air Photo Mapping Project' by West Yorkshire Archaeological Services, which plotted all known aerial photographs across a 100km² centred on the complex itself (Deegan 2005); and the recently published 'Swale-Ure Washlands Project' which considered geomorphology and environment since the end of the last Ice Age (Bridgland *et al* 2011; see also Long *et al* 2004).

2.6   A contested early 21st-century landscape

Other developments were broadly contemporaneous with these research projects. The re-emergence of a strong local interest in the complex is most clearly demonstrated by the villagers who got together in 2003 to establish the Friends of Thornborough. This voluntary campaign group is dedicated to preventing further damage to the area's archaeology and landscape whilst improving its conservation and presentation. It believes that the local community must be directly involved at every level in deciding on Thornborough's future, but its appeal has extended well beyond those who live in this part of Yorkshire, for at its height it could boast support from over 13,000 people from around the world. No doubt this success reflects broader socio-political developments like the 'greening of our consciousness' (Bender 1998, 5; see also Macinnes and Wickham-Jones 1992) and a growing interest in alternative or pagan religions. But it was also connected to specific local factors, notably the operation of a now closed household waste landfill site at the old quarry to the west of the central henge, and, most controversially, the continuing extraction of minerals. The opening in 1995 of the large quarry to the north of the village of Nosterfield by Tarmac Northern Ltd saw the destruction of a further 106ha (Fig 2.9), whilst a quarry extension by Hanson Aggregates, on the banks of the River Ure at Bellflask Farm, less than 1km to the south-east of the southern henge, resulted in more destruction. Local villagers, the vast majority of whom were either members or supporters of the Friends of Thornborough, became acutely concerned about the impact of these two new quarries within a short walking distance of the henges.

They have not been assuaged by the archaeological investigations associated with this new quarrying, arguing that nationally important archaeology and its setting should be preserved in situ as part of a long-term management plan. In 1990 an archaeological evaluation, including geophysical prospection, surface collection, test-pitting, and trial-trenching, was completed at Bellflask Farm by Bradford Archaeological Science Service (Cheetham and Clarke nd). The only prehistoric evidence was two worked flints, a result perhaps of the area being cut and recut by successive river channels since the end of the medieval period (Neil Campling, pers comm). Salvage excavation of two large undated pits immediately to the north of the northern henge was also undertaken by North Yorkshire County Council during the construction of a quarry haulage road (Neil Campling, pers comm). More extensive and long-running work, completed on behalf of Mike Griffiths and Associates, took place at Nosterfield Quarry between 1991 and 2003 (Dickson and Hopkinson 2011). Its discoveries included a cluster of 83 Neolithic pits, some with 'Grimston Ware', Peterborough Ware, and Grooved Ware, a large number of widely dispersed pits and scoops, three ring-ditches and cremations of probable Bronze Age date, six possibly prehistoric pit alignments and a further ditch/pit alignment, and two small square-ditch enclosures and a horse burial of Iron Age date. The fieldwork was accompanied by a desk-based assessment (Roe 2003). These results provide what the Interim Report describes as a 'unique opportunity to discuss the changing use of a wide tract of landscape from the Mesolithic to the modern day' (Copp and Toop 2005, 130). It was a landscape seen as fast disappearing under the plough, with excavation in advance of quarrying, rather than unrecorded destruction by farming, believed to be preferable (Mike Griffiths, pers comm). By contrast, the Friends of Thornborough thought new conservation initiatives were a better solution to its future degradation.

Unease amongst local villagers was exacerbated when Tarmac proposed the further extraction of sand and gravel at Ladybridge Farm, immediately to the east of the existing Nosterfield Quarry, and across Thornborough Moor (the area to the south of the road). In 2004 it submitted a planning application for the Ladybridge Farm site immediately across the road to the east of the existing quarry, supplemented in the following year by the results of the archaeological evaluation undertaken on behalf of Mike Griffiths and Associates (Garner-Lahire *et al* 2005). The application was greeted with dismay and anger, leading to a high-profile national campaign by the Friends of Thornborough and other voluntary campaign groups opposed to further extraction. Regional and national archaeology bodies also became involved, with the Yorkshire Archaeological Society, the Council for British Archaeology, the Prehistoric Society, and English Heritage all formally opposing further quarrying on the grounds that Ladybridge Farm was an essential part of the complex's setting. This campaign resulted in what is a rarity – an editorial in a national newspaper about British archaeology. On 20 February 2006 *The Guardian* wrote of Thornborough's landscape setting:

> for this to be imperilled by a gravel extraction scheme for Tarmac … beggars belief, particularly when the company has shown sensitivity to the core of the henge site, which would not be damaged by the proposed work. Recent archaeology shows unanswerably how the circles need their setting to be understood, and to create that numinous atmosphere which will bring visitors, and their money. Of course this farming and quarrying part of North Yorkshire has to earn a living. It will not do so by digging up its finest asset.

Thornborough's claim to national recognition appeared irresistible and the following day the planning application was rejected by North Yorkshire County Council.

A new narrative has therefore arisen. At its heart is the question of who 'owns' what the then Chief Archaeologist for English Heritage described as 'the most important prehistoric site between Stonehenge and the Orkneys' (David Miles, pers comm).

It is certainly not the first time such a debate has raged around a Neolithic monument, for it seems ever to have been so at Stonehenge (Chippindale *et al* 1990; Bender 1998), but unlike the endless controversies surrounding this chalkland henge, those at Thornborough are closely connected to the needs and aspirations of local villagers. In the same way that the medieval and early historic periods presumably saw conflict between those dividing and fragmenting a landscape, and those concerned with its everyday and open use, this present-day narrative is based on deep-rooted disagreement between the local community, the site's current custodians, and vested financial interest. It challenges those involved with managing Thornborough's future to move away from an approach which 'pickles the past, negates the present, and excludes very large numbers of people from the story', to return to the quote of earlier. Crucially, people are now returning to this contested place. The media attention of recent years – including a dedicated episode in the BBC2 *Time Flyers* series entitled 'The Stonehenge of the North' – has resulted in the complex's growing popularity. Other initiatives contributed to its newly won recognition, including a Countryside Stewardship Agreement in 1998 whereby the central and southern henges, along with a linking area, were converted to permanent grassland. Apart from its obvious advantages for preservation, this provides a defined area within which people can explore the earthworks, and accordingly, the sites were opened to those formally requesting access.

3 Physicality of presence

3.1 Introduction

This chapter examines the physical character of Thornborough's monuments and landscape. It starts with an overview of the topography, geology, watercourses, and soils of the VMNLP and ALSF Project study area and its immediate hinterland. The focus will be on those geomorphological characteristics likely to have been physically discernible, and therefore potentially meaningful, to people during the Neolithic and Bronze Age. Reference will be made wherever appropriate to the results from the Late Quaternary Landscape History of the Swale-Ure Washlands Project (Bridgland *et al* 2011), the Ouse Catchment Project (Howard *et al* 2000; see also Macklin *et al* 2000), and the watching brief at Nosterfield Quarry (Dickinson and Hopkinson 2011; see also Berg 1991; Copp and Toop 2005; Long and Tipping 1998; Rutherford nd; Tipping 2000). What little is known about vegetation cover during the Neolithic and Bronze Age, exclusively the result of other projects (4.1), is mentioned in 4.9 and 5.5. The chapter also explores the condition and original appearance of all known or probable Neolithic and Bronze Age monuments by drawing on the full range of available evidence from aerial photography, field observation, survey, and geophysical prospection. This excludes those discovered during the watching brief at Nosterfield Quarry, which are fully published elsewhere (Dickson and Hopkinson 2011). As will become apparent, the evidence differs greatly in quality, but especially noteworthy are the well-preserved northern and central henges. The other monuments, by contrast, now exist largely as cropmarks.

3.2 The landscape setting

The distinctiveness of Thornborough's landscape partly reflects its location on a shelf of Permian limestone and marl (Fig 3.1) no more than 5–6km across which runs north–south from the River Tees to as far as Nottingham (Edwards and Trotter 1954, 4, fig 2; Powell *et al* 1992, 12, 14). This outcrop is sandwiched between geologically and topographically contrasting areas. To the east is more low-lying Triassic sandstone, which, at about 3km from Thornborough, forms the Vale of Mowbray, or the northern narrowing extension of the Vale of York, reaching heights of usually no more than 30–35m OD. Some 5km to the west is the more elevated millstone grit of the Pennines which at Nidderdale rises to around 350m OD. The shelf itself consists of two narrow and broadly parallel belts of limestone which outcrop as eastern-facing escarpments (Scale 1:50,000 Solid Geology Sheet 52). The most pronounced of these is to the west where the Lower Magnesian Limestone is as high as 140m OD before sloping down to meet the Pennine Millstone Grit; within the VMNLP and ALSF Project study area, this ridge runs between West Tanfield and Well with heights of 45–75m OD. To the east the Upper Magnesian Limestone forms a much lower and gentler drift-covered escarpment, which nonetheless forms a barrier with the lowland vales to the east. Between these two limestone escarpments lies a belt of marl which outcrops as lower flatter ground, giving the shelf its overall bowl-like appearance (Scale 1:50,000 Solid Geology Sheet 52). The Thornborough complex is sited here on the middle of the shelf flanked by the two limestone escarpments (Fig 3.2A). As a result, it possesses a physically distinctive setting with topographically discernible boundaries to the east and west.

Natural features also provide boundaries to the north and south. The limestone and marl shelf is bisected at West Tanfield by the River Ure flowing west to south-east out of Wensleydale with little or no gradient along its course. Certainly in the early post-glacial it was a fast-flowing and anastomosed river, its multiple channels migrating frequently across the valley floor, but whether this was replaced by a single thread channel later in the early Holocene is a matter of speculation (see Bridgland *et al* 2011, 279; Howard *et al* 2000, 39). There is some indication that a more stable medium-energy river system developed before or during monument building (Bridgland *et al* 2011, table 3.32; Howard and Macklin 1999, 532–4), but the radiocarbon dating of geomorphological deposits lying between the southern henge and the Ure – work completed as part of the Prospection in Alluvial Environments Project by Andy Howard at the School of Geography, Leeds University – points towards a long history of river formation with significant episodes of aggradation and incision as recently as the late Iron Age and early Romano-British period (Andy Howard, pers comm). Hence, it seems likely that the henges, once built, were a little closer to the river than at present (Bridgland *et al* 2011, 48), and whatever its exact form, the Ure must have been a formidable, and at times, lethal, barrier to the south and south-west of the complex. Palaeoenvironmental evidence from Bellflask Quarry, only 1.5km to the south-east, suggests its migration had resulted in wet marshland by the Bronze Age (*ibid*, 147–51). That areas of wetland continued to exist here into the historic periods is suggested by the name 'Flask', which means an area of pools or marsh,

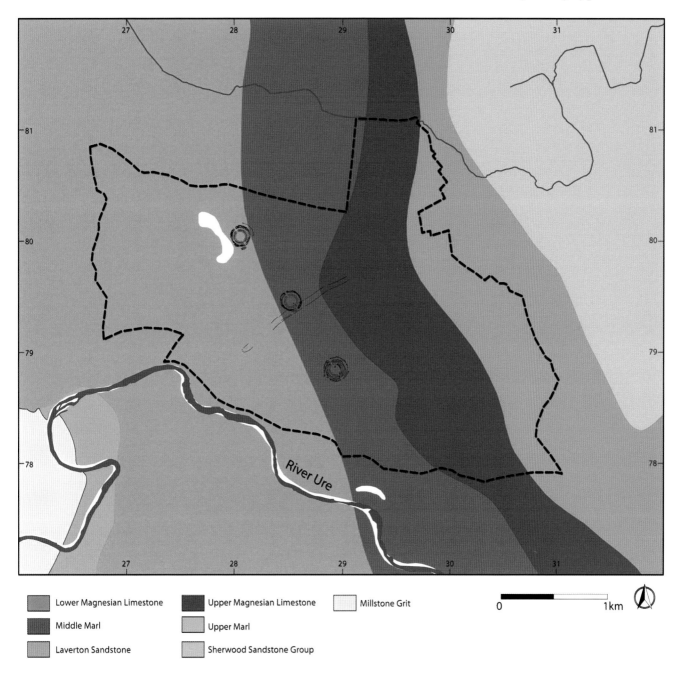

Fig 3.1   Solid geology of the study area

Lower Magnesian Limestone   Upper Magnesian Limestone   Millstone Grit

Middle Marl   Upper Marl

Laverton Sandstone   Sherwood Sandstone Group

0   1km

and the nearby farm of Mire Barf, whose name also suggests a link with marshland (Ekwell 1960, 181 in Roe 2003). Given this evidence, it seems highly probable that an extensive riparian wetland existed during prehistory.

Water also played an important role in defining the northern extent of Thornborough's landscape. Around 1.5km to the north of Nosterfield is a limestone ridge rising above 50m OD in the area of Langwith (Fig 3.2B). The ground slopes gently downwards to the south, and the resulting basin, known as The Flasks, was extensively waterlogged prior to draining in the 19th century. Evidence from Nosterfield Quarry suggests a small lake during the Devensian late glacial which was then terres-

trialised by phragmites peat, or what is sometimes called reed swamp or fen peat, under the warming Holocene climate during the 9th millennium BC (Berg 1991; Dickson and Hopkinson 2011, 31–32; Innes nd; Long and Tipping 1998; Rutherford nd; Tipping 2000). Open pools and fen-carr wetland scrub remained across this now well-wooded landscape during the mid-Holocene (Bridgland *et al* 2011, 103–5, 111–12). Wetland herbaceous vegetation expanded with subsequent climatic deterioration, and waterlogging clearly continued into the historic periods, for the name 'Langwith' is of Viking origin and probably means something like long ford, a reference perhaps to pathways which stretched across The Flasks, whilst documentary

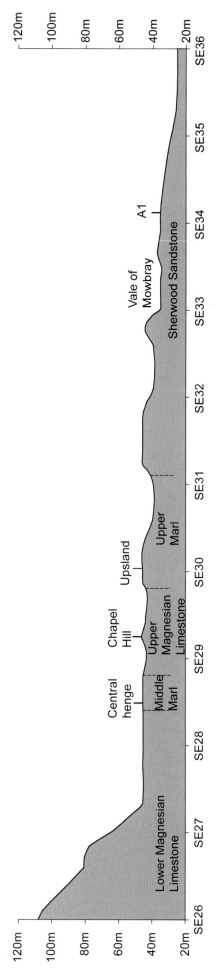

A. West to east through central henge (with solid geology)

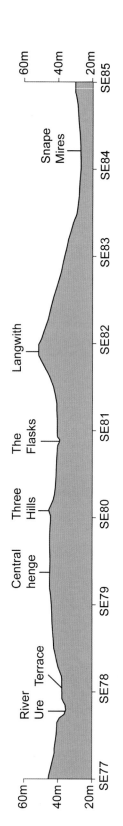

B. South to north through central henge

Fig 3.2 Schematic generalised sections of the study area and surrounding landscape. The vertical scale is ×20 greater than the horizontal scale

evidence confirms a swamp existed to the south of Langwith Wood during the Middle Ages (Roe 2003). Moreover, beyond Langwith lies Snape Mires (Fig 3.2B), a drained marshy area of *c* 9km² which even today sees mounds of wet peat forming over its numerous springs (Powell *et al* 1992, 81; Bridgland *et al* 2011, 81–7). Originally covered by a glacial lake during the last Ice Age, it gradually infilled, with shallow pools remaining in lower areas; throughout the early Holocene it was colonised by woodland and marshy vegetation (Bridgland *et al* 2011, fig 1.5, 48, 79–87, 170–203). During late prehistory the area is likely to have been covered in extensive peat deposits. This and The Flasks would have therefore formed a wide and at times almost impregnable barrier to the builders and users of the monument complex, most likely only traversed with difficulty and perhaps only by those with an intimate knowledge of this landscape.

At the centre of this neatly bounded landscape is the plateau which today is a relatively flat and open tract of land between 40m and 45m OD, characterised by a lack of trees, large arable fields, and extensive quarries. It predominantly consists of undifferentiated fluvio-glacial terrace deposits (Fig 3.3; Scale 1:50,000 Drift Geology Sheet 52), created by extensive outwash as ice sheets retreated, which form a flat-topped terrace cut and straddled by a large number of palaeochannels (Fig 3.2B; Powell *et al* 1992, 79; see also Bridgland *et al* 2011, fig 5.3, 244). The latter were probably associated with fan aggradation during the late glacial and are unlikely to have been visible waterways or relict channels during later prehistory (Deegan 2005, 10). This outwash was laid down in an area of undulating till, some of which survives as ridges which rise marginally above the plateau to heights of 45–53m OD. Within the study area, these ridges exist at Chapel Hill to the east of the southern and central henge, at Upsland where it forms the north-eastern boundary of the study area, and, more extensively, to the south-east of the southern henge (Scale 1:50,000 Drift Geology Sheet 52). Between these ridges lie ribbon-like terraces of sand and gravel. Overall, these till deposits give the eastern half of Thornborough's landscape a more undulating or hummocky appearance (Fig 3.2A). Most of the monuments are located immediately to the west across the flatter ground. The southern edge of the plateau was formed by water erosion, beyond which the land slopes down onto younger undifferentiated river terrace deposits at heights of 38–45m OD (Powell *et al* 1992, 79). Between this and most of the course of the River Ure, to as far southwards as Ripon, is an uneven belt of fluviatile alluvium formed of redeposited terrace deposit overlying gravel (Fig 3.3; *ibid*, 80–1). This occurs at a lower level than the terrace at a height of 35m OD or less.

Geology is responsible for another highly visible feature of the landscape. The two bands of marl which are part of the Permian shelf to the north of Ripon are characterised by thick beds of gypsum (Powell *et al* 1992, 94). These soft deposits of calcium sulphate are especially prone to dissolution by ground water and the area between Ripon and the village of North Stainley, a few kilometres to the south of the monument complex, possesses a large number of subsidence hollows, whilst Snape Mires is characterised by the almost complete dissolution of its gypsum beds (Cooper 1986; Powell *et al* 1992, 15–8, 94–5). These near-circular cylindrical shafts or conical depressions can be substantial in size, commonly 10–30m in diameter and up to 20m deep, or even larger when they coalesce to form collapses up to several hundred metres across (Cooper 1986, table 2, fig 2). They were encountered during the course of gravel extraction at Nosterfield Quarry – and are known from across the neighbouring farmland of Langwith to the north – where three were excavated (Long and Tipping 1998; Rutherford nd; Tipping 2000). Mistakenly identified as anthropogenic in origin, they were formed during the late glacial and were 2.2–4m in diameter and 2.5–2.8m deep. There appears to have been 'a continuous history of subsidence during Flandrian times' (Cooper 1986, 131) and its impact on areas to the north and south of Thornborough should not be underestimated. These collapses would have been an intricate part of the wetlands mentioned above which so neatly defined the northern and southern extent of Thornborough's landscape. As will be discussed in Chapter 6, gypsum is likely to have played an important role in the physical and spiritual life of those who built and used its Neolithic and Bronze Age monuments, and it seems highly improbable that these peoples were unaware of, or unconcerned by, its subsidence hollows.

These geologies are overlain by a stony but generally fertile soil, supporting a largely open landscape of intensive arable farming with modestly sized areas of improved, semi-improved, and unimproved pasture. With the exception of the area to the north of Nosterfield (R I Bradley 1987), these soils have only been mapped to a scale of 1:250,000 (Sheet 1). Typical brown earths of the Wick Series (541r) cover most of the study area. These coarse loamy and sandy soils are well-draining and found to survive to depths of 0.18–0.44m. The ridge of Lower Magnesian Limestone, between West Tanfield and Well, is covered by shallow, easy to work and freely draining calcareous fine loamy soils of the Aberford Series (511a). To the south-east of the study area, covering the ridge of till around the Rushwood Hall estate and Mire Barf Farm, is a pocket of stagnogley soils of the Salop Series (711m). These slowly permeable reddish clayey or loamy soils can become seasonally waterlogged when undrained and are difficult to work: unsurprisingly, a significant part of this area remains unploughed, being used today for grassland pasture. It also supports the wooded remnants of the parkland associated with Rushwood Hall. Similarly prone to seasonal waterlogging are the loamy stagnogley soils of the Dunkeswick Series (711p) at The Flasks to the north, and the

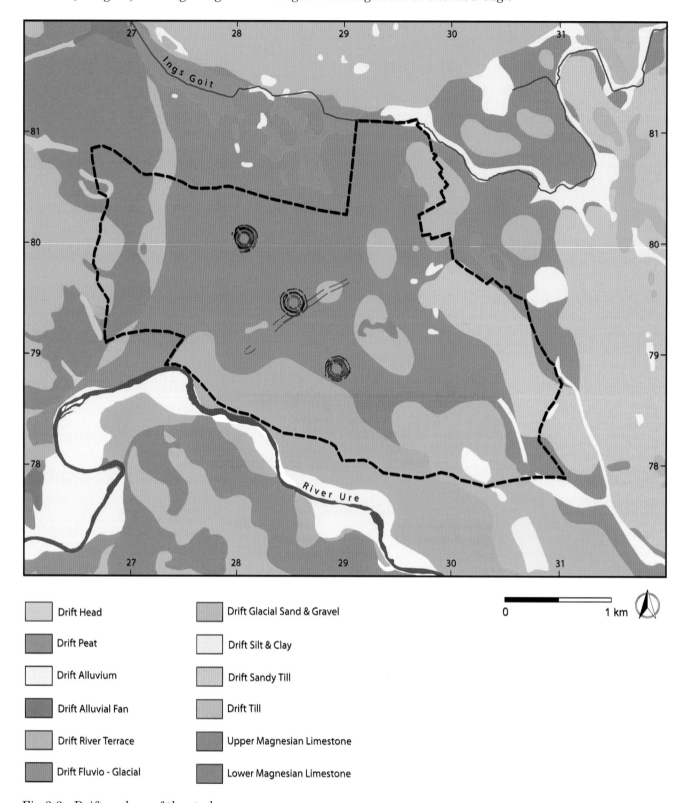

Drift Head

Drift Peat

Drift Alluvium

Drift Alluvial Fan

Drift River Terrace

Drift Fluvio - Glacial

Drift Glacial Sand & Gravel

Drift Silt & Clay

Drift Sandy Till

Drift Till

Upper Magnesian Limestone

Lower Magnesian Limestone

Fig 3.3   Drift geology of the study area

adjacent narrow band of loamy river alluvium of the Enborne Series (811a) along the course of Ings Goit. More detailed soil classification around the edge of the ancient lake at Nosterfield identified that the area's humified peat is overlain by between 0.1m and 0.6m of a slightly calcareous sandy silty loam of the Colthrop Series, with a sandy or clayey loam of the Ellerbeck Series across the marginally higher ground to the north (Berg 1991; R I Bradley 1987). The Flasks today would be extensively waterlogged if it was not for the area's system of drains. Those unquarried areas to the north of Nosterfield are characterised by a higher incidence of grassland and by small copses and woods.

The landscape as a whole is characterised by intensive economic exploitation. The quarrying of limestone, and much more importantly, gravel and sand, has already been mentioned (2.4), and its impact on the landscape is marked by visually significant lakes, a landfill site, and disused unrestored quarries. Cultivation has a long history on the better soils. The earliest evidence for arable farming, possibly dating from the later Bronze Age or Iron Age, is the large rectilinear enclosure and pit alignments, associated with increased cereal pollen, from the south-west of Nosterfield Quarry (Dickson and Hopkinson 2011, 143–6, 156–64). Recent aerial photography suggests they were part of a very much larger field system that may once have formed the southern extent of an agrarian estate, which continued to operate during the Roman and early medieval periods, mostly located on the limestone escarpment to the west and north of Nosterfield and around Well (*ibid*, 44–5; Griffiths and Timms 2005). The quarry also produced a possible Roman corn-drying kiln (Dickson and Hopkinson 2011, 168–70). Interestingly, there are no aerial photographs of likely Iron Age or Roman fields, boundaries, trackways, or enclosures from the plateau on which the henges are found (Deegan 2005, 14; see Fig 3.4), suggesting that early arable farmers avoided this area, as they also did over the following thousand years. The medieval and post-medieval townships were associated with their own composite open-field systems (2.2), traces of which are visible as ridge and furrow on aerial photographs near Thornborough, West Tanfield, East Tanfield, Nosterfield, and Sutton Howgrave further east (Deegan 2005, 16). Ridge and furrow also occurs around Upsland and Chapel Hill, but not across the plateau near the southern and central henges. By contrast, early enclosure maps indicate that few areas were not being ploughed by the beginning of the 19th century (2.3), and over 80% of today's unquarried landscape, including until recently the interiors of both the central and southern henges, is regularly cultivated. Arable farming is therefore likely to have had a substantial impact on the current condition of monuments and landscape alike, and the detrimental impact of modern ploughing is certainly illustrated by the rarer incidence of ridge and furrow on recent aerial photographs.

3.3   The monument complex *by Jan Harding and Benjamin Johnson*

A large number of Neolithic and Bronze Age monuments survive as upstanding remains or cropmarks. The three massive henges are substantial earthworks approximately 0.55km apart on a north-west to south-east axis (Fig 3.4, a–c). The now flattened cursus, parts of which have been destroyed by quarrying, is at right-angles to the henges, its cropmark running for at least 1.2km on a south-west to north-east course (Fig 3.4, d). The small oval enclosure, discovered as a cropmark and thought to be a Neolithic long mortuary enclosure, is just a short distance to the south-east of the cursus on the immediate outskirts of Thornborough (Fig 3.4, e), and there is the excavated double pit alignment directly to the west of the southern henge, running north-north-east to south-south-west for over 350m (Fig 3.4, f). Aerial photographs also show the faint cropmark of a possible cursus parallel to the northern henge (Fig 3.4, g) and another oval enclosure or possible long mortuary enclosure (Fig 3.4, h). At least ten round barrows and a further five ring-ditches have been recorded: four barrows formed the inappropriately named Three Hills Barrow Group *c* 0.4km to the east of the northern henge (Fig 3.4, i, j, k, l); the Centre Hill barrow was on the mid-point of the axis between the central and southern henges, not far from the northern end of the double pit alignment (Fig 3.4, m); the triple-ditched round barrow was 0.4km to the east-south-east of the southern henge (Fig 3.4, n); and the cropmark of a ring-ditch lies at the southern end of the double pit alignment (Fig 3.4, r), with another two further to the south-east on or near the axis of the three henges (Fig 3.4, s, t). In addition, quarrying led to the destruction of two probable round barrows immediately to the south-west and west of the central henge (Fig 3.4, p, q), and another 'tumuli' [*sic*] is recorded on a 19th-century map along the ridge to the west of the complex (Fig 3.4, o). Finally, a number of smaller ring-ditches, a large oval enclosure, and single pit rows are also known (Fig 3.4, u, v, w, x).

Until recently there had been few attempts to record the state of Thornborough's monuments and, consequently, little is known about their history of preservation and rate of destruction. Unsurprisingly, the prominent henge earthworks have attracted most attention, generating a large collection of aerial photographs, along with plans and cross-sections completed in the 19th century (2.3). There is also an original earthwork plan of the central henge and a profile of the northern henge in the excavation report by Nicholas Thomas (1955, figs 2–3). The results of more recent topographic surveys demonstrate that all three sites, and especially the northern and central henges, still survive as impressive monuments (Fig 3.5 and D1.3). Geophysical prospection at the southern and central henges, and part of the cursus (Figs 3.6 and 3.7), reveal a range of new features. Round barrow dimensions were recorded by Revd W C Lukis in 1864 (published 1870b) and Leslie Grinsell in 1952 (published in Thomas 1955, appendix 2), but topographic survey at six of these sites by the ALSF Project demonstrates they are now largely levelled. Geophysical prospection suggests differing levels of preservation. It was also completed at the double pit alignment, the oval enclosure, and the possible cursus (Fig 3.6), but poor results exclude their mention in this chapter. Further information, along with a full description of all the topographic surveys and geophysical prospection completed as part of the VMNLP, ALSF Project, and by other broadly contemporary initiatives, can be found in D1. Other monuments are known only as cropmarks or as cartographic references.

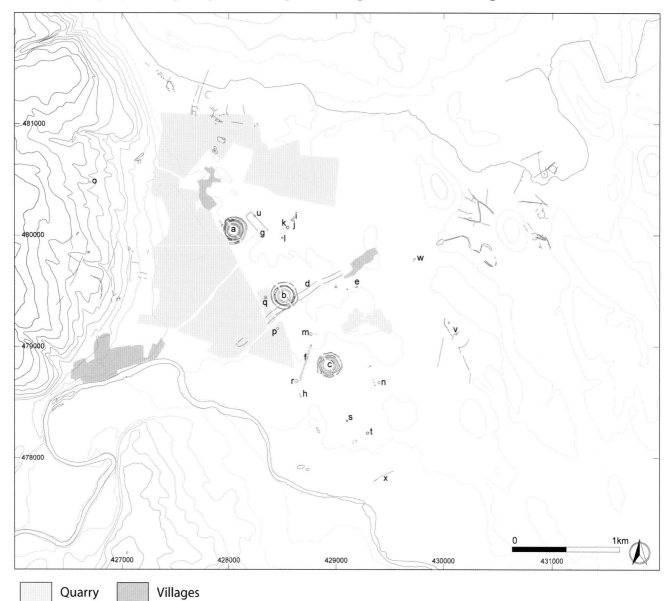

Quarry   Villages

Fig 3.4   Cropmarks and earthworks of Neolithic and Bronze Age monuments (excluding discoveries in the Nosterfield Quarry): a, northern henge; b, central henge; c, southern henge; d, cursus; e, oval enclosure; f, double pit alignment; g, possible cursus; h, possible oval enclosure; i, Three Hills Barrow Group 1; j, Three Hills Barrow Group 2; k, Three Hills Barrow Group 3; l, Three Hills Barrow Group 4; m, Centre Hill Barrow; n, triple-ditched round barrow; o, round barrow; p, round barrow (destroyed); q, round barrow (destroyed); r, ring-ditch; s, ring-ditch; t, ring-ditch; u, possible ring-ditch; v, single pit rows, enclosure and ring-ditches; w, single pit row and ring-ditch; x, single pit row

3.3.1   *Cursus* by Jan Harding, Benjamin Johnson, and Alan Biggins

The much-photographed cursus cropmark is aligned north-east to south-west across the flattest and widest expanse of the plateau (Fig 3.8). An extensive length of the monument, including its rounded western terminal – which appears to have been broken by at least three causeways – was only partially recorded prior to destruction by quarrying. Thomas and Vatcher found a U- or V-shaped ditch 2–3m wide and 0.6–0.9m deep whose fill suggested

either an inner or an outer bank (2.4). As Loveday has recently commented, 'care was obviously taken with its rounded western terminal ... Thereafter alignment and ditch regularity degenerates' (2006, 120–1). Certainly to the east of Green Lane the monument curves gently north-eastwards and widens. Aerial photographs also show a linear feature running parallel with the southern flanking ditch between the quarried area and the central henge, although there is uncertainty about the status of this feature (4.5). From the central henge the monument curves gently south-eastwards and

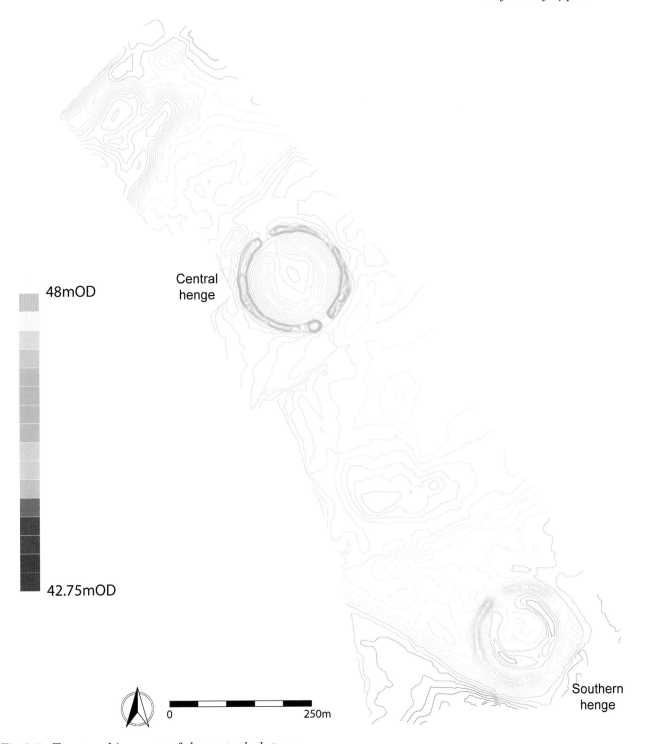

48mOD

42.75mOD

Central
henge

Southern
henge

0   250m

Fig 3.5   Topographic survey of the central plateau

then straightens out as it passes over a very slight
knoll of till. Beyond this point there is confusion
as to its exact course. The original plan in Vatcher
(1960, fig 2), based on air photographs and following
the course of the cropmark on the ground, shows a
gap in the monument, which broadly corresponds
with a now-destroyed field boundary, before it
straightens out and continues towards Thornborough. The monument narrows and its flanking
ditches end at the boundary of the first residential
property (*ibid*, 173). However, CUCAP XA9, taken

in July 1958, shows both the southern and northern
cursus ditches as very faint cropmarks terminating
at the residential garden, but also what may be the
northern cursus ditch continuing the other side of
this garden, before disappearing again under the
village (Fig 3.9; *pace* Deegan 2005, 11). It is therefore
possible that the monument actually ends further
to the east on the slightly elevated ridge of till on
which the village is located.

Vatcher accurately recorded the cursus to be at
least 1.2km long and 44m wide (1960, 178). Plots of

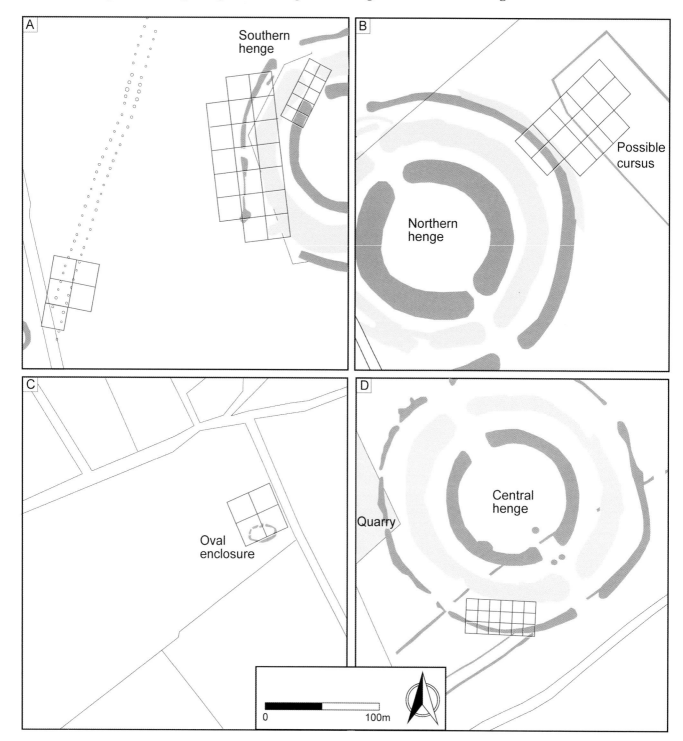

Fig 3.6   VMNLP geophysical survey: A, southern henge and double pit alignment; B, possible cursus; C, oval enclosure; D, central henge. © Crown Copyright / database right 2013. An Ordnance Survey / EDINA supplied service

the cropmark show its width varying between 38m and 66m. Its less than straight course and differing width suggest it was constructed in sections and these variations are most evident towards the middle where it appears to have been very deliberately referenced by the central henge (Fig 3.8). Geophysical prospection has added to the available information about this part of the cursus and its relationship with the later monument (D1.2). The ALSF Project magnetometer survey of the central

henge detected its northern ditch which crosses just inside the inner edge of the southern entrance to the henge (Fig 3.22, 39). Interestingly, the feature disappears short of the eastern terminal of the inner henge ditch, and, whilst this could result from truncation, it could equally be an original causeway. The cursus ditch is also pit-like in appearance immediately to the east of the henge ditch. A curving and interrupted anomaly (Fig 3.22, 40) may connect the northern and southern cursus ditches (Fig 3.22, 41),

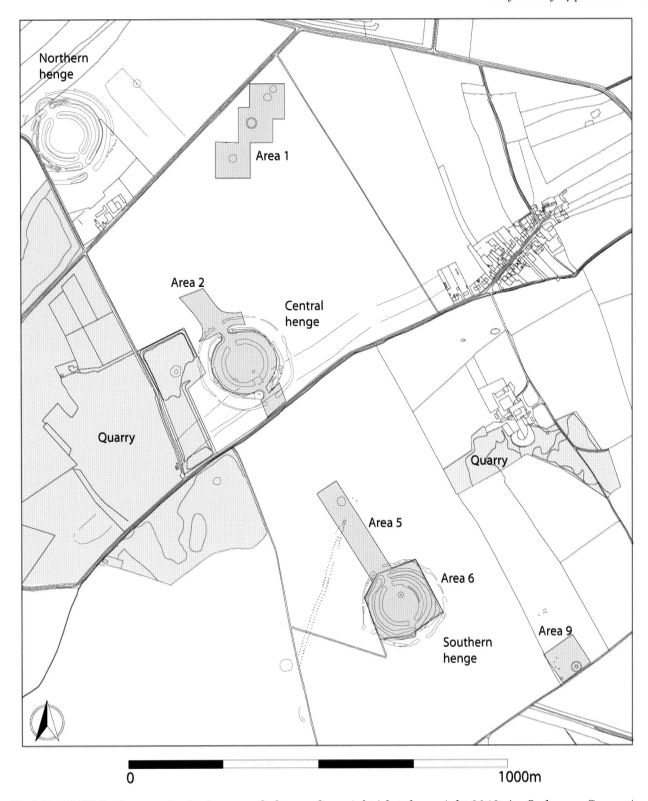

*Fig 3.7   ALSF Project geophysical survey. © Crown Copyright / database right 2013. An Ordnance Survey /
EDINA supplied service*

a parallel perhaps to the internal divisions recorded
at a number of Scottish pit-defined cursuses (Loveday
2006, 28–9). The southern cursus ditch, just inside
the outer henge ditch, also appears to consist of post-
pits, and as it approaches the eastern terminal of the
latter (Fig 3.22, 43) it too fades slightly, supporting
the suggestion of post-deposition disturbance to the

earlier monument. A separate magnetometer survey
conducted immediately to the south-west, across
a section of the cursus and the outer henge ditch,
also highlighted anomalies of significant archaeological importance (Fig 3.20). Part of its aim was to
locate the southern cursus ditch; instead it found a
similarly aligned anomaly nearly 20m to the north-

over 65m
over 60m
over 55m
over 50m
over 45m
over 40m

Quarry

0   1km

Fig 3.8   The cursus monument. © Crown Copyright / database right 2013. An Ordnance Survey / EDINA supplied service

Fig 3.9   Looking south at the eastern section of the cursus in July 1958 (CUCAP XA9). The cropmark towards the bottom of the photograph shows a former field boundary (Copyright reserved Cambridge University Collection of Aerial Photography)

west (Fig 3.20, 2), along the approximate centre of the cursus.

Ascertaining whether these geophysical anomalies are of archaeological origin and associated with the cursus must await further fieldwork, but a VMNLP excavation at the south-western section of the outer henge ditch surveyed by magnetometry suggests that many may be. It found a complex layout of inner features, including a platform or low mound into which were inserted stakes, posts, and even circles of small stone, overlying an earlier dug feature at the centre of the monument (4.5). It is impossible to say if such features are from just the central section of the cursus, or along its entire length – it is worth noting in this regard that a ditch of unknown date and purpose, which may have been just outside the southern side of the cursus, was sectioned by Faith Vatcher (1960, 178, fig 3) – but the subsequent building of the central henge signifies that this place had special importance. It is both the flattest and highest part of the plateau. From here the land slopes down gently and gradually in all directions. The western cursus terminal is marginally lower-lying and overlooks the terrace and the nearby Ure at the point where it shifts its course south-eastwards. If the other end of the cursus was on the outskirts of Thornborough then it too was less elevated, but if it continues under the village its termination is at a comparable height to its central section. The impression is of a monument which deliberately straddled a landscape physically discernible to those areas immediately beyond its terminals.

3.3.2 *Henges by Jan Harding, Benjamin Johnson, Alan Biggins, Ed Dennison, and Armin Schmidt*

The three henges are sited across the axis of the cursus. The central henge's superimposition, incorporating so exactly the flanking cursus ditches within an enclosure at right-angles to the earlier monument, suggests a 'symbolic geometry' may have been at play here. A similar observation can be made in regard to how the henge axis uses the landscape's subtle topography (Fig 3.5). Located along the principal north-west to south-east alignment of the plateau, the central henge is marginally more elevated, at 45.5m OD, than the other two sites. To the south the ground slopes very gently downwards with the southern henge at 44.3m OD. Immediately beyond the latter monument, it drops away more sharply to the terrace. To the north of the central henge is a slight ridge at 46m OD, the ground then sloping down over a distance of 170m to form a shallow basin 1.5m lower than the surrounding area. The landscape rises sharply by 2.5m over the next 30m, only to descend again, this time by 3m over a distance of 90m, where it is partly obscured by the road. The northern henge is located at a height of 43m OD. The geomorphological context for the

topographic fluctuations between the central and northern monuments is unclear, but they are unique for the plateau, indicating that the enclosures were perhaps deliberately positioned in relation to them. If so, they surely had a purpose for those moving between monuments.

The henges themselves survive in part as extremely impressive earthworks which were once very similar to one another, many of their currently visible variations the result of plough disturbance and other acts of post-depositional destruction (see D1.1.3, D1.2.3, D1.3.3). The best-preserved sections of earthwork are at the northern henge, now covered by dense and long-established woodland (Figs 3.10–3.12). Despite this, most of its outer ditch, and parts of its inner bank to the north-west, west, and south-west, have been destroyed or greatly disturbed by agriculture, quarrying, and road construction. The bank of the central henge is also impressive, especially around its southern entrance where we get a glimpse of the earthwork's original monumentality, despite parts of it being removed for road building or disturbed by sheep and rabbits, and whilst the inner ditch has now been largely filled in, it nonetheless survives as an eroded earthwork (Figs 3.10 and 3.13). With the exception of a truncated section to the north-west, the central henge's outer ditch has more-or-less been levelled by the plough. Unfortunately, the southern henge has been extensively disturbed by agriculture and related activities, especially on its eastern, southern, and western sides, making it the least well-preserved of the three henges. Much of this destruction is clearly not modern since the site was described in 1859 as lacking 'much of its original magnitude' (Hall 2005, 2). However, its inner ditch and bank are still visible today (Figs 3.10 and 3.14), and there are faint traces of the outer ditch to the north and north-west. Overall, the northern, central, and southern henges possess diameters of 220m, 224m, and 235m respectively, but if we consider the evidence from aerial photographs, which show more of their outer ditch, they have maximum diameters of 244m, 238m, and 244m respectively (Harding and Lee 1987, 314, 317). Their remarkable similarity in size, along with the near-perfect circularity of their inner ditches and banks, emphasises the homogeneity of all three henges.

The northern henge's inner ditch is remarkably well preserved and provides a good indication of the feature's original steep-sided appearance (Fig 3.11). Its eastern half is currently some 20m wide and 2.6m deep with the western half slightly less impressive at 18m wide and 2.2m deep (Fig 3.10), the result in all likelihood of increased slumping and vegetation deposition rather than a real difference in construction. This compares well with the 2.8m deep ditch recorded in 1816 ('9ft 2in', Fig 2.2), or the anonymous reference in 1859 to a feature '10 feet deep in some parts' (Hall 2005, 1). A small excavation of the ditch-bottom by Nicholas Thomas found 'almost 2 feet of clean yellow sand exactly resembling

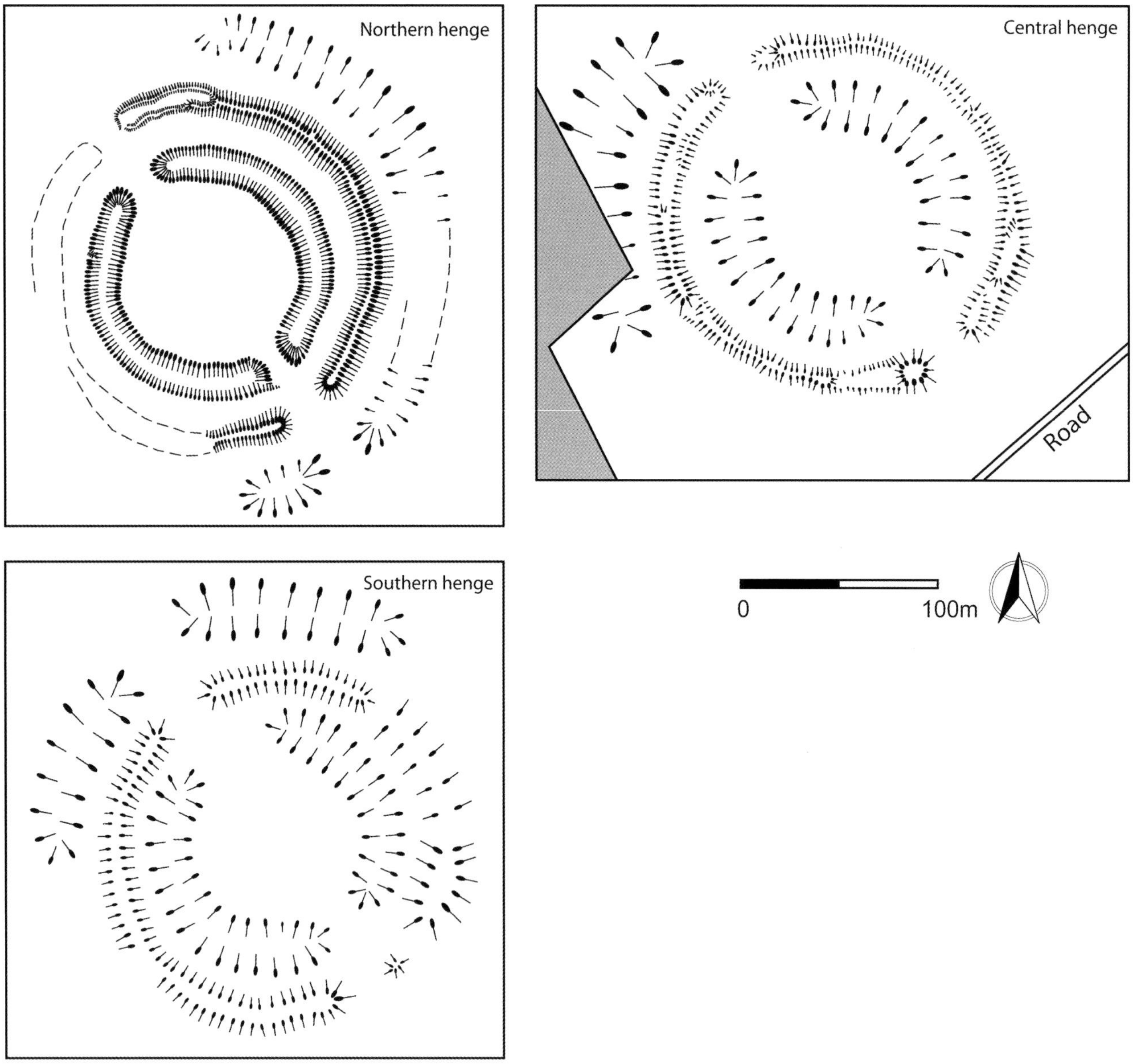

Fig 3.10   Hachured earthwork plans of the henges. The survey of the northern henge was conducted by Ed Dennison and surveys of the central and southern henges by the VMNLP

that in the ditch-bottom in the central circle', making the original earthwork over 3m deep (Thomas 1955, 434). The particular alignment of the ditch's inside edge suggests it was gang-dug from the interior as short straight sections subsequently linked together to form a 'circle'. Ditch width at the northern henge accords with a relatively well-preserved section of inner ditch to the south-west of the southern henge, which was 18.3m across, but unfortunately, the same feature at the central henge is too heavily truncated to offer meaningful comparison. Originally these inner ditches were separated from the bank by a flat wide berm which, at the northern henge, is on average 13m across. Well-preserved sections of bank can be found around the eastern half of the northern henge, where it was typically 20.5m wide and 3.2m high, and around its western half, where it was typically 18m wide and 3m high (Fig 3.10). It

still survives here as a steep-sided earthwork with a flat top 1–2m wide (Fig 3.12). These excellent levels of preservation suggest that its current size may not be too different to what originally existed; the same can be concluded for the western half of the central henge where it is on average 3m high (Figs 3.10 and 3.13). However, the bank was recorded as much as '15 feet in height' (4.6m) in 1859 (Hall 2005, 1), although this could refer to a uniquely monumental part of the site (see below). Despite this evidence, it is difficult to ascertain if each henge had a bank of standard width and height: it certainly could have been slighter to the north-east of the central henge, where it is now only about 12m wide and 0.85m high. Erosion scars at both the northern and central henges suggest it was made up of loose rounded pebbles and gravelly soil. Thomas notes its composition at the latter as consisting of 'alternate layers of

Fig 3.11 Looking west from the south-east entrance at the inner ditch of the northern henge in autumn 1994. Photograph reproduced courtesy of Ed Dennison

Fig 3.12 Looking east at the south-east bank terminal of the northern henge in August 2003

Fig 3.13 Looking south at the inner ditch and bank of the central henge in September 2012

mottled orange-brown earth and pure gravel', suggesting it 'may originally have been constructed in a series of heaps of earth and gravel, later joined together and smoothed off; for the various layers in it tend to tip' (1955, 433). There is some evidence from the southern henge for an inner timber revetment (D1.1.4).

Entrances are aligned north-west to south-east, but not all on exactly the same axis (Fig 3.15). Dymond (1963, 103) recorded the entrance

Fig 3.14 Looking south at the inner ditch and bank on the western side of the southern henge in August 1994

alignments, from north to south, as 143°/323°, 145°/325°, and 155°/327° respectively. These variations were surely deliberate and could be highly significant. Other differences are apparent. At the well-preserved southern entrance into the northern henge, the inner ditch gap is 9m wide but the bank gap much wider at 15m (Fig 3.10). The northern entrance, by contrast, is 14m wide at both ditch and bank. Bank gaps appear bigger at both the central and southern henges: at the southern entrance of the central henge the bank and ditch gaps are 19m and 17m respectively, whilst the northern entrance is 17m wide. The northern entrance of the southern henge is 19.3m wide at the inner bank but 25.5m wide at the inner ditch, reflecting the shortened section of ditch on the monument's eastern side (Fig 3.10). The three henges tend to have squared-off and steeply faced earthwork terminals, with the exceptions of the rounded ditch terminals at the northern entrance of the northern henge. It also appears bank ends were enlarged. This is still visible at the southern entrance of the northern henge, to the north-west of the southern henge, and at both central henge entrances, including most dramatically on the south-western side where it stands 21.9m wide and 4.5m high (Fig 3.16). Physically enhanced bank terminals occur at other henge monuments (Harding 2003, 63–4), but the rounded profile on the south-western side of the central henge

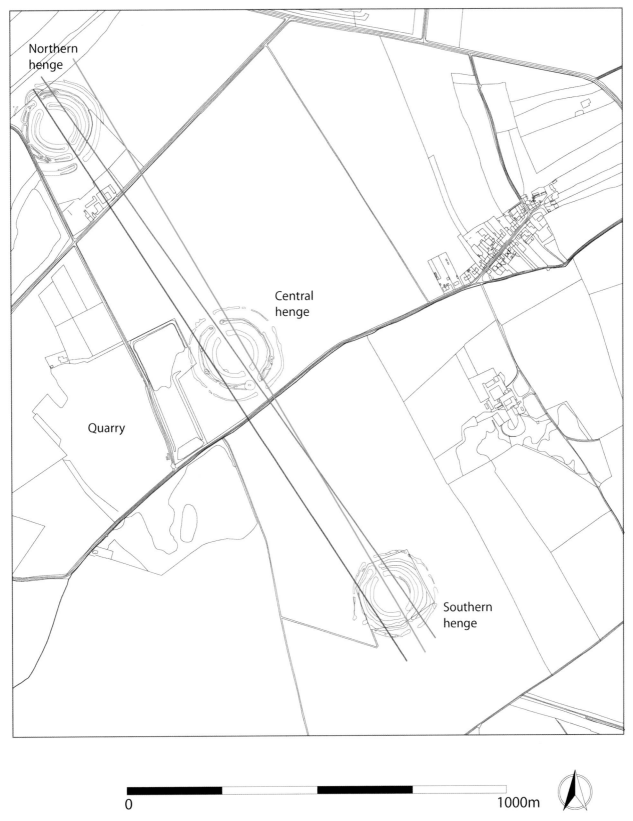

0   1000m

Fig 3.15   The differing orientation of the northern (red), central (blue), and southern (green) henges. © Crown Copyright / database right 2013. An Ordnance Survey / EDINA supplied service

is very reminiscent of a round barrow. A more definitive answer about its true origin must await further fieldwork, but round barrows are known to have been incorporated into or added to henge banks at Arbor Low in Derbyshire (Barnatt and Collis 1996,

133–6), Mount Pleasant in Dorset (Wainwright 1979, 65–8, 245), Big Rings at the Dorchester-on-Thames complex in Oxfordshire (Whittle *et al* 1992, 147, figs 3 and 26), and Catterick, just 20km to the north, where a large chambered cairn became part of what

Fig 3.16   Looking north-west at the southern entrance of the central henge, with the larger western bank terminal on the left, in August 2003

is now thought to be a henge bank (Moloney *et al* 2003). Similarly, at Ferrybridge in West Yorkshire, a ring-ditch appears to have been cut by the henge ditch (Roberts 2005, 195). A comparable development is very much a possibility for Thornborough, highlighting interesting questions about the development of its henges, and more generally, about the monumentalisation of the plateau.

The outer ditches at Thornborough have been affected by the plough and only survive as greatly denuded earthworks to the east and south of the northern henge, to the north-west of the central henge, and around the northern half of the southern henge (Fig 3.10). The best-preserved section is to the south of the northern henge in an area of pasture (Fig 3.17). Here the ditch is 21m wide and 1.2m deep with a 15m wide gap opposite the inner earthwork's southern entrance. Elsewhere the outer ditch exists as a cropmark – although only 50 years ago it was 'still clearly visible' at the central henge (Thomas 1955, 433) – and as geophysical anomalies at the southern (Fig 3.21, 67) and central (Figs 3.20, 1 and 3.22, 27, 43–4) henges. In each instance the outer ditch is interrupted opposite the entrance through

the inner ditch and bank by a gap of similar width (Fig 3.18), and at the central henge, geophysical survey shows it with squared-off ends (Fig 3.22, 27, 43). As with the inner earthworks, the ditches on either side of these entranceways are distinctive in other ways. Aerial photographs suggest that some of the terminals were wider, and the circuit is flattened either side of the southern entrance into the southern and central henges (Fig 3.18). The latter does not appear to be the case at the northern henge, although a vertical aerial photograph, taken in 1930 (NMR 2880/1), shows what could be an alignment of eight or so large pits or postholes running just outside the outer ditch to the east of its southern entrance (Fig 3.18). Their straight course suggests they could be the remains of a flattened façade structure. By contrast, ditch terminals flanking the northern entrances of the northern and southern henges were turned outwards, but at the central henge turned inwards (Fig 3.18). These characteristics illustrate the distinctiveness of the sections of outer ditch interrupted by the main entrances.

Whether the outer ditch of the central and southern henges was originally irregular and inter-

Fig 3.17   Looking west at the outer ditch on the southern side of the northern henge in August 2003

rupted is far from clear (Fig 3.18). Its more-or-less continuous and regular appearance around much of the northern henge appears authentic, for its southern and eastern sides are depicted as such on the Ordnance Survey Map of 1856, and around all but its western side on a map which accompanies Lukis's (1870b, plate I) account of barrow-digging. Its siting on the grazing land of Thornborough Common until enclosure in 1799 would certainly account for its better preservation. Thomas (1955, 433–4) believed the outer ditches were once more-or-less unbroken at all three henges, and since the amount of spoil needed to create the bank of the central henge is roughly twice that obtained from the inner ditch alone, he concluded the outer ditch served primarily as a quarry which 'resembled the inner one closely in size and shape, as does the outer ditch of the Big Rings at Dorchester-on-Thames'. However, there does appear to be some similarity in the location of gaps to the west, north-east, and south-west of both the central and southern henges (Fig 3.18). At the southern henge, the interruption to the south-west corresponds with what has been identified as a possible 'scoop around the bank'

(Deegan 2005, fig 4), the result perhaps of material being scraped together for building the earthwork. More telling evidence comes from the small-scale excavation of the southern henge's outer ditch which demonstrates that the cropmark gap in its western section was indeed an interruption (4.6.2). Hence, ploughing alone may not adequately explain its irregularity at two of the three henges.

The construction of the outer ditch in discontinuous sections of varying width and depth would certainly explain some of its peculiarities. The cropmark evidence from all three henges hints at the southern and south-south-east sections of the outer ditch originally being wider than elsewhere, corresponding, at both the central and southern henges, with its flattened course (Fig 3.18). Such physical exaggeration and modification is understandable if people proceeded into the complex from the south, for it resembles an earthwork façade whose straightened layout necessitated the circuit's abrupt shift northwards further round to the east. The digging-out of a true circle does not appear to have been of greatest concern here and the same may be said of the outer ditch to the west of the

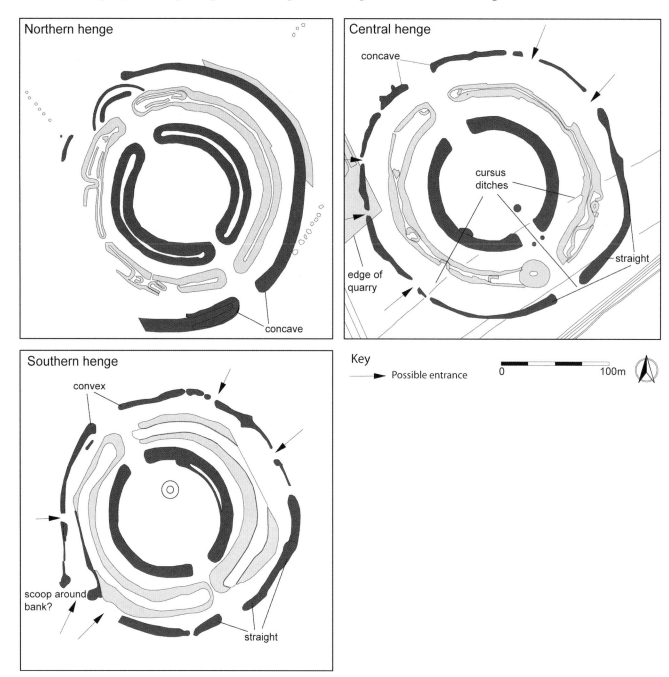

Fig 3.18   Plans of the henges using both earthwork and cropmark evidence (based partly on Deegan 2005, fig 4)

southern henge. Aerial photographs demonstrate that immediately to the south of its causeway the ditch narrows and straightens for some 40m before disappearing completely (Fig 3.18). Here the feature looks more like a bedding-trench than a henge ditch, suggesting this part of the southern henge was defined by a fence-line or palisade. Unfortunately, the geophysical survey conducted across the western side of this monument detected only the bulbous end of this straightened section (Fig 3.19, i), despite showing the ditch further to the north (Fig 3.19, d), and confusingly, another anomaly continues straight in a south-easterly direction (Fig 3.19, a). The latter is in fact evident on a number of

the better aerial photographs of the monument and is in line with an extremely narrow bedding-trench, perhaps for a fence rather than a palisade, located during the small-scale excavation of the southern henge's outer ditch (4.6.2). It does not continue as a cropmark to the north of the excavated ditch-end. The feature remains undated, and could conceivably have been an integral part of the monument or a later prehistoric land boundary. Most likely it post-dates the henge. Whatever its exact interpretation, the south-eastern section of the monument's outer ditch differed to its appearance elsewhere.

Obviously, Thomas lacked this cropmark evidence when arguing 'that the outer ditch must have

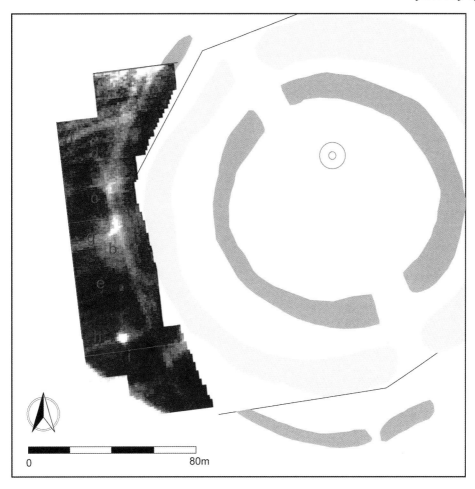

0   80m

Fig 3.19   Earth resistance survey at the outer ditch of the southern henge

resembled the inner one closely in size and shape'. There are other uncertainties as to his assertion that this feature served exclusively as a quarry for the inner bank. Aerial photographs of the northern henge appear to show the cropmark of an outer bank about 4m wide on its north-eastern side (Fig 3.18; Deegan 2005, fig 4). This is matched at the southern henge by the discovery of a 3.5m wide bank on the western side of the narrow bedding-trench mentioned above (4.6.2), and whilst it could be a lynchet formed against a later land boundary (Fig 3.21,70), it ends opposite the interruption in the course of the outer ditch, suggesting its broad contemporaneity with the monument. In neither case is there evidence for a berm between bank and ditch. Yet no mention was made of outer banks during the 19th century, and indeed, none was detected by geophysical prospection across the outer perimeters of the central and southern henges (Figs 3.19 and 3.20). They would have been largely levelled by ploughing – except for, in part, at the better-preserved northern henge – but the excavation at the central henge found no evidence for such an earthwork, despite finding traces of other probably earlier sub-surface features (4.5.2). It again appears there was notable variation around the henge's outer perimeters, with only some sections associated with an outer bank. If this was the case, then the appearance and purpose of the

outer earthwork was very different to that of the inner bank and ditch.

The arresting monumentality of the earthworks cannot be over-exaggerated, especially if, as seems likely, their inner banks were coated in gypsum (6.3). Forming an alignment some 1.7km long they would have visually dominated the plateau and orchestrated movement and activity across the largely flat terrain. They surely imposed themselves on those gathered within. Their insides are proportionally modest areas between 83m and 92m across, and as such, lay deep within the earthworks, emphasising the physical and symbolic importance the builders placed on separating them from the external world (Harding 2003, 63–8). They also appear to have contained few enclosed features. Magnetometry across the interiors of both the central and southern henges found few anomalies, and much of what was found may relate to later activity (D1.1.4 and D1.2.4). Offset from the centre of the southern henge, and associated with possible pits, was a flattened V-shaped anomaly with its ends on the site's main axis (Fig 3.21, 74). It could represent the remains of a ditch or bedding-trench for a timber structure. Also, a single aerial photograph taken in March 1998 (NMR 17105/22) shows what looks like a small and poorly defined ring-ditch, possibly with an inner pit, near the monument's centre (Fig 3.18), although

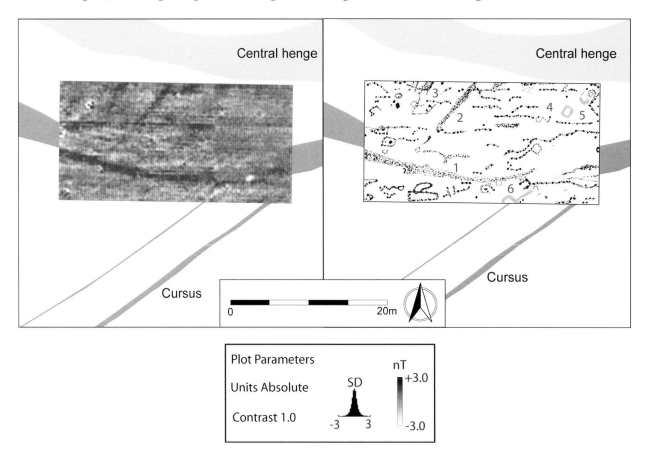

Fig 3.20   Magnetometer survey at the outer ditch of the central henge

it went largely undetected by geophysical prospection. These possible features are unmatched at the central henge, although there are some ill-defined anomalies across its central area (Fig 3.22, 34). It did, however, produce a strong positive anomaly near the southern entrance on its axis (Fig 3.22, 38). This feature is visible on aerial photographs, and, given its size and location, could be a large pit or a substantial posthole. It coincides with a linear anomaly running along the centre of the site (Fig 3.22, 26B), which, at first glance, looks like a land drain: curiously, though, it fails to continue outside the henge, the fainter response beyond the northern entrance being on a marginally different alignment (Fig 3.22, 26). The discontinuous circular anomaly found around the berm between the inner ditch and bank at both the southern and central henges (Fig 3.21, 70 and Fig 3.22, 31 respectively) is best interpreted as a lynchet which formed when these sites were under cultivation.

Whilst magnetometer survey at the southern henge found little of interest in its causeways, except for two sub-circular and rhomboid-shaped anomalies at its southern entrance (Fig 3.21, 78), an earlier earth resistance survey located a patch of low resistance along the northern edge of the north-west inner ditch terminal and across its entrance (Fig D1.12). Subsequent excavation showed it to be the badly disturbed and undated

remains of a banked feature (4.6.3). If it hints that some of the henge entrances were anything but empty, then the results of magnetometry at the central henge suggest the same. Again, it is the northern entrance which is of interest. A strongly responsive negative and positive linear feature crossed between the outer edges of the earthwork, closing off the entrance (Fig 3.22, 30). It was crossed transversely by a positive linear anomaly which runs inside the monument (Fig 3.22, 29). Even more intriguing is the positive linear anomaly running from outside the monument and through the centre of its northern entrance (Fig 3.22, 26). Just in front of the inner ditch terminals it passes through the middle of four positive paired lateral point anomalies, set at right angles, and a number of possible pits (Fig 3.22, 26C). At the other end of this 100m or so linear anomaly lies another possible feature with similarities to 26C (Fig 3.22, 23). There is little on which to reconstruct their appearance, but given the complex entrance features excavated at Stonehenge (Cleal *et al* 1995, figs 68, 156), it is not over-stretching the evidence to imagine that palisades or fences divided this entranceway. Also, two circular cropmark patches show just outside the southern causeway of its inner ditch (Fig 3.18). Finally, the recent Thornborough Henges Air Photo Mapping Project detected the cropmark of two concentric semi-circular ditches with widths of 2m

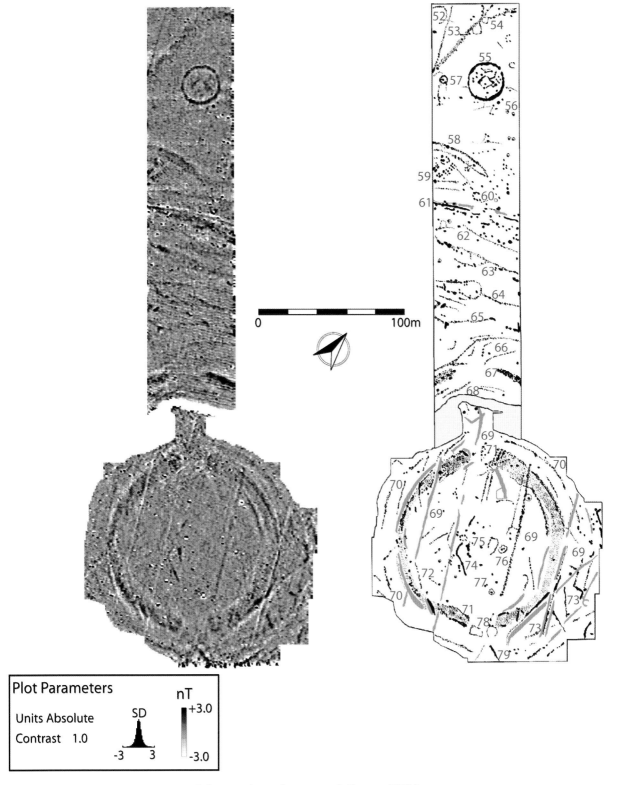

Fig 3.21 Magnetometer survey of the southern henge and Centre Hill barrow

and 4m immediately inside the northern entrance of the northern henge (Fig 3.18; Deegan 2005, fig 4). Tree cover here makes it impossible to say if they continue under the inner earthwork, thus predating the henge. They have an internal diameter of 31m.

If these features were broadly contemporary with

the construction and use of the henges, and assuming that those located between the bank terminals of the central henge were not later in date (see 2.2), this suggests that considerable significance was placed on the act of crossing into or out of the henges. The flattened sections of outer ditch to either side of two of the southern entrances could have attracted people

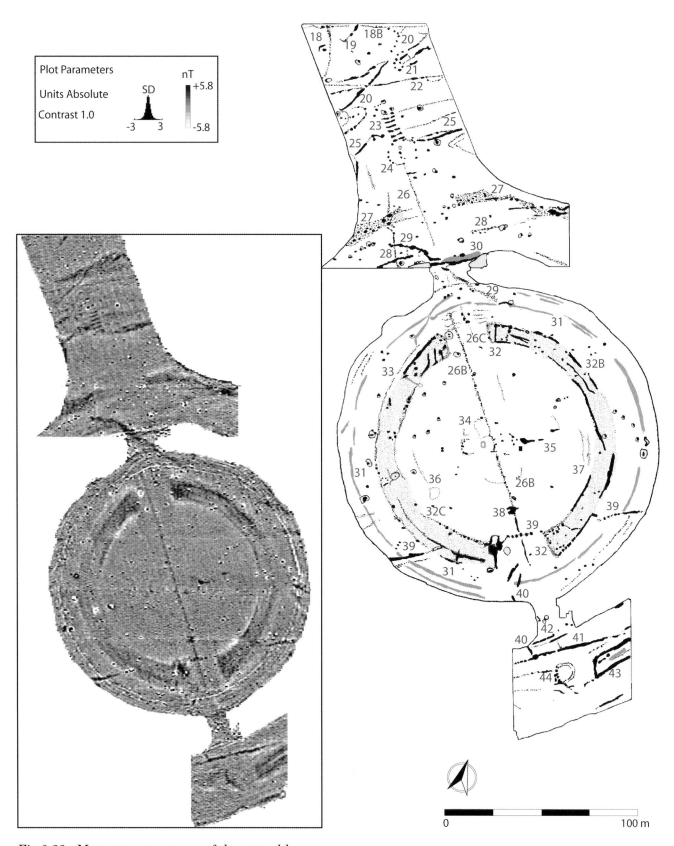

Fig 3.22 Magnetometer survey of the central henge

to a point of entry, serving a specific purpose which complemented the possible entrance structures exclusively associated with their northern causeways.

The orchestration of movement and activity may also have occurred as people travelled between the henges, for geophysical prospection has detected possible features in the intervening space. Magnetometry immediately to the north of the southern henge detected a large number of anomalies (Fig 3.21), but these are probably of geomorphological or agricultural origin. More convincing evidence for prehistoric structures can be found to the north of the central henge. The linear anomaly running through the henge entrance appears to terminate with six, or possibly seven, pairs of positive anomalies, placed some 1.5m apart and with a central gap aligned transversely at right-angles to the henge axis (Fig 3.22, 23). They are very like the feature at the northern end of the double pit alignment (Fig 3.21, 59; see also 4.7 and Fig 2.6). Each anomaly is approximately 7m long and 1.5m wide. Although they appear solid, they could consist of closely spaced postholes. Two strong bipolar responses occur immediately to the north of this intriguing feature, and to its south it joins a circular anomaly 16m across which appears to consist of pits or postholes with a positive linear anomaly running off to the east (Fig 3.22, 24 and 25 respectively). Two linear anomalies to the north are known to be field boundaries (Fig 3.22, 20, 22). Whilst there is no direct evidence for the date or original appearance of these features, their form and location suggest they were connected to the functioning of the henge. Equally enigmatic is the cropmark of a single pit alignment at the northern henge. It consists of widely spaced pits and runs for around 30m from its north-west section of outer ditch on the same axis as the henges (Fig 3.18; Deegan 2005, fig 5). It is presumably connected to the two large U-shaped pits excavated by North Yorkshire County Council in advance of the building of a quarry haul road a further 40m to the north-west (Neil Campling, pers comm; see also 5.5). Stone packing suggests that one of these may have held a timber upright.

3.3.3 *Round barrows and ring-ditches* by Jan Harding, Benjamin Johnson, and Alan Biggins

The ten known round barrows are found largely on the plateau. Three of the four which make up the Three Hills Barrow Group, labelled THBG2, THBG3 and THBG4, are sited in a line along a low triangular-shaped gravel ridge 268m by 132m (Fig 3.4, j, k, l; Fig 3.23). The ridge is 1.5m higher than the surrounding plateau, rising from 42.5m OD to 44m OD, with gentle slopes except to the south-west where it is somewhat steeper (see D1.4.3). Their vantage point offers good views of the nearby northern and central henges. The remaining barrow, THBG1, is on the northern slope of the ridge (Fig 3.4, i; Fig 3.23). A barrow 186m south-south-west of the central henge was destroyed by quarrying (Fig 3.4, p), and nearby, the Centre Hill barrow (Fig 3.4, m) seems to have been deliberately sited on a low gravel ridge running east to west between the central and southern henges. A large ring-ditch at or close to the south-western end of the double pit alignment (Fig 3.4, r), and located just below the water-eroded southern edge of the plateau on the river terrace, is considered to be almost certainly a round barrow. To the east, at the edge of the plateau, is the excavated triple-ditched round barrow on a slight gravel ridge which rises 0.5m above its immediate landscape to 42.5m OD (Fig 3.4, n). If the relationship between the cursus and later henges suggests a 'symbolic geometry', then the same is also perhaps true of the relationship between the henges and the round barrows, for the latter clearly gravitate towards the enclosures. The exception is the barrow on the elevated limestone ridge between West Tanfield and Well at a height of 75m OD (Fig 3.4, o); it could,

Table 3.1 Recorded sizes of round barrow mounds

Previous names	ALSF Project name	Plan of 1816	Lukis 1864	Grinsell 1952	ALSF 2003
Three Hills North Grinsell 27	Three Hills Barrow Group 1	56ft (17.1m) diameter 3ft (0.9m) high	Not recorded	60ft (18.3m) diameter 1ft (0.3m) high	Not evident as an earthwork
Three Hills Centre Grinsell 26	Three Hills Barrow Group 2	56ft (17.1m) diameter 3ft (0.9m) high	Not recorded	60ft (18.3m) diameter 1ft (0.3m) high	Not evident as an earthwork
Three Hills South Grinsell 25	Three Hills Barrow Group 3	77ft (23.5m) diameter 5ft (1.5m) high	c 50ft (15.25m) diameter c 3ft (0.9m) high	80ft (24.4m) diameter 3ft 6in (1.1m) high	41m diameter 0.5m high
Not recorded	Three Hills Barrow Group 4	Not recorded	Not recorded	Not recorded	Diameter unclear but visible as a slight earthwork 0.15m high
Centre Hill Grinsell 5	Centre Hill	Not recorded	c 60ft (18m) diameter 3ft 6in (1.1m) high	90ft (27.5m) diameter 3ft (0.9m) high	28.8m diameter 0.3m high
Grinsell 6	Triple-ditched round barrow	Not recorded	Not recorded	100ft (30.5m) diameter 4ft (1.2m) high	Not evident as an earthwork

however, have enjoyed extensive views of the plateau and of the henges.

Five of these monuments had previously been recorded as earthworks by Revd W C Lukis in 1864 (published 1870b) and Leslie Grinsell in 1952 (Thomas 1955, appendix 2) (see Table 3.1). Of these, the largest was the triple-ditched round barrow which excavation confirms was once an impressive mound (see 4.2). It went unrecorded by Lukis, despite being marked on the OS map from which he took other information, but was noted by Grinsell as 1.2m high and 30.5m across. It is sobering that only 60 years later this substantial earthwork is barely visible (Fig 3.23). Seemingly not as large, though still substantial, was the Centre Hill barrow. Lukis observed a mound 'about sixty feet in diameter, and three feet six inches high' [c 18 × 1.06m] (1870b, 119), but Grinsell records it as 'spread by ploughing' across 27.5m, despite allegedly only losing 0.2m of its height. Problems of identification are presumably responsible for this discrepancy. The rate of destruction clearly accelerated in the post-war years and the earthwork is currently 28.8m across, close to Grinsell's recorded diameter, but substantially lower at a height of only 0.3m (Fig 3.23). Marginally larger was THBG3, described in 1864 as 'a prominent object' to the right of the lane leading from West Tanfield (Lukis 1870b, 120). Its mound has now been spread over an area 41m across, despite still reaching a height of 0.5m (Fig 3.22). This is presumably the site recorded on the 1816 plan as '77 feet' (23.5m) across and '5 feet' (1.5m) high (Fig 2.2), but if so this contradicts the later measurements by Lukis, who recorded it with a diameter of only 15.25m. The other two Three Hills barrows on the 1816 plan were considerably smaller with diameters of '56 feet' (17.1m) and heights of '3 feet' (0.9m). Their comparability is also illustrated by Grinsell who records both as 18.3m across, but with heights of only 0.3m: it seems likely that ploughing led to their mounds being spread downslope of the Three Hills gravel ridge (see 4.8). They no longer survive as earthworks.

Geophysical prospection discovered significant buried archaeology at these greatly denuded barrows. The triple-ditched round barrow produced strongly positive responses (Fig 3.24, 90). Two possibly interrupted ditches, one of which may have been recut, enclose an area with an overall diameter of 25.7m. Two strongly negative features, or possible stone features, lay between them on either side (Fig 3.24, 91–2), and within were the remnants of what appeared to be a third circular ditch, four inner pits, and a rectangular-shaped anomaly. Excavation confirmed this was indeed a monument of some complexity (4.2). The ring-ditch of the Centre Hill barrow, which from the air encloses a central feature, was also highly visible (Fig 3.21, 55). At 26.7m across it was very similar in size to the surviving earthwork. The ditch was 2.5m wide with an interruption to the north. A squarish positive anomaly at its centre could conceivably be the remains of Lukis's

excavation trench, whilst other positive anomalies, including two immediately outside the ditch (Fig 3.21, 56), were perhaps the remains of pits or even secondary burials.

The results from Three Hills were less discernible, although they do show the incomplete ditch of THBG2 (Fig 3.25, 1) and the more complete ditch of THBG3 (Fig 3.25, 6), each with an approximate diameter of 22m. Both are associated with positive anomalies, or what may be internal pits, and a small rectilinear-shaped negative anomaly within THBG2 could be a stone structure. The third barrow in the survey area was THBG4, but any trace of its existence is far from obvious, despite being visible from the air as a ring-ditch 18m across with a central pit. It is most likely represented by a cluster of negative and positive responses to the south-west, including a strongly positive anomaly rectangular in shape, 6m long, with flanking pit-like features (Fig 3.25, 13). There was no trace of THBG1, and although this may suggest its destruction, the site has been photographed as a cropmark ring-ditch with a diameter of about 20m. These barrows are surrounded by other positive and negative anomalies, some of which, such as those that appear to be squarish or circular post-pit structures (Fig 3.25, 4–5, 10–12), show promise as being of archaeological significance. The two prominent bands of negative and positive responses (Fig 3.25, 8) are palaeochannels surrounding the gravel ridge.

Less is known about the other four likely round barrows. The quarried site near the central henge (Fig 3.4, p) was marked as an earthwork on the 1856 OS map, but went unmentioned by Lukis (1870b), despite appearing on his reproduction of this first edition map. It was subsequently recorded by Grinsell in September 1952 for the Ordnance Survey Archaeology Division – and included in his published gazetteer as No. 4 (Thomas 1955, appendix 2) – as a spread earthwork with a diameter of '50 yards' and a height of '2 ft' [c 46 × 0.6m]. Unfortunately, it was not photographed from the air prior to destruction. Only 47m to the west of the central henge was another probable round barrow (Fig 3.4, q). The faint cropmark of a large ring-ditch with an approximate diameter of 27m was photographed in July 1948 and July 1951 (CUCAP O10 and GU68–69 respectively), and the slight earthwork of a mound recorded for the Ordnance Survey Archaeology Division by Leslie Grinsell in 1952. Whilst not included in his published listing of sites, its size and location is certainly suggestive of a round barrow. A ring-ditch some 31m in diameter at the south-western end of the double pit alignment is shown in a number of aerial photographs (most notably, CUCAP CDK21, 26, and CQJ16–18 taken in July 1979 and July 1984 respectively; see Fig 2.7). Its impressive size is similar to that of Centre Hill and its siting mirrors the offset location of this barrow at the other end of the pit alignment; there seems little doubt it is indeed a levelled round barrow. Finally, a 'tumuli' [*sic*] on the limestone ridge between West Tanfield

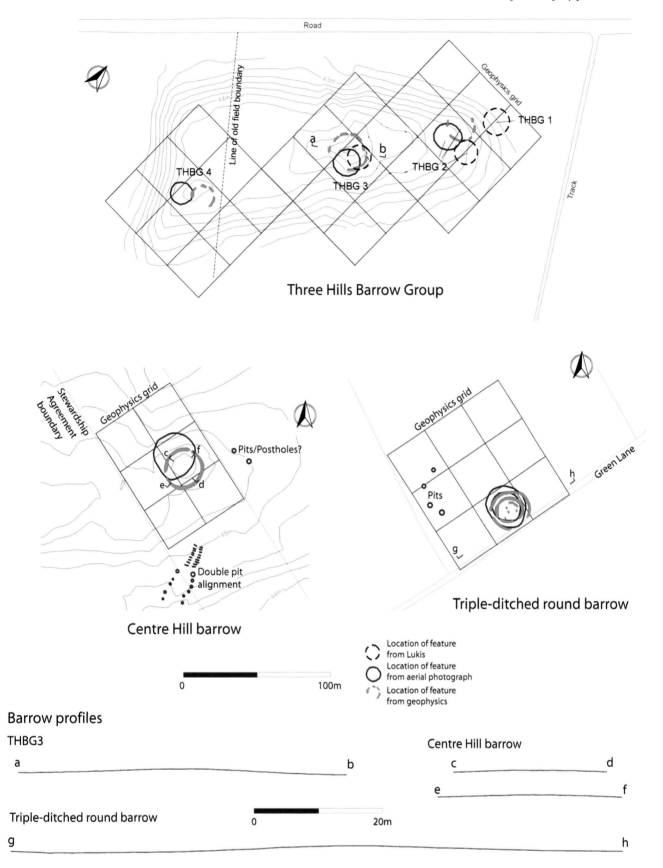

Fig 3.23 The Three Hills Barrow Group, Centre Hill barrow, and triple-ditched round barrow. Measurements are metres Ordnance Datum

and Well is shown on the 1856 OS map (Fig 3.40). At over 1km from the complex it is sited in an area which has not benefited from aerial photography,

and, whilst no trace of an earthwork now survives, it is nonetheless considered a probable round barrow. Other ring-ditches may be plough-razed round

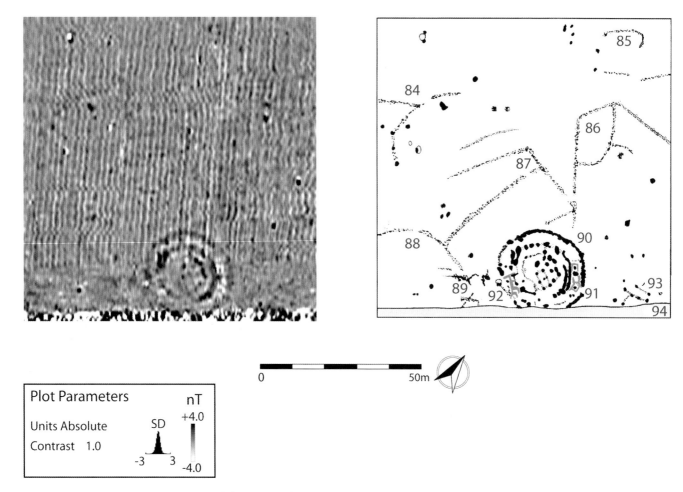

Plot Parameters	nT
Units Absolute	SD +4.0
Contrast 1.0	-3 3 -4.0

Fig 3.24   Magnetometer survey of the triple-ditched round barrow

barrows. Some 98m to the east of the northern henge is the faintest of ring-ditches with a central pit (Fig 3.4, u; DNR 541). Nothing else is known, yet its location is similar to the two round barrows by the central henge. Another ring-ditch, 21m in diameter, has been photographed on the river terrace 0.6km south-east of the southern henge (Fig 3.4, t; NMR ANY163/16–7). Its precise siting along the southern extension of the henge axis indicates that it too may have been a round barrow, and if so, the 'symbolic geometry' played out by these monuments clearly extended off the plateau. Nearby is the cropmark of a smaller oval-shaped and interrupted ring-ditch 10m by 14m across (Fig 3.4, s; NMR ANY163/16–17). The cropmarks of other similarly small ring-ditches have been photographed elsewhere (Fig 3.4, v, w) and, whilst their association with linear boundaries may suggest a much later date, the evidence from Nosterfield Quarry highlights the possibility they too were Bronze Age. The largest of the ring-ditches in the quarry, and almost certainly a round barrow, was a cropmark 17m across cut by a later pit alignment (Dickson and Hopkinson 1836–7, 215). An inner cremation, radiocarbon dated to 1980–1760 cal BC (SUERC-3786), was regarded as a primary burial, and an inhumation from just outside its ditch provided a date of 1530–1380 cal BC

(SUERC-3779; 3190±BP) (Dickson and Hopkinson 2011, 137).

A few possible round barrows have been excluded from this study. Intriguingly, Thomas Pennant, on his visit to Thornborough in 1774, refers in passing to three tumuli shown on a plan to be north-west of the central henge. He was clearly familiar with such sites, having visited Three Hills, but writes that these others 'escaped my notice' (1804, 51). No such plan has been found and it seems likely that the area in question was quarried in the 1970s. Lack of more accurate information prevents their inclusion despite the potential importance of three further barrows in an area of unknown archaeological significance. In addition, the recent Thornborough Henges Air Photo Mapping Project identified the diffuse cropmark of what may be a barrow mound, some 19m across, just 51m to the east of the northern henge (SE 2825 8005; Deegan 2005, fig 5). However, one would expect that if a barrow had been located here, so close to the henge and on Tanfield Common, it would have been recorded as an earthwork by Lukis, Grinsell, or someone else, whilst if its mound had been completely levelled, it would be shown as a ring-ditch on at least one of the aerial photographs. There must, therefore, be serious doubts about the site's original status, and

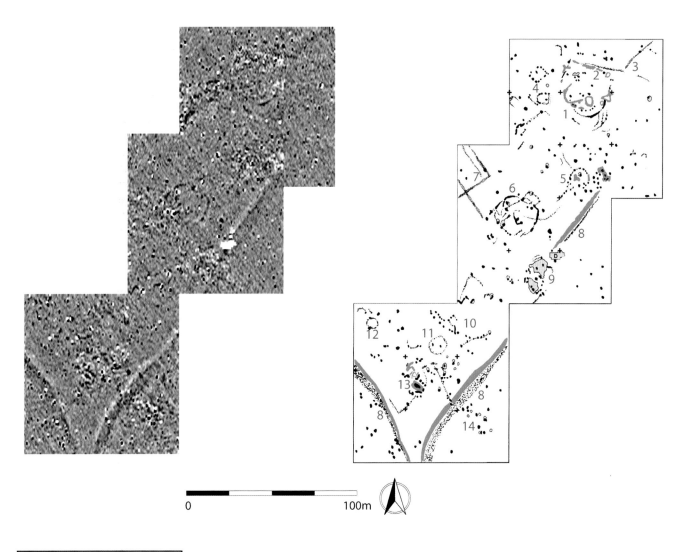

Plot Parameters

nT
+1.3

Units ± 2.0 S.D.
Contrast 1.0

-3   3
-1.2

0   100m

Fig 3.25   Magnetometer survey of the Three Hills Barrow Group

consequently, it is excluded from further consideration as a round barrow.

3.3.4   *Other monuments* by *Jan Harding and Benjamin Johnson*

The cursus could be associated with other broadly contemporary monuments. Four aerial photographs (Ordnance Survey 73 199; CUCAP BTY42–3; DNR 541) of the field to the east of the northern henge appear to show the faintest cropmark of what may be two parallel ditches 72m apart on a north-west to south-east alignment (Fig 3.4 g). They run from the West Tanfield to B6267 road for a length of 240m and may end with an irregular squared terminal. Given that it is barely visible on only four photos,

and altogether absent from many more besides, its status is uncertain (also see Deegan 2005, 11). It could be of agricultural origin, and is certainly on the same axis as the shortest of the enclosing field boundaries, with the eastern side of the cropmark aligned within a few metres of a now ploughed-out hedgerow. Yet it was located on the former Tanfield Common in an area never divided into strip-fields (Roe 2003). Alternatively, the cropmark may be a second cursus, and it was for this reason that a small earth resistance survey was conducted over part of its length (Fig 3.6B). Except for a possible ring-ditch some 12m across (Fig 3.4, u), the results showed nothing of archaeological interest (D1.7), and so it is thought unlikely that the cropmark is a prehistoric monument.

A single aerial photograph (Fig 3.26) of Chapel Hill

Fig 3.26   The oval enclosure in July 1975 (CUCAP BTY30). (Copyright reserved Cambridge University Collection of Aerial Photography)

Farm, immediately to the south of Thornborough, produced far clearer evidence for a 4th-millennium monument (Fig 3.4, e). Located in a field used periodically for pasture over the last four decades (Doreen Benson, pers comm) was the oval enclosure. It was 17m by 25m, had flattened ends, a causeway in the middle of its western terminal, and possibly another in the middle of its eastern terminal. The enclosing ditch is irregular in appearance and its north-western quadrant interrupted twice by either original gaps or plough damage. There may be an off-centre pit in its interior. The enclosure looks like a ploughed-out oval long barrow or a so-called 'long mortuary enclosure' (Atkinson *et al* 1951; Buckley *et al* 1988; Loveday 1985; Loveday 2006, chapter 5; Loveday and Petchey 1982; Vatcher 1961), and is only 161m south-east of the cursus. Indeed, if the latter

terminated on the eastern outskirts of the village, then the enclosure actually lies adjacent to and level with its terminal. Geophysical prospection produced inconclusive results (D1.6), but the following excavation confirmed the presence of an enclosing ditch (4.4). There was no dating evidence, but the cropmark's distinctive appearance and location strongly suggests it is a Neolithic monument. The aerial photograph also shows the cropmark of what looks like two large pits immediately to the west of the oval enclosure, and beyond this, a rectilinear enclosure with a rounded and partly open north-western end which shares the same approximate east–west alignment (Fig 3.26). Elsewhere, the Thornborough Henges Air Photo Mapping Project located the cropmark of another oval enclosure, to the south-west of the southern henge on the river terrace (Fig

3.4, h; CUCAP CAL53). Its eastern half is obscured by a modern track, but like the other site, it consisted of a segmentary ditch with what could be an inner pit, was around 20m in length, and aligned north-north-west to south-south-east (Deegan 2005, 11).

Immediately to the west of the southern henge lies the large double pit alignment (Fig 3.4, f). Originally discovered and published as a cropmark in 1977 (see 2.4), then incorrectly rectified by the VMNLP – producing a plan reproduced elsewhere (Harding 2000, fig 2.2; 2003, fig 65; Harding *et al* 2006, figs 1–2) – it consists of two largely straight rows of pits 10–12.5m apart, extending on a north-north-east to south-south-west alignment for at least 350m with pits spaced every 5–7m. Its northern end, which lies near the axis of the southern henge, consists of two groups of nine closely set and narrow parallel trenches, each about 3m long and spaced approximately 2.5m apart, on either side of a 1.7m wide central gap with their long axes at right angles to the alignment (Fig 2.6). Geophysical prospection by the ALSF Project suggests these 'trenches' were actually lines of either two or three contiguous postholes (Fig 3.21, 59; D1.1.4). About 80m to the north-east are the cropmarks of what look like two large pits, and whilst these are on the same axis as the double pit avenue, their relationship with it is uncertain, especially since they align on the triple-ditched round barrow. The excavation of the double pit alignment confirmed it had originally been a timber avenue (4.7). Its architecture was therefore very different to Thornborough's other monuments, and the same can be said of its topographic setting, for it avoids the flat expanse of the plateau, being sited over its gently sloping southern limits and adjoining terrace at 43.75–45.5m OD. As mentioned, a round barrow is offset at or possibly close to each of its ends. The cropmark of a possible double pit alignment running south-west towards the northern henge looks unconvincing, and is only visible on two photographs taken in July 1991 (NMR 12110/24–25), although a single pit alignment excavated in the Nosterfield Quarry (see below) does extend as a cropmark into the same field (see Fig 5.39). The Nosterfield excavations revealed another double pit alignment north-west of the northern henge (Dickson and Hopkinson 2011, 119–25). These will be discussed in 5.5.

Other single pit rows are known. Three were excavated in the Nosterfield Quarry, two of which were found to be of Iron Age or Roman date (*ibid*, 156–64), comparing well with evidence from elsewhere (Waddington 1997). By contrast, the third site, which as noted above heads out of the quarry towards the northern henge, could be of Neolithic or earlier Bronze Age date (Dickson and Hopkinson 2011, 101–5). It comprised 39 fairly regularly spaced pits on a sinuous north-east to south-west course. Cropmark evidence also demonstrates single pit rows to the east and south of the henges (Fig 3.4, v, w, x). Around 1km to the east of the southern henge are two alignments, one of which is more irregular,

on approximately the same axis as the henges, and associated with a large sub-circular enclosure approximately 139m across (NMR 17610/24–7). The latter's association with the single pit row suggests it is later than the monument complex, yet the possibility of a broadly contemporary date cannot be discounted, and if this was to prove the case it would be an important discovery. Also of interest is another long pit row to the south-east of the henges cutting across their axis (Fig 3.4, x; CUCAP BZG87, CKD20). Its location on the lower terrace, whose formation is known to have continued into the late Iron Age and early Romano-British period (3.2), highlights the need for caution when assuming it too may be of prehistoric date, yet its positioning in relation to the henges is intriguing.

3.4   Conclusion

There is a contrast at Thornborough between the plateau, with Neolithic and Bronze Age monuments, and its more undulating hinterland, where such sites are rare. Given this, its description as a 'sacred plateau', or a topographically bounded area across which religiosity was firmly embedded, seems especially apt, and would account for the close and deliberate relationship between successive monuments. This contrast also appears to have been played out over the following millennia. As Alison Deegan (2005, 14) states

It is interesting to note that fields, boundaries, trackways and enclosures of possible Iron Age and Roman date appear to be absent from the low-lying flat area on which the henges sit, although crop marks of earlier monuments do show in this area. On this limited evidence it appears that the area immediately around the henge monuments was not settled or cultivated during these periods.

It is tempting to argue that a distinction between the monuments of the long dead and a surrounding agricultural landscape resulted from conscious choices based on the specific social and religious value of particular places. These factors may have been reworked in the following centuries to produce current patterns in the preserved archaeology. It has been claimed that most of the plateau's archaeology is so badly damaged that it is of little value (Griffiths and Timms 2005, no page number) – and the rapidly deteriorating condition of the round barrows starkly illustrates the plough's propensity for destruction – but a more impartial examination of the evidence also highlights the plateau's remaining and impressive archaeological potential. That a large part of it may not have been ploughed until relatively late in the landscape's history certainly explains why each of the henges continues to survive as pronounced earthworks, with the northern site's location on the open common of Nosterfield township responsible for its almost intact state. It would also account for the success of geophysical prospection in detecting a complex array of buried features whose conservation should be considered an urgent priority. The results highlight how the area around the cursus and henges is likely to have been anything but empty.

Much is left to do with the basic characterisation of the monument complex and its immediate landscape. Little is known about all but a small part of the plateau, and its further investigation by extensive geophysical prospection and limited excavation will undoubtedly add greatly to our understanding of the layout, use, and development of the monument complex. Equally beneficial would be further study of the cursus and henge interiors, especially at the central henge, where it seems a special relationship emerged between two very different types of monument, and where the bank of the later site seals a presumably well-preserved section of cursus. Subtle uses of topography, along with the available archaeological evidence for free-standing structures both within and without these enclosures, suggest experience across the sacred plateau was highly orchestrated. Cursuses have long been seen as processional routeways, but all too often, as empty processional routeways (see Johnston 1999). At Thornborough, by contrast, we may be dealing with a monument whose interior was far more complex. That henges may also be part of processional routeways has been highlighted before (eg Loveday 1998; Parker Pearson and Ramilisonina 1998), yet only by understanding better what happened within and between them can we start to grasp why it was necessary to create three massive enclosures. Further characterisation of the plateau's archaeology is also necessary if we are to understand the relationship between older monuments and the later round barrows and pit alignments. The excavated double timber avenue suggests monumentalisation being used to create defined routeways, in this instance linking two round barrows, but what about the other places and spaces of the 2nd-millennium landscape? Only through further fieldwork can we start to address these relationships.

4   Acts of monument construction

4.1   Introduction

The VMNLP and the ALSF Project excavations (see Table 4.1 and Fig 4.1) addressed fundamental issues of chronology and structural sequence. It was thought likely that the ditched cursus – which Thomas (1955, 436) saw as belonging to the 'Atlantic or Pre-Bronze Age climatic phase', but which is a monument class generally dated to 3600–3200 BC (see Barclay and Bayliss 1999) – would be associated with other broadly contemporary monuments, for which the nearby oval enclosure, which closely resembled excavated 'long mortuary enclosures', was a promising candidate. Four small evaluation trenches were dug here to ascertain its original appearance and date (4.4). The triple-ditched round barrow was also possibly of 4th-millennium date (see Harding 1996; Kinnes 1979) and its ploughed ditch had produced sherds from a probable carinated bowl (see D4.1.2). Hence, it was evaluated by a single trench (4.2) with two large test-pits opened at a nearby cluster of pits (4.3). Next to nothing was known about the chronology of the three henges. Thomas had highlighted a lengthy interval between the cursus and their construction in the early Bronze Age (2.4), but such a date was based on the flimsiest of evidence. Not only are henges now known to have been built in the later Neolithic, but those at Thornborough possess outer ditches whose irregular and segmentary appearance is reminiscent of the earliest of these (Harding 2003, chapter 1). It was therefore essential to explore the original form of these perimeters and ascertain whether they were earlier than the very different looking inner earthworks. Consequently, small-scale excavations were undertaken across the outer ditches of the southern and central henges and at the north-west terminal of the southern henge's inner ditch (4.5 and 4.6).

Table 4.1   VMNLP and ALSF Project excavations

Site (Trench Code)	Date of excavation	Size of excavation	Single Context Records	Method of excavation
Oval enclosure (TRN 5 & TP1–3)	August–September 1996	Two 4m × 1m Two 5m × 1m Three 1m × 1m	501–22	Topsoil removed by hand, features cleaned and excavated by hand, features and topsoil dry sieved
Outer ditch, southern henge (TRN 4)	August–September 1996	7.5m × 9m (maximum)	401–36	Topsoil removed by hand, features cleaned and excavated by hand, features and topsoil dry sieved
Inner ditch, southern henge (TRN 6)	August–October 1997	20m × 15m	601–45	Mechanical stripping of topsoil, features cleaned and excavated by hand, features and sample of topsoil dry sieved
Outer ditch, central henge (TRN 7)	August–October 1998; February–May 1999	20m × 20m	701–99 7001–14	Mechanical stripping of topsoil, features cleaned and excavated by hand, features and sample of topsoil dry sieved
Double pit alignment (TRN 1, 2 & 3)	September 1994 and 1995	2.5m × 2.5m (maximum) 2m × 2m 4m × 4m	101–9 & 121–30 201–8 301–8	Topsoil removed by hand, features cleaned and excavated by hand, features and topsoil dry sieved
Double pit alignment (TRN 8 & 9)	August–September 1998 and 1999	350m × 30m	801–50 901(01)–988(02)	Mechanical stripping of topsoil, features cleaned and excavated by hand, features dry sieved
Three Hills round barrow (TRN THRB)	August 2003	60m × 3m	001–013	Mechanical stripping of topsoil, features cleaned and excavated by hand, features and sample of topsoil dry sieved
Triple-ditched round barrow (TRN DRD)	August–September 2003	35m × 3.6m	DRD 001–048	Mechanical stripping of topsoil, features cleaned and excavated by hand, features and sample of topsoil dry sieved
Pit cluster (TRN DRDTP1)	August 2003	5m × 5m	DRDTP1 001, 003, 005–13, 018, 022	Topsoil removed by hand, topsoil dry sieved, features cleaned and planned
Pit cluster (TRN DRDTP2)	August 2003	6.5m × 5m	DRDTP2 002, 004, 014–17, 019–21, 023–27	Topsoil removed by hand, features cleaned and excavated by hand, topsoil and features dry sieved

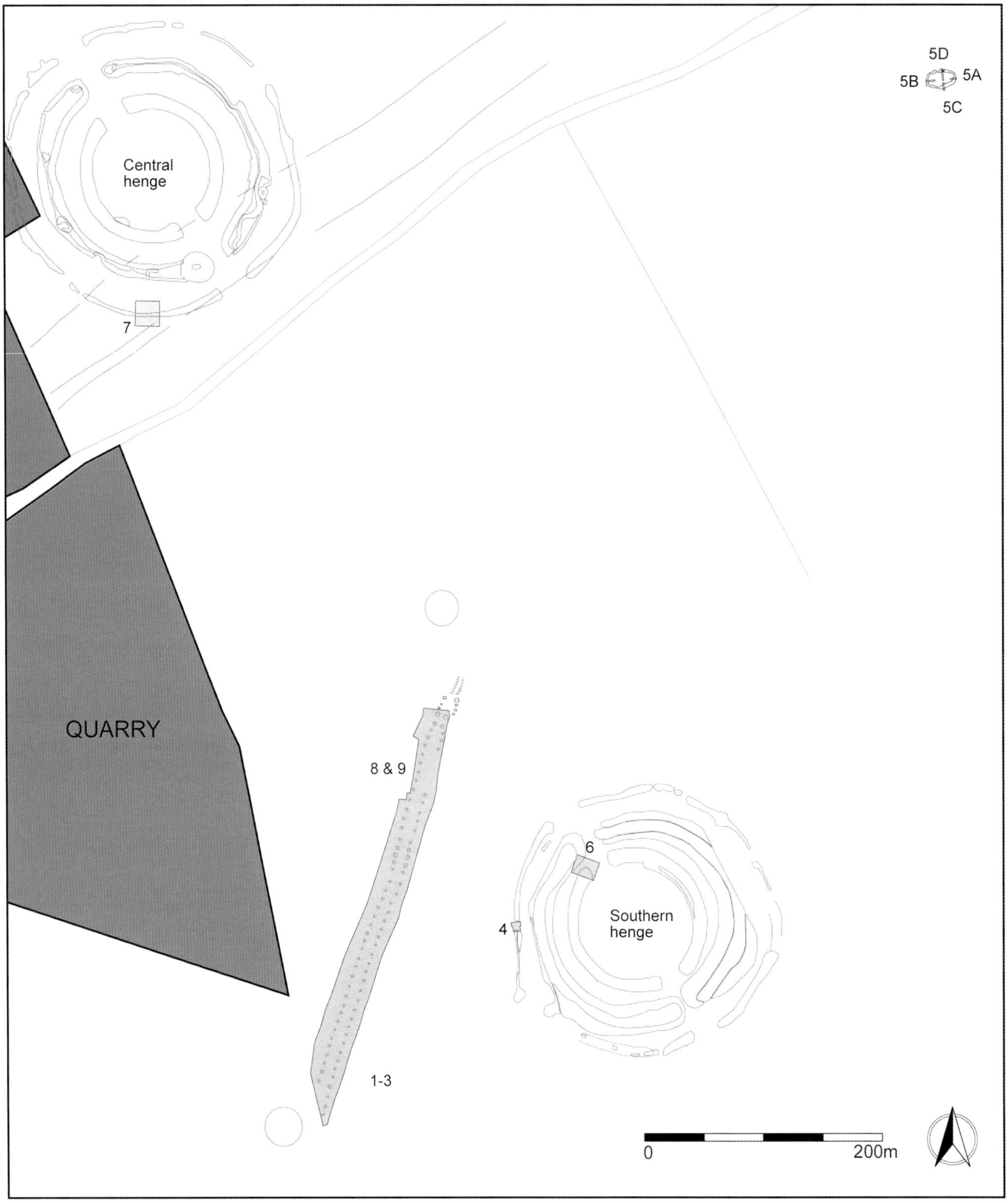

Fig 4.1   VMNLP excavation trenches at Thornborough. © Crown Copyright / database right 2013. An Ordnance Survey / EDINA supplied service

Also completed were the large-scale excavation of the double pit alignment (4.7) and the evaluation of the worst-preserved of the Three Hills barrows (4.8) in order to ascertain if these monuments were broadly contemporary with the henges or were later additions to the complex.

Ultimately, the small areas opened for all but one of these excavations, along with the frustrating tendency of the monuments to produce little or no material culture or organic remains, meant the above programme failed to establish a dated sequence for the construction and use of the complex. Looking back it seems hopelessly naïve to have believed this could ever have been achieved by limited excavation,

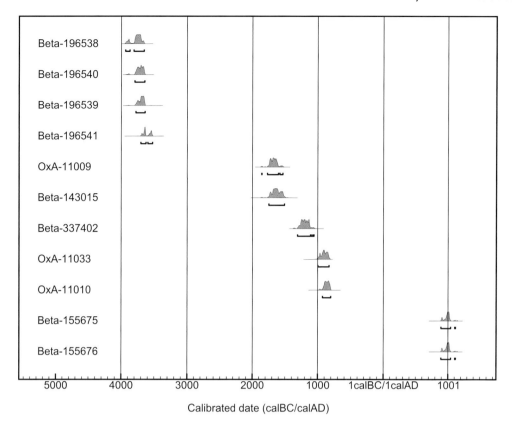

Fig 4.2 Radiocarbon dates from the excavations. All have been calculated using the computer program OxCal v.4.1.7 (Bronk Ramsey 2010) with atmospheric data from Reimer et al 2009

and a more careful calibration of project objectives and likely outcomes would have resulted in a better thought-through, and perhaps more ambitious, programme of fieldwork. Nevertheless, the following excavation results are presented in the order in which the monuments were most likely built, and an attempt is made to identify sequences of activity at individual sites. Eleven radiocarbon dates were obtained (Fig 4.2; see D5 for details). Very little is known about the complex's development during the earlier and middle Neolithic and there are no dates for the cursus and oval enclosure. Fortunately, the triple-ditched round barrow, the only site to produce human bone, was more forthcoming, providing four radiocarbon assays in the first half of the 4th millennium BC (Fig 4.2; Beta-196538–41). It may have been the earliest monument at Thornborough. The excavations also failed to verify whether the outer henge ditches were built before their inner earthworks, or to produce any useful relative or absolute dating evidence for the enclosures. A single radiocarbon date in the early Bronze Age from the inner ditch of the southern henge (Beta-143015) fails to indicate their likely date of construction. The only large-scale excavation, at the double pit alignment, produced sherds from vessels of Bronze Age date (D4.1.2), and radiocarbon dates in the 2nd millennium BC (OxA-11009, Beta-337402) and early 1st millennium BC (OxA-11010, OxA-11033). Finally, there are two identical radiocarbon dates in the late 1st millennium AD and very early 2nd millennium

AD for the outer and inner ditches of the central and southern henges respectively (Beta-155675, Beta-155676).

One other major shortcoming of the evidence is worth mentioning. Despite seven seasons of excavation, next to nothing is known about the immediate setting of these monuments. This is certainly true of the Neolithic and Bronze Age environment, for a combination of relatively high pH and large sediment particle size meant that pollen grains were largely destroyed by microbial attack, with submitted samples from the excavations at the southern henge and the oval enclosure containing little or no pollen (Moores nd). As a result, no other pollen samples were taken during the course of the VMNLP and ALSF Project. Bulk soil samples from the triple-ditched round barrow, the Three Hills round barrow, some of the features which make up the double pit alignment, and the inner ditch of the southern henge were submitted for flotation, but again, the results – integrated here into accounts of individual sites – were unimpressive (see also D4.5). Little is also known about the network of contemporary structures which most likely existed around and between the monuments. Fieldwork elsewhere has demonstrated how cursuses and henges were often only one part of more complex landscapes, surrounded by features like single pit alignments, small enclosures, timber settings, and stone walls or buildings, as is spectacularly demonstrated by the impressive remains recently discovered between

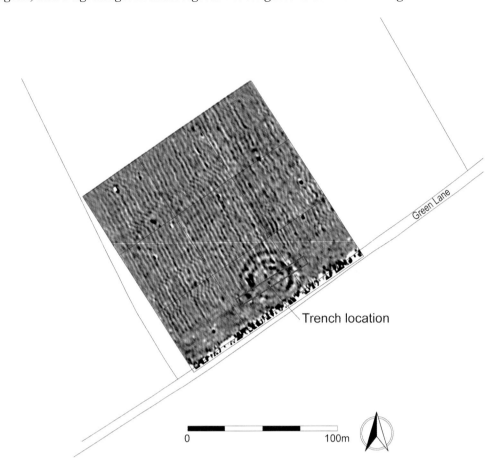

Fig 4.3   Excavation at the triple-ditched round barrow

the Ring of Brodgar and the Stones of Stenness in Orkney (Card 2010), or indeed, by the hengiforms and timber circles found next to the Ferrybridge henge in West Yorkshire (Roberts 2005, fig 128). These more modest structures were essential to the ways in which people moved around, encountered, and interpreted larger monuments, but at Thornborough no attempt was made to evaluate the full extent of Neolithic and Bronze Age archaeology across the plateau itself. This failure greatly limits what can be realistically said about the use and development of this remarkable monument complex.

4.2   Triple-ditched round barrow *by Jan Harding, Benjamin Johnson, Sarah Groves, and Simon Mays*

4.2.1   Introduction

An excavation trench 35m by 3.6m was located across the centre of the greatly denuded triple-ditched round barrow to evaluate the condition, preservation, date, and use of a range of possible features detected by geophysical prospection (Fig 4.3). The monument was 25.7m across, consisting of two roughly circular ditches, another possible inner enclosure, and what could be internal pits (3.3.3). A chert flake and flint core had been found at the site during an earthwork survey in 1952 (Thomas 1955, appendix II), and an inspection of the monument in 1997 revealed two small sherds of a probable carinated bowl from the freshly ploughed-out soilmark of its innermost ditch (D4.1.2). Topsoil was stripped by machine and the remainder excavated by hand; a quarter of the former, and all of the latter, was sieved for finds.

4.2.2   Excavation results

Excavation revealed three ditches encircling small central features (Fig 4.4). These circuits are likely to be the product of different phases of activity and may suggest three episodes of mound construction. The almost completely destroyed condition of the latter made its stratigraphic exploration impossible. A number of inner features had been cut into the mound, but again, it is impossible to ascertain their wider relationship with the rest of the monument. The site produced the largest artefact assemblage from any of the excavations. There were 497 worked lithics, largely from the plough-disturbed horizon and mostly of Mesolithic or earlier Neolithic date, with a further 93 pieces, mostly of irregular waste,

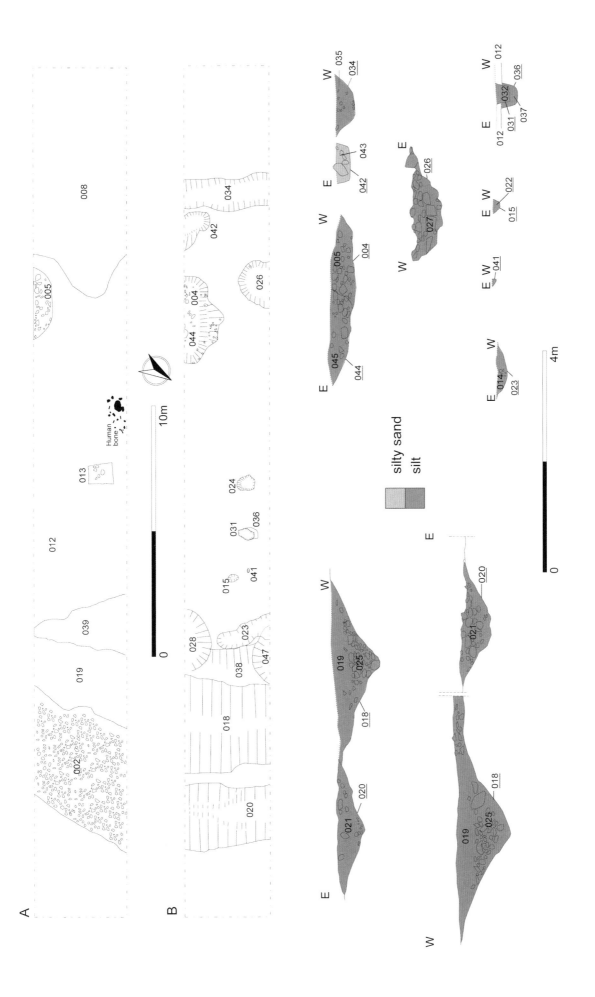

Fig 4.4 The triple-ditched round barrow: A, plough-disturbed upper fills; B, excavated features

from the bulk sieving of soil samples. The collection is summarised in Tables D3.6, D3.9, D3.13, D3.16, D3.20, D3.22, and D3.26. There was also human bone, its importance only diminished by much of it being from a disturbed context (D4.3). Four statistically consistent radiocarbon dates for the stratified human bone fall between 3920 cal BC and 3530 cal BC (see D5), and whilst it is not possible to create a chronological sequence, they most likely date the earliest burial(s) and the first phase of monument construction.

Plough-disturbed horizon and pre-barrow activity

The removal of the topsoil, 001, which averaged about 0.29m deep, revealed the plough-disturbed upper fills of a number of features (Fig 4.4A). Extending across the middle of the trench was a distinctive reddish-yellow silty gravel deposit, 012, with large numbers of small stones usually between 0.05m and 0.1m in size. The deposit is presumed to be the remnants of the barrow mound. Towards its centre was 013, an ill-defined spread of both human and animal bone and tooth fragments sitting in a matrix of loose brown gravelly silt. This rectilinear-shaped deposit was approximately 0.8m by 0.45m, and was subsequently recognised as the truncated upper fill of 024, a pit dug into the mound (Fig 4.4B). Immediately to the east of the mound remnant were two distinctive deposits. The first of these was 002, a linear band of cobbles and loose brown silt around 4m wide. It was subsequently recognised as overlying 021, the truncated upper ditch fill of the monument's outer ditch, and may represent redeposited mound material. Abutting the western side of 002 was 019, a linear band of loose strong brown silt about 3.9m wide. This was the truncated upper fill of the barrow's middle ditch (Fig 4.4B). The removal of the ploughsoil from the western half of the trench revealed 005, a loose brown silty deposit with many large cobbles, subsequently shown to fill 004, a ditch butt-end (Fig 4.4A). Plough marks, orientated east to west along the field's headland, were very visible along the length of the trench. The western end of the trench is downslope of the small ridge on which the monument is located; it appeared more heavily truncated, with neither surviving subsoil nor remnant mound material. Here the ploughsoil sat directly on top of natural gravel (008).

The heavily disturbed mound material was subsequently removed, revealing a number of additional features (Fig 4.4B). That it appeared to cover some features and not others, irrespective of their apparent sequence in the phasing of the monument (see below), is due to the mound's almost complete but irregular destruction by the plough. In the eastern half of the trench it covered, or appeared to cover: 023, a linear feature curving inwards towards the north, and filled by 014, a silty deposit with large numbers of cobbles and pebbles; 015, a small oval pit filled by 022, a loose silt; 024, a plough-

damaged pit near the centre of the trench, filled by 013, a loose silt containing deposits of human bone; and 036, another plough-damaged pit, again near the centre of the trench, and filled by 037, a very loose silty gravel. The vigorous cleaning of the trench also revealed two additional features from its western half: 026, or what appeared to be another ditch butt-end, filled by 027, a loose silty deposit with large cobbles; and 042, a narrower ditch terminal, filled by 043, a loose silty sand with large cobbles. The site's remaining features (028, 034, 038, 041, 047) were only revealed later in the excavation after the natural gravel, into which they were cut, had weathered. All these features, with the possible exception of 041, a dubious stakehole only 0.09m across and 0.09m deep, are integral to the monument and described below.

The plough-disturbed horizon produced a large quantity of largely fragmentary human bone. From 001 and 012 came 206 fragments, including 26 from long bones, along with 3 hand phalanges, 5 other complete bones, and the remains of 2 teeth. This material was fairly equally divided between the two contexts. There were also a few pieces of animal bone and teeth. A similarly large quantity of human bone came from 013, described below, and the very top of 039, the fill of 038, produced two very small fragments of bone. The freshly broken nature of much of this material attests to the effects of the plough, but some of the breaks appear older, and may even suggest that the bone was redeposited as part of original funerary practice. The fragmentary nature of these unstratified remains and their considerable admixture makes it difficult to identify discrete individuals, but much of the bone comes from a single adult male who may have originally been deposited in pit 024 (see below). That a significant amount of the bone relates to this particular deposition is confirmed by the refitting of fragments from 001 and 013, the pit's heavily truncated fill. This plough-disturbed material also includes the remains of two other adults, represented in one instance by several teeth and bone fragments, and in the other, by a vertebra, and a single juvenile, represented by a tooth and a pair of fragmentary clavicles.

There were also 381 worked lithics, 76.7% of the excavated total from the site, of which the majority were from the topsoil. There was a sizable Mesolithic component, and among the most diagnostic artefacts of this date are four microliths: a complete obliquely blunted point of chert and three flint fragments, including two further obliquely blunted points (eg Fig 4.5, 3), which would, when complete, have fallen within the relatively large size range of early Mesolithic forms. There is also an opposed platform blade core (Fig 4.5, 1) and several bladelets. Beyond these, there is every reason to think the Mesolithic element is substantial, perhaps more so than anywhere else at Thornborough, whether from an excavated site or the ploughsoil. Blade production is well-represented, by both blades and further blade cores (Tables D3.6,

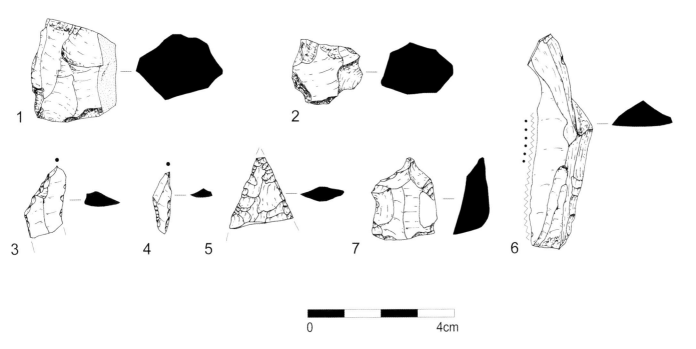

Fig 4.5 Selected lithics from the excavation of the triple-ditched round barrow: 1, context 012, opposed platform blade core; 2, context 027, multi-platform flake core; 3, unstratified, fragmentary obliquely blunted point; 4, context 019, rod microlith; 5, unstratified, fragmentary leaf arrowhead; 6, context 001, serrated blade; 7, unstratified, borer

D3.26). Linear and punctiform butts are frequent here (Table D3.12), as are feather terminations and core rejuvenation flakes (Table D3.6), reflecting systematic care in core maintenance and knapping. Many of these characteristics mark earlier Neolithic industries as well as Mesolithic ones. Two fragmentary leaf arrowheads (eg Fig 4.5, 5) are certainly of this date, as may be a serrated blade (Fig 4.5, 6) and a long scraper. The only artefact which stands out as possibly later is a borer made on a broad-butted, hard hammer-struck flake with unresolved cones of percussion on its ventral face (Fig 4.5, 7), a kind more likely encountered in Bronze Age industries.

The 116 flint and chert artefacts from the undisturbed ditch and pit fills (see below) were in similarly variable condition to those from the plough-disturbed horizon in terms of the frequency of breakage, post-depositional damage, cortication, and other surface modification, suggesting that many of them were redeposited, whether from the surface and topsoil as the various stages of the monument were built, or from the mound as it weathered into the ditches. They also matched the superficial material in their predominantly Mesolithic or earlier Neolithic technology and typology.

The high incidence of debitage of all kinds from the plough-disturbed horizon and buried features alike (Table D3.6) suggests the location was used for knapping. At the same time, the low frequency of cortical flakes (Table D3.20 and D3.22) indicates that most flint was brought here in an already partly decorticated state. A breakdown of the flint artefacts for which a source can be determined shows that while till flint, the largest single category of raw material from the site (Table D3.9), accounts for more than 75% of the flakes, blades, and retouched pieces, it accounts for only 30% of the cores. This may reflect an originally larger size for till flint cores, each yielding more removals than those of other materials. It may also indicate that till flint cores, from more distant sources (see D3.2 for discussion of sources) and less readily replaced, were considered of higher value than more locally available material and were removed elsewhere. The three discarded examples had been worked down to very small sizes, each weighing less than 10g. Other flints and cherts may have come from local fluvial deposits; they could even have been gathered from a nearby watercourse, now surviving as a palaeochannel (5.4). Some or all of the 62 pieces of chert may reflect the opportunistic knapping of pieces found when the ditches were being dug (see D3.2). These materials were used less parsimoniously, some chert and gravel flint cores being discarded at weights of over 20g.

Earliest monument

The earlier Neolithic lithic material from the plough-disturbed horizon may be closely associated with the first act of monument construction. This would appear to include the digging of pit 036 which was sub-oval in plan and aligned north-east to south-west (Fig 4.4B). Upon excavation it was found to be 0.98m long, 0.55m wide, and 0.35m deep, and to contain a human cranial vault fragment and an intermediate human hand phalanx (D4.3). Bulk sieving produced two further human hand phalanges, possibly from different adult individuals. The cranial fragment and hand phalanx yielded two statistically consistent (T'=3.1; T'(5%)=3.8; =1) radiocarbon dates of 3790–3650 cal BC (Beta-196540; see D5) and 3680–3530 cal BC (Beta-196541; see D5) respectively, but it is impossible to say if the bone was from the same adult individual. The disturbance of this feature by pit 031, a feature which also contained human bone, suggests that more skeletal material may have been present but was redeposited within the later pit, and the dated cranial fragment fits with a parietal bone fragment from the latter. Given this disturbance, it is unclear whether the material had originally been articulated or not. The presence of small hand bones suggests it was, or at least that there was partial articulation, but basing this interpretation on just three fragments is inconclusive, especially since the pit appears too small for a whole body. The deposition of articulated body parts is an alternative explanation. It is also difficult to ascertain whether the feature was left open or immediately backfilled, although its filling, 037, was homogeneous in character. This loose brown gravelly silt was associated with a very large number of gypsum specks, especially around its edges, and many of the small pebbles in the fill had been stained white, presumably by the same material. That the gypsum would have created a localised environment with a less acidic matrix is one explanation for the small number of land snail shell fragments from both *Cepea hortensis* and *Cepea nemoralis* found in 037, but both are burrowing species and may be a more recent introduction (D4.4). It is of interest that what was used as a repository for human bone appears to have been lined with gypsum (see 6.3 for a fuller discussion). Bulk sieving produced nineteen pieces of irregular waste and one small core fragment, all of flint.

This feature was then presumably enclosed by the inner ditch of the barrow, identified at the east end of the trench as 038 and at the west end as 004 (Fig 4.4), and perhaps covered by a mound. Later activity made their identification difficult and they did not survive in section, but both were probably the same feature, enclosing an area at least 11m across with a causeway to the west. Their fills, 039 and 005, were virtually identical, consisting of a brown silt containing large cobbles, and both cuts had a shallow flat-bottomed U-shaped profile. They had also both been recut, by 028 and 047 into the south and north sides respectively of 038, and by 044 into the east side of 004. These broadly comparable recuts, each around 2.5m across and about 0.45m deep, are again seen as the result of a single act of ditch-digging; if correct, the monument may have now possessed causeways on both sides. They were filled by 029, 048, and 045, each of which was broadly alike, consisting of a loose brown or yellowish-red stony silt with large cobbles towards its top. These fills were so similar to those in the earlier ditch that the recuts were only visible in section, perhaps suggesting they occurred shortly after the infilling of the initial ditch. Both are therefore ascribed to the same general phase.

Unfortunately, neither the earliest ditch nor these later recuts produced organic samples suitable for radiocarbon dating and the only excavated find was the proximal fragment of a flint blade from 029. Bulk sieving of a soil sample of the latter produced six pieces of irregular waste, one very small core fragment, and one small flake, all of flint.

Enlargement

The middle ditch appears to have been opened next. It respected the earlier ditch and causeway on the western side of the monument, but to the east it cut into the original feature and closed off the existing gap. The new ditch is represented by 018 on the monument's eastern side, and 026 and 042 to the west (Fig 4.4B), all three with similar fills of densely packed cobble and loose brown or dark brown silt. Ditch 018 was 3.8m wide and 1m deep with a V-shaped profile, whilst 026 and 042 were 2.1m wide and 0.67m deep and 0.8m wide and 0.38m deep respectively, both having a shallow U-shaped profile. The basal fill of the feature on the monument's eastern side was 025, a distinctive layer filling the bottom 0.6m of the ditch, of which about 90% were large cobbles separated by many voids (Fig 4.6). It produced a small quantity of unidentifiable animal bone and the tooth of a cow. Large cobbles were also present in 027 and 043, the fills of 026 and 042 respectively, although not in the same quantity. This primary fill, on both the eastern and western side of the monument, is interpreted as deliberate backfilling, and the absence of an underlying wash of gravel or sand suggests it happened immediately after construction or that the ditch bottom was cleaned prior to dumping. It is impossible to ascertain whether this phase of activity, which enlarged the area enclosed by the ditch to nearly 15m across, included the building of a larger inner mound. Bulk sieving of 019, the upper fill of the ditch on the monument's eastern side, produced two fragments of barley grain and one carbonised weed seed.

Most of the lithics from the middle ditch were from its eastern side. The twenty pieces associated with 025 consisted of a complete serrated flint blade, two flint scraper fragments, a microlith fragment, two multi-platform flake cores (one of flint and one of chert), seven flakes, four blades, two chips, and one piece of irregular waste. The bulk sieving of soil samples produced another thirteen pieces of flint irregular waste. This small collection, no doubt the result of redeposition during the feature's deliberate backfilling, is chronologically indistinguishable from the 39 pieces found in 019, the overlying and largely stone-free deposit of loose strong brown silt which then naturally infilled the feature. The material from here consisted of a complete rod microlith of later Mesolithic date (Fig 4.5, 4), a complete bladelet and the fragments of two others, two blade cores, one of them with opposed platforms, five blades, twenty flakes, and eight chips. Most of this material was

Fig 4.6 Triple-ditched round barrow: looking south at cobble fill 025 in bottom of ditch 018

actually from the bottom of 019, close to the under-lying cobbles, suggesting that they too may have been rapidly redeposited prior to natural infilling. A further sixteen pieces of irregular waste, one core fragment, and one flake fragment were found from bulk sieving. The fill of the 026 ditch terminal on the western side of the monument produced a complete flint multi-platform flake core (Fig 4.5, 2), a core tablet, and two flakes, and its bulk sieving produced three further flint flakes, one of which was burnt.

Final phase

The outer ditch is represented by 020 to the east and 034 to the west (Fig 4.4B); 020 was at most 2m wide and 1m deep, but irregular in profile, varying from a shallow U-shape in the north to a V-shape in the south (Fig 4.7); 034 was 1.5m wide and 0.6m deep with a steep-sided U-shaped profile. It was not broken by a causeway on its western side and is accordingly thought to post-date the middle and inner ditches, rendering the existing causeway obsolete. Its digging enlarged the enclosed area to over 22m across. The truncated upper fill of the eastern section of outer ditch, 002, was 3.6m wide and spread over part of the upper fill of the middle ditch, implying that the latter was dug before the outer ditch. The primary fill of the outer ditch,

021 to the east and 035 to the west, consisted of a loose light brown silt with medium or large cobbles throughout. The stony and homogeneous nature of the fills again suggests deliberate backfilling, and on its eastern side it was then covered by 002, which in large part was a deposit of cobbles (Fig 4.8). This is presumably redeposited mound material and could be nothing more than plough-spread with the stones settling in the softer ditch fill. Alternatively, it could be a deliberately deposited layer of cobbles, and if so, may have been the final act of building at the monument.

The outer ditch produced 31 worked lithics, eleven of which were chert, divided more-or-less equally between its eastern and western segments. There was a serrated flint flake, the fragment of a flake core and a tested nodule (both of chert), three reju-venation flakes, seventeen flakes, six blades, and two chips. Bulk sieving of 021 and 035 produced five pieces of irregular waste and four small flakes, two of which were burnt, with another trimming or thinning flake. All were of flint.

Other features

A number of internal features (023, 024, 015, 031) from the eastern half of the trench (Fig 4.4B) lack stratigraphic evidence about their relationship

Fig 4.7   Triple-ditched round barrow: looking south at ditch 020 after excavation

with the above sequence. They are near the centre of the barrow with three out of the four appearing to have been an integral part of funerary practice. The exception is 015, a shallow sub-oval depression, 0.25m long, 0.2m wide, and 0.15m deep, with an irregular U-shaped profile. It was filled by 022, a loose brown silt deposit with pebbles. It does not resemble a posthole, was cut into 012 but not the natural gravel, and could be nothing more than the indent of a large stone removed previously by topsoil stripping.

Feature 023 was a shallow ditch running along the inside edge of the inner, and earliest, of the above circuits. It was 1.1m wide and 0.48m deep, with a flattened U-shaped profile. A section some 2.25m in length was present in the trench, running out on the north side (Fig 4.9). It was filled by 014, a loose dark brown silt with many cobbles and pebbles, some of which showed evidence of burning, and one very large and perhaps deliberately placed stone. The fill also contained a large amount of charcoal, and one flint chip, which had not been burnt. Bulk sieving produced six pieces of irregular waste, three small flakes, one of which was burnt, and a large flake most likely from an opposed platform core, all of flint. That it abuts 038 and closes off the causeway formed by the recutting of this feature suggests it is later than this initial phase of building, but it proved impossible to ascertain the stratigraphic relationship between 023 and 047. The geophysical results indicate that 023 may have continued around to the north, and perhaps even the south and west, forming a squarish feature whose eastern side was convex-shaped (Fig 4.3). Its butt-end may have been part of an original causeway.

Pit 024 was at the centre of the monument. This could indicate that it belonged to the earliest monument, but had clearly been cut into the mound and was very badly plough-damaged. Sub-rectangular in plan, it was 0.8m long, 0.45m wide and 0.3m deep, with a shallow U-shaped profile and flat base. Filled by 013, a loose brown gravelly silt deposit

Fig 4.8   Triple-ditched round barrow: looking west at cobble fill 002 in top of ditch 020

Fig 4.9 Triple-ditched round barrow: looking south at ditch 023 after excavation

whose truncated upper reaches had been visible immediately after topsoil stripping (Figs 4.4A and 4.10), it contained over 160 disturbed human bone fragments, including cranial pieces, long bones, ribs, and hand bones (D4.3). It is suggested that the majority of bone comes from a single individual, an adult male, over 45 years of age. This conclusion is based on many of the surviving long bone fragments being quite large and robust with pronounced muscle attachments, characteristics that are more likely to be seen in males than females. The skull and mandible fragments are also more masculine in appearance. The wear patterns on some of the teeth suggest an old individual, as does the presence of osteoarthritis in several of the vertebrae and areas of remodelled bone at some of the muscle and ligament attachment sites. These changes can be caused by high levels of physical activity or repeated stress or trauma to a muscle. The feature contained one complete multi-platform flake core of chert. Bulk sieving of the soil sample produced four pieces of irregular flint waste.

Pit 031 was cut through the mound and into pit 036. Sub-oval in plan, it was 0.7m long, 0.5m wide and 0.3m deep, with a steep-sided and flat-bottomed profile. The feature, whilst heavily truncated, was partly covered by two large stones which had offered it some protection from the plough. These were some of the largest found on site and may have been deliberately placed. The pit was filled by 032, a loose light brown gravelly silt,

Fig 4.10 Triple-ditched round barrow: looking south at 013 showing bone fragments and teeth

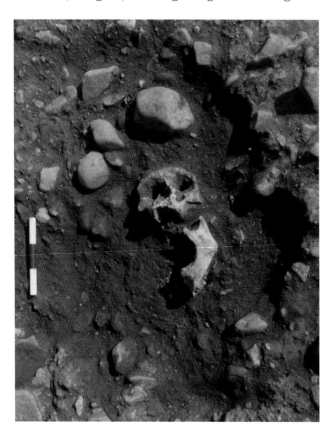

Fig 4.11   Human cranium and mandible in fill 032

and 24 pieces of human bone, including a substantially complete cranium and mandible (Fig 4.11), 5 other cranial vault fragments, teeth, hand and foot bones, rib fragments, and vertebrae. The majority of the breaks were old. It is not certain that the cranium and mandible were from the same individual, but their semi-articulated position during excavation, along with similarities in their morphology, suggest that they were. If so, this is most likely the skull of a male aged between 40 and 60 years. Two hand bones were dated to 3920–3660 cal BC (Beta-196538; see D5) and 3780–3640 cal BC (Beta-196539; see D5) respectively. These measurements are statistically consistent (T'=1.1; T'(5%)=3.8; ν=1) with each other, with a weighted mean of 4950±29 BP, calibrated at 2 sigma to 3800–3650 cal BC, but also with the measurements from pit 036 (T'=6.5; T'(5%)=7.8; ν=3). It is impossible to say if the dated bone from both contexts was from the same adult individual or from separate adult individuals. That this feature so neatly intruded on 036 is unlikely to be accidental and the earlier pit could have been marked in some way. The deposit also contained a single flint flake fragment, animal bone fragments and teeth, largely of rodent, one fragment of barley grain, and, like the fill of 036, a small number of land snail shell fragments identified as *Cepea hortensis* and *Cepea nemoralis*. Bulk sieving produced six pieces of irregular waste and a small flake, all of flint.

4.2.3   Discussion

The excavations provide an insight into the changing significance of the site, from a place of sporadic and short-term knapping, possibly located near a watercourse and ready supply of flint, to one used for the deposition of human bone. Mesolithic and earlier Neolithic activity, represented by the sizable lithic collection, appears to be residual within the excavated deposits at the barrow. The earliest phase of the monument saw the excavation of the inner ditch around pit 036 (Fig 4.12). The former was then recut, presumably only a short time after its initial construction, with causeways both to the east and the west. Whether this recutting was combined with the excavation of the middle ditch, also interrupted to the west, is thought unlikely. It was probably dug during a second phase of activity, and followed by the outer ditch during a third phase of activity (Fig 4.12). The geophysical results suggest the latter may have been causewayed to the north-west. The monument was therefore enlarged and re-enlarged. That the disturbed remnant of its mound, 012, contained large amounts of small stone, but none of the cobbles found in 002, suggests it was capped by large stones, some of this heavier material then rolling downwards to the barrow's edge. If so, then the final mound would have extended across part of the middle ditch, at least on the monument's eastern side, and, if matched to the west, could have been as much as 18m across, making it an impressive sight. A regional parallel is provided by the water-worn sandstone cobbles covering the Neolithic round barrow of Whitegrounds on the Yorkshire chalklands (Brewster 1984). How the inner features relate to this sequence is unclear but pit 031, which so neatly cuts the monument's original central feature, probably also belongs to the first phase of the barrow. If 023 were covered by the final mound, then this linear feature would pre-date the digging of the outer ditch, and if it was part of a more continuous feature running around the monument's interior, it may be connected to the mound's enlargement during the first or second phase of building. The heavily truncated state of pit 024 indicates it belongs to the final phase of activity, and if so, it would have been dug into the centre of the newly extended mound, presumably before stone capping was added (Fig 4.12).

The four radiocarbon assays were on human bone whose condition suggests it was not terribly old when deposited. They date the monument's first phase to between 3920 and 3530 cal BC, broadly contemporary with the earliest long barrows and long cairns in southern England (Whittle *et al* 2007, 126–7) and with other Neolithic round barrows in Yorkshire (Gibson and Bayliss 2010; see also Harding 1996; 1997a, 284–7). The excavated sites of Callis Wold 275, Whitegrounds, Grindale 1, and Boynton 3, all from the east of the county, may certainly be comparable in age (Bayliss *et al* 2012, 49-50; Jordan *et al* 1994; Walker *et al* 1991, 107), and the last two

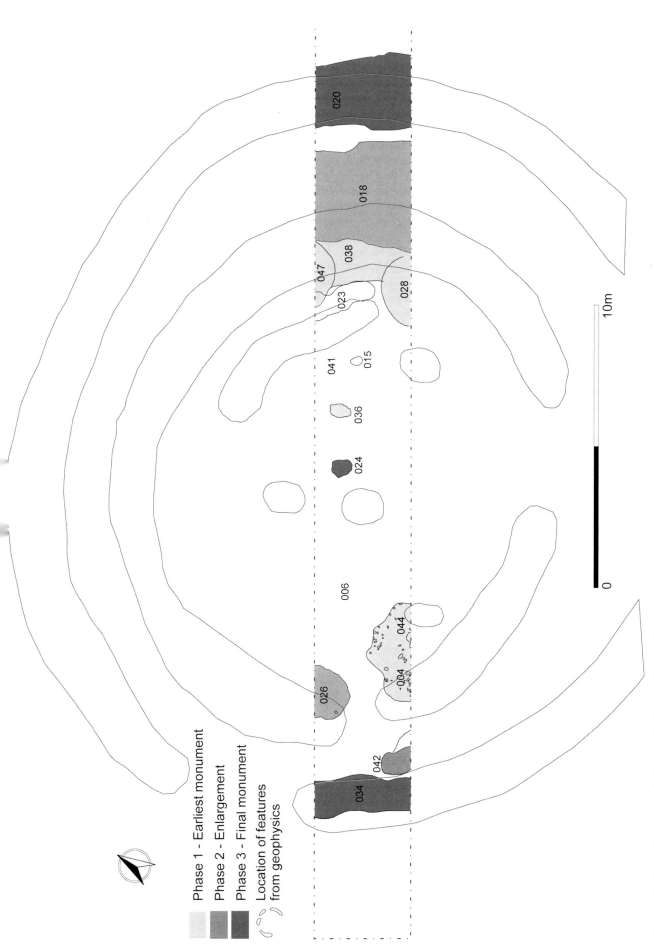

Phase 1 - Earliest monument
Phase 2 - Enlargement
Phase 3 - Final monument
Location of features
from geophysics

0   10m

Fig 4.12   Development of the triple-ditched round barrow. Ditch 023 has not been phased

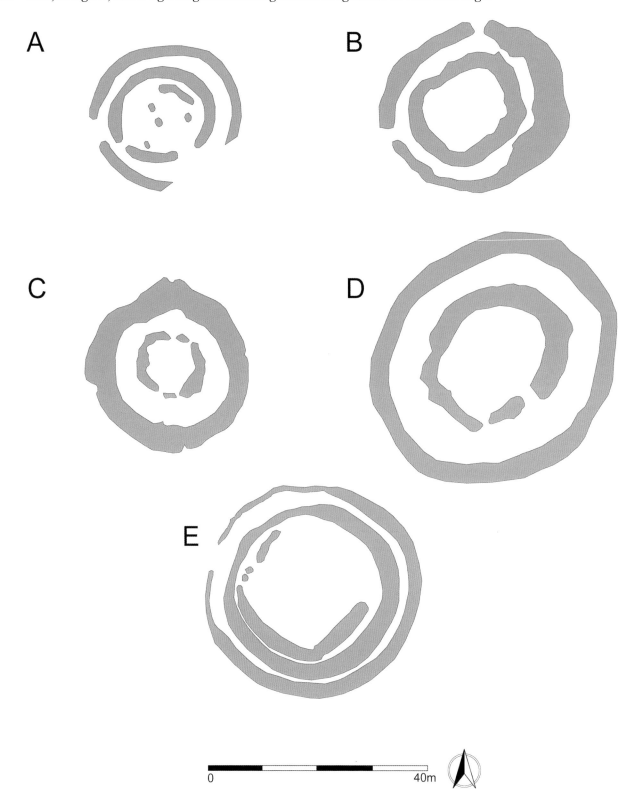

Fig 4.13   Plans of multi-ditched round barrows: A, Thornborough; B, Grindale 1 (after Manby 1980, fig 2); C, Boynton 3 (after Manby 1980, fig 10); D, Aldwincle 1 (after Jackson 1976, fig 5); E, Grendon V (after Gibson and McCormick 1985, fig 9)

are very similar in appearance to the triple-ditched barrow (Fig 4.13, A–C). Grindale 1 had a central pit containing a bone fragment and fourteen flakes, surrounded by two irregular, concentric ditches (Manby 1980, 24–33). An unweathered antler on the base of the inner and earlier ditch was dated to 3966–3378 cal BC (HAR-269; 4910±120 BP). Its outer ditch enclosed a monument similar in size to the triple-ditched barrow (Fig 4.13, B). Also close in both age and appearance was Boynton 3, even if, like

Grindale 1, it possessed only two encircling ditches (*ibid*, 38–43). The innermost of these produced a date of 3793–3377 (HAR-268; 4840±80 BP) and could provide a parallel for the squarish inner feature of which 023 may be part (Fig 4.13, C). At Boynton 3 it was tentatively interpreted as a bedding trench for timbers (*ibid*, 43). Something similar, if larger, was found at two sites in Northamptonshire. At the Aldwincle 1 round barrow three straight lengths of ditch, and possibly a fourth, formed a roughly rectangular enclosure (Fig 4.13, D) within which were postholes, a scatter of limestone, and the remains of two adults, one fully crouched and the other disarticulated and fragmentary (Jackson 1976, 13–30, 42–6). This initial structure produced a date of 3517–3027 cal BC (HAR-1411; 4560±70 BP). It was subsequently surrounded by two concentric ditches, as was the squared three-sided enclosure, with a palisade trench along its fourth side, excavated at Grendon V (Fig 4.13, E). This feature was unassociated with human remains (Gibson and McCormick 1985, 35–8, 60–4).

At Thornborough the remains of the dead were placed in pits dug into the marginally more elevated eastern half of the monument. The majority of the undisturbed skeletal material was from pit 031 and appears to represent a minimum of two adults and a possible juvenile or infant. The disturbed remains of a further three adults and one juvenile, the majority from a single adult associated with pit 024, were found at the centre of the monument. These features share an approximate north–south orientation and geophysical results suggest there may be others within the monument (3.3.3 and D1.5). Despite their truncated state, it seems unlikely they were ever large enough to have contained complete articulated individuals, the deposition of disarticulated or partially articulated human bone appearing more probable. The excarnation of the dead prior to burial may be supported by the heavily eroded character of some of the skeletal material, although the general absence of bleaching raises the possibility that local soil conditions, and the presence of gypsum, was responsible for their condition (D4.3). Other likely evidence for the practice includes the under-representation of distal hand and foot phalanges and other small bones of the hands and feet, along with the under-representation of long bone joint surfaces and pelvic bones. Early 4th-millennium round barrows from elsewhere across the region have produced both articulated and disarticulated deposits (Brewster 1984; Coombs 1976; Kinnes 1979, 12–13; Moloney *et al* 2003, 6). Indeed, both were evident at Whitegrounds where an entrance grave was associated with three decapitated inhumations and the disarticulated remains of a further five individuals (Brewster 1984). Its excavator also described a 'nest of skulls' from two adults and a juvenile (*ibid*, 8), providing a parallel for the complete cranium and mandible placed in pit 031.

There are indications that the monument's development may not have spanned too lengthy a period of time, although it is impossible to say if we are dealing with as brief a chronology as recently reported for some of the southern English long barrows and long cairns (Whittle *et al* 2007, 129, 131–2). The very deliberate way in which pit 031 cut pit 036, the two contexts producing the radiocarbon dates, suggests a short timescale, during which bone was redeposited into the more recent feature. The same can be concluded for the deliberate backfilling of the middle and outer ditches before the accumulation of primary fill. That the monument was definitely in use during the first half of the 4th millennium, but not necessarily any later, accords with Neolithic round barrows in eastern Yorkshire. Here there is some evidence for a trend whereby the number of bodies buried together declined during the latter half of the 4th millennium to between one and three individuals (Harding 1996, 71). This is demonstrated at Whitegrounds where the earlier entrance grave was succeeded by a single male inhumation placed in a pit and dated to 3520–3020 BC (Brewster 1984; Bayliss *et al* 2012, 49–50). The association of the latter with a jet slider and flint axe typifies the connection between this development in burial practice and the more ready inclusion of grave goods (Kinnes 1979). Special objects like these were absent at Thornborough, although an earlier 4th-millennium parallel for the two unstratified leaf arrowheads could be the three incorporated into the burial deposits at Callis Wold 275 (Coombs 1976).

4.3   Gypsum pits
by Jan Harding and Benjamin Johnson

4.3.1   Introduction

An aerial photograph of the triple-ditched round barrow, taken in July 1979 (CUCAP CKD24), showed the cropmarks of what looked like at least four pits to the north-west of the monument. Possibly another four, albeit more closely set and with poorly defined edges, lie directly to its west. Two of the first group were detected by geophysical prospection at the barrow, showing as circular positive anomalies (Fig 4.14; D1.5.4). There is no trace of the others, which largely fell outside the survey area, but three further anomalies not visible on the aerial photograph were discovered. These features may be of particular significance given their proximity to the triple-ditched round barrow and, to the north-west, the southern henge. Excavation was therefore undertaken in August 2003 with the aim of evaluating and ascertaining their general condition, preservation, date, potential, and significance. Two small 5m by 5m trenches (DRDTP1, DRDTP2) were opened at the northernmost pair of geophysical anomalies (Fig 4.14). DRDTP2 was extended eastwards by 1.5m to expose the full extent of a feature. They were excavated by hand with all spoil sieved.

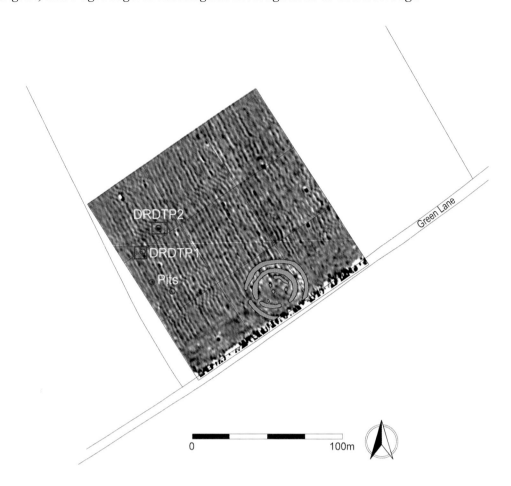

Fig 4.14   Excavation of the gypsum pits

4.3.2   Excavation results

The truncated fills of six features were discovered in the two trenches, four in DRDTP1 and two in DRDTP2 (Fig 4.15). All were cleaned and recorded, but only one of these, 015 in DRDTP2, was excavated, the others left in situ. This was a large pit with a strongly cemented primary fill of gypsum. The other unexcavated features are assumed to be broadly similar. The excavation produced an unremarkable collection of 68 worked lithics which were mostly from the plough-disturbed horizon. They are summarised in Tables D3.6, D3.9, D3.13, D3.16, D3.20, D3.22, and D3.26. There were no diagnostic pieces, inviting comparison with their low frequency at the triple-ditched round barrow. The role and date of these unusual features is unknown, but they could be connected to the use of gypsum at either the triple-ditched round barrow, the southern henge, or the Centre Hill barrow.

DRDTP1

The topsoil, 001, was a firm dark reddish-grey silty loam, which reached depths of 0.25–0.39m. Its removal revealed four irregular plough-disturbed patches of a very pale brown silty sand, each interpreted as the upper fill of a cut, three of which were largely outside the trench (Fig 4.15): 008, an oval feature 3.3m across; 007, the northern edge of a probable sub-circular feature; 012, the southern edge of a probable sub-circular feature; and 010, the south-eastern part of another probable sub-circular feature. None was excavated and their significance is unclear. It is highly likely, though, that they are related to the excavated oval-shaped feature in DRDTP2, appearing to be broadly similar in size, in outline, and in the composition of their upper fills. The plough-disturbed horizon produced a total of 37 worked lithics, consisting of the fragment of a chert core, a flint core rejuvenation flake, seventeen flint flakes and seven chert flakes, a flint bladelet, two flint blades, and eight flint chips. The majority of pieces were incomplete. The flint was either from till/gravel or possible till sources.

DRDTP2

The removal of the topsoil, which was the same as in DRDTP1, but reaching a depth of 0.41m, revealed two irregular plough-disturbed patches, each interpreted as the upper fill of a cut: 014, an oval of

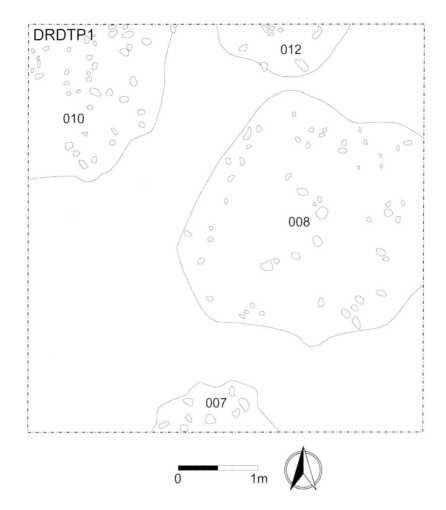

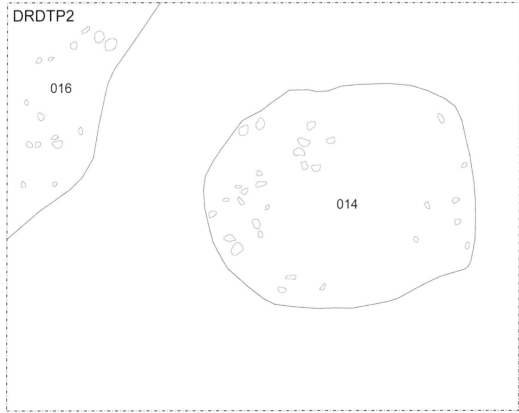

Fig 4.15   Top of features in DRDTP1 and DRDTP2

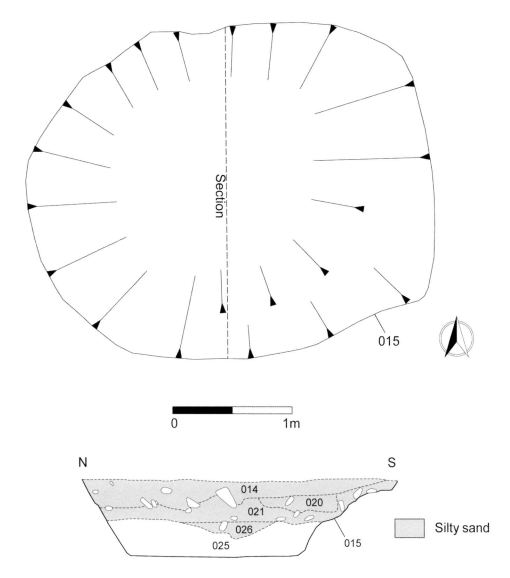

Fig 4.16   Plan and section of pit 015

dark yellowish-brown silty sand, measuring 3.48m east–west and 2.7m north–south in the centre of the trench; and 016, a very pale brown silty sand of unknown size and shape, extending beyond the north-west corner of the trench (Fig 4.15). The first of these appeared comparable to the possible features in DRDTP1, despite its fill being different in colour, and consequently, was selected for excavation. The possible second feature gives the impression of being larger in size than the others. The plough-disturbed horizon produced a lithic collection similar to that from DRDTP1. There was a total of 26 worked pieces, consisting of the fragments of a flint blade core and flint multi-platform flake core, sixteen flint flakes and two chert flakes, two flint blades, two pieces of irregular flint waste, and two flint chips. The majority of pieces were again incomplete and largely from till/gravel or possible till sources, although there was also one possible piece from the chalklands of eastern Yorkshire.

On excavation, 014 was found to be the top fill of a large steep-sided pit, 015, which also measured 3.48m east–west by 2.7m north–south, and was 0.83m deep with a flat base (Fig 4.16). Fill 014, was 0.16m deep, and below it was a very similar deposit, 021, of dark yellowish-brown silty sand, 0.2m deep. Across its south-western quadrant was 020, also a dark yellowish-brown silty sand, but slightly looser than 021. It could be an area of disturbance. The pit's primary fill was a strongly cemented layer of a whitish-grey material 0.47m thick at the centre but lensing up the sides of the cut (Fig 4.17). It was so hard it had to be removed with a pick. At the time of excavation the TV programme *Time Flyers* was being filmed and their geologist completed on-site testing, concluding it was gypsum (Dr H Cockburn, pers comm), an interpretation later confirmed by the British Geological Survey (A Cooper, pers comm). This deposit was slightly dished in the centre and filled with 026, a reddish-brown sandy silt. The recovery of a chert flake and two chert blades in exceptionally fresh

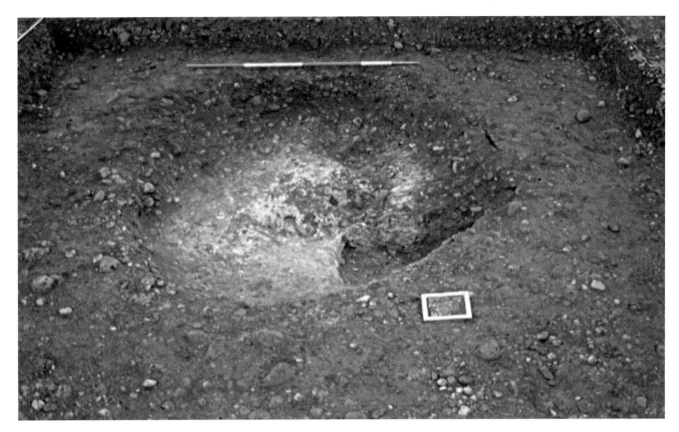

Fig 4.17   Looking east at gypsum in the bottom of pit 015

condition from 014 and 021 suggests this readily available raw material was worked on site. These two contexts also produced a flint blade and flint flake.

4.3.3   Discussion

Interpreting the excavated feature is difficult. The most likely explanation is that the primary fill is a deliberate deposit of burnt gypsum – burning the soft rock reduces it to a more manipulative raw material – which had reset as plaster (A Cooper, pers comm). If correct, there is no sign the burning was completed in situ, so the pits may have been used for either storing the resulting powder, or, more likely, for mixing into a paste. The slight dish at the centre appears to have infilled naturally given its fine-grained deposit, but if so, the latter's absence from elsewhere is unexplained. The fill above, 021, has an irregular top and contains large cobbles, most likely suggesting it was deliberate backfilling. There are no indications of the date of the pit, but it could have been associated with the monument complex. Gypsum was used at three nearby sites: at the neighbouring triple-ditched round barrow, where it appears to have been deliberately deposited in an inner burial pit (4.2.2); at the three henges, where it may have coated the inner bank (6.3); and at the Centre Hill barrow, where Lukis discovered that a 'kind of basin, 18 inches deep, had been cut

out of the natural soil to receive the coffin, and that the bottom of the basin or cist had been lined with a coarse concrete, 10 inches thick in the middle, diminishing to nothing at the edges and so hard that the pick pierced it with difficulty' (Lukis 1870b, 119). The digging-out of the pit, and perhaps the other surrounding features, could therefore have been connected to the preparation of gypsum for use at one of more of these monuments, with the contents of this specific pit not entirely used, explaining the colour difference between its fill and the fills of the other exposed features.

The results of the excavation suggest that those features visible on the aerial photograph and geophysical results were part of a larger group of very densely packed pits. The aerial photograph may even show another group approximately 100m to the north. It seems unlikely that such a large number of pits had been employed in the preparation of gypsum solely for the triple-ditched round barrow – unless, of course, it had also been used in contexts other than inner burial pits – suggesting they were either connected to more than one of the above monuments, making them multi-period, or had been used for the only site big enough to require the large-scale preparation of gypsum, the southern henge. If the latter is correct then there may be good reason for why they were sited 0.4km from the henge: given the results from surface collection (see Chapter 5), it may well be that the preparation of gypsum was prohibited across the plateau during the later Neolithic, occurring instead around its edge. It is impossible to say if this embellishment of the southern henge occurred rapidly, involving large numbers of people, and presumably many pits, or if it occurred periodically as people added to or renewed the covering of the bank. It does, however, beg the question of whether similar pits exist closer to the central and northern henges.

4.4   Oval enclosure *by Jan Harding and Joshua Pollard*

4.4.1   *Introduction*

Geophysical prospection had failed to detect the oval enclosure (D1.6) clearly evident as a 17m by 25m cropmark on a single aerial photograph (Fig 3.26). Despite this, a small trench was excavated across each of its four sides (Fig 4.18) to evaluate the possibility that it was either a ploughed-out oval-shaped long barrow or a 'long mortuary enclosure' (3.3.4). These four trenches were located using the plot of the cropmark. They were sited along, and at right angles to, the east–west axis of the enclosure. The two trenches across its side ditches were 4m by 1m in size (TRN5C, TRN5D), whilst the two across its end ditches both 5m by 1m (TRN5A, TRN5B). Three 1m by 1m test-pits (TP1–3) were also located on the same axis as the trenches to ascertain the existence of features within the enclosure's central area. The excavation was conducted by Joshua Pollard in August and early September 1996. Excavation was by hand with all spoil sieved. The only find was the proximal fragment of a flint flake from the subsoil of TRN5D.

4.4.2   *Excavation results*

A topsoil, 501, of 0.10–0.15m thick grey-brown clayey loam overlay a subsoil, 502, of grey-brown sandy loam which sat on natural gravel at a depth of 0.18–2m (Fig 4.18). Both contained 10–20% small to medium-sized gravel. Its removal revealed the enclosure ditch in three of the evaluation trenches (Fig 4.18). In TRN5A its cut, 505, possessed a flattened U-shaped profile 2.70m across at its top with a rounded bottom at a maximum depth of 0.53m. In TRN5D the ditch, 521, was narrower and more steep-sided, with a U-shaped profile, a width at its top of 2.35m, and a maximum depth of 0.70m. It was different again in TRN5C, where the excavation failed to locate both edges of the cut. The ditch, 509, was steep-sided to the south, but rose gently on its other side. It had a maximum depth of 0.63m. The aerial photograph hints at a possible causeway immediately to the west of TRN5C, where the cropmark narrows, but it is too ill-defined to appear on the plan. The ditch sloping up into a rounded terminal would certainly explain its shallower depth of 0.40m in the east-facing section of TRN5C. In all three trenches the outer edge of the ditch was steepest, indicating that the enclosure was dug from the inside.

The excavated segments of ditch produced a fairly homogeneous sequence of fills (Fig 4.18). Inspection of the sections revealed a thin lens, approximately 70mm thick, of loose gravel and dark brown loamy sand lining the bottom and inside edge of the ditch cut in TRN 5A, 5C and 5D. This initial erosion was followed by backfilling (Robert Shiel, pers comm), represented by a homogeneous firm, fine-grained brown loamy sand with quantities of very small to medium stone (504, 508, 513, 520, 522), and 519 in TRN5D, a firm fine-grained deposit of dark reddish-grey sandy loam with a large amount of small to large stone. The asymmetrical nature of the latter suggests the raking back of material from the enclosure interior. The backfilled ditch in TRN5C had been recut by 507, but only for 0.5m along its length, ending in a squarish terminal: it may have respected the earlier possible causeway. This steep-sided recut had a maximum width and depth of 1.1m and 0.29m respectively. It had infilled naturally with 506, a dark greyish-brown silty loam, with a slip of loose gravel along the cut and quantities of small or medium stone throughout. It was mottled with darker patches of leaf mould. Tertiary ditch fills, 503 and 518, survived in TRN5A and 5C. This fine-grained dark brown loamy sand contained loose gravel and limited amounts of very small and small stone.

The remaining evaluation trench, TRN5B, missed the enclosure ditch at its western end (Fig 4.18), but provided other valuable evidence. Apparent at a depth of only 0.25m was 510, a 0.15m thick band of fine-grained brown loamy sand, with quantities of very small to very large stone, deposited directly on the natural gravel. At most it was 2.2m wide, making it a similar width to the enclosure ditch, and its composition was almost identical to this earthwork's backfill. These characteristics could indicate it was possibly the remains of an inner bank built *c* 2m inside the ditch, and the continuation of such a feature along the enclosure's northern side may have been the source of 519, the redeposited ditch material found in TRD5D. However, if such an earthwork existed, it failed to respect an adjacent gap, some 0.6m wide, in the cropmark ditch, and the fact that it sits directly on the natural gravel, and very broadly corresponds to an oval-shaped area of low resistivity extending over and well beyond the western half of the enclosure (D1.6.3), suggests it may alternatively be the remnants of a natural feature. This geophysical anomaly corresponds with an especially stony and gravelly patch in the ploughed field.

Other possible features were revealed by two of the three test-pits (Fig 4.18). In TP3 was 515, a semi-circular patch of mottled but compact fine-grained orangey brown sandy silt with dark grey-brown humic patches. Similar in shape was 516 in TP2, a loose deposit of gravel within a matrix of greyish-brown loam. Neither was excavated since they had

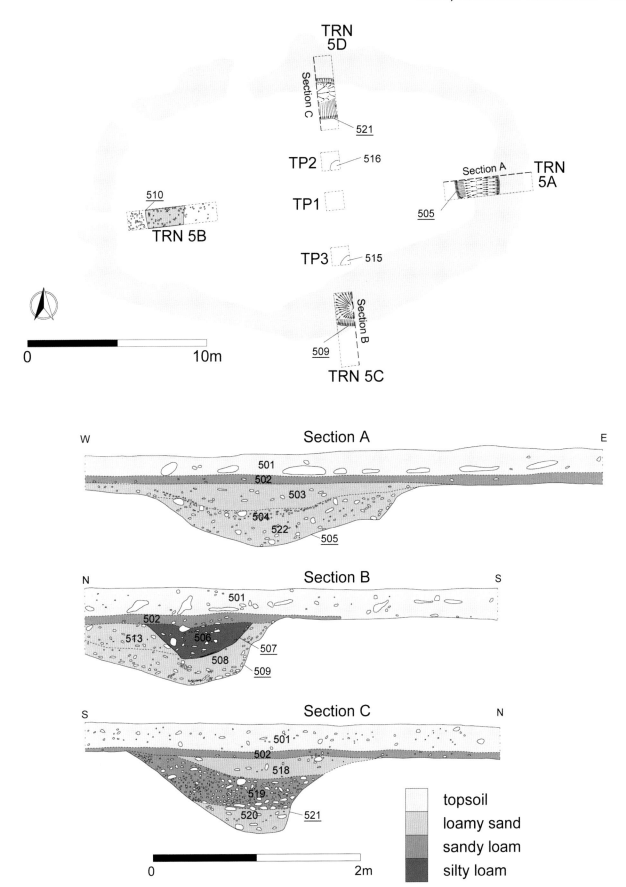

Fig 4.18 The excavation of the oval enclosure

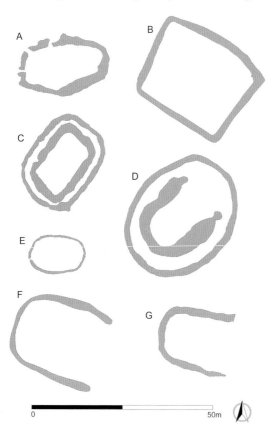

Fig 4.19   Plans of enclosures at: A, Thornborough; B, Sonning (after Slade 1963–64, fig 2); C, Barrow Hills (after Bradley 1992b, fig 2); D, Lower Horton (after Ford and Pine 2003, fig 2.6); E, Maxey (after Pryor et al *1985, fig 44); F, Barford (after Loveday 1989, fig 4:5); G, North Stoke (after Case 1982, fig 34)*

only been partially exposed. Their location was close to the cropmark of what may have been an off-centre pit (3.3.4).

4.4.3   Discussion

The excavations were inconclusive as to the date of the enclosure, yet in layout it is broadly comparable with a number of excavated enclosures dating to the latter half of the 4th millennium. Comparisons can be made with: the inner features already mentioned at Aldwincle 1 and Grendon V in Northamptonshire (Fig 4.13, D, E; Jackson 1976, 13–30, 42–6; Gibson and McCormick 1985, 35–8, 60–4); the rectangular enclosure at Sonning in Berkshire (Fig 4.19, B; Slade 1963–64); U-shaped and completely enclosed monuments at Barrow Hills in Oxfordshire (Fig 4.19, C; Bradley 1992b), Lower Horton in Berkshire (Fig 4.19, D; Ford and Pine 2003), and Maxey in Cambridgeshire (Fig 4.19, E; Pryor *et al* 1985, 62–6, 233); and U-shaped enclosures at Barford in Warwickshire (Fig 4.19, F; Loveday 1989) and North Stoke in Oxfordshire (Fig 4.19, G; Case 1982).

Some of these have been classified as belonging to a heterogeneous group of usually rectilinear or oval-shaped 'long enclosures', but Loveday (2003, 30–2; 2006, 54–6) notes this class's general similarity with partially or totally ditched long barrows, preferring to see most as the ploughed-out remains of what were originally mounded monuments (see also Jones 1998). Certainly the enclosure constructed and redeveloped in the first three phases of Barrow Hills was most likely associated with a mound, and even if it was not, the site subsequently turned into a short oval-shaped long barrow now known to be characteristic of the middle Neolithic. The same was also possibly the case at Lower Horton, and the enclosing ditch at Maxey held either a freestanding timber setting, which was later covered by a mound, or revetment for a contemporary barrow. By contrast, those 'long enclosures' never covered by an earthwork – Normanton Down in Wiltshire (Vatcher 1961), Dorchester VIII in Oxfordshire (Whittle *et al* 1992, 148–52, 195–6), Raunds in Northamptonshire (Harding and Healy 2007, 94–9), and perhaps Inchtuthil in Perthshire (Barclay and Maxwell 1991; *pace* Loveday 2006, 75) – tend to be very much wider, longer, and more rectangular than Thornborough's oval enclosure. Whilst there is no evidence from the latter for a mound, this is unsurprising in such an intensively farmed landscape, and its inner size closely corresponds with the maximum 10–14m width of most accurately recorded long barrow mounds (Loveday 2003, 32; 2006, 62). If this earthwork did originally exist then the source of the material needs explaining given the prompt back-filling of the enclosure ditch. Loveday believes that many of these subsequently flattened barrows were turf-built, their generally slight ditches providing nothing more than capping (Loveday 2006, 62). The building of a mound at the oval enclosure is therefore a possibility, although the probable causeway in its western terminal suggests it was built after the site's original if short-lived use as an enclosure.

These excavated comparisons indicate that the oval enclosure is most likely middle Neolithic, and its location, immediately to the south-east of the cursus and possibly adjacent to and aligned upon its eastern terminal (3.3.4), supports this interpretation. Long enclosures and barrows of this period are often to be found in such close association, forming broadly contemporary monumental foci (for examples, see Bradley 1991; Loveday 1989, 71–4; 2006, 56), and the U-shaped sites at Barford and North Stoke were sited along the very ends of a cursus and bank barrow respectively. Indeed, if the oval enclosure was not of 4th-millennium date then the Thornborough cursus would be highly unusual in not being sited alongside other broadly contemporary monuments. Nearby are the cropmarks of what look like two large pits, and beyond this, a small rectilinear enclosure with a rounded and partly open north-western end and a squared-off south-eastern end (Fig 3.26). The latter, which shares the same approximate east–west alignment as the oval enclosure, may have inner features. It bears some similarity to what is most likely a middle Neolithic rectangular feature excavated at New Wintles Farm in Oxfordshire, consisting of two 6m long ditch segments, about 3m apart, with pits at each end, and surrounded by a discontinuous outer ditch (Kenward 1982). It produced a few burnt child cranial fragments. The further exploration of this area and the determination of where the cursus actually ends (3.3.1) is vital to understanding Thornborough's 4th-millennium landscape, especially given the quarrying-away of its western terminal and surrounding landscape.

4.5 Central henge and cursus
by Jan Harding and Blaise Vyner

4.5.1 Introduction

The geophysical survey across a south-west portion of the central henge showed its outer ditch as a curving anomaly running east–west (see Fig 3.20, 1; D1.2.4). The eastern end of the feature is less easy to follow, although aerial photographs demonstrate its continuous and uninterrupted nature. The survey was less successful in locating the southern cursus ditch. During the fieldwork it was incorrectly believed to be the short linear anomaly on a north-east to south-west alignment (see Fig 3.20, 6; 3.3.1). The source of this misidentification was an error in the layout of the grid which saw it positioned further to the west than intended, an error

which went undiscovered during the excavation, shortly afterwards, of a 20m by 20m trench. Hence, the latter missed the southern cursus ditch, despite its aim of exploring the relationship between the cursus and outer henge ditch at a point where the aerial photographs suggested the latter widened significantly (Fig 4.20). The trench was also positioned to evaluate some of the geophysical anomalies either side of the outer henge ditch, interpreted as possible pits or postholes (Fig 3.20). The excavation was largely undertaken in August and September 1998, although not finally completed until May of the following year. Topsoil was stripped by machine and the remainder excavated by hand with all spoil sieved.

4.5.2 Excavation results

The excavation revealed three major features (Fig 4.21). The most visible was the outer henge ditch running along the length of the trench. On either side, but originally part of the same feature, was what was interpreted as a deliberately deposited layer or low platform, very possibly an original element of the cursus interior subsequently cut by the digging of the henge ditch. Small timber uprights and placed circles of small stones may have been associated with this feature. It overlay two shallow cuts, one of which, to the north-west of the excavation trench, was associated with post settings. Both are again assumed to be part of the cursus. The third major feature looked like a bedding trench for a palisade or fence-line to the south-east of the excavation trench. It terminates short of the outer henge ditch, suggesting it is later, but otherwise its date and relevance is unknown. This interpretation of the excavation results replaces an alternative mentioned elsewhere (Harding 2000, 35–6). The excavation failed to produce any worked lithics or any other prehistoric finds. Later ditch fills produced a single radiocarbon date in the 10th or early 11th century AD (see D5) and seventeen pieces of medieval and post-medieval pottery, along with roof tile (D4.1.3).

Plough-disturbed horizon

The plough-disturbed horizon consisted of a topsoil, 701, of soft dark brown silt 0.11–0.28m thick which overlay a subsoil, 702, of soft dark brown sandy silty loam 0.04–0.16m thick. Both contained 35–40% small to medium-sized stone. Its removal revealed four distinct deposits (Figs 4.21, 4.22, 4.23): 705, the plough-disturbed upper level of the outer henge ditch; 703, a linear band in the south-east corner of the excavation trench mistakenly identified as the cursus ditch; and 706 and 707, to the south and north of the henge ditch respectively, and extending across the western half of the excavation. The only finds from the plough-disturbed horizon were a

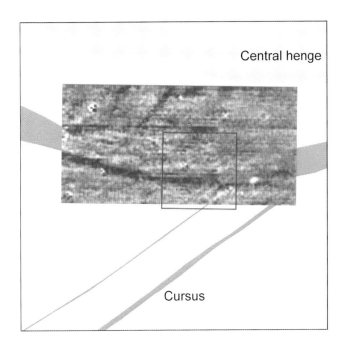

Central henge

Cursus

0   20m

Fig 4.20 Location of excavation trench at the central henge in relation to geophysical results

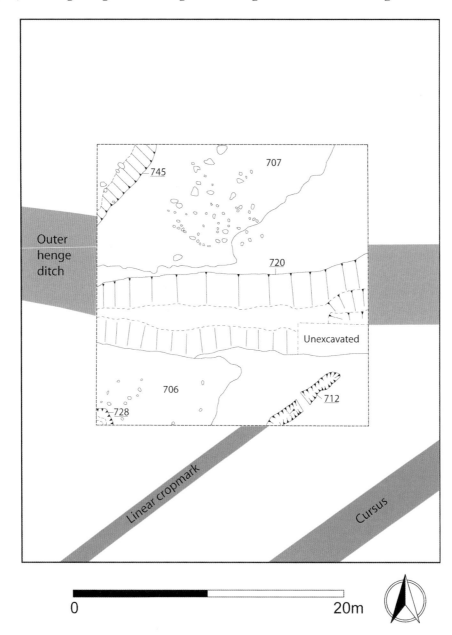

Fig 4.21   Plan of excavation trench at central henge

Fig 4.22   Looking north-east at the excavation trench of the central henge's outer ditch after the removal of topsoil and subsoil

single plainware sherd from a medieval Humber Ware drinking jug, a scrap of post-medieval purple-glazed redware, and three pieces of post-medieval roof tile.

Possible inner cursus features

Across the south-west quadrant of the excavation trench, and under its baulks to the west and south, was 706, a deposit 0.1–0.25m thick (Figs 4.21 and 4.23). It continues to the east for approximately 8m and then tapers down into a shallow lens which extends for a further 3.5m, before ending just short of 712, the later linear feature. The character of 706 varied, consisting to the west of patches of compact yellowish-brown silty sand which capped a band, no more than 1m across, of comparable material except

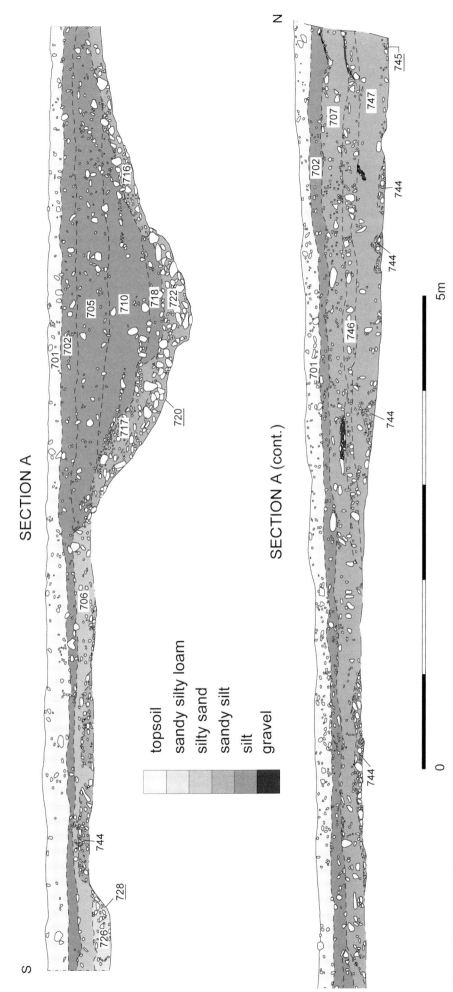

SECTION A

SECTION A (cont.)

topsoil
sandy silty loam
silty sand
sandy silt
silt
gravel

S

N

5m

0

Fig 4.23 Central henge: east-facing section of the excavation trench

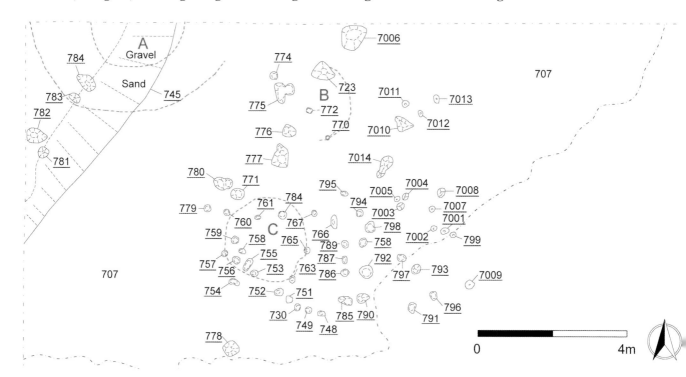

Fig 4.24   Central henge: detail of features to the north of the outer henge ditch, including the possible arcs of stone (A, B and C)

for its dark yellowish-brown colour and large number of small sub-rounded stones and gravel. However, the majority of 706 was soft sandy silt identical in colour to the band but with far fewer stones. On the other side of the henge ditch, and covering much of the northern half of the excavation trench, was 707 (Figs 4.21 and 4.23), a deposit very similar to 706. It consisted largely of a firm yellowish-brown sandy silt, again with a large number of sub-rounded stone and gravel, but with a thin lens of pure sand and gravel extending for around 2m to the east and south of the north-west corner of the trench. The excavation's east-facing section (Fig 4.23) indicates that 706 and 707 were cut by the outer henge ditch, so both were most likely part of the same layer of deliberately deposited material, now surviving to between 0.1 and 0.5m thick. Parts of it sat upon 744, a firm dark yellowish-brown sandy silt with a large number of stones, of differing sizes and shapes, and a high gravel content. Its presence beneath 706 and 707, but absence elsewhere in the excavation trench, suggests it was the remnants of an old land surface.

In two places this buried surface had been cut into before the deposition of 706 and 707. In the south-west corner was 728, which, whilst only partly in the excavation trench, appears to be part of a sub-circular feature, with steep sides, a flat bottom, and a depth of 0.21m (Figs 4.21 and 4.23). It had been immediately backfilled with 726, a soft dark yellowish-brown sandy silty loam with large quantities of small or medium-sized stones around its edges. The feature had been capped by 706 and broadly corresponds with the band of slightly

different material mentioned above. In the north-west corner of the excavation trench was 745, the gently sloping cut of a flat-bottomed feature 0.35m deep (Figs 4.21 and 4.23). It also continued beyond the excavation trench, making it difficult to interpret, but does seem to parallel the north-north-east to south-south-west alignment of a linear positive geophysical anomaly only 5m to the west (Fig 4.20). It had been deliberately filled with 747, a relatively stone-free deposit of firm yellowish-brown sandy silt, but not before clods of the old land surface had ended up along its bottom. It was then capped by 746, an almost identical deposit of firm dark yellowish-brown sandy silt 0.07–0.21m thick, with more small rounded stones and pebbles. These two deposits, which were only really distinguishable from each other in section, spread beyond, but parallel with, the edge of the cut, perhaps originally forming a very low raised area or mound prior to the deposition of 707. Four sub-circular, steeply sloping, and flat-bottomed postholes (781, 782, 783, 784), 0.26–0.66m across and 0.23–0.62m deep, were found along the bottom edge of 745 (Fig 4.24). It is not known with any certainty if their timbers had been freestanding or inserted into the cut's backfill, but the former is considered more likely given that the postholes were only discovered after the complete removal of the fill.

The deposition of 706 and 707 established a very much wider platform or low mound. It may have been associated with other features. A large number of vertical or steep-sided postholes and stakeholes, largely corresponding with the extent of 706 and 707, were discovered after the removal of these

Fig 4.25   Central henge: the western (A), eastern (B), and southern (C) stone arrangements

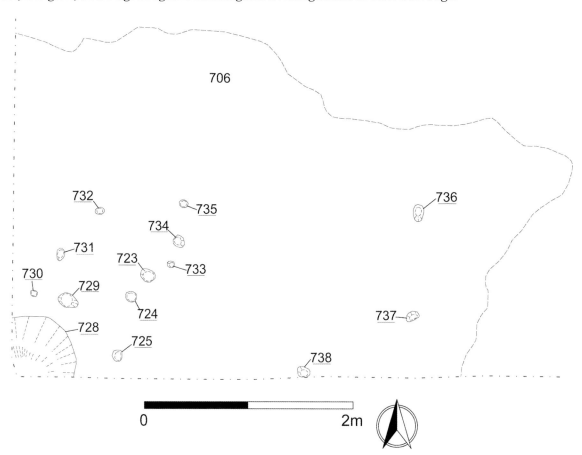

Fig 4.26   Central henge: detail of features to the south of the outer henge ditch

two contexts. To the north of the henge ditch was a wedge-shaped arrangement of 59 features (Fig 4.24). The largest formed two rows of postholes – to the west 723, 771, 775, 777, 780, and 7006, and to the east 778, 7010 and 7014 – whose north-east to south-west alignment mirrored the nearby cut of 745 and its four posts. They were irregularly shaped and at most 0.26–0.78m across and 0.25–0.58m deep. Running south-eastwards at right angles from the southern end of the two rows were smaller and shallower closely set stakeholes (730, 748–9, 751–7), defining the cluster's southern edge. They possessed diameters and depths of 0.16–0.26m and 0.13–0.27m respectively. Most of the other features were more widely and irregularly spaced stakeholes to the east of the two rows, and some of these may again have been set at right angles to the latter. They varied in size, with a few over 0.4m deep. The cluster's overall layout is confusing, although the two rows, presumably containing the largest posts, would have defined a largely undivided area approximately 6m long and 2m wide. The thirteen postholes or stakeholes to the south of the henge ditch had a simpler layout (Fig 4.26). The majority formed two irregular rows converging upon 728 in the trench corner, and of these, 723–5 and 733–5 were broadly aligned with the easternmost posthole row to the north of the henge ditch. They possessed diameters and depths of 0.16–0.44m and 0.13–0.27m respectively.

There may have been other embellishments to the north of the henge ditch (Figs 4.24 and 4.25). There are signs that small and medium-sized stone, often in conjunction with sand and gravel, had been deliberately arranged into similarly sized arcs or circles within 707 at depths of 0.4–0.5m from the top of the trench. The most distinctive of these formed a semicircle, about 3m across, presumably continuing under the south-facing baulk (Fig 4.24, A). It encloses a spread of gravel and was set within the diffuse patch of pure sand mentioned above to extend across the north-west corner of the excavation trench. Less clear, although nonetheless suggestive, were two arcs of stone, again with patches of internal gravel, which, had they originally formed circles, would have been about 2.5m across (Fig 4.24, B–C). That both were located between the two posthole rows, with the southernmost circle possibly enclosed by timber uprights on three sides, suggests these arrangements may not simply be fortuitous; rather, they may have been part of the same structure as the posts and stakes, and, if the stone settings had been deliberately laid across the surface of 707, then they indicate this earthwork was originally insubstantial in height, its surviving top no more than 0.1–0.2m above 744, the underlying buried surface. It looks more like a decorative layer than a mound or raised platform.

These deliberately deposited layers, underlying cuts, and stakeholes and postholes look unified in

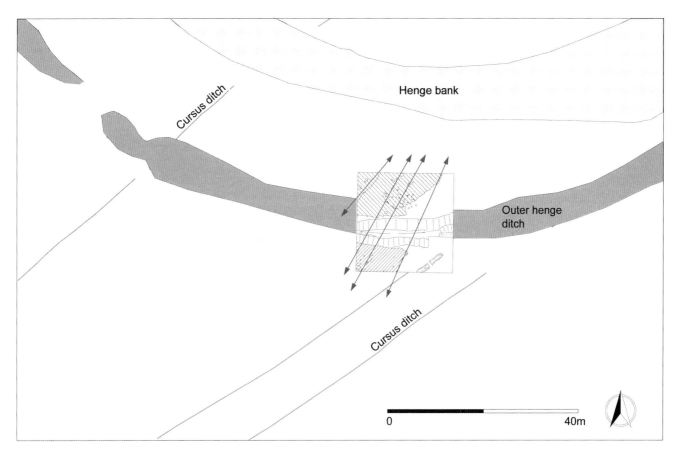

Fig 4.27 Central henge: the excavated features in relation to the cursus

their overall layout, for they share the same north-north-east to south-south-west alignment (Fig 4.27). If so, then they are broadly contemporary, earlier than the henge, and perhaps, therefore, originally part of the cursus interior. This is certainly the interpretation favoured here. However, there is actually no direct evidence linking these features with the cursus and their alignment differs from the north-east to south-west axis of the cursus ditches. If not associated with the cursus, then they attest to complex patterns of pre-henge activity across this central and clearly significant part of the plateau. Only new evidence from further fieldwork offers the chance of understanding the original appearance of these structures and their likely relationships with both the cursus and henge.

Outer henge ditch

The plough-disturbed upper level of the outer henge ditch, 705, ran east to west along the length of the excavation trench (Fig 4.22). It consisted of a diffuse band of dark yellowish-brown silt ranging in width from 4.75m in the west to 8.25m in the east. Its wider easternmost section was also considerably stonier. Upon excavation 705 was found to be 0.3–0.6m deep and closely related to 720 (Figs 4.21 and 4.23), the cut of a substantial ditch, which at the western end of the trench was 4.7m across, but widened to 6.9m

at its eastern end. In its east-facing section it was a flattened V-shape with a maximum depth of 1.0m. It then formed a flat but irregular bottom some 0.5m wide, which, by the eastern trench edge, had widened to approximately 1.4m across. Its increased breadth, as it started to curve very slightly inwards, was also matched by the deepening of the feature, surviving to a maximum depth of 1.3m in the west-facing section. The northern side of the cut was more irregular and gently sloping than its wavy southern side, suggesting it had been dug from the inside by regularly spaced individuals or teams.

The ditch fill varied greatly, making its interpretation difficult. Extending across the entire width of its bottom and southern face for the easternmost 14m was 722 (Fig 4.23), a distinctive deposit mainly of large quantities of cobbles and irregularly shaped medium and large stones, within a matrix of brown sandy silt. Natural processes could not account for the transport of such a large quantity of stone and cobbles, suggesting, as does their almost imbricated orientation parallel with the ditch cut, that they had been deliberately dumped from outside the monument (Raimonda Usai, pers comm). The absence of any underlying sand or gravel in-wash suggests this happened immediately after the digging of the ditch. The spread of 722 along the bottom of the ditch broadly corresponds with the extent of 706 to the south of the feature, and it is possible it derived from here, the result perhaps of an attempt to level off the area immediately around the henge. This would imply, however, that the inner cursus feature was capped by a stony deposit which no longer survives on either side of the henge ditch. Whatever its origin, the deposition of 722 was far from casual. That it was consistently about 0.3m thick along the bottom of the ditch and had undergone moderate compaction suggests care had been taken.

By contrast, the primary fill elsewhere was 716, a soft dark yellowish-brown sandy silt with large quantities of small to medium rounded stone and an underlying lens of gravel and sand (Fig 4.23). It reaches a thickness of 0.37m in the deeper west-facing section, but less elsewhere, and tapers up the gently sloping northern side of the ditch. It probably resulted from natural in-wash and the erosion of the earthwork, thereby accumulating over a far longer timespan than 722. The same processes were responsible for the formation of 717 along the southern ditch face (Fig 4.23), and along the middle section of ditch it is up to 0.4m thick, resembling a distinct slump of material. It was a compact brown sandy silt with pebbles, cobbles, and medium-sized sub-rounded stone. A quantity of larger rounded stone lay at the foot of this deposit and was most likely tumble, forming a ledge beyond which 718, a wind-blown deposit of soft brown silt, had gradually accumulated along the ditch bottom (Fig 4.23). The latter was mottled with darker patches probably caused by decaying vegetation. A piece of *Betula* sp. charcoal, from the top of 717 and very close to its interface with both 710 and 705, was dated to cal AD 910–1030 (Beta-155675; see D5). The sample was either residual or intrusive, but the resulting date is identical to that from stratified charcoal in the upper ditch fill of the southern henge, both perhaps indicating an extensive phase of activity across the surrounding landscape at that time.

Subsequent fills were also most likely wind-blown deposits with the occasional in-wash of small stone and gravel (Fig 4.23). The secondary fill along the entire ditch length was 710, like 718 a soft brown silt, with some small and medium-sized rounded stone. It was as much as 0.45m thick. Overlying this, and described above, was 705, which had also clearly developed over a prolonged period of time. The only finds from throughout the ditch deposits came from the middle and lower depths of 705 and the top of 710: there were ten sherds of medieval plainware and two sherds of medieval glazed vessels including a rim (D4.1.3), as well as the badly corroded and fragmentary remains of an iron nail. The plainware includes a single sherd of a thin-walled jar from Winksley, near Ripon (Bellamy and Le Patourel 1970) and four gritty ware sherds, in colours varying from white to pink, again possibly of local manufacture. The glazed ware, which consists of a rim sherd of a reduced grey ware jug and a body sherd in a gritty fabric, is of uncertain origin. Like the larger collection of pottery from the southern henge (4.6), these are probably largely from the 13th

and 14th centuries, suggesting that well over half the ditch was infilled by the beginning of the later medieval period. The history of this feature therefore contrasts with the results from the earlier excavation of the central henge's inner ditch, where sherds, dating to between the 12th and 15th centuries, were found as far down as the bottom of the secondary fill (Thomas 1955, fig 3, 438–9). That this ditch remained virtually unfilled until then necessitated 'cartloads of material' being brought 'to level up the ditch for cultivation' during the medieval period (*ibid*, 432). The implications of these very different histories will be explored below (4.6.4).

Later linear feature

Extending across the south-east corner of the excavation trench and under the north-facing baulk was 703, a distinctive linear band of soft brown silt, approximately 1m wide, with a large quantity of differently shaped medium and large stones. It ran south-west to north-east for 6m before terminating just short of the outer henge ditch. It was found to be a 0.3m thick upper fill of 712, a 0.52–1.12m wide cut divided into three distinctive parts on account of slight but nonetheless visible variations in appearance (Fig 4.28). Its westernmost section, running from under the baulk, was U-shaped and 0.95m deep with a flat base 0.3m wide. Its bottom then rose into a V-shaped cut with a depth of between 0.7 and 0.8m. What may have been two extremely shallow post sockets were cut into its floor. The easternmost length of the ditch, just over 1m in length, was the shallowest part of the feature. This was again V-shaped, but its bottom rose to form a rounded terminal. Along the feature's entire length was 708, a soft dark brown sandy silt with a large quantity of differently shaped small and medium-sized stone, no doubt the result of backfilling immediately after it had been dug out. In Section A it closely resembled a bedding trench for a small palisade or fence (Fig 4.28).

Dating the feature is problematic. The fact it runs broadly parallel with the cursus, albeit veering off very gradually to the south-west, suggests an association with this monument. Certainly sections of the nearby Scorton cursus were defined by a pair of ditches along both its sides (Topping 1982, 7, fig 1; see also Harding 1997b), and postholes are known to run parallel to either the inside or outside of cursus ditches elsewhere (Loveday 2006, 38–9). Against such an association is its termination short of the outer henge ditch. Even if the latter was earlier than the rest of the henge, there is nothing to suggest that cursuses and the first henges overlap chronologically, or indeed, that the latter pre-dates the former. Hence, it most likely post-dates the henge. It runs at a right-angle from the hedge immediately to the east and is parallel with the field boundary along the northern edge of the now quarried-out L-shaped enclosure (Roy Loveday, pers comm). However, none of the maps

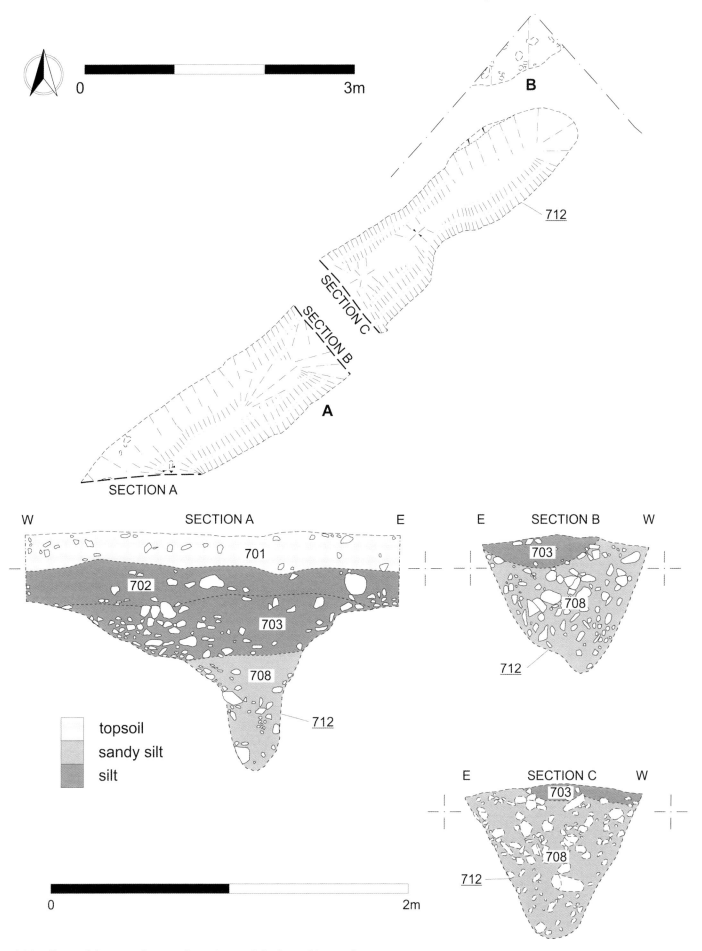

4.28 *Central henge: plan and sections of the later linear feature*

shows a field boundary here, so if it did play such a role then it certainly pre-dates the 18th century. There are parallels elsewhere. At Drayton, in Oxfordshire, a Romano-British field ditch follows the exact line of a cursus despite the latter no longer surviving as a visible earthwork (Barclay *et al* 2003). Loveday (2006, 40–3), who puts the continuation at Drayton down to the presence of a hedgerow in the narrow gap between the cursus and the later boundary, provides other examples of where the course of a cursus had determined the layout of much later landscape divisions. It therefore remains a possibility that the feature was a very deliberate attempt to redefine the earlier cursus alignment, whether it was for reasons of farming or to meet more arcane special needs.

4.5.3   Discussion

These results may offer an insight into the layout of the cursus interior. The few excavations completed elsewhere across the insides of these monuments have produced contrasting evidence about the extent to which they were built within and used. The eastern terminal at Springfield in Essex produced pits and part of an impressive timber circle (Buckley *et al* 2001), whereas the two earthwork cursuses at Holywood in Dumfries (Thomas 2007), and another two at Eynesbury in Cambridgeshire (Ellis 2004, 6–7, 100) may have enclosed what were empty spaces. The relatively well-preserved remains at Thornborough, with its unusual suite of inner structures, are different again. Their interpretation is difficult, and it is far from clear if they were indeed contemporary with the enclosing bank and ditch; but if they were integral to this earthwork then a significant part of the enclosed area along this section of the monument may have been built upon, and on more than one occasion. The partially exposed cuts in the south-west and north-west corners of the excavation trench – the latter, along with its associated postholes, apparently running along the centre of the cursus on approximately the same alignment – may even pre-date the flanking ditches and banks, as has been suggested for the seemingly ceremonial group of pits and a series of posts erected inside the Holywood South and Holywood North cursuses respectively (Thomas 2007, 237–41). At Thornborough, these features were backfilled and capped by a long raised area or layer, which was then extended by the deposition of a new platform into which were placed both wooden stakes and circles or arcs of small stones, the layout of these embellishments suggesting they were part of a coherent design. The latter are especially intriguing, and perhaps paralleled in part by the 'unusual use' of small distinctive stones at the two excavated Holywood cursuses (*ibid*, 242), or indeed, by the more substantial oval stone settings found outside the entrances to both tombs at the passage grave of Knowth (Eogan 1986, 46–8, 65, pl 6).

The presence of some form of inner platform or

layer invites comparison with the nearby Scorton cursus, where a series of contiguous interior mounds were constructed along the length of the monument (Topping 1982, 10–13). Further afield, comparison can be made with Stanwell in Middlesex (Lewis 2010) and Cleaven Dyke in Perthshire (Barclay and Maxwell 1998), where similar if narrower banked features existed down the centre of these monuments. At Scorton, these remains extended across its entire inner width, making it unclear if they 'only occupied the centre of the site and have been spread by plough-damage, or whether they formed a long uneven linear mound extending from ditch edge to ditch edge to give the monument an almost cambered appearance' (Topping 1982, 13). At Thornborough the arcs of stone suggest minimal plough-spread, implying that it originally covered just the central part of the inside. A recent observation by Roy Loveday uses other evidence to support the idea of a central feature at Thornborough. He notes that the monument's western terminal was:

> constructed separately it seems by those with a knowledge of the procedures ... It does not represent a full semi-circle or chord, however. At its centre there is an approximate 8m length of straight ditch. From this run curves on quite different arcs ... This could suggest the site was laid out by eye alone but the good general correspondence of each arc to circles of some 20m and 15m in diameter perhaps argues for layout either side of a now vanished central obstacle corresponding to the straight central element. Interestingly the excavators recorded the discovery of an unaccompanied crouched burial in a stone cist set about 4.5m back along the centre line of the cursus from the terminal ditch. It is conceivable that this lay under the end of an axial mound, akin to that of the nearby Scorton cursus (Loveday 2006, 120–1).

Clarification as to the layout of this inner earthwork and the earlier dug features must await further fieldwork, but a central platform or mound would have acted as a 'dramatic focal point' (Buckley *et al* 2001, 155), like the timber circle within the eastern terminal of the Springfield Cursus.

The excavation fails to tell us anything new about the central henge's sequence of construction, or more specifically, whether the outer ditch is earlier or later than its inner earthwork. Indeed, the unexpectedly large size and regularity of the excavated section of outer ditch highlights a similarity to the inner feature, reducing the likelihood that the former belonged to an earlier 'formative' phase of henge building (3.3.2). That is not to say there were no differences between these two earthworks. Apart from the larger size of the inner ditch, as recorded by Thomas (1955, 432), there were contrasts in the sequence of infilling. Unlike the central henge's inner ditch, which appears to have infilled naturally until the medieval period (*ibid*, 432, fig 3), the above indicates an episode of backfilling early in the history of the outer ditch. As mentioned above, one explana-

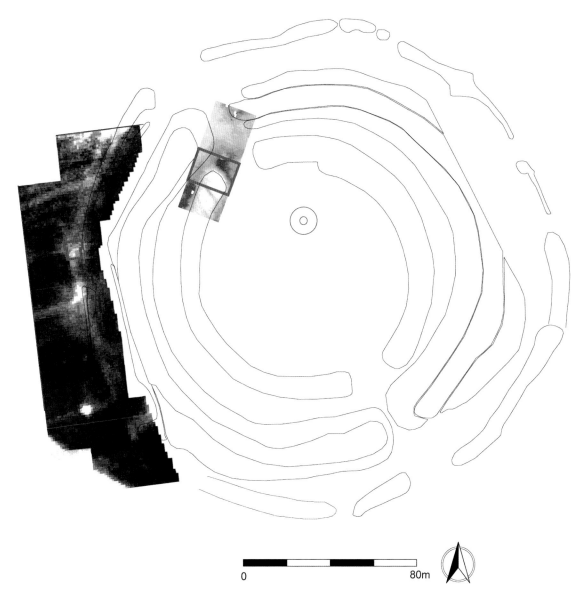

Fig 4.29 Excavation trenches at the southern henge

tion is to see this as a result of the partial levelling of the raised feature within the earlier cursus. Whatever the motivation, it suggests that if both henge ditches were contemporary then they were used in very different ways, with less importance being attached to maintaining the outer earthwork. Perhaps its primary role was to provide spoil, for as Thomas notes 'The amount of soil in the bank is roughly twice the volume of gravel to be obtained from the inner ditch alone' (*ibid*, 433). Even if dug for that purpose, however, its layout reflects the importance the henge-builders placed on establishing a wide berm between the earthworks.

4.6   Southern henge

4.6.1   Introduction

Geophysical survey across the western edge of the southern henge, and around its northern entrance, clearly showed the outer and inner ditches prior to excavation (Fig 4.29; see D1.1.4). A small excavation trench, 6m by 6m, was located across an apparent outer ditch terminal and gap, and subsequently extended 1.5m to the north with 1m by 3m extensions to the north-east and north-west quadrants (Fig 4.29). Excavation was by hand, with all spoil sieved, in August and September 1996. The following year a larger excavation trench, 20m by 15m, was positioned over the relatively well-preserved earthwork of the north-west inner ditch terminal and part of the adjoining entrance where geophysical prospection had detected a squarish patch of low resistance (Fig 4.29). Topsoil was stripped using a mini-digger and the rest excavated by hand, with all spoil sieved. It was excavated during August, September, and October 1997. The principal aim of the two excavations was to ascertain if the outer ditch was earlier in date or if both earthworks were broadly contemporary.

4.6.2   *Excavation of outer ditch*
by Jan Harding and Blaise Vyner

Three heavily truncated and poorly defined features were revealed, with others largely clustered in the south-western quadrant of the trench (Fig 4.30). The small size of the excavation, along with difficulties in identifying these features and their stratigraphy, make interpretation problematic, and what is proposed here differs, in several significant respects, to earlier accounts of the excavation. The outer henge ditch, which was very modest in size compared to that excavated at the central henge, terminates in the north-east of the trench. Its spoil was most likely used to create a modest outer bank. A low fence or small timber uprights may have been subsequently erected along the inside of the bank and across the entrance. Stratigraphy indicates this was at a much later date, and the feature appears to run parallel to the existing field boundary immediately to the east; yet it neatly delimits the eastern side of the bank and is interrupted by a narrow gap adjacent to the causeway. Its southern extension was greatly affected by other unexplained activity, probably including later animal disturbance. The excavation produced a tiny piece of possible carinated bowl and a small and unremarkable collection of twenty worked lithics (summarised in Tables D3.6, D3.9, D3.13, D3.16, D3.20 and D3.22). The latter included chert flakes struck on site and discarded at the entrance. The only diagnostic tool was a broken scraper possibly of later Neolithic date. There was also a tiny collection of medieval and post-medieval pottery from the plough-disturbed horizon (D4.1.3). With one exception, all the finds were from the disturbed horizon.

Disturbed horizon

The disturbed horizon consisted of: 401, a topsoil of firm dark brown loamy sand around 0.31m deep; 410, an underlying thin layer of stiff-grained dull yellowish-brown sand; and 402, a subsoil of weakly cemented and coarse-grained dull brown loamy sand varying between 0.02 and 0.33m deep, which was either at its shallowest or completely absent above the bank remains in the north-west quadrant. These deposits are depicted in section (Fig 4.31). In the south-west of the trench, across an area subsequently interpreted as disturbed by rabbit burrowing, were distinctive but irregular and shallow patches of sand, loose stone, and compact stone (404–7). A single plough-mark, cutting 402, was visible, running for 4.5m east to west across the centre of the trench, on approximately the same axis as a series of diffuse and parallel linear anomalies detected by geophysical prospection (Fig 3.19, e–h).

The removal of this disturbed horizon revealed three truncated features. Running north-north-west to south-south-east was 403, a clearly visible but irregular linear band of firm brown silty sand

between 0.6m and 1m wide. It initially continued across the trench, but subsequent excavation showed it turning eastward and immediately terminating with a squared-off end. It is the truncated top of a possible bedding trench. Less discernible was 409 in the north-east quadrant. This firm dark brown loamy sand extends across the outer ditch terminal, but is absent from the southern half of the excavation trench, suggesting it may be redeposited bank material, resulting perhaps from ploughing. It was, however, more compact and less stony than 402. By contrast, the western side of the trench, for about 6m from north to south, was much stonier and gravelly than elsewhere, with 403 forming a possible eastern edge. This was the remains of the bank and appeared to be made up of three distinct deposits (414, 422, 436).

Found in the area of burrowing was a very small fragment of possible carinated bowl (D4.1.2). With a dark grey internal surface, and a largely missing external surface, it possessed a dark grey fabric with numerous small and medium-sized dolerite grits and a clay fabric containing mica dust. The disturbed horizon produced other finds. There was a scraper end fragment (Fig 4.32, 1), a core fragment (Fig 4.32, 2), fifteen flakes, a bladelet, a hammerstone, and a piece of irregular waste, the majority of which were from the south-west quadrant of the excavation trench. Chert constituted more than half of this small collection, and a distinct cluster of seven large and complete chert flakes (eg Fig 4.32, 3–5), along with a single chert chip, was found to the south of the ditch terminal. The chert was in a very fresh condition and had clearly been struck on site. It may even relate to a single knapping event, associated perhaps with the heavily battered but complete pebble hammerstone of till/gravel flint found nearby. The small cluster also included a complete till flake with a faceted platform often found in Grooved Ware-associated industries (Manby 1974, 83). The scraper end fragment, again of till flint, may be of similar affinities. By contrast, the piece of a bladelet (Fig 4.32, 6) was of a character consistent with a later Mesolithic date. It certainly looked residual, possessing dense patination. Later finds consisted of three fragments of glazed medieval pottery, perhaps of Winksley manufacture, an abraded rim sherd from a medieval greyware jug, seven other small abraded medieval plainware sherds from various industries, and a small piece of post-medieval glazed earthenware bowl.

Outer henge ditch and bank

Excavating the outer henge ditch, 433, proved difficult. Its primary fill, which extended up the sides of the cut, closely resembled the top of the natural, making the feature's edges ill-defined. Given this, it is possible that its full extent was not revealed. The ditch was slight in size and irregular in appearance (Figs 4.30 and 4.31, Section A), yet there was

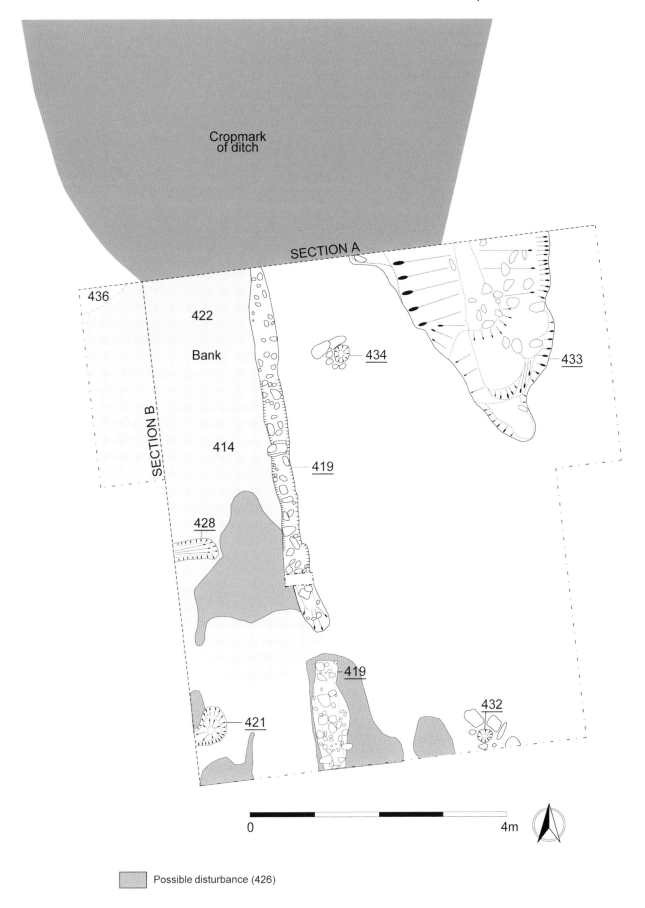

Cropmark
of ditch

436

422

Bank

434

433

SECTION A

SECTION B

414

419

428

419

421

432

0   4m

Possible disturbance (426)

Fig 4.30   Southern henge: plan of the outer henge ditch excavation. See overleaf for sections

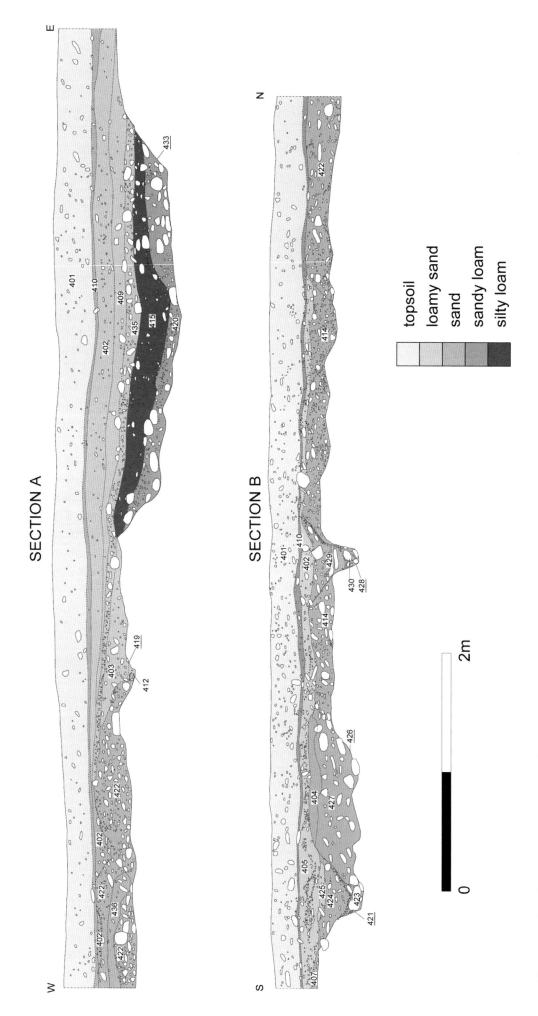

SECTION A

SECTION B

topsoil

loamy sand

sand

sandy loam

silty loam

Fig 4.31   Southern henge: sections of the outer henge ditch excavation

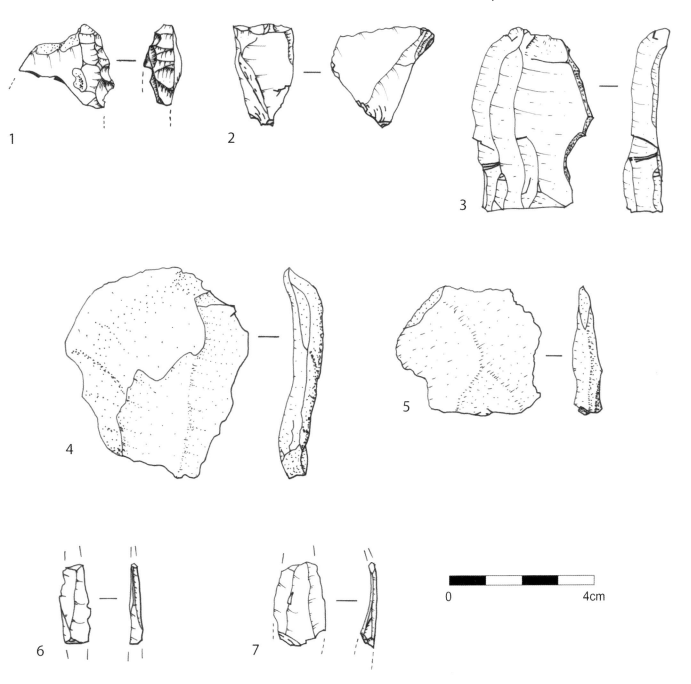

Fig 4.32   Southern henge: selected lithics from the excavation of the outer henge ditch: 1, context 401, scraper end fragment; 2, context 401, core fragment; 3–5, context 411, chert flakes; 6, context 402, bladelet fragment; 7, context 420, shouldered blade

no indication from the excavation, nor indeed from aerial photography or geophysical survey, that it was significantly wider and deeper immediately to the north of the trench. In the south-facing section the ditch had a flattened and asymmetrical U-shape with a width of 3.40m. Its eastern and western sides sloped gently to a rounded, but irregular, bottom 2.60m across. From the top of its cut it had a maximum depth of only 0.50m. In outline the ditch tapers abruptly to a sharply defined and in-turned terminal 3m from the northern edge of the trench.

The basal fill consisted of 420, a firm dark brown sandy loam with a high proportion of gravel and very small to large stones (Fig 4.31, Section A). It could have resulted from the rapid collapse of the ditch cut, but this would not explain the number of large boulders. Neither would it explain its almost flat-topped appearance nor its protrusion 1m out from the ditch's eastern side where it reaches a depth of 0.2m. Alternatively, the fill could have resulted from deliberate backfilling, but if so this was done immediately after the digging of the ditch; yet if the ditch was primarily dug as a quarry for the outer bank it seems unlikely that the latter would have been robbed for backfill so soon after construction. Given that neither of these explanations is convincing, the deposition of 420 is unaccounted for. The fill produced the only other find from the excavation, a blade fragment of till flint, with backing retouch which runs approximately a third of the way up the left and right margins (Fig 4.32, 7). It is later Meso-lithic or earlier Neolithic in date, and certainly looks residual, possessing dense patination.

The spoil from the ditch was presumably used to create an outer bank (Figs 4.30 and 4.31). It consisted of 414 and 422, both of which were stiff fine-grained sand with a high proportion of very small to large stones. They were only distinguish-able from one another by the subtle difference in their colour, 414 being brown and 422 dull reddish-brown. The sections suggest the bank was made up of separate dumps of material, possibly demonstrat-ing a sequence of construction. The initial deposit of 422 was piled outside the ditch running 1.8m from the northern baulk. The feature was extended southwards to a minimum length of 5.3m by the addition of 414. In the north-west corner of the exca-vation trench the top of 422 sloped downwards in a westerly direction before forming another smaller dump capped by 436, also of stiff fine-grained brown sand, but which, unlike the rest of the earthwork, was largely stone free. It had been overlain by a further deposit of 422. Overall the bank was at least 3.5m across, very similar to the width of the ditch, with a maximum height of 0.34m in the south-facing section.

Overlying the primary ditch fill was 415, a soft fine-grained dull reddish-brown silty loam reaching a maximum depth of 0.25m. This naturally deposited secondary fill tapers up the ditch sides to the top of the cut. It incorporated occasional flecks and small pieces of charcoal. Sloping down from the apex of the bank and forming the ditch's tertiary fill was 435, a firm fine-grained greyish-brown loamy sand with small to large stones. Absent across the southern half of the excavation trench, it is probably redeposited bank material, resulting from either a deliberate attempt to level the earthwork or from ancient ploughing. With a maximum thickness of only 0.13m, the latter of these two explanations is perhaps more plausible. It is stratigraphically later than the linear feature, and if this had held a fence or palisade it had disappeared prior to the deposi-tion of 435.

Other features

A narrow steep-sided slot trench, 419, was dug into the eastern side of the bank and across the causeway, where it appears to have been interrupted by a gap with a maximum width of 0.4m (Fig 4.30; Fig 4.31, Section A). This irregular feature was 0.25–0.38m wide and extended for 5.2m from the northern trench edge, curving inwards to a rounded terminal. It is narrowest to the north as it runs under the baulk, where its cut was only partly visible in section (Fig 4.31, Section A), possibly as a result of under-

excavation. Elsewhere it was U-shaped with a flat bottom and a maximum depth of 0.30m, although its southern end formed a flattened V-shape with a depth of only 0.22m. To the south of the interruption the feature was far less easily discernible, but wider at 0.37–0.63m across, both the result of subsequent disturbance.

The upper fill of the cut to the north of the gap consisted of 412, a firm fine-grained dull reddish-brown loamy sand with very small to medium stones. This thin deposit survives to a depth of 0.06–0.15m. Running underneath it is 413, with an identical soil matrix, but a far higher proportion of stones, of very small, small, and large size. It is 0.08–0.22m deep. The deposit is absent from the south-facing section (Fig 4.31, Section A), again the possible result of under-excavation. Both 412 and 413 are likely to have been deposited at the same time, with larger quantities of stone thrown into the lower part of the feature, perhaps as packing for small timber uprights: their distribution along 413 was certainly interspersed by relatively stone-free patches *c* 0.05–0.09m across, and one of these was associated with a possible stakehole in the bottom of the cut. Despite this, it is impossible to say with any certainty whether the feature was in fact a bedding trench. Whilst badly truncated, as indicated by 403, which survives to a depth of 0.22m in the south-facing section (Fig 4.31, Section A), any erected structure is likely to have been modest.

The date of this slot-trench is unclear. It post-dated the bank into which it had been cut, and in the northern half of the excavation trench was overlain by the two plough-disturbed layers of 409 and 435, the former producing a single sherd of medieval plainware. That it neatly delineates the eastern edge of the bank, and is interrupted where the bank terminates, hints at it being dug when the earlier earthwork still played an important role, perhaps even being part of the henge itself. On the other hand, the linear feature's striking archaeological visibility, its relatively high position in the stratig-raphy, and the fact it runs parallel to an existing field boundary immediately to the east, all suggest a more recent date. It is therefore regarded as an undated feature most likely post-dating the henge itself. Although much shallower, it resembles the linear feature at the central henge, also interpreted as post-dating the monuments.

Most of the other excavated features were located in the south-western quadrant (Fig 4.30). They were only observed as cuts into the natural gravel, despite an assumed relationship with the shallow patches of sand, loose stone, and compact stone (404–7) higher in the stratigraphy. The most clearly defined were 421 and 428 (Fig 4.31, Section B). Cut into the bank and running beyond the excavation's western edge was 428, a steep-sided linear feature 0.72m across at its top but narrowing to a rounded base just 0.12m wide. It was 0.41m deep from its truncated top and filled with 430, largely consisting of stone and gravel in a matrix of brown sand, and 429, an overlying deposit of greyish-brown sand with far less stone. Also running into the east-facing baulk was 421, a kidney-shaped feature with a U-shaped profile (Fig 4.31, Section B). Approximately 0.71m by 0.5m across at its top, but just 0.19m wide at its base, it had a depth of 0.38m. It was filled by 423, a basal deposit of loose stone and gravel, and 424, consisting of brown sand with smaller quantities of stone. The feature was partly covered by a thin layer of greyish-brown loamy sand. Abutting both and extending across the south-eastern quadrant was 426 (Fig 4.30), an irregular cut which varied greatly in shape, width, and depth. It was filled by 427, a mixed deposit of stone, gravel, and sand. Beyond the south-west quadrant were two possible stake-holes or small postholes. Towards the south-eastern corner of the trench was 432, an oval and U-shaped cut 0.2m by 0.12m across with a depth of 0.25m, and between the ditch and slot-trench, 434, also oval and U-shaped, 0.28m across, and only 0.19m deep.

It is impossible to ascertain the relationship of these features to each other, or indeed, their relationship to the excavated ditch, bank, and slot-trench. That 421 and 432 are located in the apparent causeway across the outer ditch is suggestive, yet their vicinity to 426 indicates a more recent, if unexplained, role. The various cuts and fill of 426 looks like animal-burrowing, and if the slot-trench marked the edge of a field, then this may have occurred along the unploughed boundary or in a plough headland. The stony fill of the slot-trench appears to have acted as a barrier to these burrowing animals, and if so this could have been deliberate, raising the admittedly unlikely possibility that these features, along with the bank itself, were a structurally atypical pillow-mound for the breeding of rabbits. The relationship between these features and the overlying shallow patches of sand, loose stone, and compact stone is unknown, although the distribution of 404 and 405 demonstrate there was a connection.

4.6.3   *Excavation of inner ditch*
by Jan Harding, Robert Johnston, Blaise Vyner, and Lindsay Allason-Jones

The 20m by 15m excavation revealed the north-western inner ditch terminal and the remnants of a banked or platform structure, along with five postholes, in the adjacent northern henge entrance (Fig 4.33). The entrance structure is likely to have been contemporary with the building and use of the henge's inner earthwork. An early Bronze Age radiocarbon date from the top of the primary fill of the inner ditch is of little value, but what is likely to be stratified charcoal from its later fill produced a date in the 10th or early 11th century AD (see D5). The only prehistoric finds were seventeen worked lithics, mostly from disturbed horizons (summarised in Tables D3.6, D3.9, D3.13, D3.16, D3.20 and D3.22), including three bladelets and a possible later Neolithic or early Bronze Age long end scraper.

A small yet significant collection of medieval pottery – consisting of 37 glazed sherds and 63 plainware sherds, most probably belonging to the 13th and 14th centuries (D4.1.3) – dates an episode of ditch infilling similar to that previously recorded for the central henge. This pottery could suggest the later use of the henge as a fair or for other assemblies. Other finds consisted of a 1st-century AD Roman brooch (D4.2) and three post-medieval sherds (D4.1.3) from the secondary and tertiary ditch fills respectively. Later activity included the possible erection of a boundary, most likely in the post-medieval period, across the largely levelled earthwork. Time limitations meant the western side of the trench was left largely unexcavated after the removal of topsoil. This unexcavated portion was 4–6.2m wide. The excavation of the inner ditch proceeded with a 0.8m wide step at a depth of 1.2m.

Disturbed horizon

The plough-disturbed horizon consisted of 601, a topsoil of fine-grained dark greyish-brown sandy loam 0.07–0.31m thick, and 602, a subsoil of fine-grained dark yellowish-brown sandy silty loam 0.04–0.44m thick (Fig 4.34). Both contained 10–20% very small to large stones. Stratigraphically between these deposits near the henge bank was 603, a stonier deposit of brown loamy sand with a maximum thickness of only 0.12m (Fig 4.34, Section B). Extending across the trench from the western baulk for around 3m, this is probably quite recently redeposited bank material. It was left unexcavated with the exception of a 2.8m wide section removed from the north-west corner of the trench (Fig 4.33). Ploughing is demonstrated by a single narrow mark running north to south across the north-east corner of the trench and the wavy surface of 602 in the north-facing section. The plough-mark's orientation differed to 617, a north-west to south-east linear feature in the south-west corner of the trench, disappearing under the southern baulk and possibly terminating just short of 603 (Fig 4.35). Cut into 602, this feature was around 2.5m wide at its top, with steeply sloping sides and a maximum depth of 0.5m (Fig 4.34, Section A). Its northern edge was clearly defined and relatively straight, with its southern edge more irregular. The fill of 617 consisted of soft fine-grained very dark greyish-brown sandy silty loam with substantial quantities of medium, large, and boulder-sized stone. Towards its centre the fill was almost entirely of densely packed cobbles and boulders, sitting in a loose soil matrix, whose heaped but regular appearance suggests it was once a structure. The larger stones tended to be to the north. There is little to indicate that 617 was the bedding trench for a stone wall, the piled cobbles more probably acting as packing for upright timbers. That it was once a field boundary is suggested by the surface of its fill being more regular than the wavy top of abutting 602 to the east (Fig 4.34, Section A) –

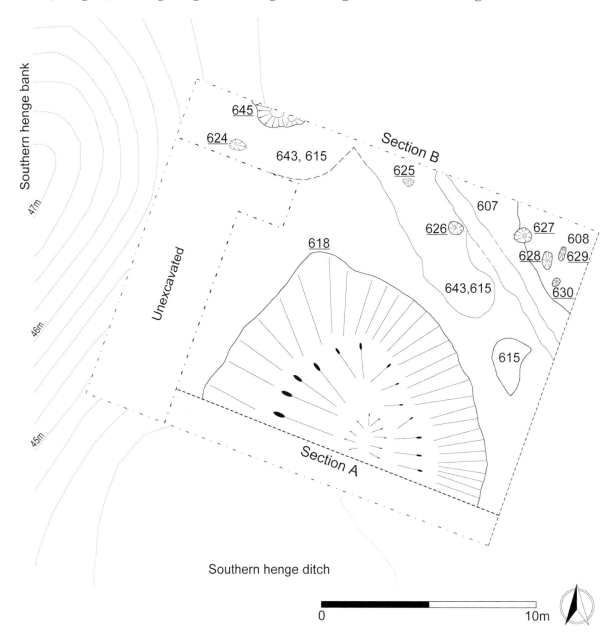

Fig 4.33   Southern henge: plan of the inner henge ditch excavation

the latter perhaps the result of ploughing – but the feature seems unnecessarily wide for this role. The creation of a substantial agricultural division across the limited space of the henge's inner area is curious, and the excavation's northern baulk gave no indication of ploughing. Pottery from the underlying ditch fill indicates this structure post-dated the 13th and 14th centuries AD.

The removal of the plough-disturbed horizon indicated the remains of three features (Fig 4.34). Much of the southern half of the trench was covered by 604, the truncated top fill of the henge ditch. It was immediately distinguishable during excavation by the high concentration of stone compacted into its surface, presumably dragged there by the plough before settling in the yielding fine-grained dark yellowish-brown loamy sand. Interspersed across its

western extent, and to one side of 617, was 609, a fine dark brown sandy loam with many small pebbles. No more than 0.1m thick, its stratigraphic relationship with 603, which was similar in appearance and also found on the side of the trench closest the bank, is unknown; it too may result from quite recent disturbance, perhaps by rodents, for it produced three pieces of late 19th- or early 20th-century pottery, a small sherd of modern-looking clear glass, and a few unidentified pieces of badly corroded iron, along with medieval pottery and worked flint (see below), one of the latter showing signs of plough-damage. In the north-east corner of the excavation trench was 608, and running parallel with it, then curving around to the west and running beyond the excavation trench, 643 (Fig 4.33; Fig 4.34, Section B). Both these deposits appear to be part of the entrance

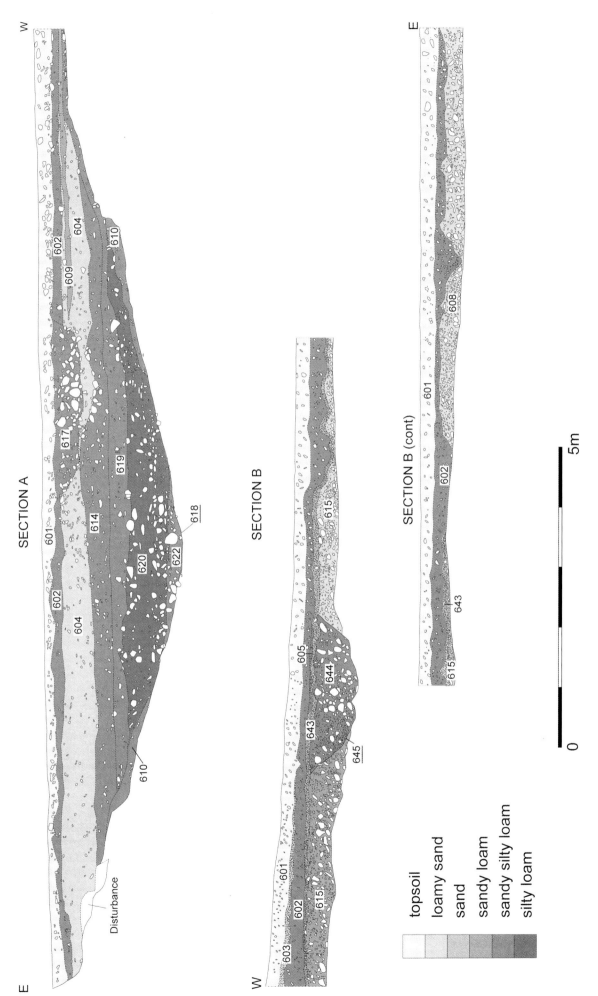

SECTION A

SECTION B

SECTION B (cont)

topsoil
loamy sand
sand
sandy loam
sandy silty loam
silty loam

0   5m

Fig 4.34 Southern henge: sections of the inner henge ditch excavation

Fig 4.35   Southern henge: looking east at the later linear feature (617)

structure. The third feature was 605, located against, and under, the northern baulk (Fig 4.34, Section B). This thin lens of soft dark yellowish-brown loamy sand was some 2.7m across and sits on 643 directly above 645, a large pit of unknown date and use.

These disturbed contexts produced fifteen worked flints – two from 601, seven from 602, one from 603, and five from 609 – half with signs of plough-damage. They included a complete long end scraper of a form more frequently encountered in later Neolithic or earlier Bronze Age assemblages (Fig 4.36, 1; see Manby 1974, fig 33), and two bladelet fragments (Fig 4.36, 2–3). There were also two edge-retouched flake fragments (eg Fig 4.36, 4), nine further flakes or blades, five of which were crude or chunky in appearance (eg Fig 4.36, 5–6), and a single flint chip. With the exception of three patinated pieces (eg Fig 4.36, 7), which are likely to be earlier and residual, the collection seems broadly contemporary with the monument, and at least half were deposited in a complete and fresh state, presumably across the enclosed inner area and the bank. However, the absence of flint from the ditch itself (see below) highlights the possibility that this small collection actually post-dates the construction and initial use of the monument. All but one of these pieces was of olive-grey till flint.

A total of 43 medieval and post-medieval pottery sherds were found, largely from 609, in a generally small and variably abraded state. A range of medieval wares is represented (D4.1.3). Nine jug sherds with a brown or green glaze, some decorated with simple rouletting or incised cordons, and a buff-brown to orange fabric were most probably the product of local kilns, including those at Winksley, near Ripon (Bellamy and Le Patourel 1970). They include a base fragment with internal glazing. Possibly from further afield in Yorkshire are: a battered sherd with brown-green glaze over a pink fabric, which may be from Brandsby or nearby in the Howardian Hills; a fragment of jug in a fine buff sandy fabric with olive-green glaze and decorated with incised cordons; another sherd, with splash glazing over an additional buff sandy fabric, from an unknown source, but also found at Ripon (Mainman 1997, 137); and from north-east Yorkshire, or possibly more local (*ibid*, 132), a handle join to a jug with a green glaze over a white slip covering a fine sandy fabric. The thirteen sherds of medieval plainware included a body sherd from a Winksley product and a sherd in a buff-white fabric perhaps from the Hambleton Hills (Jennings 1992, 18). 609 also produced three sherds from what is probably the same small black-glazed late 19th- or early 20th-century jug.

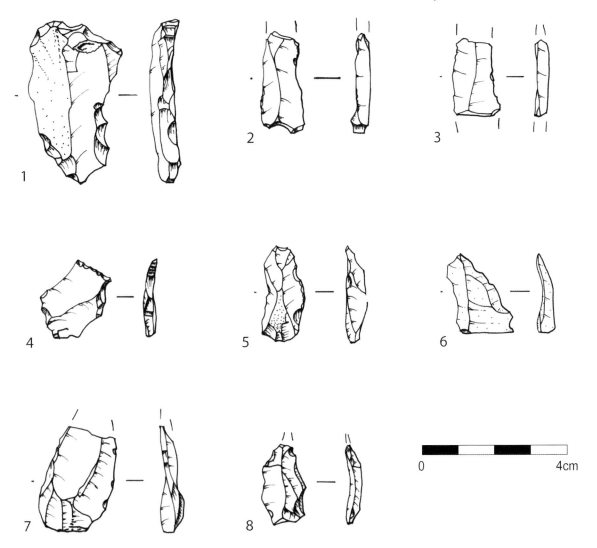

Fig 4.36   Selected lithics from the excavation of the inner ditch at the southern henge: 1, context 609, long end scraper; 2, context 602, bladelet fragment; 3, context 602, bladelet fragment; 4, context 602, edge-retouched flake fragment; 5, context 601, blade; 6, context 602, blade; 7, context 602, retouched flake; 8, context 610, flake

Inner henge ditch and later use of monument

The inner henge ditch, 618, is broadly comparable in profile to the same excavated feature at the central henge (Fig 4.37). Whilst its cut is more irregular, it is nonetheless closely similar in shape and size, and at both sites the ditch cut is asymmetrical, being marginally longer on the side nearest the bank, and consequently, slightly steeper on the opposing face. These characteristics no doubt reflect a shared method of digging the feature. The southern henge terminal curves irregularly around from the east with a more straight-sided western edge (Fig 4.33). At the baulk the width across its top is 13.2m. In section it has a flattened U-shaped cut, both sides interrupted about one-third of the way from the top by an abrupt break of slope before sloping gently again to an off-centre bottom some 1.5m across (Fig 4.34, Section A). The cut is least abrupt on its northern side where it slopes up to form an irregularly squared-off terminal. The ditch has a maximum

depth of 1.96m from the top of its cut. Its marginally narrower width and depth when compared to the feature at the central henge, where it was recorded with an approximate depth and width of 2.10m and 17.70m respectively (Thomas 1955, 432), may simply be because it was a terminal.

The ditch was intermittently waterlogged immediately after construction. The natural into which it was cut consisted of a gravelly matrix of very fine yellowish-brown sand, the top of which had undergone gleying, transforming it into a sticky deposit with extensive dark grey, dark greyish-brown, and very pale brown mottling. This was most intensive along the middle third of the ditch bottom, but gleying had also evidently occurred along the more gently sloping western side as far up as the abrupt break of slope. The basal ditch fill, 622, was also a gleyed deposit (Fig 4.34, Section A). Consisting of a fine brownish-yellow sandy loam, it had been transformed into a very sticky deposit with extensive dark grey mottling except for nearer

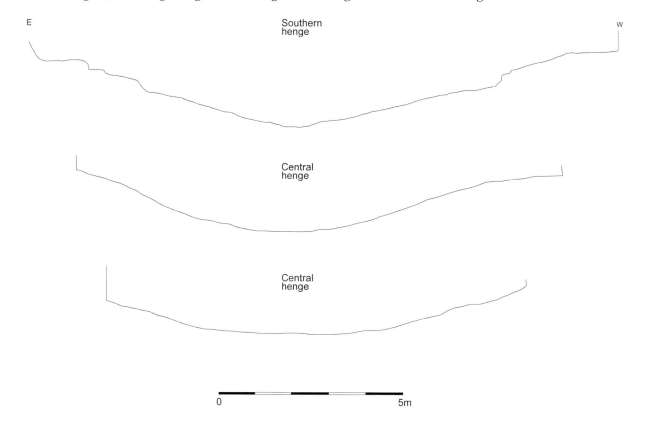

Fig 4.37 The excavated inner ditch cut at the southern henge compared with the results of Thomas' (1955, fig 3) earlier excavations at the central henge. Henge interior to left

its edges where it retained its original colour. At no more than 0.28m thick, it was a little shallower than the '1–2 feet of clean yellow sand' excavated at the ditch bottom of both the central and northern henge (Thomas 1955, 432), and it too presumably resulted from the natural erosion of the freshly cut ditch, albeit in this instance undergoing gleying. It was different to the primary fill at the other two henges in another respect. It consisted of a significant amount of small to large stones whose incorporation probably resulted from a process other than natural erosion. They could be the product of deliberately tidying up and dumping some of the larger stone left littering the henge.

A single radiocarbon date came from the very top of the primary ditch fill. A small piece of *Corylus* roundwood, found on the interface between 622 and the overlying secondary fill of 620, produced the date of 1745–1515 cal BC (Beta-143015; see D5). It is impossible to ascertain the extent to which it post-dates the actual digging of the inner ditch, but the extent of gleying suggests a lengthy interval. That the earthwork may have been largely stable after an initial episode of erosion is also suggested by the leaf mould covering the primary fill at the northern henge (Thomas 1955, 434). It is also likely that this small charcoal fragment was redeposited from above to the top of the gleyed deposit since there were seven charcoal fragments throughout the bottom of 620, but no others from 622. The radiocarbon date is therefore of limited value.

Running down part of the eastern and western sides of the ditch cut, for 2.5m and 2.8m respectively, was 610, a fine brown sandy silty loam with many gravel inclusions and some very small to medium-sized stones (Fig 4.34, Section A). It has a maximum thickness of around 0.2m and is shallower lower down the ditch cut. This material presumably accumulated through the erosion of the ditch sides and the deposition of wind-blown surface material. Its absence from the bottom half of the cut could reflect the earthwork's intermittent waterlogged condition, and if so, it suggests that during wetter times of the year the water was at least 0.5m deep. Its interface with 614 produced a single sherd of medieval plainware and a complete flake of till flint, which, like the lithics in the plough-disturbed horizon, was most probably of later Neolithic or earlier Bronze Age date (Fig 4.36, 8).

Subsequent deposits consisted of 620, a homogeneous secondary fill of fine dark yellowish-brown silty loam with a maximum thickness of 0.77m (Fig 4.34, Section A). It is likely that it resulted in part from wind-blown deposition, but the presence of significant amounts of medium to large stone, especially in its bottom half, suggests natural tumble from the top of the ditch cut and/or deliberate dumping. Again, there may have been a conscious effort to keep the monument clear of surface debris. The later ditch fills of 619 and 614 (Fig 4.34, Section A) were similar in appearance, consisting of fine brown sandy silty loam and fine dark yellowish-brown sandy silty loam

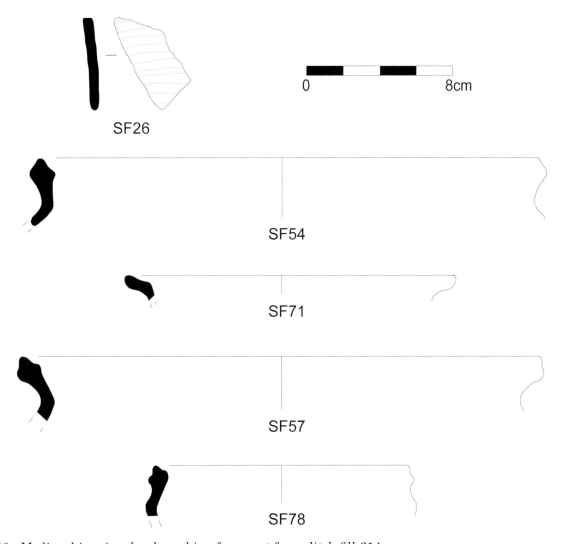

0 ▬▬ 8cm

SF26

SF54

SF71

SF57

SF78

Fig 4.38 Medieval jar rim sherds and jug fragment from ditch fill 614

respectively. In section both possessed a relatively low stone content, but their excavation involved the removal of large quantities of boulders. There were two irregular and dense concentrations of stone in 614, the largest of which spread as much as 5.2m by 4.2m across the north-western top of the ditch; and the boulders were denser in 619, particularly towards the edge of the cut. Fills 614 and 619 were up to 0.35m thick, but the former was shallower and more undulating towards the west, below and to one side of the more recent stone feature noted above, raising the possibility that this later structure replicated an earlier wall or boundary. The final ditch deposit was 604, a fine dark yellowish-brown loamy sand with a maximum thickness of 0.61m (Fig 4.34, Section A). As noted above, its western side may have been disturbed by 609.

The quantity of stone in 619 and 614 is reminiscent of the 'major phase of destruction' represented by dumping in the inner ditch of the central henge (Thomas 1955, 439). This episode was dated to between the 12th and 15th centuries by the discovery of stratified medieval sherds (*ibid*, 429, 432, fig 3), and the chronology of infilling at the

southern henge may have been broadly similar. In the eastern half of 619, and towards its bottom, was a discrete but irregular L-shaped dump of cobbles some 2.5m by 2.5m in extent. Mixed within the stone were a poorly preserved piece of unidentifiable bone and three charcoal fragments of *Sorbus* sp, *Rosa* sp, *Acer* sp, *Betula* sp, and *Rosaceae* indet. One of these pieces, representing a mix of *Acer*, *Betula*, and *Rosaceae*, was dated to cal AD 910–1030 (Beta-155676; see D5). Its position within the stone dump means the charcoal fragment is unlikely to have got there through bioturbation from a higher level, and since all the taxa are short-lived, it is unlikely to be significantly older than their context. Accordingly, the date provides a *terminus ante quem* for the underlying deposit. It implies that in contrast to the results from the central henge, the ditch was anything but 'virtually as it was when prehistoric man first dug it' (Thomas 1955, 439) when dumping took place between the 12th and 15th centuries.

It seems likely that 619 and 614 formed rapidly. Closer to the top of 614 was medieval pottery, and as with the collection from the disturbed horizon, its 57 sherds were generally small and in a variably abraded state. They also appear to date to the 13th and 14th centuries. There were 24 pieces of glazed pottery, all body sherds with the exception of two rims and part of a rod handle. They included four pieces of jug, with simple rouletted cordon decoration glazed in brown or green over a buff-brown to orange fabric, most likely the product of nearby Winksley. A further three undecorated sherds, again with either brown or green glaze, were of the same fabric. The glazes of the remaining sherds were either olive-green, green over a white slip, brown-green, or splash glazing, these covering three different fine sandy fabrics and a fourth gritty fabric. They were probably from both local sources and from further afield, although, with the exception of the three sherds possibly from Brandsby or nearby in the Howardian Hills, these remain unidentified (eg Fig 4.38, SF26, SF54, SF78). Five of these, decorated with simple rouletting and incised cordons, may also be from north-east Yorkshire. The 33 plainware sherds are largely undiagnostic, consisting for the most part of sandy fabrics in varying shades of orange-brown. The exception was two body sherds and three jar rim sherds (eg Fig 4.38, SF57, SF71), two of which were probably from the same vessel, from Winksley, and a single sherd in a buff-white fabric perhaps from the Hambleton Hills (Jennings 1992, 18). A similar range of plainware was discovered at St Agnesgate in Ripon (Mainman 1997, 130–2) and it therefore appears likely that most was the product of local industries.

The only other find from the secondary and tertiary fills was also from 614, albeit from a lower level than the medieval pottery. Discovered during section cleaning, close to its interface with 610 on the eastern side of the ditch, was a copper-alloy Roman brooch, its hinge not surviving other than as a soil stain (Fig 4.39; D4.2). It is a basic version of the 'Aucissa'-type bow brooch introduced to Britain at the time of the Roman invasion, but which appears to have no longer been produced after AD 65 (Snape 1993, Type 1.5). That the fragile hinge was intact at the time of deposition could certainly be taken to suggest it was in situ, yet the 10th- or early 11th-century AD date from underlying 619 indicates otherwise. It could be an heirloom placed here or lost at a much later date, or, as seems more likely, was redeposited, perhaps during an episode of medieval dumping. The original findspot, if there was one, must remain a mystery, but there is every possibility that the brooch was deliberately deposited at the henge, perhaps in an act of veneration or commemoration, many centuries before it moved. A local metal-detectorist is known to have found a Roman brooch of unidentified type in the plough soil above the outer ditch of the central henge.

It therefore appears that 614 resulted from deliberate and rapid infilling at around the same time as similar events at the central henge. Whilst it contained none of the distinct dumps of gravel observed at the central henge, and taken as 'representing cartloads of material put there to level up

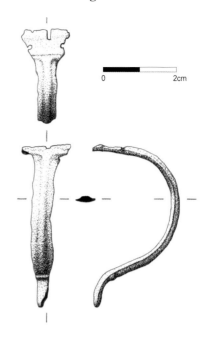

Fig 4.39   Roman brooch from ditch fill 614

the ditch for cultivation' (Thomas 1955, 432), the quantity of stone suggests something similar. It seems likely that the underlying deposit of 619 was also backfill, but the absence of medieval pottery from here suggests it pre-dates the 13th and 14th centuries. Sieving of bulk samples showed that small fragments of charcoal were relatively common in this deposit. If the levelling at the southern henge occurred in advance of farming, then it is possible that 604 was the cultivated soil – yet if so, the absence of finds from here is puzzling, as is the thickness of the deposit. This is the more surprising given the close similarities between the medieval pottery in 614 and the smaller collection from the higher disturbed horizon. Both collections seem certain to be connected to the same phase in the monument's use, but the absence of pottery in intervening 604 suggests the pottery in the disturbed horizon was redeposited from elsewhere, the likeliest candidate being the nearby bank. The only other finds from the secondary and tertiary ditch fill were a fragment of a till flint flake and a large unidentified piece of badly corroded iron, both from 614.

Entrance features

Located along the western side of the henge's northern entrance were the remains of three incomplete earthen features, seven postholes or stakeholes, and part of a large pit (Fig 4.33; Fig 4.34, Section B). The most obvious of the positive features was 607, a linear band of compact stone and gravel, sitting in a matrix of fine dark brown loamy sand, no more than 0.88m wide with a possible causeway around 1m across. With a thickness of only 0.05–0.13m the feature was invisible in the south-facing section, and at just 0.3m from the trench top it was clearly separated from the upper surface of 615 by a continuous spread of subsoil, suggesting it was later in date. Stratigraphically it matches 617, in the opposite corner of the trench, and both share the same north-west to south-east orientation. Whilst 607 is narrower and shallower than 617, lacking also its cobbles, these may nonetheless be related and quite recent features, corresponding with the linear anomalies detected by geophysical prospection (Fig 3.21, 69). If so, they enclose an area 11m across.

The other two positive features, 608 and 615, share the same north-west to south-east orientation as 607, but in contrast, may have formed part of an earlier entrance structure broadly contemporary with the henge. Sitting on the natural in the north-east corner of the excavation trench was 608, a fine brown loamy sand, with significant quantities of gravel and small to large stone, between 0.21 and 0.39m thick. It resembles the truncated remains of a bank at least 4m wide. Extending for 3m along the south-facing section it then slopes down abruptly, almost to the top of the natural, for the next 0.4m, before again rising and continuing for another 2.69m, suggesting its construction in two parts. The top of 608 produced a single sherd of brown-green glazed medieval pottery over a pink fabric which may be from Brandsby or nearby in the Howardian Hills. Four likely postholes and stakeholes with similar depths were found after the removal of 608. The largest of these was 627, an oval feature with a maximum diameter of 0.58m, its U-shaped cut sloping more gently towards its top. It survived to a depth of 0.42m. More irregular was 628, 0.77m by 0.43m across, its U-shaped profile 0.43m deep. The others, 629 and 630, were vertical-sided and flat-bottomed with depths of 0.47m and 0.42m respectively. In size they were 0.48m by 0.35m (629) and 0.33m across (630).

Larger and more difficult to interpret was 615, a fine dark brown loamy sand with substantial quantities of stone. Despite being treated as a single context, it possessed an irregular shape and varied between 0.03m and 0.58m in thickness, raising the possibility it was deposited for different reasons and perhaps even at different times. It is least substantial in the north-east quadrant of the trench, where it runs parallel with 608: surviving to a maximum height of only 0.24m, its greatly undulating top suggests extensive plough-damage. It too may have originally formed a bank, at least 2m across and most likely interrupted by a causeway some 1.5m wide. Despite disappearing shortly after this gap, it may have once continued beyond the eastern limit of the excavation. The feature was associated with two irregularly shaped possible postholes or stakeholes: 625 was V-shaped with a flat bottom and a maximum diameter of 0.62m; 626 was U-shaped with a maximum diameter of 0.47m. Both were only visible once the natural gravel had been cleaned

and were shallow with depths of only 0.25m (625) and 0.29m (626).

The extent of 615 differed noticeably in the north-west quadrant of the trench. At almost the point where the feature runs into the south-facing section, it curves sharply to the south-west and rises significantly in section. It contained larger stones than elsewhere in the context, especially throughout its bottom half, and small pieces of gypsum were found towards its top. Whilst it continues into the unexcavated area along the western side of the trench, making its interpretation problematic, this part of 615 could either be redeposited material from the henge bank terminal or the remains of a platform or mound abutting the entrance. The latter is perhaps more likely given this material's close similarities with 615 in the north-east quadrant. Indeed, the plausibility of the entire context belonging to the same broadly contemporary structure is highlighted by 643, a shallow band of gravel and very small or small stone in a matrix of soft dark yellowish-brown sand capping all of 615. It was cut by 645, a large steep-sided pit 2.54m wide in section with an uneven bottom and a maximum depth of 0.75m (Figs 4.33 and 4.34, Section B). At least half of it was outside the area of excavation. It was filled by 644, a soft dark brown sandy silty loam with a significant number of stones, the largest of which could suggest packing for a pair of timber uprights. Nearby was 624, a possible U-shaped posthole or stakehole 0.55m by 0.37m at its top (Fig 4.33). It was only visible upon cleaning the natural gravel, surviving to a depth of just 0.18m.

4.6.4 Discussion

The excavation offers some useful insights into the monument's appearance and history. The excavated section of outer ditch was narrower and shallower than this feature at the central henge (4.5.2), but both saw differing degrees of backfilling immediately after digging, suggesting that little importance was attached to maintaining their original appearance. Irrespective of whether the southern henge's outer ditch was larger elsewhere around its circumference, it seems improbable it was dug along this section of the monument to provide spoil for the imposing inner bank. Rather, it was more likely used for a closer, and less substantial, outer bank, which could conceivably have been reinstated by the addition of a modest palisade or fence. If so, the discovery of this earthwork complements the aerial photograph of a similar feature at the northern henge (3.3.2). When this building took place remains unknown, as does its sequential relationship to the similarly undated inner ditch, the radiocarbon date of 1745–1515 cal BC from the top of the primary fill being of little help. Neither do the small collection of worked lithics and tiny fragment of what is possibly a carinated bowl shed any light on sequence or chronology.

Given the contrast between the modest outer

earthwork and the imposing inner bank and ditch, it seems reasonable to conclude that the monument's users would have had very different experiences of each, with the latter providing a smaller and very much more physically bounded arena, especially if there had been standing water in the ditch at certain times of the year. The extent to which the latter was planned is debatable, there being no evidence for waterlogging at the other two henges (see also Richards 1996, 330–1). It was most likely an accidental outcome of hitting the water table during the digging of the ditch, but, irrespective of intention, the presence of water added to the enclosure's physical effectiveness at separating space. The extent of gleying along the ditch bottom and sides certainly suggests a substantial if intermittent accumulation, which, according to our own field observations following excavation, would have drained away very slowly. The same can be concluded for the banked feature in the henge's northernmost entrance. The earth resistance survey conducted immediately before excavation had exposed an area of low resistance here and this can be seen extending across the causeway towards the opposing ditch terminal (Fig D1.12). It may match the 'pair of conjoined parallel lines like an elongated H' shown by an aerial photograph in the southern entrance of the nearby and now largely denuded Cana Barn henge (Harding and Lee 1987, 304–5). Architecturally elaborate entranceways have been demonstrated for other henges, with Stonehenge being the finest example, and these undoubtedly emphasised, and perhaps even orchestrated, the act of moving into and out of the monuments (Harding 2003, 65–6). The interpretation of Thornborough's possible entrance feature is made the more difficult by a number of linear negative anomalies discovered by geophysical prospection to be running across the henge. Their regularity suggests they are agricultural features of a later date, and one of these, extending along the ditch terminal in the same place as the excavated feature (Fig 3.21, 69), probably relates to 607 (Fig 4.33).

The subsequent history of the southern henge is similar to that of the central henge. The inner ditches of both were partially levelled in the medieval period, itself an impressive feat suggesting a clear need, but the greater quantity of pottery at the southern henge suggests this was more of a focus for activity than the other monument, at least during the 13th and 14th centuries. That 50% of this collection was derived from glazed jugs compares favourably to the results of limited excavation at the medieval village of High Worsall, on the Tees west of Yarm, where plainware composed 80–100% of the collection from 'low-status' areas such as the village green but 22–50% in 'high-status' areas near the church and presumed manorial site (Vyner 2009). One explanation for the greater incidence of high-status pottery at the southern henge might be its use for fairs, races, and other assemblies, and, as previously discussed (2.2), the enclosing henge earthwork would have made for an ideal gathering

place. Unfortunately, there is no direct evidence for what exactly was happening here, and the small and abraded state of this pottery suggests that if the monument was used in this way then such activity was followed by a phase of ploughing well before the construction of 617. As discussed above, the interpretation of the latter is also problematic, but irrespective of whether it is the remains of a stone wall or some form of timber boundary, this structure was clearly on a different alignment to 607 and its associated geophysical anomalies, suggesting a complex sequence of activity following the levelling of the earthwork in the 13th and 14th centuries. Presumably, much of it was agricultural in origin.

4.7   Double pit alignment *by Jan Harding, Benjamin Johnson, Blaise Vyner, and Peter Makey*

4.7.1   *Introduction*

The excavation of the double pit alignment (Fig 4.40) was undertaken periodically over five years (2.5). Initial geophysical prospection in 1994 had detected its southern extent nearest the then extant track (D1.1.4), and, as a result, three small trenches, each no more than 4m by 4m, were located over the most obvious anomalies. These were excavated by hand, with all spoil sieved, in September of 1994 and 1995, resulting in the discovery of three pits, each given its own series of context numbers (beginning 100, 200 and 300). These modest investigations were followed in 1998 and 1999 by more substantial excavations. In August and early September of 1998 a 28m by 16m trench was opened towards the monument's northern end, and a further six pits excavated, allocated context numbers with the numerical prefix of '8'. This trench was enlarged significantly in August 1999, resulting in an area 30m wide and extending for 350m south-south-west towards the track. Its width ensured the alignment could be chased irrespective of any shifts in course. This large trench revealed 84 pits, again associated with their own series of context numbers, this time with a numerical prefix of '9'; it included the three previously excavated from its southern end, renumbered 966 (100), 971 (200) and 973 (300) (Fig 4.40). In both 1998 and 1999 topsoil was stripped by machine as far as the truncated tops of the pits, as was the surrounding subsoil to the depth of the natural gravel. This was done under close supervision. All features were then cleaned and excavated by hand, with their deposits always sieved. They were recorded by an individual feature number after the prefix in their order of discovery (eg the 23rd feature discovered in 1999 was given the context '923'), so the numerical sequence does not always proceed logically along the monument's course. Fifty-two pits were completely excavated (in two halves) in 1998–99 – recording sections on both sides of a temporary baulk – but in order

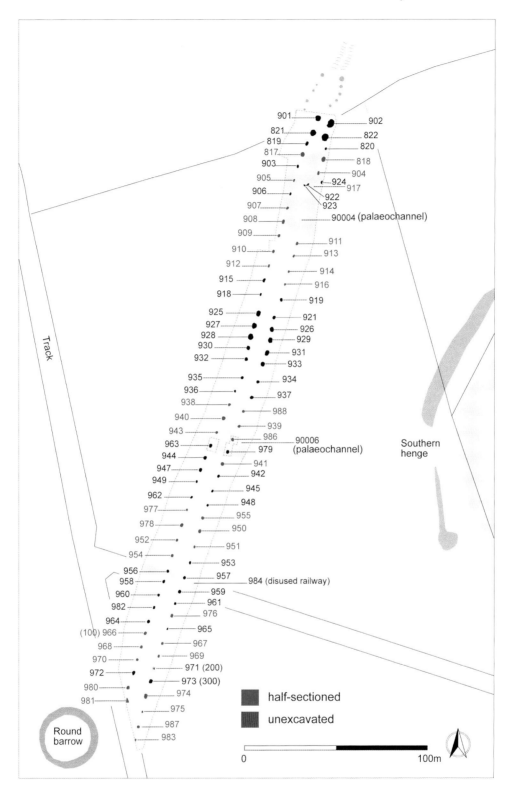

Fig 4.40 Plan of double pit alignment excavation. © Crown Copyright / database right 2013. An Ordnance Survey / EDINA supplied service

to conserve some of the monument a further 32 were only half-sectioned, their remaining northern half usually left intact (Fig 4.40). Six pits at the southern end were planned but unexcavated (Fig 4.40).

4.7.2 Excavation results

A total of 90 pits were found divided into a western row of 44 pits and an eastern row of 46 pits (Fig 4.40). The rows are 10–12.5m apart with individual

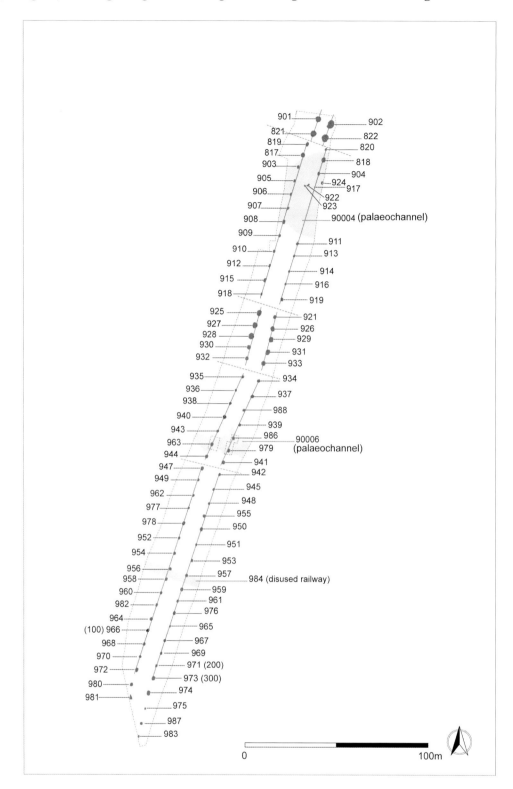

Fig 4.41   Changes in the course of the double pit alignment

pits spaced every 5–7m along them. The symmetry between these rows suggest the pits were deliberately paired in a broadly north-north-east to south-south-west direction, but the monument subtly changes course at least four times (Fig 4.41). These shifts correlate with topographic factors and distinct variations in the morphology of the pits themselves,

suggesting significant differences in appearance and perhaps even use as the alignment crosses the gently sloping river terrace. The eastern row has a large gap 33.75m wide which is likely to have been an original feature. In all probability, the majority of pits originally held timber uprights, some of which were fairly substantial. Unlike earlier accounts of the excavation, it is not now thought that the pits were recut, with posts being left to rot rather than deliberately removed. Aerial photography demonstrates the existence of a further ten pits to the north of the excavated area, along with an unusual end-feature (3.3.4), but the alignment may have also continued beyond its southern extent, past the now ploughed-out track. Given this, it is impossible to identify the monument's total length, although its southern end is most likely in the vicinity of the cropmark of what appears to be a round barrow (3.3.3). The pit rows cut two palaeochannels, and were subsequently cut by the old railway, which fortunately does not seem to have destroyed any earlier features. The excavations produced only 68 largely redeposited worked lithics, the majority of which were flakes. The collection is summarised in Tables D3.6, D3.9, D3.13, D3.16, D3.20 and D3.22. The site did, however, produce the largest collection of prehistoric pottery from any of the monuments, albeit just four sherds from a possible early Bronze Age vessel, 167 sherds of a middle Bronze Age vessel, a single sherd also possibly of this date, and an additional sherd of possible Neolithic pottery (D4.1.2). Two medieval sherds came from the top of 966 (D4.1.3). Four 2nd-millennium BC and early 1st-millennium BC radiocarbon dates were of limited value (see D5), but suggest it was most likely constructed and used in the middle Bronze Age.

Plough-disturbed horizon and railway

The plough-disturbed horizon consisted of topsoil and subsoil with a thickness of 0.25–0.32m and 0.07–0.30m respectively. Generally, the plough-disturbed horizon deepened from north to south as the plateau sloped down, but there was considerable variation along the uneven drift geology. The mechanical removal of the topsoil and the uppermost subsoil revealed the tops of the pits as clearly discernible and usually quite regular patches of reddish silt, often with fewer stones than the surrounding surface. These normally corresponded very closely to the excavated pits, suggesting that many features had only been marginally truncated by ploughing. Disturbance was most pronounced across the sloping northern half of the monument, especially at the palaeochannel, where the plough horizon was shallowest. Other indicators of disturbance were seen in the upper fills of pits 925 and 927, each producing a single piece of flint with slight traces of stubble burning, and from the top of pit 929, where two medieval pottery sherds of likely 13th- or 14th-century date were found, including a single jug sherd of Brandsby-type ware (D4.1.3). These three pits were along its northern section on an elevated gravel ridge.

At the southern end of the excavation trench was 984, the highly visible remains of the disused Thirsk to Masham railway line that ran south-east to north-west across the trench (Fig 4.40). In the west-facing section the feature was 7.23m across, reaching a maximum thickness of 0.27–0.32m for a width of *c* 1.2m at its approximate centre, before tapering gently to its edge. It consisted of 98403, a basal deposit of stiff reddish-yellow clay with a large quantity of gravel and stone, and a maximum thickness of 0.19m. At its southern edge, after narrowing, it turned upwards and rose to the surface. Overlying this for 4.19m from its northern edge was 98401, a discontinuous deposit of clinker and burnt coke. Its curves slightly upwards along the northern edge of the feature and reaches a maximum thickness of 0.18m at the centre of the feature.

The double pit alignment

The morphology and fills of the 90 pits, which are fully described in Table 4.2, vary greatly along the course of the monument. They can be divided into four basic types: pits with post-pipes, usually in association with large cobbles, which unambiguously attest to the original existence of timber uprights; pits whose profile or slumped fills, again often in association with large cobbles, suggest posts; pits, usually containing one or two fills, about which it is impossible to say if they held timbers; and most rarely, pits whose shape, profile, or depth suggest they never held uprights. These distinctions are not always clear-cut – sometimes the interpretation depends on evidence from only one of its two recorded sections – especially with those pits classified as never having held posts. Nonetheless, these differences are believed to correlate with significant variations in the monument's original appearance, use, and perhaps even development. Most noticeably, those pits which unambiguously held timber uprights occur along the more elevated sections of the monument, whilst those which are least likely to have done so are found close to its wide gap (see Fig 4.62).

The four largest pits (the pair of 901/902 and 821/822) are at the northern end of the excavation where the monument is narrowest (Fig 4.40). These substantial sub-circular features were 3.06–3.65m in diameter at their top, with steep sides, flat bases, and depths of 1.01–1.63m (Figs 4.42 and 4.43). The two eastern pits are the largest of each pair and also the most off-line with other pits to the south, limiting the inside of the monument to a gap only 2.5m across. Post-pipes at the bottom of 901 and 902 indicate central timber uprights of *c* 0.45–1.2m diameter, and both were immediately backfilled with large cobbles and what appears to have been a largely silty deposit. A small fragment of *Quercus* charcoal from 90207, the post-pipe in 902, was dated to 1750–1525 cal BC (OxA-11009; see D5). This is the only sample of oak from the monument, and is unlikely to be the result of bioturbation given its location amongst the stony fill. Therefore, it could conceivably have come from the post (see below). Both 821 and 822 are similar in profile, and indeed deeper, indicating they

Table 4.2   The double pit alignment

Pit	Cut description (including maximum size at top of feature and maximum depth)	Fill descriptions from south-facing sections (from bottom to top)	Post
817	Sub-oval, 1.9m × 1.18m; 0.8m deep; steep sides, flat base	813, a friable brown sandy silt 0.2m thick with cobbles; 832, a firm dark brown silt 0.15m thick with cobbles lensing to east and west; 805, a firm red silt	Yes
818	Sub-oval, 1.9m × 1.15m wide; 0.6m deep; moderate to steep sides, flat base	837, a firm brown silty clay 0.12m thick with cobbles; 814, a firm dark brown sandy silt 0.17m thick with cobbles lensing to east and west; 806, a firm red silt	?
819	Sub-oval, 1.9m × 1.35m; 0.7m deep; steep sides, shallow U-shape base	825, a friable reddish-brown silt 0.35m thick with large cobbles; 808, a firm red silt with cobbles; 823, a loose reddish-brown sandy silt	Yes
820	Sub-oval, 1.65m × 1m; 0.6m deep; steep sides, flat base	838, a firm sandy clay 0.08m thick with cobbles; 829, a firm dark red silt 0.28m thick with cobbles lensing to the east and west; 830, a firm brown-black sandy silt 0.15m thick lensing to the east and west; 809, a friable red silt	Yes
821	Sub-circular, 3.1m diameter; 1.63m deep; steep sides, flat base	840, a loose dark yellowish-brown silty sand 0.41m thick lensing to east and west; at the centre 850, a very loose sandy silt 0.3m thick with large cobbles; 836, a friable dark red-brown sandy silt lensing to east and west; 811, a firm yellowish-red sandy silt	Yes
822	Sub-circular, 3.65m diameter; 1.33m deep; steep sides, flat base	847, a brown sandy silt 0.3m thick lensing to the east and west; 843, a friable brown sandy silt 0.3m thick with large cobbles; 810, a friable red silt	Yes
901	Sub-circular, 3.06m diameter; 1.01m deep; steep sides, flat base	90106, a firm brown slightly sandy silt 0.38m thick lensing to the east and west; at the centre 90105, a firm dark brown sandy silt 0.27m thick with large cobbles; 90101, a stiff brown silt	Yes
902	Sub-circular, 3.2m diameter; 1.2m deep; steep sides, flat base	90209, a firm dark brown sandy silt 0.17m thick lensing up the sides; 90206, a firm dark brown sandy silt 0.27m thick with cobbles; 90207, a stiff dark yellowish-brown silt 0.39m thick with large cobbles; 90205, a stiff dark brown silt 0.18m thick lensing to the west; 90201, a stiff dark yellowish-brown slightly sandy silt with large cobbles	Yes
903	Sub-oval, 0.63m diameter; 0.44m deep; steep sides, flat base	90303, a loose dark brown sandy silt 0.2m thick lensing up the sides; 90302, a loose dark brown silty sand 0.14m thick with cobbles; 90301, a loose very dark brown silt	Yes
904	Sub-oval, 1.45m × 0.83m; 0.24m deep; steep sides, flat base	90402, a firm very dark greyish-brown sandy silt 0.09m thick with cobbles; 90401, a friable very dark brown sandy silt with cobbles	No
905	Sub-oval , 0.85m diameter; 0.1m deep; shallow sides, flat base	90501, a loose black silt with cobbles	No
906	Sub-oval, 0.87m × 0.76m; 0.19m deep; steep sides, flat base	90601, a loose black silt with cobbles	No
907	Sub-circular, 0.85m diameter; 0.12m deep; shallow sides, shallow V-shape base	90701, a loose very dark greyish-brown silty sand with cobbles	No
908	Sub-oval, 1.2m diameter; 0.05m deep; shallow sides, flat base	90801, a loose dark brown silt with cobbles	No
909	Sub-circular, 1.45m diameter; 0.25m deep; steep sides, flat base	90902, a soft brown clay 0.13m thick with cobbles; 90901, a loose brown sand	?
910	Sub-circular, 0.65m diameter; 0.54m deep; steep sides, irregular flat base	91004, a loose dark reddish-brown silt 0.13m thick with cobbles; 91003, a loose dark reddish-brown silt 0.15m thick; 91001, a very soft dark reddish-brown silt	Yes
911	Sub-oval, 1.63m × 0.91m wide; 0.32m deep; moderate sides, flat base	91101, a loose dark brown sandy silt with cobbles	?
912	Sub-oval, 1.5m × 0.65m; 0.49m deep; vertical sides, shallow U-shape base	91004, a loose dark reddish-brown sandy silt 0.15m thick; 91202, a loose dark reddish-brown sandy silt 0.2m thick lensing to the east and west; 91201, a soft very dark brown slightly sandy silt	Yes
913	Sub-oval, 1.65m × 0.95m; 0.43m deep; steep sides, shallow U-shape base	91304, a loose dark brown sandy silt 0.11m thick lensing to the east and west; 91303, a loose dark brown sandy silt 0.14m thick lensing to the east and west; 91301, a friable reddish-black silt	Yes
914	Sub-oval, 1.86m × 1.18m wide; 0.44m deep; steep sides, shallow U-shape base	91403, a loose dark yellowish-brown sand 0.15m thick; 91402, a loose dark yellowish-brown silt 0.14m thick with large cobbles; 91401, a friable reddish-brown silt	Yes
915	Sub-rectangular, 1.89m × 0.98m; 0.50m deep; steep sides, shallow U-shape base	91503, a loose dark reddish-brown slightly silty sand 0.2m thick; 91502, a loose dark reddish-brown slightly sandy silt 0.14m thick with large cobbles; 91501, a soft dark brown silt	Yes

Table 4.2 (*cont.*) **The double pit alignment**

Pit	Cut description (including maximum size at top of feature and maximum depth)	Fill descriptions from south-facing sections (from bottom to top)	Post
916	Sub-oval, 1.51m × 1m; 0.47m deep; steep sides, shallow U-shape base	91603, a loose dark reddish-brown sandy silt; 91601, a friable dark brown sandy silt with large cobbles	Yes
917	Irregular, 1.2m × 1m; 0.18m deep; shallow sides, shallow U-shape base	91701, a firm brown silty sand with cobbles	No
918	Sub-rectangular, 2.02m × 1.03m; 0.47m deep; near vertical sides, flat base	91802, a firm dark brown sandy silt 0.34m thick with cobbles; 91801, a friable dark brown silt	Yes
919	Sub-oval, 2.22m × 1.17m; 0.61m deep; steep sides, flat base	91903, a loose very dark brown slightly silty sand 0.17m thick; 91902, a firm dark brown sandy silt with large cobbles; 91901, a firm dark reddish-brown slightly sandy silt	Yes
921	Sub-oval, 2.65m × 1.6m wide; 0.7m deep; steep sides, flat base	92102, a stiff very dark brown sand 0.18m thick; at the centre 92104, a loose reddish-brown sand with large cobbles 0.23m thick; around the edges 92103, a firm reddish-brown sand 0.28m thick lensing up the east and west; 92101, a firm dark reddish-brown silt	Yes
922	Irregular, 0.66m × 0.84m; 0.21m deep; shallow U-shape	92201, firm brown silty sand with cobbles at the centre	?
923	Irregular, 0.64m × 1.06m wide; 0.15m deep; shallow sides, shallow U-shape base	92302, a loose reddish-brown sand 0.08m thick with cobbles; 92301, a friable dark brown silt	?
924	Irregular, 0.58m wide; 0.15m deep; shallow U-shape	92401, a friable dark brown silt [description from west-facing section]	?
925	Sub-circular, 2.9m diameter; 0.95m deep; steep sides, flat base	92503, a stiff yellowish-brown sand 0.1m thick lensing to the east and west; 92502, a friable dark yellowish-brown sandy silt 0.15m thick with large cobbles; at the centre 92504, a firm dark brown silt 0.2m thick with large cobbles; 92501, a friable brown silt with some cobbles	Yes
926	Sub-oval pit, 3.55m × 2.3m; 1.2m deep; shallow sides steepening to vertical sides with a flat base	92608, a loose brown sand 0.35m thick; at the centre 92606, a firm dark brown silty sand with large cobbles 0.32m thick; to the west 92604, a firm dark brown sandy silt with large cobbles 0.3m thick; to the east 92605, a firm slightly sandy silt with large cobbles 0.35m thick; at the centre 92603, a firm dark brown sandy silt 0.3m thick; 92602, a friable dark brown sandy silt with some cobbles; at the centre 92601, a loose dark reddish-brown silt 0.1m thick	Yes
927	Sub-circular, 2.1m diameter; 1.5m deep; steep sides, shallow U-shape base	92707, a firm dark brown sandy silt 0.3m thick lensing to the east and west; 92706, a firm dark brown sandy silt with large cobbles 0.5m thick; 92704, a firm dark brown silty sand 0.6m thick; to the east 92703, a charcoal lens 30mm thick; 92701, a firm dark brown silt with cobbles	Yes
928	Sub-circular, 2.5m diameter; 1.3m deep; steep sides, flat base	92804, a stiff dark brown slightly sandy silt 0.75m thick with numerous large cobbles; to the east and west 92803, a firm dark brown sandy silt 0.2 thick lensing to the east and west; 92802, a firm dark brown silt 0.7m thick with large cobbles; 92801, a loose dark brown silt with cobbles	Yes
929	Sub-oval, 2.7m × 1.65m wide; 0.85m deep; steep sides, flat base	92907, a firm dark brown sandy silt 0.3m thick lensing to the east and west; 92903, a firm dark brown slightly sandy silt; 92905, a firm dark brown slightly sandy silt, very similar to 92903, 0.3m thick; 92901, a firm dark brown sandy silt	Yes
930	Sub-circular, 2.4m diameter; 0.83m deep; steep sides, flattish base	93005, a firm brown sandy silt 0.15m thick lensing to the east and west; at the centre 93004, a stiff dark brown silty sand with large rounded cobbles; to the east and west 93008, a loose dark brown sandy silt; 93001, a firm dark brown silt	Yes
931	Sub-circular, 1.7m diameter; 0.70m deep; steep sides, flattish base	93104, a firm brown slightly sandy silt 0.15m thick lensing up the sides to east and west with a number of large rounded cobbles to its centre; 93103, a firm dark brown sandy silt; to the centre 93102, a soft black silt only 0.25m wide and 0.02m thick; 93101, a stiff dark brown sandy silt	Yes
932	Sub-oval, 2.5m × 2m; 1.6m deep; steep sides, flattish base	93205, a loose dark brown sandy silt 0.25m thick lensing up the sides to the east and west; 93204, a firm dark brown sandy silt 0.45m thick with many large rounded cobbles; 93201, a firm dark brown sandy silt	Yes
933	Sub-oval, 2.2m × 1.3m; 0.82m deep; steepish sides, shallow U-shape base	93305, a loose very dark brown sandy silt 0.18m thick lensing up the sides of the pit to the east and west; at the centre 93308, a loose very dark brown sandy silt with many large rounded cobbles 0.23m thick; 93302, a loose dark brown sandy silt 0.22m thick; 93301, a loose brown slightly sandy silt	Yes
934	Sub-oval, 2.5m × 2m; 0.55m deep; shallow sides, flat base	93403, a firm dark brown sandy silt 0.13m thick lensing up the sides to the east and west; 93402, a firm dark reddish-grey silt 0.4m thick with large rounded cobbles; 93401, a firm dark brown slightly sandy silt	Yes

Table 4.2 (*cont.*) **The double pit alignment**

Pit	Cut description (including maximum size at top of feature and maximum depth)	Fill descriptions from south-facing sections (from bottom to top)	Post
935	Sub-circular, 1.36m diameter; 0.47m deep; steep sides, flat base	To the south 93506, a firm dark brown sandy silt with some large cobbles 0.18m thick lensing up the side; to the north 93501, a firm dark brown sandy silt with some large cobbles 0.47m thick lensing up the side; 93503, a firm dark brown slightly sandy silt with a few large rounded cobbles 0.35m thick; 93502, a firm dark brown slightly sandy silt 0.23m thick [description from west-facing section]	Yes
936	Sub-oval, 1.7m × 0.98m; 0.79m deep; steep sides, irregular U-shape base	93606, a loose dark brown sandy silt 0.20m thick; 93605, a loose dark brown sandy silt 0.21m thick; 93603, a loose dark brown silty sand; 93601, a loose very dark brown silty sand	Yes
937	Sub-oval, 2.22m × 1.91m wide; 0.56m deep; steep sides, irregular flat base	93706, a firm very dark brown sandy silt 0.16m thick; 93705, a firm very dark brown sandy silt 0.33m thick; 93701, a firm very dark brown sandy silt with a few large cobbles	Yes
938	Sub-circular, 1.1m diameter; 0.39m deep; steep sides, flat base	93805, a firm dark brown sandy silt 0.09m thick lensing up the sides; 93804, a stiff dark brown silty sand 0.12m thick; 93801, a stiff dark brown sandy silt with large cobbles [description from east-facing section]	?
939	Sub-oval, 1.21m × 0.74m; 0.23m deep; irregular sides, flat base	93902, a loose black slightly sandy silt 0.28m thick with numerous large cobbles lensing up the sides; 93901, a loose black silt 0.18m deep	?
940	Sub-oval, 1.15m × 1.62m; 0.48m deep; shallow sides, U-shape base	94003, a loose very dark brown sandy silt with numerous large cobbles 0.18m thick; 94001, a loose dark brown silty sand 0.28m deep	?
941	Sub-circular, 1.68m diameter; 0.65m deep; shallow sides, flattish base	94101, a friable dark brown silt 0.2m thick lensing up the sides to the east and west; 94103, a soft dark brown silt with a few large cobbles	?
942	Sub-oval, 1.26m × 1.02m wide; 0.37m deep; shallow sides, shallow V-shape base	94101, a loose very dark brown silt with a few large cobbles to the centre	?
943	Sub-oval, 2.05m × 1.35m wide; 0.38m deep; shallow sides, flat base	94302, a friable brown slightly sandy silt 0.16m thick and lensing to the edges with a few large cobbles to the centre; 94301, a friable brown slightly sandy silt 0.22m thick	?
944	Sub-circular, 1.52m diameter; 0.54m deep, moderately steep sides, flat base	94401, a firm dark brown silt	?
945	Sub-oval, 1.04m × 0.79m; 0.25m deep; shallow sides, flat base	94501, a loose very dark brown silt	?
947	Sub-oval, 1.48m × 0.98m; 0.45m deep; moderately steep sides, flat base	94701, a loose dark brown silt with large cobbles	?
948	Sub-oval, 1.14m × 0.66m; 0.54m deep; steep sides, flat base	94802, a loose very dark brown silt 0.22m thick with cobbles lensing up the sides; 94801, a loose very dark silt with large cobbles	?
949	Sub-oval, 1.12m × 0.74m; 0.29m deep; moderately steep sides, flat base	94901, a loose very dark brown silt with large cobbles	?
950	Sub-oval, 1.60m × 1.19m; 0.39m deep; moderately steep sides, flat base	95001, a firm dark brown silt with large cobbles	?
951	Sub-oval, 1.33m × 0.88m; 0.4m deep; steep sides, flat base	95102, a firm dark grey silt 0.15m thick with cobbles lensing up the sides; 95101, soft very dark grey silt 0.25m thick with angular cobbles	?
952	Sub-circular, 1.03m diameter; 0.35m deep; steep sides, irregular flat base	95202, a soft dark brown silt 0.22m thick; 95201, a firm dark brown sandy silt 0.17m thick with large sub-angular cobbles	?
953	Sub-oval, 1.04m × 0.78m; 0.39m deep; moderately steep sides, U-shape base	953001, a loose very dark brown silt	?
954	Sub-oval, 1.52m × 0.88m; 0.49m deep; moderately steep sides, irregular U-shape base	95401, a loose very dark brown silt	?
955	Sub-oval, 1.74m × 0.97m; 0.59m deep; moderately steep sides, flat base	95502, a loose very dark brown silt 0.38m thick; 95501, a loose very dark brown silt 0.21m thick	?
956	Sub-oval, 1.8m × 1.64m wide; 0.56m deep; moderately steep sides, flat base	95603, a soft brown sandy silt 0.14m thick and lensing up the sides; 95602, a soft dark reddish-brown silt 0.21m thick; 95601, was a firm dark brown slightly sandy silt 0.26m thick with some cobbles	?
957	Sub-oval, 1.8m × 1.4m; 0.55m deep; steep sides, shallow U-shape base	95704, a soft yellowish-brown sand 0.06m thick; 95702, a friable dark grey slightly sandy silt 0.17m thick and lensing up the sides; 95701, a soft dark reddish-brown silt 0.45m thick with some large cobbles	?
958	Sub-oval, 1.8m × 1.4m; 0.4m deep; moderately steep sides, shallow U-shape base	95802, a friable dark grey sandy silt 0.28m thick; 95801, a soft dark reddish-brown silt	?
959	Sub-oval, 1.75m × 1.29m; 0.53m deep; steep sides, flat base	95901, a loose dark brown sandy silt with some cobbles	?

Table 4.2 (*cont.*)   **The double pit alignment**

Pit	Cut description (including maximum size at top of feature and maximum depth)	Fill descriptions from south-facing sections (from bottom to top)	Post
960	Sub-oval, 1.39m × 0.89m; 0.49m deep; steep sides, flat base	96001, a loose dark brown sandy silt with some cobbles	?
961	Sub-oval, 1.1m × 0.73m; 0.29m deep; moderately steep sides, flat base	96001, a loose dark brown sandy silt	?
962	Sub-oval, 1.55m × 0.97m; 0.52m deep; steep sides, flat base	96202, a friable dark brown sandy silt 0.21m thick lensing up the sides of the pit with some small cobbles; 96201, a soft brown silt with some small cobbles	?
963	Sub-oval, 1.98m × 1.47m wide; 0.37m deep; moderately steep sides, shallow U-shape base	96301, a soft dark reddish-brown silt	?
964	Sub-oval, 1.8m × 1.25m; 0.4m deep; moderately steep sides, irregular U-shape base	96401, a soft dark reddish-brown silt	?
965	Sub-oval, 0.76m × 0.48m; 0.08m deep; shallow sides, flat base	96501, a loose dark reddish-brown silt	No
966 (100)	Sub-circular, 1.43m diameter; 0.73m deep; steep sides, shallow U-shape base	108, of soft yellowish-brown sand 0.25m thick lensing to the east; 106, a soft dark yellowish-brown sandy silt 0.05m thick lensing to the east; 107, a soft very dark greyish-brown sandy silt with a few cobbles	?
967	Sub-oval, 1.72m × 1.34m wide; 0.33m deep; shallow sides, steepening towards a shallow U-shape base	96701, a soft dark brown silt	?
968	Sub-oval, 1.6m × 1.2m; 0.4m deep; moderate irregular sides, shallow U-shape base	96801, a soft dark brown silt	?
969	Sub-oval, 1.54m × 1.05m; 0.29m deep; moderately steep sides, flat base	96901, a firm very dark grey slightly sandy silt	?
970	Sub-oval, 1.53m × 1.17m; 0.35m deep; moderate irregular sides, flat base	97001, a firm very dark grey slightly sandy silt	?
971 (200)	Sub-circular, at least 2m diameter (its extents lay outside the trench); 0.73m deep; moderately steep sides, shallow U-shape base	207, a soft brown sandy silt, 0.36m thick; 205, a soft dark yellowish-brown sandy silt 0.13m thick and thickening to the east; 204, a loose dark yellowish-brown sand	?
972	Sub-oval, 1.98m × 1.31m; 0.41m deep; moderately steep sides, flat base	97201, a firm very dark brown silt	?
973 (300)	Sub-oval, 2.2m × 1.65m; 0.5m deep; shallow sides, shallow U-shape base	305, a soft dark brown sandy silt 0.13m thick lensing to the east and west; to the west 307, a soft dark yellowish-brown sandy clay, 0.43m wide and 0.2m thick; 306, a soft yellowish-brown silty sand with large cobbles; 302, a soft dark brown silty sand	Yes
974	Sub-oval, 2.8m × 1.98m	Unexcavated	N/A
975	Sub-oval, 1.32m × 0.85m	Unexcavated	N/A
976	Sub-oval, 1.89m × 1.52m; 0.19m deep; shallow sides, shallow V-shaped base	97601, a soft very dark brown silt	No
977	Sub-oval, 1.18m × 0.93m; 0.62m deep; steep sides, irregular flat base	97702, a loose very dark brown silt 0.2m thick with small cobbles; 97701, a loose very dark brown silt with some small cobbles	?
978	Sub-oval, 1.67m × 1.33m; 0.42m deep; moderately steep sides, flat base	97802, a soft very dark greyish-brown slightly clayey silt 0.19m thick with cobbles; 97801, a firm brown sandy silt with cobbles	?
979	Sub-oval, 1.76m × 1.01m; 0.46m deep; shallow sides, shallow U-shape base	97901, a loose very dark brown silt	?
980	Sub-oval, 1.82m × 1.49m	Unexcavated	N/A
981	Sub-oval feature, minimum of 2.5m × 1.48m	Unexcavated	N/A
982	Sub-oval, 1.46m × 1.03m; 0.25m deep; steep sides, flat base	98201, a loose very dark grey sandy silt [description from west-facing section]	?
983	Sub-oval, minimum of 2.42m × 1.83m	Unexcavated	N/A
986	Sub-oval, 1.85m × 1.5m; 0.3m deep; moderately steep sides, flat base	98601, a friable very dark grey slightly sandy silt with cobbles	?
987	Sub-oval, 1.48m × 1.19m	Unexcavated	N/A
988	Sub-oval, 1.64m × 1.33m; 0.46m deep; moderately steep sides, shallow U-shape base	98801, a friable dark brown silty sand with cobbles	?

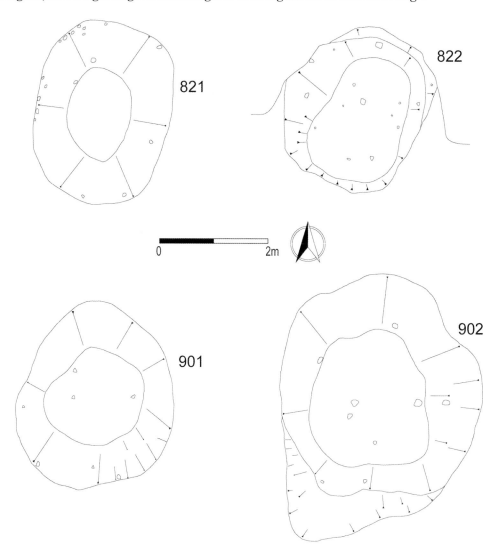

Fig 4.42   Plans of pits 821, 822, 901, and 902

too once held timbers. The former presence of a post could account for 850, in pit 821, a deposit of sandy silt and large cobbles so loose it collapsed into voids upon excavation. The secondary fills in both 821 (836) and 822 (843), complete with a thin deposit of gravel (848) and a narrow band of medium-sized cobbles (844) respectively, is interpreted as backfill, which in the case of the former had clearly slumped after the timber upright rotted.

To the south the monument widens to 12.5m across and both rows assume a straight course for as far as 918/919, broken only by the 33.75m wide gap on the eastern side (Fig 4.44). The proximity of the latter to the northern entrance of the nearby henge adds to the likelihood that this is an original feature. The 24 pits along this section of the monument, many of which were cut into an existing palaeochannel (see below), vary greatly, but are all much smaller than the four already described. To the north of the gap, across sloping terrace, are 819/820, 817/818 and 903/904. These sub-oval pits are largely steep-sided with either a flat or U-shaped base and are 0.83–1.9m across at their top with a depth of 0.24–0.8m (Figs 4.45 and

4.46). Pit 819 contains a well-defined post-pipe 0.43m in diameter, complete with many large cobbles. It had been immediately backfilled with sandy silt around the post. The near-vertical sides of the bottom half of 817, 820, and 903 imply that they also held timber uprights, as does the fact that their fills and large cobbles had slumped inwards towards the centre of the pits, their tertiary silts most likely eroding into the void left by the decayed post. If correct, the upright in 903 was perhaps the smallest, and indeed, there may be a trend whereby the posts decreased in size from the northern end of the excavation trench. More difficult to interpret are 818 and 904, although large cobbles at the centre of the former may have been stone packing for an upright. The shallowness of 904 could be the result of heavy truncation, and it is cut into the palaeochannel, whose softer deposit would be more yielding to the plough. Yet the presence of two thin fills indicates it originally lacked depth, and is therefore unlikely ever to have held a post despite the large cobbles. Its closeness to the gap in the eastern row may suggest it fulfilled a different role. The clayey material across the bottom of 818 and 820

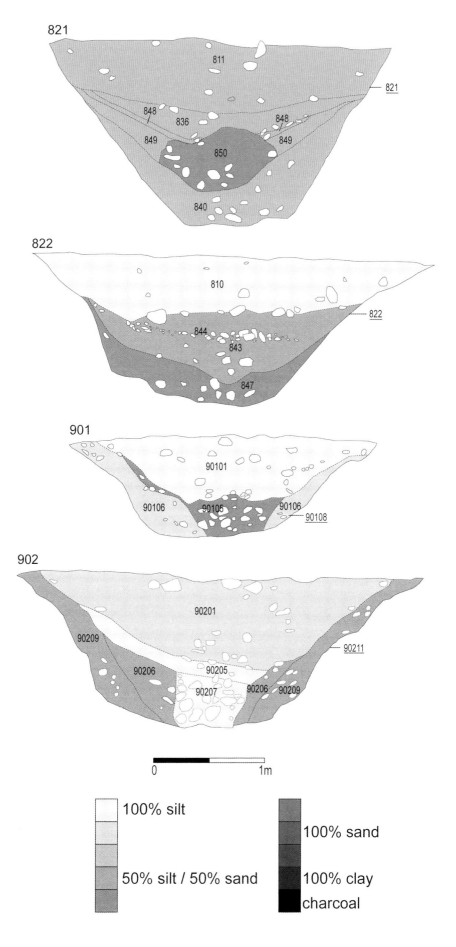

Fig 4.43   Sections of pits 821, 822, 901, and 902

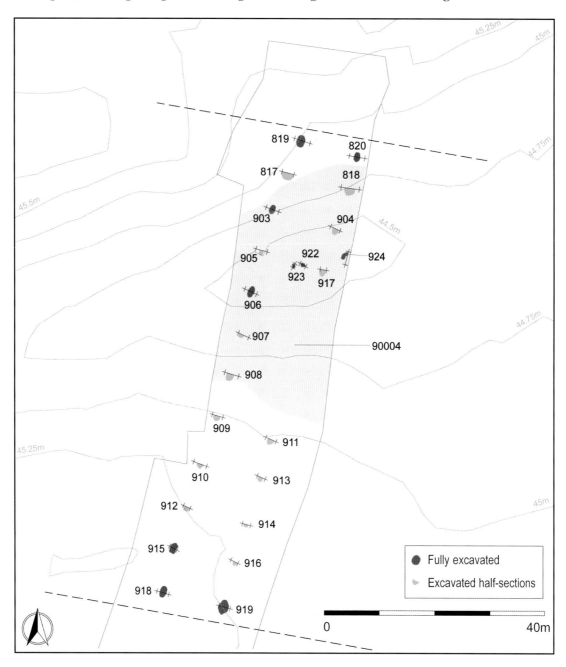

Fig 4.44   Plan of the northern section of the double pit alignment

is unlikely to have had a practical benefit, given it was deposited to a maximum thickness of only 0.12m. It probably came from the palaeochannel.

The pits immediately to the north of the gap (905/917), and the three opposite it (906, 907, 908), are also cut into the palaeochannel and show similarities to 904. They are generally more elongated than those to the north, varying between 0.76m and 1.2m across at their top (Fig 4.45). They are also extremely shallow with depths of 0.05–0.19m, each containing a single fill and large cobbles (Fig 4.46). This could again be due to increased plough damage across the palaeochannel, although these features were protected by more overburden than elsewhere along the monument's northern half. There is no reason to assume they were originally like the larger pits to the north of the palaeochannel, and their differing shape

– with their long axis orientated along the monument's alignment – and correspondence with the gap highlights their distinctiveness. They are therefore considered to have been without posts. Very similar in size, but not part of the pit rows themselves, were 922, 923, and 924 (Fig 4.44). The first two were sited only 0.50m apart, between pits 905 and 917. They were 0.64–1.06m across, with a maximum depth of 0.21m (Figs 4.45 and 4.46). Immediately outside the eastern row and running under the west-facing baulk is 924, a curving negative feature 0.58m across and 0.15m deep. It is impossible to determine the date and role of these three features, yet their location on the northern side of the gap, and similarities with other nearby pits, suggest they were once part of the monument.

The remainder of this straight section, running from

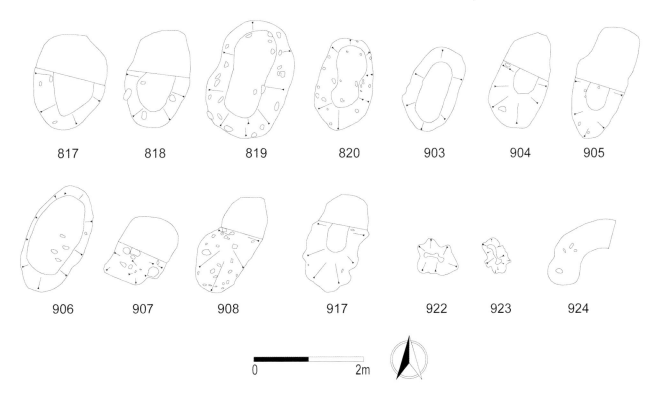

Fig 4.45   Plans of pits 817–20, 903–8, 917, and 922–4

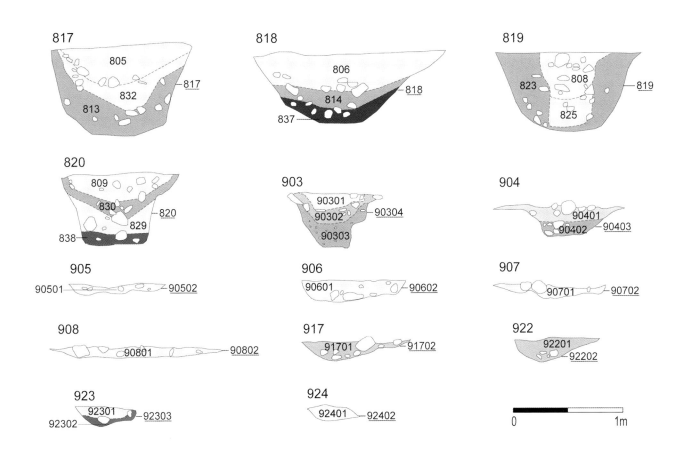

Fig 4.46   Sections of pits 817–20, 903–8, 917, and 922–4. See Fig 4.43 for deposit types

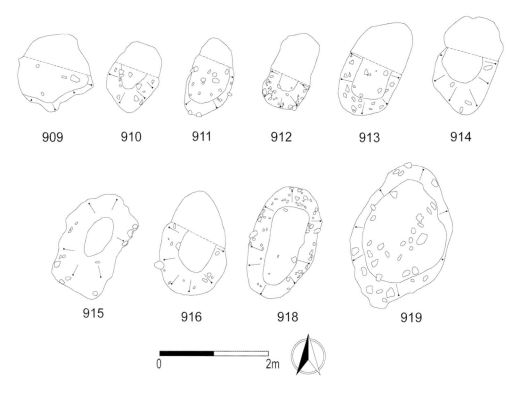

Fig 4.47   Plans of pits 909–16 and 918–19

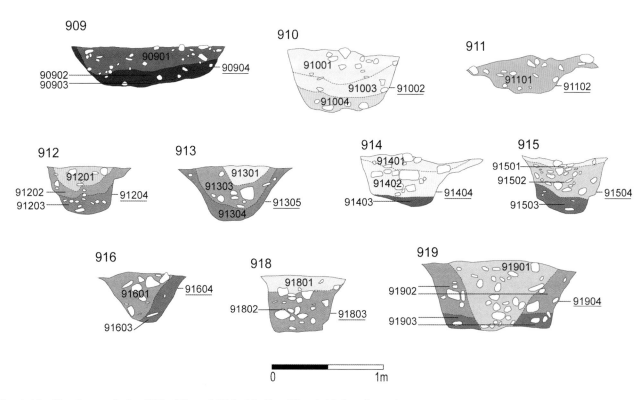

Fig 4.48   Sections of pits 909–16 and 918–19. See Fig 4.43 for deposit types

the southern edge of the palaeochannel until a gravel ridge, is made up of five pit pairs (909/911, 910/913, 912/914, 915/916, 918/919), each a little more widely spaced along the rows than is the case to the north. They are sub-circular, sub-oval, or sub-rectangular in shape, and vary between 0.65m and 2.22m across

at their tops (Fig 4.47). With an average of 1.43m, they are generally larger than the pits found across the palaeochannel, and the biggest, 918/919, are at the southern end of this section. The pits nearest the palaeochannel, 909/911, are less steep-sided than the rest and shallower, with depths of only 0.25m and

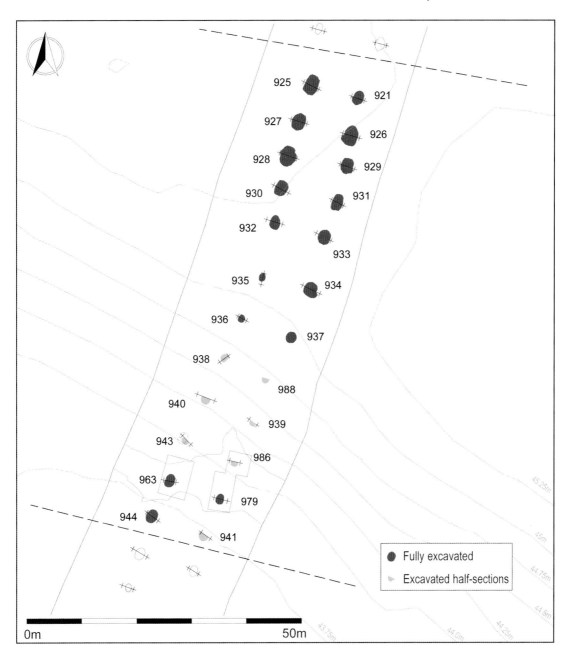

Fig 4.49   Plan of the central section of the double pit alignment

0.32m respectively (Fig 4.48). Neither produced good evidence for posts and may be more intact versions of the shallow features cut into the palaeochannel. The single fill of sandy silt in 911 certainly matches the contents of the latter, but 909 is altogether different, containing a basal deposit of soft clay, and unusually, a deposit of loose sand. The rest of these pits are steep or vertical-sided, 0.43–0.61m deep, and largely with U-shaped bases, the exceptions being 918/919 at the southern end of the section, which have flat bases. They all most likely held posts and had been immediately backfilled: they contain large cobbles, especially at their centres, 919 had a post-pipe 0.36m across at its base, and the fills of 910, 912, 913, and 915 had slumped inwards. Tertiary deposits probably resulted from the silting in of the depressed top of the pits or of infill into the void left by the decayed post.

After a larger gap of 9m the pit rows shift direction slightly southwards (Fig 4.41). This new alignment is shared by five closely spaced pairs of pits (925/921, 927/926, 928/929, 930/931, 932/933) – albeit with 929 and 931 marginally offset from the eastern row – running along a pronounced gravel ridge (Fig 4.49). These sub-circular or sub-oval features are substantial. They are 1.6–3.55m across at their tops, with an average size of 2.52m, and possess steep sides, flattish bases, and depths of 0.7–1.6m, with those in the eastern row generally being shallower than those in the western row (Figs 4.50 and 4.51). There is every indication they held timber uprights and had been immediately backfilled. Extensive use was made of cobbles for stone packing and nine out of the ten pits have post-pipes 0.46–0.85m across; the exception is 928, but even here the profile of its

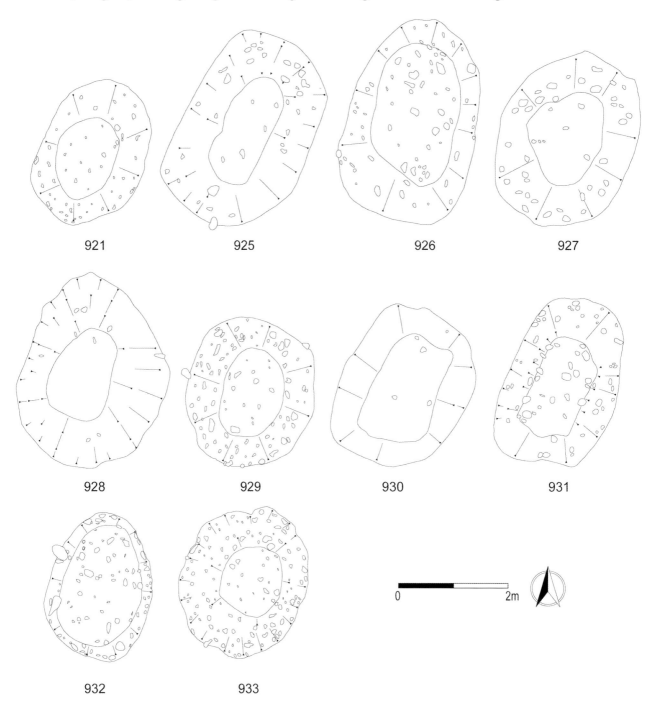

Fig 4.50   Plans of pits 921 and 925–33

initial fill and dense stone packing across the bottom of the pit indicates a post about 0.44m across. The backfill is normally of sandy silt, but also includes deposits of sand (921, 926) and silt (921, 925, 928). It appears that the backfilling of these large pits would have left shallow depressions in the ground surface, at least in 927 where it reached a depth of 0.25m. It was within the centre of this slight hollow, directly on the interface with the underlying backfill of 92704, that an irregular lens of *Corylus* charcoal and burnt shale, some 0.6m across and 30mm thick, was found. It produced statistically consistent (T'=0.8; T'(5%)=3.8; ν=1) replicate dates of 925–800 cal BC (OxA-11010) and 1000–825 cal BC (OxA-

11033) respectively. There is every possibility this is the remains of in situ burning, the implications of which will be discussed below.

South of these pits the ground slopes down sharply and the avenue starts again in a new more westerly direction after a gap of 9m (Fig 4.41). Continuing on this alignment until the south side of a second palaeochannel are seven pairs of pits (935/934, 936/937, 938/988, 940/939, 943/986, 963/979, 944/941), with 988 marginally off-line (Fig 4.49). These sub-oval and sub-circular features are most like the pits between the gravel ridge and the palaeochannel to the north, albeit a little larger at 0.74–2.5m across, their biggest at each end of the section. There are

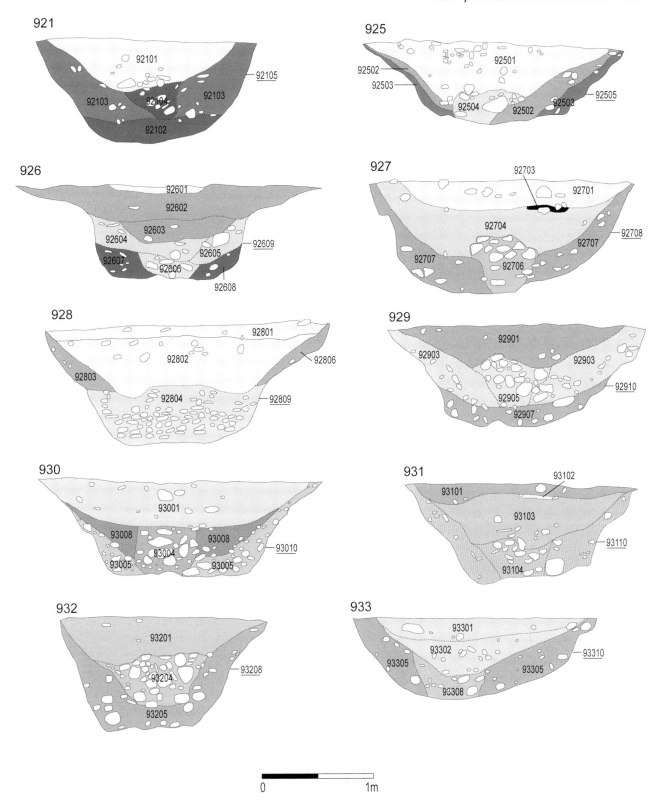

Fig 4.51 Sections of pits 921 and 925–33. See Fig 4.43 for deposit types

differences between them (Figs 4.52 and 4.53). At the northern end of this section are 935/934 and 936/937, with steep sides, depths of 0.47–0.79m, dense large cobbles at their centre, generally more complex fills, and in 935 a post-pipe 0.57m across. It is likely all four held timber uprights. They contrast with the other pits along this section which vary between 0.23m and 0.65m deep. Concentrations of large cobbles occur in the next two pairs, 938/988 and 939/940, but these are generally less steep-sided and shallower, whilst 940 and 988 possessed simple fills, all characteristics of the remaining pits to the south. Of these, 943/986 and 963/979 are basically bowl-shaped – three of these were cut into the pal-

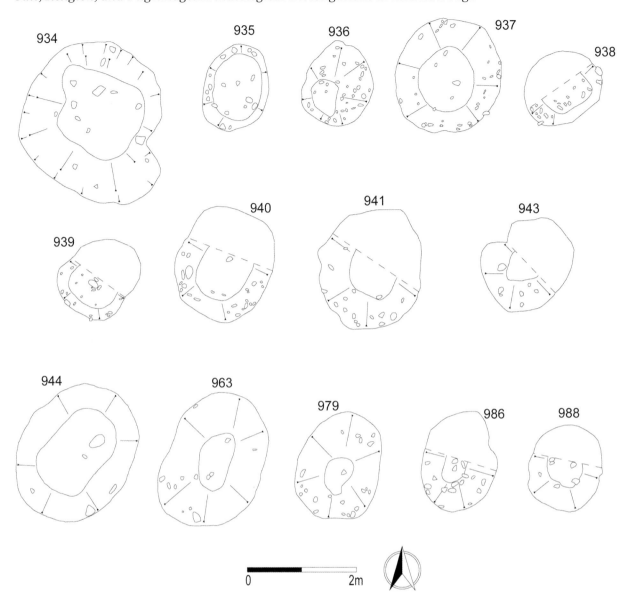

Fig 4.52   Plans of pits 934–41, 943–4, 963, 979, 986, and 988

aeochannel – but the end pair of 944/941 were much larger and deeper with straighter sides and flat bottoms. It is impossible to say which of these had originally held timber uprights, although it does seem likely for at least 941.

The rest of the monument continues on a new course after 944/941 (Fig 4.41). This section consists of sixteen pairs of excavated pits, 947/942, 949/945, 962/948, 977/955, 978/950, 952/951, 954/953, 956/957, 958/959, 960/961, 982/976, 964/965, 966/967, 968/969, 970/971, 972/973, whose general similarity matches their shared alignment (Fig 4.54). They occur across ground which is less steep than to the north of the monument and which gets flatter as you move south. The pits are largely sub-oval, 0.48–2.2m across, normally with moderately steep sides and either flat or shallow U-shaped bases, and depths of 0.08–0.73m (Figs 4.55 and 4.56). Many contain a single fill, more often than not of silt, and compared with elsewhere there are few cobbles. In these instances,

it is impossible to say with any certainty if they held wooden uprights, although their profile is often suggestive. Conversely, the shallowness of 976 and 965, next to each other along the eastern row, is taken to militate against the presence of posts. A smaller number of pits in this section of the monument had two or three fills, and some of these certainly possess what looks like stone packing or slumped fill. Yet with the exception of 973, which unambiguously had a 0.52m diameter post-pipe (from its north-facing section), none can be said with certainty to have held a timber. It is impossible to say if the six unexcavated features (980/974, 981/975, 987, 983) at the monument's southern end can be considered part of this section, given the lack of evidence about their appearance (the tops of these features are depicted in Fig 4.57), but they may possibly form a new, slightly more southerly, alignment which commenced with 972/973, the last and largest of the excavated pits along this section.

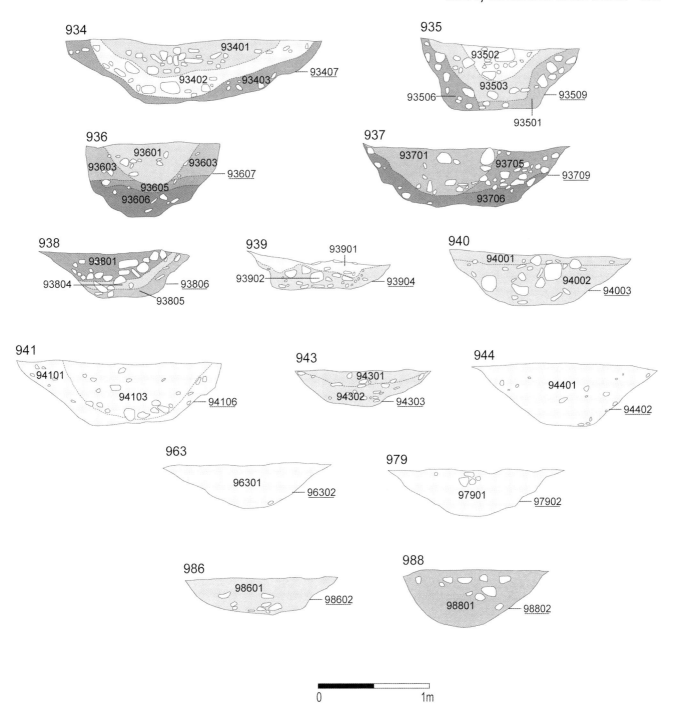

Fig 4.53   Sections of pits 934–41, 943–4, 963, 979, 986, and 988. See Fig 4.43 for deposit types

It is therefore apparent that the majority of pits along the northern half of the monument originally held posts, whilst this can only said with any certainty for one of the features along its southern half. It is difficult to account for this contrast: whilst those pits with posts are generally wider and deeper than those without (Fig 4.58), there is considerable overlap between their sizes, suggesting that both types may actually be part of a continuous single series. The entire monument may best be interpreted as a timber avenue – although whether its posts were freestanding or connected by fences is impossible to ascertain – with pit variation linked to changing topography, its

northern half on the southern slopes of the plateau, its southern half on the more gently sloping terrace. There would clearly have been variations in post size. The largest were inserted in 901/902 and 821/822 at the monument's northern end, which could have held uprights *c* 1m across, and the pits dug into the gravel ridge, which were up to 0.85m across. Elsewhere, the timbers may have been 0.5m or smaller in diameter, which compares closely with an average of 0.47m for the wider double pit alignment excavated in nearby Nosterfield Quarry (Dickson and Hopkinson 2011, 121), or with post diameters of 0.3–0.75m estimated for the much narrower double pit alignment at

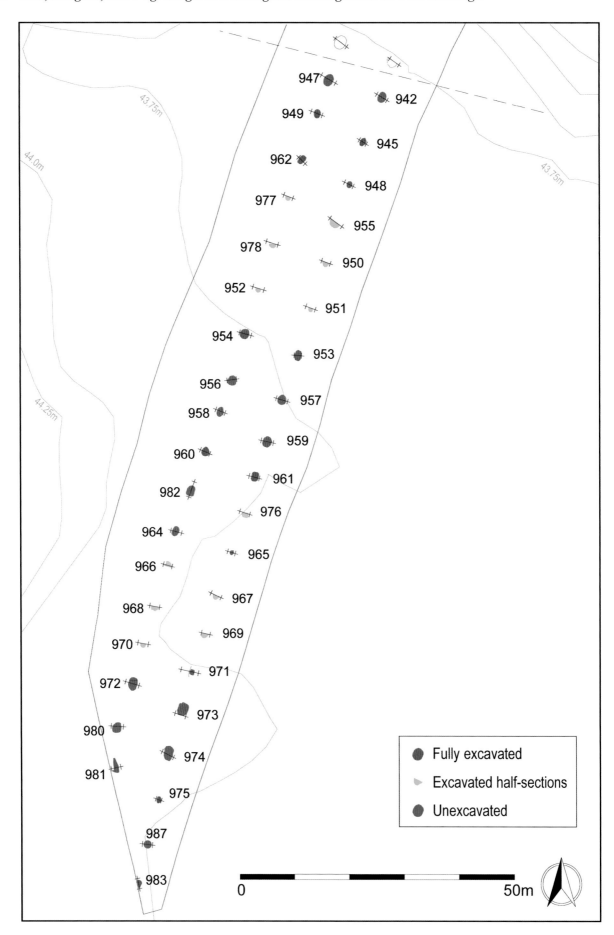

Fig 4.54   Plan of the southern section of the double pit alignment

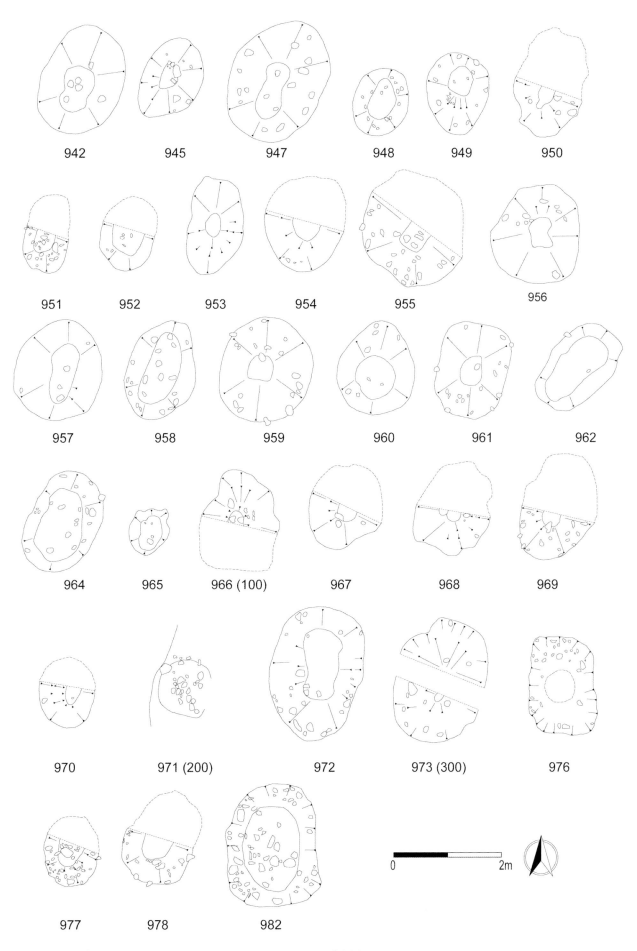

Fig 4.55 Plans of pits 942, 945, 947–62, 964–73, 976–8, and 982

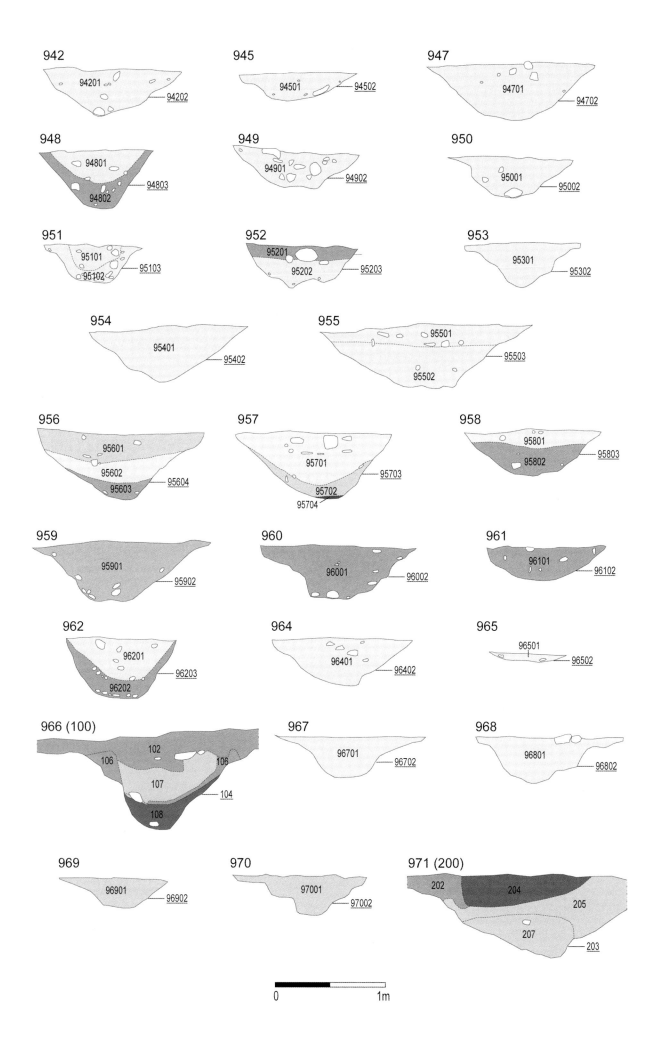

942
94201
94202

945
94501
94502

947
94701
94702

948
94801
94802
94803

949
94901
94902

950
95001
95002

951
95101
95102
95103

952
95201
95202
95203

953
95301
95302

954
95401
95402

955
95501
95502
95503

956
95601
95602
95603
95604

957
95701
95702
95703
95704

958
95801
95802
95803

959
95901
95902

960
96001
96002

961
96101
96102

962
96201
96202
96203

964
96401
96402

965
96501
96502

966 (100)
102
106
106
107
104
108

967
96701
96702

968
96801
96802

969
96901
96902

970
97001
97002

971 (200)
202
204
205
207
203

0   1m

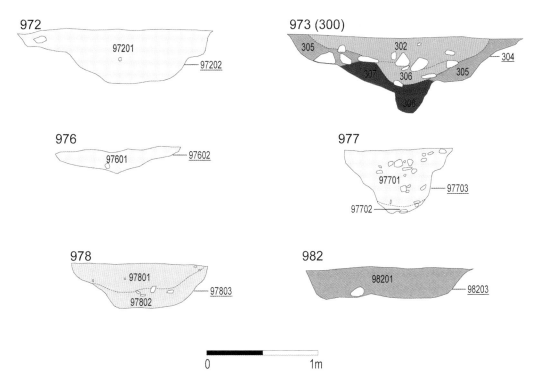

Fig 4.56 (above and left) Sections of pits 942, 945, 947–62, 964–73, 976–8, and 982. See Fig 4.43 for deposit types

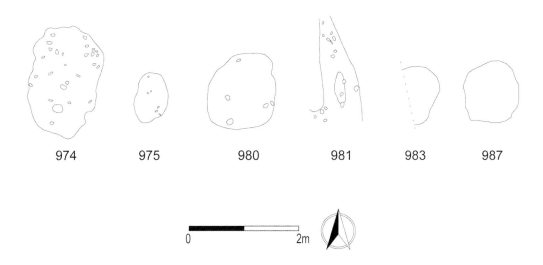

Fig 4.57 Plans of unexcavated pits

nearby Marton-le-Moor (Tavener 1996, 186). Gauging their height is even more problematic. If between a quarter and a third of each post was buried (see Miket 1981, 145), then the largest would have stood 3.2–4.8m above ground, with an average height along the northern half of the monument of 1.6–2.4m. As mentioned, some of the pits were definitely without timbers, all but two of which are opposite the gap, cut into the relict streambed. That this part of the monument did indeed look different is highlighted by the fact that by far the smallest pits which definitely held posts, 910 and 903, occurred at either end of this particular section.

The lack of naturally eroded material from the bottom of these pits suggests they were all immediately backfilled. Heavy tamping would be essential if the posts were to stay upright, and this could certainly account for the distinctiveness of some of the deposits in the bottom half of the pits, and the survival of post-pipes here. Higher in the fills, where the material had not been rammed and was consequently looser, they tended not to survive, their voids being filled by indistinguishable surrounding material. If tamping suggests the expertise of the builders, then more puzzling is the choice of material for backfilling. If the spoil just dug out had been used,

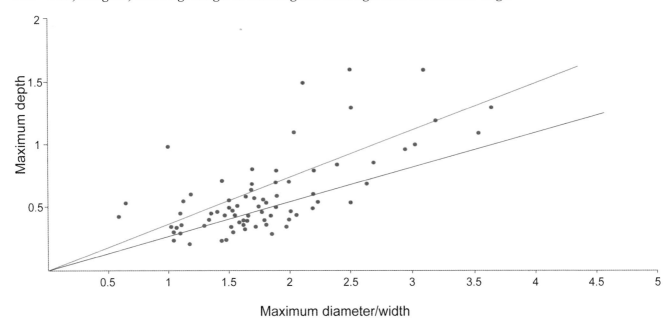

- pits with posts
- pits without definite evidence for posts

Fig 4.58   Comparative sizes of pits with posts and those where the presence of posts is uncertain. The 'pits without definite evidence for posts' category excludes 922, 923, 924 and any others unlikely to have held timbers

the lower portions of the fills would be dominated by gravelly sand, and indeed, such material makes an ideal backfill for posts. Yet only rarely was it found within the pits, their fills commonly consisting of sandy silts – albeit along with naturally occurring cobbles, regularly exploited as stone packing during the construction of the northern half of the monument – or pure silts, as in the majority of pits between the southernmost palaeochannel and the railway line (Fig 4.56). If these pits held posts, then the use of this backfill rather than the excavated sand appears wholly irrational: silty soils lose their structure once disturbed, and, as a consequence, are less likely to keep larger posts upright. This could suggest other less mundane motivations, and, in turn, could be connected to the presumed origin of a lot of backfill – the surrounding topsoil. The use of the latter would certainly correspond with the condition of the tiny amounts of *Quercus*, *Corylus*, and *Alnus* charcoal fragments discovered in the fills, the small size and abraded nature of these fragments implying they came from weathered surface or topsoil material incorporated into the pits. Equally curious is the incorporation of thin deposits of clay into the bottoms of 818, 820, and 909, on either side of the northernmost palaeochannel, which appears to be without practical benefits. One can only speculate whether ritual was dictating the use of these materials.

The fills produced only 68 worked lithics – consisting of 45 flakes, seven retouched pieces, seven pieces

of irregular waste, six blades, and three cores spread randomly throughout the fills of individual pits. The majority were found in those dug into the gravel ridge, including pit 930, which produced 23 worked pieces (Fig 4.59). Such locations were certainly favoured for occupation during the later Mesolithic (5.4), and indeed, some of the pits produced worked flint of this period: there was a complete edge-blunted point microlith of till flint from pit 927 (Fig 4.60, 1), and a little to the south of the gravel ridge in pit 936, the proximal fragment of a till flint bladelet. These two pieces are patinated, and this is also a trait of four other undiagnostic flints in pits from the gravel ridge (921, 926, 932, 933). All these pieces are undoubtedly residual, and supplemented by a larger number of later date, including the fragment of an edge-retouched till flake of Neolithic character in pit 933 (Fig 4.60, 2), and six complete till flakes reminiscent of later Neolithic industries from pits 925, 929, 927, 928, and 930. The pits from the gravel ridge also produced all but two of the 32 pieces of worked chert from the monument (Fig 4.59), this material constituting a relatively high percentage of the collection when compared to other excavated sites at Thornborough (Table D3.6). The largest cluster consisted of the twelve flakes and six pieces of irregular waste in pit 930, all of a pale yellow-brown chert, and these, along with a partially flaked single-platform flake core of the same material from adjacent 928 (Fig 4.60, 3), suggest the expedient knapping of local material on this gravel ridge. A

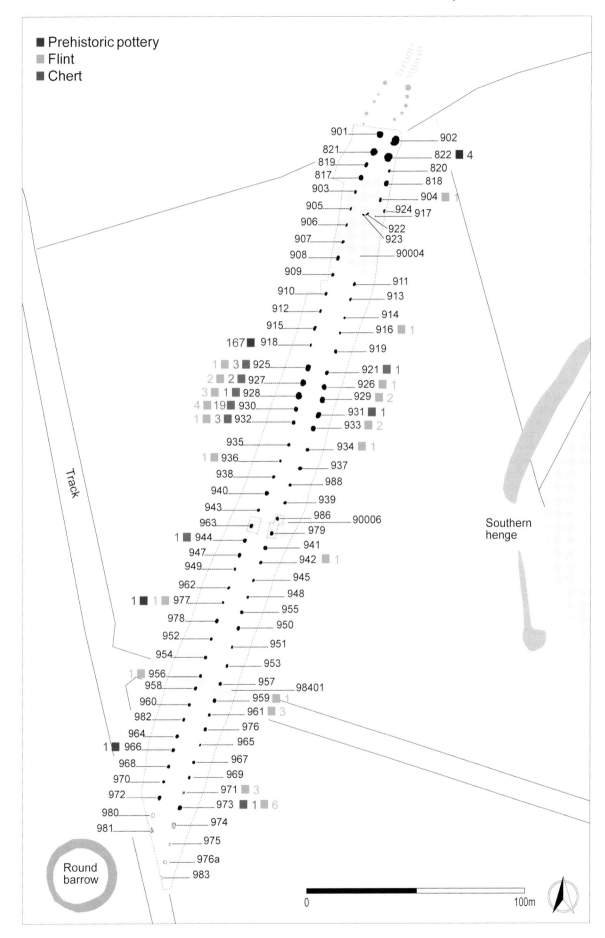

Fig 4.59   Distribution of prehistoric pottery and worked lithics from the double pit alignment.
© Crown Copyright / database right 2013. An Ordnance Survey / EDINA supplied service

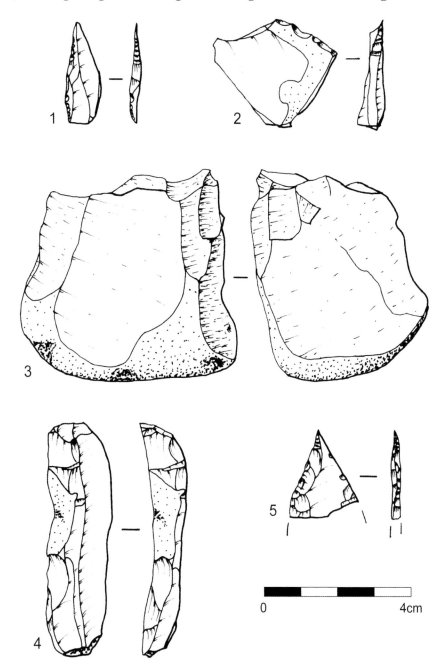

Fig 4.60   Selected lithics from the excavation of the double pit alignment: 1, pit 927, edge-blunted point microlith; 2, pit 933, fragmentary edge-retouched flake; 3, pit 928, single-platform chert core; 4, pit 977, long end scraper; 5, pit 973, fragmentary leaf arrowhead

crude and unclassifiable core of greenish-grey chert was found in pit 931.

Most of the very small number of lithics found in pits off the gravel ridge (Fig 4.59) were flakes, but pit 977 produced a complete long end scraper, manufactured on a cortical blade support of till flint (Fig 4.60, 4) and typical of pieces found in either Mesolithic assemblages or Peterborough Ware assemblages (eg Rudston, Corner Field Site 2: Manby 1975, 35, fig 7.14). Pit 973 produced two conjoining fragments of a leaf arrowhead, representing the tip and medial section of a very fine specimen of Green's (1980) class 3 B(r), manufactured on a fine-grained till flint (Fig 4.60, 5). The outline of the arrowhead

was formed by minimal marginal retouch and is almost of ogival form. Such fine pieces are found infrequently in this region and although few come from stratified contexts the known associations tend to be with burials associated with Towthorpe Ware (Manby 1980, 52). This arrowhead may also be residual, yet the breakage probably occurred after discard, and the fineness and relative intactness of the tip suggests it cannot have moved far from its original position of deposition or loss. Leaf arrowheads of ogival form are thought to have been deliberately manufactured as prestige goods (Green 1980, 85) and it has long been recognised that such pieces tend to have a relationship to monuments

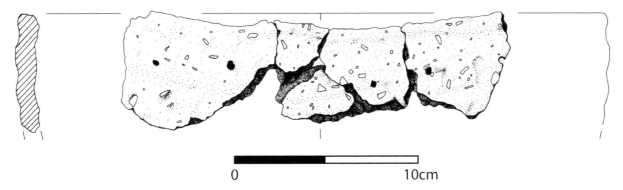

0   10cm

Fig 4.61   Rim sherds with jabbed impressions from the Middle Bronze Age vessel found in pit 918

(Thurnam 1867). The find is very delicate and strikingly similar to one excavated from a pit within a re-cut of the eastern ditch of the Rudston A cursus on the Yorkshire Wolds (Makey 1997). The similarities between the two pieces are so striking that both could have been manufactured by the same hand.

Despite the small number of diagnostic pieces, it appears that this collection is largely of later Neolithic date. This is certainly indicated by the size and shape of most of the flakes and other debitage, an impression reinforced by the lower incidence of linear and punctiform butts when compared with the collections from the triple-ditched round barrow, the gypsum pits, and Three Hills (Table D3.16). Yet there is no reason to assume that any of it was actually connected to the construction and use of the monument. This later material was mixed randomly with lithics of an earlier date, and there was an absence of anything demonstrably Beaker or later. It is therefore probable that most, if not all, was residual, as was the possible sherd of Neolithic pottery from pit 966 (see D4.1.2). The high tertiary flake element, complete absence of primary material, and low incidence of cores and irregular waste, suggests the collection came from a light multi-period background scatter, albeit one clustered on the gravel ridge, which was then incorporated into the pits when the surrounding soil was exploited as backfill, or subsequently by erosion and other factors into the depressions left by the rotting posts and collapsing fills. Such a low level of activity corresponds with the sterile nature of these deposits: the processing of bulk soil samples produced little charcoal (other than in 92703), just one charred cereal grain of possible barley (*Hordeum* sp), also in 927, and two charred rhizomes, in pits 929 and 979. It is no coincidence that two of these pits are found on the gravel ridge.

Prehistoric pottery was found in the upper fills of four pits (Fig 4.59). The single largest find comprised 167 sherds, weighing 2810g, from a single vessel in 91801. Its external surface varied from dark grey to grey-brown with some patches of buff-brown, and the internal surface was dark grey to mid-brown. Numerous medium (3–6mm) and many large (6–9mm) angular dolerite fragments were present within the fabric, along with a few small quartz grains, and mica grains within the clay matrix. Wall thickness was

10–12mm. The interior had a carbonised accretion to within 20mm of the rim, whilst the exterior had a carbonised accretion on only the uppermost 20mm of the vessel. The form of the vessel appeared to be a straight-sided or bucket-shaped jar. The plain rim, represented by 28 sherds weighing 655g, was near vertical and slightly in-turned, with a low, raised cordon 35mm wide on average and 2–3mm high at its centre below the rim exterior (Fig 4.61). A single row of impressed jabs, 25–33mm below the rim, 4–5mm in diameter, and 40–45mm apart, follow the line of the cordon. These extend almost through the wall of the vessel, but were clearly not intended to penetrate it, as in one instance where the wall was pierced a small amount of clay was luted to the internal surface. One rim sherd had two small patches of a shallow impression, possibly from a coarse rope or mat, probably a chance acquisition when the vessel was newly formed. The exact size of the vessel was difficult to establish given the lack of base and large body sherds, but the rim is likely to be between 300mm and 400mm across.

It belongs to a class of middle Bronze Age vessels, poorly represented in Yorkshire, which has a row of point decoration below the rim as a diagnostic trait (Longworth *et al* 1988, 41–9). Few good comparisons are known. From Flaxby, 22km south-east of Thornborough, was a shallow pit within which was a bucket urn with a pronounced raised cordon beneath a row of pierced holes (Addyman *et al* 1964, 187–90, fig 2). A pit cut into a round barrow at Ganton, on the Yorkshire Wolds, contained a barrel urn with a raised cordon below the rim interior, beneath which was a row of pierced holes (Kinnes and Longworth 1985, 42). The inner ditch of the 11th- and 10th-century BC enclosure at Paddock Hill, Thwing, also on the Yorkshire Wolds, contained bucket urn P39, which has a very similar style and decoration to the Thornborough vessel, though with a slightly more incurving rim (Manby 1988b; forthcoming). Parallels may also be found amongst the published ceramics from Mam Tor, Derbyshire (Challis and Harding 1975, figs 1.3 and 2.2). More generally, comparisons can be drawn with the large plain jars of so-called Green Knowe style, suggested to date from the late 2nd millennium BC in Northumberland and Scotland (Halliday 1985, 243–5). These are in bucket and barrel forms with simple rims, some having shallow raised cordons similar to that seen on the Thornborough vessel, although lacking the row of pierced holes. They are found on settlements and have been described as the domestic pottery of the period (Burgess 1995, 152), although they probably served a variety of functions.

The distribution of sherds within only the northern half of the upper pit fill of 918 is suggestive. As already described, the pot itself had been differentially fired, with some surfaces dark grey and others buff-brown, but during excavation this was mistakenly identified as two different fabrics, the first concentrated on the north-west side of the pit, the second on its north-east side. This observation indicates that either great care was taken with arranging sherds to represent a previously broken vessel, or alternatively, that the vessel was complete during deposition, then smashed, whether deliberately or as a result of post-depositional factors. The presence of rim sherds, but absence of base sherds, suggests the vessel was deposited inverted into the depression left by the rotted post, with the base and lower parts of the sides, along with the top of the pit, subsequently lost to ploughing. However, this would not explain why only around 20% of the rim was actually present, and hence it is most likely it was originally deposited against the post, then smashed with only some of the upper sherds from one side of the vessel subsequently eroding into the void left by the rotted timber. The carbonised accretion of likely foodstuffs from the pot's inner surface produced a radiocarbon date of 1300–1120 cal BC (Beta-337402; see D5), and it is assumed that this is the remains of cooking associated with the original act of deposition.

Other pits produced very little pottery. In fill 810 of pit 822 were four sherds from what is assumed to be a single vessel. They possess an internal, dark grey surface, a mid-brown external surface, a dark grey fabric with numerous small and medium dolerite grits, and a wall thickness which varied between 10mm and 13mm. A single sherd had traces of impressed cord decoration. The vessel is thought to be of early to middle Bronze Age date. The only other ceramic, from 97701, is more likely to belong to the latter part of this horizon. It consists of a single highly fired rim or edge piece with mid-grey surfaces and fabric, numerous small, and a few large, angular and rounded cavities in the light and porous fabric, and a typical wall thickness of 20mm. The cavities indicate the former presence of grits, now leached or burnt out, and the imprint of a sea shell and a fossil crinoid suggest the grit was limestone. Also present in the clay matrix are mica dust and a small fragment of quartz. There appears to be traces of moulded rib decoration on the exterior.

4.7.3 Discussion

Double pit alignments have been discovered elsewhere (Waddington 1997). Apart from Thornborough, which could be the longest yet recorded, five others are known from the area. Nearby in Nosterfield Quarry, excavations revealed an impressive double alignment, its seventeen pits 1.45–3.02m across and 0.92–2.4m deep (Dickson and Hopkinson 2011, 119–25). Whilst undated, its layout in relation to the complex, and impressive width of 21–27m, could suggest a role as an avenue to and from the northern henge (see 5.5). Less than 3km to the south-east of Hutton Moor and Cana Barn was a slightly curving double pit alignment, its 65 postholes 0.65–1.4m in diameter and 0.6–1.8m deep, forming two closely spaced and parallel rows only 1.8–2.7m apart (Tavener 1996, 184–5). It produced a range of mid-3rd-millennium BC radiocarbon dates (Abramson 2003). Tavener (1996, 186) also notes two similar sites found during excavations *c* 200m to the west of the Devil's Arrows further downstream at Boroughbridge, and yet another was recently discovered at Hollow Banks, Scorton (Greg Speed, pers comm); the former produced Grooved Ware pottery and the dates of 3030–2570 cal BC (RCD-1596) and 3350–2600 cal BC (RCD-1597), the latter a date of 2200–1890 cal BC from what may be residual charcoal. Notable examples further afield include the unexcavated 'segmented embanked pit-alignments' of the North York Moors, their pits between parallel banks and tangentially aligned on burial mounds (Lofthouse 1993; see also Vyner 1995); the two irregular but parallel alignments at Heslerton, Yorkshire, which seem to have held posts and been of later Neolithic date (Powlesland 1986, 65–75); the final Neolithic 'avenue' of paired timber posts close to the Milfield North henge, Northumberland (Harding 1981); and the excavated alignment at Ogden Down, Dorset, where two closely spaced rows of posts were built towards the end of the 2nd millennium BC (Green 2000, 113–16, pls 19–20). Taken together, this evidence indicates that double pit alignments are a phenomenon spanning the later Neolithic and Bronze Age (Waddington 1997, 29, table 1) and may often have held posts; as such, they were extended versions of the entrance 'avenues' at many earlier and broadly contemporary monuments, such as the large later Neolithic posts discovered leading into the enclosure at Forteviot, Perthshire (Noble 2009, 230–1). The alignment at Ogden Down connected two ring ditches, built much earlier in the later Neolithic but subsequently reused for the insertion of at least one cremation, suggesting its use as a procession-way for both the living and the dead.

The date of 1750–1525 cal BC from the post-pipe at Thornborough broadly accords with the monument's tangential association with two round barrows (3.3.3). Centre Hill, at its northernmost end, was excavated by the Revd W C Lukis in 1864. Under the middle of the mound, and presumably its primary burial, was a coffin, 'the remains of which, reduced to dust, were very discernible' (Lukis 1870b, 119). Within it were found small fragments of unburnt bone, a large flake 'elaborately chipped to a sharp edge' (*ibid*, 126, pl III) – which could be an irregular scale-flaked knife, on the same spectrum as more regularly and fully flaked plano-convex knives (Frances Healy, pers comm) – and about half of a food vessel or what was described as a 'rudely ornamented jar … of coarse earthenware, on its side, empty, and much injured by moisture and the pressure of the superincumbent earth' (*ibid*, 119, pl II). Subsequently restored, the food vessel has been described by Stuart Needham (pers comm) as 155mm high, 175mm in diameter at the mouth and 180mm at the shoulder, with a slightly sandy fabric with grog and surface colour red to buff. Its decoration is continuous from its insloping bevel to just below the shoulder, comprising poorly organised rows of rough stab marks made with a sharp point. It possesses a slightly pinched out shoulder and thick rim with flattened external lip. The coffin, and gypsum-lined pit in which it was placed (4.3.3), are clearly unusual, but food vessels are often found in the region's barrows, as at nearby Quernhow, where three were found with cremations and a further two unaccompanied by burials (Waterman 1951). They are generally thought to date to 2050–1700 BC (Needham 1996; Manby *et al* 2003, 61, 64), partly overlapping with the radiocarbon date above. Secondary cremations may also have been deposited at this monument. Leeds Museum possesses several hundred very small fragments of unidentified cremated bone, along with a chip of possible ochre and five burnt pebbles, from a barrow 'between the two Thornborough Rings', donated by Edwin Kitson Clark in 1927–28 (Katherine Baxter, pers comm). There is also a record of 'large bones' of a 'woman between 20 and 30' which were sent to the Leeds School of Anatomy. Centre Hill is the only site which fits this description, although Lukis makes no mention of cremations. If they are from here, they were presumably found later by someone else.

However, the double pit alignment is probably not as early as the Centre Hill barrow. The middle Bronze Age pottery vessel from pit 918 was most likely placed against a standing post, its dated burnt foodstuffs contemporary with this event. This means the monument was certainly in use between 1300 cal BC and 1120 cal BC. The discrepancy between this and the earlier radiocarbon date could be explained if the monument developed intermittently, its earliest section being the northern end near the Centre Hill barrow, but the chronological difference seems too lengthy for such a cogently planned monument. Hence, the double pit alignment is regarded as a single-phase avenue constructed and used in the middle Bronze Age, with the oak charcoal producing the earlier date either residual, or if originally from the post, part of a tree which lived many centuries before the timber was inserted into the ground. By implication, the small quantity of potentially early Bronze Age pottery in pit 822 was also residual. That this is a middle Bronze Age monument is supported by the autoduplicate dates of 925–800 cal BC and 1000–825 cal BC from the in situ burning in pit 927. Previous accounts had recorded this thin spread of charcoal as coming from the bottom of a recut, and indeed, it was believed many of the pits had been dug

into in an attempt to extract the posts and decommission the monument. However, these 'recuts' were surprisingly regular and absent from some of the larger pits. Closer scrutiny suggests that their identification had been confused with the way in which these features were backfilled and with the subsequent infilling of voids or depressions. The burning in 927 was compacted into the top of the underlying material, suggesting its deposition after the standing post had rotted and any resulting void been infilled – a process presumably taking no longer than *c* 200 years – but before the depression left by the pit had completely disappeared. Its early 1st-millennium date would certainly accord with the monument's use in the 12th and 11th centuries BC.

This was a carefully constructed monument employing shifts in orientation, differences in post size, and subtle changes in topography to vary the experiences of those moving along its course (Fig 4.62). Architecture and landscape seem deliberately fused together, perhaps to create a narrative or story. Its northern end, with what appear to be the alignment's largest timber uprights, sits on the southern edge of the plateau at a height of 45.25m OD, and its unexcavated section would have been marginally higher at 45.5m OD. That this was the most elevated part of the monument emphasised its terminal location around 35m from the Centre Hill barrow sited up-slope; if the mound of the latter (3.3.3) was already built when the alignment was in use, this juxtaposition must have been visually striking. The double pit alignment is narrowest at the northern end – to the extent that any movement between the posts is unlikely to have been more than three abreast – then appears to widen again outside the excavated area, finally terminating in two groups of nine closely set and narrow parallel trenches each about 3m long and 2.5m apart on either side of a 1.7m wide central gap. This distinctive feature, located close to the axis of the southern henge, may originally have held parallel posts or fences (3.3.4). It is of unknown function, but may be paralleled by a very similar arrangement to the north of the central henge (3.3.2). Whatever its exact role and appearance, it must have orchestrated the experience of anyone moving along the interior, even perhaps invoking a claustrophobia which contrasted with the vista enjoyed at the Centre Hill barrow, with its views across the river terrace to the south and south-west and the central henge to the north.

Variations elsewhere along the alignment's course correspond just as closely with local topography (Fig 4.62). Immediately to the south of its northern end it again shifts direction as the ground slopes down to a basin at 44.5m OD, and here its gap, and surrounding pits which seemingly lack substantial uprights, could have been deliberately designed to connect the monument's users with its immediate setting, and more specifically, the nearby henge. Outside of the western row of pits, by contrast, the ground slopes up, minimising contact with the surrounding landscape. As the ground rises again to the south there is evidence

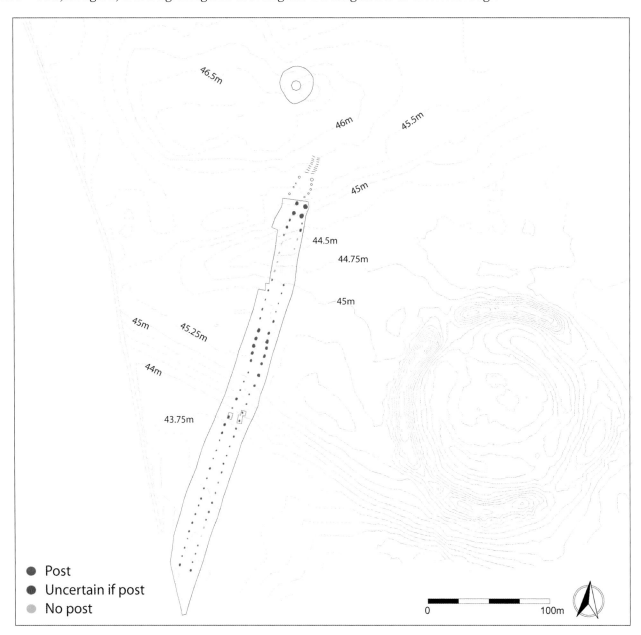

Fig 4.62   Interpretative plan of the double pit alignment and topography

of standing posts, and atop the gravel ridge at 45.25m OD, the alignment once more shifts course. This is the second highest point along the monument and it is surely no coincidence that it was on this rise that large posts were again used. They must have been an impressive sight, especially looking from the south, where the monument runs along the lower-lying and flatter river terrace. Irrespective of whether people were moving from north to south, or south to north, this ridge clearly represents an important point in its course – indeed, it is perhaps no coincidence that the monuments to the south and the north of the gravel ridge are not clearly inter-visible with each other. At the southern edge of the ridge the monument makes its most pronounced change of direction before running down a relatively abrupt break of slope on to the river terrace. At around 43.75m OD, after the second palaeochannel, there is the final change of direction, and it now runs across relatively flat ground adjacent to the unexplored round barrow. Only further fieldwork will ascertain if it ends there or continues further along the terrace.

4.8   Three Hills round barrow *by Jan Harding and Benjamin Johnson*

4.8.1 Introduction

The Three Hills Barrow Group appeared very badly damaged, and as part of the ALSF Project, THBG2 or what was previously known as 'Three Hills Centre', the northernmost and worst-preserved of the barrows, was chosen for evaluative excavation (2.5 and 3.3.3). This site had been previously excavated by the Revd W C Lukis in 1864 when it still survived as an earthwork (Lukis 1870b); no topographic trace was found by survey, however, and it existed as barely dis-

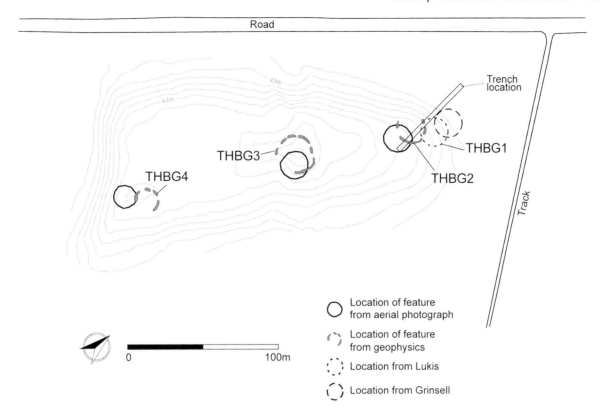

Fig 4.63 Excavation at the Three Hills Barrow Group (THBG)

cernible geophysical anomalies of its incomplete ditch and some possible internal features (Fig 3.25, 1). The evaluation in August 2003 consisted of an excavation trench 60m long and 3m wide, located to sample the barrow ditch and continue across a palaeochannel to the north which surrounds much of the Three Hills gravel ridge (Fig 4.63). Topsoil and the palaeochannel were stripped by machine and the remainder excavated by hand with all spoil sieved.

4.8.2 Excavation results

The excavation revealed two segments of the barrow's ditch, on its northern and southern sides, and downslope of this, a horizon of redeposited material and the palaeochannel. No internal features or intact mound material was found. A small and unremarkable collection of 65 worked lithics, including a fragment of what may be a knife, came largely from the redeposited context. The lithics are summarised in Tables D3.6, D3.9, D3.13, D3.16, D3.20, and D3.22. The excavation by Lukis found 'a few fragments of pottery … layers of grey and ferruginous clay, and a circular cist two feet in diameter and eighteen inches deep, filled with burnt bones and charcoal' (Lukis 1870b, 120).

Plough-disturbed horizon

The location of THBG2, across the break of slope on the northern edge of the gravel ridge (Fig 4.63), made it vulnerable to the plough. The excavation of the topsoil, 001, a deposit with a depth of 0.21–0.40m, exposed subsoil whose patchy distribution is telling. At the southern end of the trench, closest to the summit of the ridge, was 006, a brown subsoil 0.34m thick with pockets of clay and medium-sized cobbles. It got gradually shallower, disappearing completely within the barrow's interior (Fig 4.64). Between the latter and the northernmost ditch segment the ploughsoil sits directly on top of the natural gravel (005). The subsoil reappears the other side of the barrow as 002, a loose dark yellowish-brown silty gravel, which, despite lacking a stratigraphic relationship to the monument, is interpreted as a mixed horizon of barrow material, subsoil, and old ploughsoil redeposited downslope by plough action. Its thickness varies greatly, but at most is only 0.18m. It extends for *c* 14.5m downslope of the monument, disappearing as the ground levels off. From this point on lies the palaeochannel (see below).

Gravel 002 produced the majority of finds from the trench. There was modern pottery and glass, a few tiny fragments of unidentified cremated bone, a large number of charcoal fragments, and 58 pieces of worked flint and chert. The lithics consisted of one core fragment, two core rejuvenation flakes, twelve pieces of irregular waste, 29 flakes, and ten blades. There were also four retouched pieces, three of which were miscellaneous retouched flakes, the only diagnostic from the entire collection being the proximal fragment of what would have been a large till flint knife of possible later Neolithic date. Despite this, the collection shares many traits with

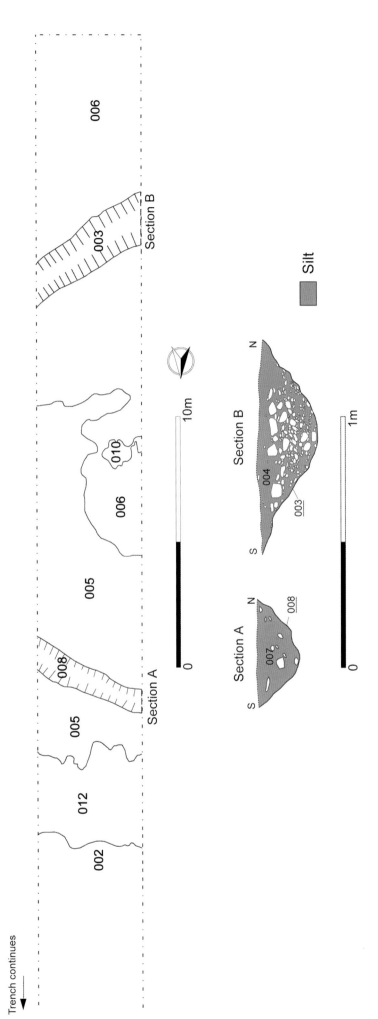

Fig 4.64 Plan and sections of THBG2

the Mesolithic and earlier Neolithic material from the triple-ditched round barrow (4.2). It possesses a significant element of controlled blade production, directly evidenced by the relatively high number of blades, indirectly by cognate knapping practices seen in punctiform and linear flake butts, with diffuse bulbs of percussion and feather terminations. Also, the retouch on a complete flake of till flint resembles that seen on microliths. Hence the collection may have belonged to two distinct periods, and even two distinct types of activity, with its largest element being Mesolithic or earlier Neolithic, the residues perhaps of a short-term camp site. There was a fragment of an exceptionally large flake from the exterior of an elongated, rounded nodule of brown flint, corresponding to descriptions of the till flint on Flamborough Head (eg Manby 1974, 83). The large size, dark colour, and thick cortex of a fragmentary core rejuvenation flake and a fragmentary crested flake would be compatible with a source on the southern English Chalk.

Barrow ditch

The two segments of barrow ditch were presumed to be part of the same feature, but recorded separately, as 003, to the south and on the ridge summit, and 008, around 0.5m lower to the north (Fig 4.64). The southernmost segment was more substantial, its truncated top as much as 1.7m wide, whilst that to the north, on the slope, was only 0.8m wide at its top. These features had irregular sides and a shallow U-shaped profile, their southern and northern sections 0.8m and 0.4m deep respectively. They were filled by 004 and 007, a loose strong brown silt with gravel, and medium and large cobbles which closely resemble those from the nearby palaeochannel. The density of stone along the centre of the fill's bottom half suggests deliberate backfilling, followed by natural silting with what are most likely wind-blown deposits. The smaller dimensions of the downslope ditch segment certainly reflects the impact of the plough beyond the crest of the ridge, and its edges were diffuse and its fill more disturbed, yet differences in the profile of these two segments suggest this feature may have originally varied in appearance. The ditch enclosed an area 16.9m across, close to Grinsell's 1952 description of the earthwork mound as 18.3m across and 0.3m high (Thomas 1955, appendix II). Inside it was empty apart from 010, initially thought to be remains of Lukis's robber trench. On excavation this irregular feature, 1.3m long, 0.9m wide, with an irregular base around 0.1m deep, was thought to be natural. It contained a loose fill of yellow silt.

The only finds were seven worked lithics from the southern ditch segment (004). Four flakes of grey chert, of which three were complete, may suggest the exploitation of material possibly discovered during the digging of the ditch, and may, therefore, be contemporary with the barrow – indeed, two chert cobbles were found in the bottom of the ditch. Three

of these flakes belonged to the primary or secondary stages of reduction. Also found in the ditch was a flint chip, perhaps from retouch or from the edge of a core platform, another flint chip, possibly a Janus flake, and a fragment of a flint flake. It is impossible to say whether these were also contemporary with the barrow or a residual component of the Mesolithic and earlier Neolithic occupation represented in the plough-disturbed horizon. Bulk soil samples of 004 and 007 produced a very small fragment of burnt mammal bone and a charred barley grain respectively. There were also occasional land snail shells of various species found in a variety of different habitats.

Palaeochannel

Immediately outside the northern ditch segment was 012, a loose yellowish-brown silty sand 0.31–0.46m thick and overlying the natural gravel (Fig 4.64). It extended for 23m along the trench, largely under 002. To the north it overlay 011, the palaeochannel, and may therefore be a related riverine deposit. The palaeochannel extended 13m across the northern end of the trench. It was only between 0.10 and 0.24m deep, comprising a loose brownish-yellow gravelly silt with pebbles and cobbles. It was unsuitable for the preservation of palaeoenvironmental material, but is likely to be many millennia earlier than the barrow given its location high on the gravel terrace and its relationship to the Three Hills ridge.

4.8.3   *Discussion*

The excavation results highlight the potential significance of the Three Hills gravel ridge for occupation and the possibility that it had been intermittently settled from as early as the Mesolithic or earliest Neolithic. This preference for raised areas has been identified elsewhere across the terrace and will be more fully explored in the next chapter. As will be discussed, these places often witnessed monument building, and this was especially the case with the construction of the linear cemetery of four barrows here during the early Bronze Age, at what was surely one of the most physically obvious of these locations. They must have been an impressive sight. It is not clear from Lukis's cursory description if his clay layers, sealing a pit approximately 0.6m in diameter, 0.45m in depth, and filled with charcoal and burnt bone, were at the centre of the barrow. This does seem likely, however, given their similarity to what he found 'At a depth of about six inches from the apex' (Lukis 1870b, 120, pl V) of nearby THBG1. If this is correct, his robber trench was most probably located immediately to the west of this more recent excavation. It is impossible to say if the pit discovered by Lukis, or any other internal features, still survive. The excavated ditch fill raises the possibility that the site was remodelled, a common characteristic of early Bronze Age round barrows, but it is impossible to verify this without new evidence. Whilst the evaluation of THBG2 failed to locate stratified material culture, it does suggest that the intensively ploughed terrace still contains significant archaeological deposits, and as such, highlights the potential of THBG3, which appears to be the best-preserved Three Hills barrow.

4.9   Themes in the development of the monument complex

There is every chance that the triple-ditched round barrow was a 'founder monument'. In use early in the 4th millennium BC, it could have played a role in bringing about the development of a 'new' Neolithic society. Its siting at a place of earlier sporadic and short-term knapping was surely deliberate – as at the comparable monument of Grindale 1 in eastern Yorkshire (Manby 1980, 24, 31, 33) – this veneration of an earlier place invoking familiarity, and hence, offering a thread of continuity between past and present generations. Yet from the outset what was undertaken here surely possessed the qualities of strangeness, originality, and novelty: the creation of a small gypsum-lined pit, the insertion of body parts from different individuals, and the digging of an encircling ditch and building of a mound, brought a small group of people together to experiment with new possibilities and transformative potentials. Whilst of only limited scale and duration, this initial manipulation of the dead, and of a mineral originally from deep in the ground whose colour resembled clean human bone (see 6.3), made these activities physically arresting and intellectually poignant. Sacred 'double mediation' was at play here (1.3), drawing people into repeated conversations about their changing world as they returned, deposited further excarnated body parts, and on two occasions rebuilt the site. There is no reason to consider this as anything other than the acts of a few families, but the outcome was monumental all the same. The final mound, as much as 18m across and capped by large pale grey cobbles, must have been impressive, its location on a ridge possibly making it highly visible from across the terrace and the southern half of the plateau. The result was a public symbol whose history may have united, and indeed, divided, families.

The triple-ditched round barrow was probably out of use by the second half of the 4th millennium BC, and if so, the abandonment may be broadly contemporary with other changes in Britain (eg Harding and Healy 2007, 90, 110–11). This is certainly around the time of the earliest ditched cursuses (Barclay and Bayliss 1999; Thomas *et al* 2009), and whilst the one constructed at Thornborough is undated there is no reason to doubt it too belongs to the period around 3600–3200 BC. It is impossible to say if its building overlapped with the use of the triple-ditched round barrow, if it was built immediately after the latter's abandonment, or if there was a hiatus between the two. There is every reason, however, for regarding the building of the cursus, and any related sites like the oval enclosure, as a new beginning. To build it would have certainly involved communal effort – Loveday (2006, 145) has recently calculated that it would have taken 5747 labour hours, or the equivalent of 100 men working 10-hour days for 6 days, just to dig its ditch – even if lack of knowledge about population makes it impossible to gauge whether this proved a challenge to its creators. What is more important, perhaps, is that the building of the cursus saw the monumentalisation of the plateau. By carefully positioning an earthwork stretching 1.2km or more along its central and highest point, the builders were effectively creating a level of order and alignment across what was a neatly bounded narrow neck of land, perhaps even formally demarcating a corridor or pathway only visited on certain social occasions (see Harding 1999; Last 1999; Tilley 1994, chapter 5). Much has been made of the slight size and episodic construction of cursus ditches and banks (Barclay *et al* 2003, 240; Loveday 1999, 56–7; Pryor *et al* 1985, 232; Whittle *et al* 1992, 196), and Thornborough may be no exception, its modest earthworks (see 2.4) twice shifting direction along the most elevated section of plateau before reaching the village of Thornborough. Excavation also points towards its intermittent development or embellishment: Vatcher (1960, 178) notes how at least one section of its ditch may have been deliberately backfilled, and the above provides evidence for an admittedly undated sequence of possible inner structures, the earliest of which may be a dug feature at the centre of the site. Nonetheless, its very deliberate siting suggests an overarching intention behind the monumentality. It was physically striking when first built, especially if the layer or platform of sand continued for some distance along its centre, and was surely seen as both an achievement and a radical statement.

Hence, the cursus, irrespective of its size, and whether it was built gradually or on a single occasion, could have been an attempt to bring into being new relationships and forms of identity. If so, this may have been partly achieved through what was happening within it. Its early dug features, deliberately deposited layers of sand and gravel, modest posts and stakes, and tiny stone circles suggest that, if indeed contemporary, a complex aesthetic or sacred experience was being fashioned across the cursus interior – and they all suggest something quite intimate. These features could only be appreciated by those within their immediate vicinity and it is tempting to see their scale and irregularity as a product of individuals or small groups completing private acts of symbolic expression, whether it be inserting small wooden uprights, pressing down small stones to form an arc or circle, or gathering within the narrow space formed by the two rows of posts. It remains to be seen if similar acts were completed along the entire length of the cursus, and Vatcher's earlier excavations found nothing inside its flanking earthworks other than an undated crouched inhumation (2.4), although the removal of topsoil by the quarry owners would have probably destroyed any features. What was discovered by the more recent excavations reported here, however, indicates that whilst cursuses may have brought into being extensive ritually charged spaces which drew upon and went some way to structure the wider landscape (Barrett *et al* 1991, 58; Harding 1999; Loveday 2006, 124ff; Tilley 1994, 173–200), they also created arenas for the types of congregation and experience associated with very much smaller monuments; and at such a level of interaction, there is always room for expedient reinvention or playful innovation. New meaning may therefore have been generated through the practice of using, altering, or adding to this enclosure.

Cursuses are often linked spatially with burial monuments and may have played a role in funerary practice (eg Bradley 1991, 36–58; Loveday 2006; Tilley 1994, 170–200). If so, this engagement with – and manipulation of – ancestry could be integral to the development of new and larger socio-political identities (Harding 1995). The fact that there are only two barrows or enclosures of possibly broadly contemporary date from around Thornborough's cursus may be both genuine and revealing, adding to the impression that its construction represented a new beginning across a part of the landscape which had hitherto been little used, and which, according to the results of Vatcher's investigation, was at the time a 'deciduous forest environment' (1960, 171). That the cursus fails to reference the existing Neolithic round barrow spatially is perhaps telling. More fieldwork is certainly necessary, especially at the oval enclosure and the comparable site recently discovered by aerial photography (3.3.4), but the impression is of a cursus built across a part of the landscape not directly linked with the ancestral remains of individual groups, a landscape which was largely socially neutral or even liminal. Indeed, that the excavations within the cursus and oval enclosure failed to produce collections of earlier flint, in striking contrast to the triple-ditched round barrow, is perhaps testament to this. Its construction, then, was not some statement of territorial intent, with it being built at the heart of a landscape littered with ancestral remains, but rather an experiment in forging new relationships and identities. Given this, it would hardly be surprising if people needed to reassert and even perhaps reinvent themselves and their alliances through subsequent acts of building.

Were the same socio-political organisations, relationships, and alliances responsible for the construction of the later henges, or were these the product of something completely different? Continuity between the builders of these middle Neolithic and later Neolithic monuments may certainly be indicated by the central henge's location over

the widest section of the cursus at the very point where it shifts course slightly; that this was done deliberately and with precision is indicated by the latter's northern flanking ditch neatly delimiting the henge's southernmost entrance and the fact that the distance between the outer lip of both henge ditches is the same as the width of the cursus. This certainly suggests some form of symbolic geometry or planning whereby it was necessary for the layout of the earlier enclosure to be drawn into the design of the new monument, and that of the other two henges. Whilst it is known that the earlier cursus ditch had more or less fully silted long before the construction of the inner henge bank (Cornwall 1953, 145; Thomas 1955, 432), it is possible that the older monument was still visible through its flanking banks and any central platform or mound. If so, the relationship was not just a matter of social memory or folklore, but actually involved an intense physical connectivity, emphasising the social relationships linking generations. Indeed, it is even possible that the henge builders actually had to shift these earlier earthworks, conceivably accounting for the dumping of cobbles and sandy silt in the bottom of part of the freshly dug outer ditch, labour perhaps akin to an act of remembrance. Yet despite such hints of continuity, these circular monuments, with their radically different design, were built some considerable time after the cursus had fallen out of use (2.4), and moreover, were sited on a shared axis at right angles to the cursus. That this new enclosure cut across and manipulated the power of this earlier monument must have been apparent to its builders, and as such, their activity was not so much a reinstatement of existing structures, or the conscious commemoration of earlier meanings, as a subversion or radical reinterpretation of the complex and the social relations with which it was associated.

Such redesign is unsurprising if the henges were the manifestation of a new religion which took hold across Britain during the later Neolithic and which represented a profound break with the past (Harding 2003). It is even more understandable if we consider that their building indicates a major escalation in monumentality across the plateau, and therefore, a likely increase in the amount of labour coalescing for this purpose. It was calculated by Griffiths and Timms (2005) that each of the Thornborough henges involved the excavation and movement of 'approximately 27,000 cubic metres of earth and gravel'. If we follow Startin (1982, 153), who gives a figure of 0.68m^3 per hour for a team of picker, shoveller, and carrier working on gravel, then each henge would have taken at least 119,118 labour hours to build, an amount 21 times greater than Loveday estimated for digging the ditch of the entire cursus (see above). Of course, the henges would have placed an even greater demand on their builders if the banks had been coated in gypsum, as indeed does seem likely (2.4 and 6.3). Irrespective of the exact figures, we appear to be dealing with a hugely significant increase in the amount of committed labour, and probably in the numbers of people coming together across the plateau. Hence, the henges may be closely connected not only to a new world view, but to other changes in the socio-political geography of the Thornborough landscape and surrounding areas. This building project may have even been the means by which new organisations, relationships, and alliances came about, for, as discussed in Chapter 1, the mobilisation of large amounts of labour is responsible for generating novel institutions and systems of power in the first place.

Central to these issues is the question of when the henges were constructed, and more specifically, whether they developed gradually or were the product of a single large-scale building project. It has been suggested that double-ditched henges occurred late in the currency of these monuments (Whittle *et al* 1992, 191–2), a conclusion based largely on the two radiocarbon dates of 2279–2031 cal BC (HAR-3064) and 2199–1920 cal BC (HAR-3067) from the lower secondary silts of the inner ditch of Condicote, Gloucestershire, one of only two such sites found outside Yorkshire. The implications of their late development would be significant for Thornborough, for it means a lengthy interval after the abandonment of the cursus when there was no actively used ceremonial monument. Yet the excavation of the Ferrybridge henge, located some 58km away in West Yorkshire, suggests an earlier origin for these double-ditched henges, with the inner ditch and an initial bank 'probably constructed around 3000 BC', and additional upcast material, derived from a shallower outer ditch, being added 'at some time in the 3rd millennium BC' (Roberts *et al* 2005, 235). Here there is a complex sequence, with discrete episodes for each of these phases, and at least one hiatus lasting several decades (*ibid*, 234) – and as its report suggests for the heaps of earth recorded in the bank section by Thomas, 'it is conceivable that a similar staged construction might have occurred for Thornborough's central henge' (Roberts *et al* 2005, 235). The same may well be demonstrated at nearby Nunwick by the 'traces of tip-lines and the interleaving of loads' discovered during the 1961 excavation of its surviving henge bank (Dymond 1963, 100, fig 3). Gradual and punctuated development would certainly fit with henges being intrinsic to the emergence of new socio-political relationships (Harding 2012), rather than the product of a society which had already changed.

Reconstructing the chronology and sequence of construction at Thornborough is problematic, and unfortunately, beyond the reach of the available evidence. An argument can certainly be made for the broad contemporaneity of the inner and outer henge ditches (3.3.2), or perhaps, as at Ferrybridge, for the inner ditch being dug first, for the intervening banks require about twice the amount of spoil as is provided by the inner ditch, the rest presumably coming from the digging of the outer ditch. Indeed, the primacy of the inner ditch may be confirmed at Nunwick where

no outer ditch was dug at all. However, simply regarding the outer ditches as a response to the need to enhance the enclosed bank is not without its problems. The excavated section of outer ditch at the southern henge indicates its digging was connected to the construction of an outer bank, the former then promptly backfilled, with aerial photographs of the northern henge suggesting a similar feature was created around at least one part of its circuit (3.3.2). Neither does simple expediency necessarily explain the characteristics of these outer ditches: at the central and southern henges they are clearly more regularly interrupted, with the siting of these causeways suggesting some deliberation behind their design; and at both, their layout deviates significantly from the near-perfect circularity of their inner earthworks, assuming a more flattened course to the south and south-south-east, where the ditch is clearly wider, and curving sharply in the immediate vicinity of three of their four major entranceways (Fig 3.18). The overwhelming impression is that the outer ditches played an important role in the use of these monuments – perhaps as an earthwork façade or as other architectural devices choreographing experience – and consequently, were one element in a complex sequence of development. They could even have been completed intermittently, perhaps explaining their extra causeways and the deviations in their course. Furthermore, the possibility that a fence or small palisade was added at a later date to the western side of the southern henge cannot be discounted.

It seems likely that the inner henge earthworks affected movement and experience in a different way to their outer earthworks, even if their banks developed periodically. The arresting monumentality of their perimeters cannot be under-estimated. Their banks and ditches are as much as 20m across, the former standing at least 3m high, and the latter with a maximum depth of around 3m. They create an imposing barrier – which would be all the more striking given the wide intervening and apparently undisturbed berm – between the enclosed inner space and the surrounding landscape. Even the Lower Magnesian Limestone ridge immediately to the west (3.2), and the more distant Hambledon Hills to the east, are likely to have been masked by the height of the bank. The only visual connection with the outer world was through their causeways, but the remnants of a banked structure at the partially excavated northern entrance of the southern henge, along with the geophysical anomalies from the entrances of the central henge (3.3.2), suggest that these were anything but empty spaces. Each henge was therefore designed to choreograph the experience of those moving into, out of, and across these arenas, and the gypsum most probably coating their banks, along with the standing water in the inner ditch of the southern henge, all added to a sense of enclosure and separation. The henges are likely to have been the largest and most physically striking buildings their users had experienced, inducing both awe and disorientation. The bewildering quality of their architecture was perhaps complemented by a surprising claustrophobia given the proportionally modest size of their inner spaces, and at only 83–92m across, and possibly divided by a range of structures including palisades or fence-lines (3.3.2), they could have easily filled with people. That all three henges need not have necessarily held more worshippers than the earlier cursus could perhaps say a great deal about the choices now being made by their builders.

Similarity in henge design suggests that the sequence of construction, whatever form it took, was shared by all three monuments, perhaps as part of a carefully planned and long-term vision – or religious imperative – for how this landscape was to be used and perceived. At least one part of this was the need for worshippers to achieve an altered mental state or emotional catharsis through the use of an ideologically charged or sacred space buried deep within a series of imposing and long-standing boundaries or thresholds, and consequently removed from the outer more mundane world (see also 5.5). Yet the adoption and replication of these architectural principles did not necessarily mean the chronology of each monument was the same, and indeed, the different orientations of their entrances could indicate they did not develop together (3.3.2). It is impossible to confirm whether one of these monuments was built before the other two, but if this was the case then the central henge's superimposition on the cursus may suggest it was here, at the highest point of the plateau, that a sacred geometry first developed, with its orientation most closely reflected by the axis of the southern henge. Alternatively, the inter-relationship of each henge, and therefore their possible contemporaneity, is suggested by the fact that the axis, as viewed from the northern henge, is offset to the east, but conversely, offset to the west as viewed from the southern henge. Of course, none of this proves if the henges were contemporary or not, or explains why these monuments failed to share the same orientation. It does, however, hint at the importance of resolving the chronology and structural sequence of the three Thornborough henges, ascertaining the possible longevity of the timespan over which they developed, and identifying if there were hiatuses when no building took place.

Similarly, it is impossible to say if they all went out of use at the same time as part of some general phase of abandonment, or when the henges were no longer considered as sacred places with intense meaning to those using the plateau. Generally, the 'abandonment' of henges is implied through the increasing popularity of the single-grave tradition and the start of round barrow building, or what is often taken as the replacement of one type of society by another, at the end of the later Neolithic. At Thornborough and its hinterland it is difficult to see such a horizon of change. The only known Beaker burial was a crouched adult male inhumation in a grave pit nearly 2km to the west of the monument

complex on the other side of the River Ure (Mayes *et al* 1986), and across the entire Ure-Swale interfluve only small amounts of this pottery are known, from four pits at the nearby Nosterfield Quarry (Dickson and Hopkinson 2011, 134), from another at Marton-le-Moor (Tavener 1996, 183), from the cursus and a ring ditch at Scorton (Topping 1982, 10, 17–19), and from recent excavations at Catterick (Vyner 2003a, 31) and along the A1 (Vyner forthcoming). By contrast, the four barrows excavated at Thornborough by Revd W C Lukis in 1864 produced cremated human bone and later pottery types dating to the first half of the 2nd millennium (2.3; see also 4.7.3), as did his work on Melmerby Common (Lukis 1870b, 120ff) and the more recent excavations at nearby Quernhow (Waterman 1951). The same can be concluded for a ring-ditch in Nosterfield Quarry, interpreted as the plough-levelled remains of a round barrow, an inner cremation radiocarbon dated to 1980–1760 cal BC (SUERC-3786 (GU-12287); Dickson and Hopkinson 2011, 135–6). On the face of it, this evidence could support the idea that the henges were indeed late, dominating the plateau at a time when the barrow tradition was taking hold elsewhere – as at Ferrybridge, where four Beaker inhumations were buried under a barrow just a short distance from the henge (Roberts and Richardson 2005, 202–4). Alternatively, there could have been a significant hiatus between the abandonment of the henges and the deposition of these burials and their associated acts of monument building. The fact there are only ten definite round barrows from across Thornborough, compared to the sixteen or so from around the nearby Hutton Moor/Cana Barn henges (Vyner 2007, fig 7), could highlight a marked decline in the importance of the plateau during this long interval, and it has been observed that round barrow distribution shifted eastwards 'away from the valley slopes above the Ure and east onto the interfluve ridge between Ure and Swale' (*ibid*, 81).

It is very possible that the number of round barrows at Thornborough was originally higher (3.3.3), and an interpretation of 'decline' clearly simplifies a more complex story. The construction of these mounded burial places may illustrate the realignment of social values and a return to the intimacy of more limited, or family-based, activity, but if so the henges and their wider setting clearly continued to hold some meaning, either as sacred places whose veneration persisted, or as mythical spaces around which family histories were now written. These newer monuments largely cluster around the axis of the henges, and although they were never built on the enclosures – unless we consider the south-west terminal of the central henge to have been enhanced by a later earthen mound – they were often in what appear to be carefully chosen positions, as with the Centre Hill Barrow, placed as it is between the southern and central henges at the very point where the axes of both monuments intersect (3.3.3). This site could be earlier than the other excavated barrows, given its association with a food vessel, a coffin, and unburnt human bone, and if this explains its striking position, then perhaps the same could be said of the two destroyed barrows close to the central henge, or the ring-ditch to the south-west of the southern henge (see Fig 3.4). All four may be examples of what Frances Peters (2000) labelled 'conspicuous barrows' for the large, more prominently located, and early sites of the Stonehenge landscape, and certainly they are the largest mounds at Thornborough, with diameters of 27–31m (3.3.3). If so, the rights and motivations embedded in their building and use may be different to barrows like the four grouped into a linear cemetery at Three Hills, each a little smaller than those closer to the henges, at 20–24m across. They clearly demonstrate that symbolic geometry continued to be played out, the henges still determining where later monuments were built. Even more distant sites, like the excavated ring-ditch in Nosterfield Quarry, interpreted as the plough-levelled remains of a round barrow (Dickson and Hopkinson 2011, 216), or the probable site on the lower terrace (Fig 3.4, t), suggest the same, both carefully aligned on the axis of the three henges. They broadly compare to the size of the Three Hills barrows with diameters of 17m and 21m respectively.

Neither did the construction of these barrows mark the end of impressive acts of monumentalisation at Thornborough. Irrespective of when in the Bronze Age the double pit alignment was built, this avenue of posts, pits, and possibly fences, was most likely the result of larger-scale co-operation, requiring as it did a significant amount of labour. Along with its two associated and probably earlier round barrows, it would have been an imposing

sight and its construction next to the southern henge must have been deliberate. Its considerable size suggests it may even have been an attempt to replicate the achievements of the earlier builders – especially remarkable if it did indeed date to the middle Bronze Age, many centuries after the construction of these earlier enclosures. Interestingly, the excavations at Nosterfield Quarry also produced evidence for a flurry of activity in the latter half of the 2nd millennium, with an inhumation burial radiocarbon dated to 1530–1380 cal BC, a small cremation cemetery, consisting of five urned, one possible urned, and four unurned cremations, in use between 1600–1290 cal BC and 1400–1060 cal BC, and possibly two small ring-ditches (Dickson and Hopkinson 2011, 137–41). The double pit alignment may therefore fit alongside other, albeit less spectacular, attempts to renew affiliations between people and this landscape through monumentalisation and funerary practice. It would have certainly been a special place where emotion and sacredness were heightened, and if it served as a pathway by which to ascend safely and respectfully to a plateau now inescapably linked to the ancestors and distant dead, this journey was carefully orchestrated by the monument's variations and subtle use of topography. Movement along its course may have created a storyline to which the associated round barrows added genealogical richness and depth. That its users might have entered the monument near one old round barrow, then exited opposite another, which was not only in line with the henges, but also afforded a view across to the already ancient triple-ditched 'founder monument', attests to the importance of the past.

5   Experiencing the landscape

5.1   General issues

From the outset the fieldwork at Thornborough was concerned with the relationship between the monuments and broader patterns of activity across the surrounding landscape (2.5). Taking a lead from the collection and analysis of surface lithic scatters at Neolithic and early Bronze Age complexes in southern England, most notably at Stonehenge (Richards 1990) and Cranborne Chase (Barrett *et al* 1991), it was believed that Thornborough's plough-soil held vital clues about how this 'sacred landscape' was perceived, organised, and used. One obvious question was whether people were actually living here, be it during intermittent and short episodes of activity, perhaps as normally dispersed groups got together at given times of the year to build and use the monuments, or as a result of more permanent occupation. Of course, it was possible that both residential patterns existed together, as people's circumstances changed and monument construction pulsated. Alternatively, was it that only more specialised tasks, perhaps taking just a few hours, were deemed appropriate to such a landscape? The evidence from the wider landscape was also seen as essential to appreciating the monuments themselves. It could offer valuable insights into whether they 'belonged' to a single community or a wider social network, and crucially, help us understand how people experienced these places. Sacred architecture is designed, built, and enlivened within a physical setting, and its hinterlands are often essential to the religious 'double mediation' discussed in the first chapter, manipulating worshippers' memories and understanding of everyday life as they approach and enter monuments. It seemed possible the distribution of surrounding lithic scatters would reflect this reality.

Significant problems confront any such investigation. Surface lithic scatters constitute the majority of British occupation evidence from this period, and over the last two decades much has been written about 'the identification of Neolithic activity in the ploughsoil, how it may be distinguished from earlier and later periods, and how specific activities may be represented in the form of surface artefact collections' (Schofield 1987, 269). Yet these remains are no more than a partial and incomplete signature of original activity, and as such, necessitate the need for a systematic and intensive examination of the ploughsoil *and* underlying sub-surfaces, employing a wide range of techniques including geophysical prospection and geochemical analysis (R Bradley 1987b; Entwistle and Richards 1987; Ford 1987b). This still rarely happens, surface collection often being undertaken in isolation, or not at all in the case of some developer-led archaeology. Where the detailed investigation of surface scatters has been completed, the exercise has not always proved productive, the archaeology proving resistant to a 'marriage of methodologies' (Schofield 1987, 273). There are examples where little or nothing has been exposed through excavation (eg Edmonds *et al* 1999, 49–50; Ford 1987b, 128), and to make matters worse, it is sometimes far from clear whether this reflects the destructive properties of post-depositional factors like ploughing or the fact that subsoil features never existed in the first place, as suggested for many lithic assemblages dating to the 3rd and 2nd millennium BC (Healy 1987; 1988). Such problems reinforce the image, created earlier in the 20th century (Childe 1940, 98–9; Hodges 1957; Piggott 1954), and perpetuated until recently, that most peoples lived in flimsy, short-lived, and what are now, largely *unrecoverable* settlements. Accordingly, 'it is not surprising that so many narratives … are constructed around the archaeology of monuments, material practices and the relations of social power, rather than dwelling' (Pollard 1999, 77–8).

These problems can be at least partially overcome by drawing widely on the range of available evidence and developing a conceptual framework for interpreting lithic scatters. Some interpretations of surface archaeology have successfully distinguished between different types of scatters, most notably between settlements, special purpose or extractive locations, and the localised flint source or quarry, making a positive contribution to understanding regional settlement systems (Clark and Schofield 1991, 103; Schofield 1987; Edmonds *et al* 1999, 71–2; Ford 1987a). These approaches are often coarse-grained, however, with little room for the subtleties of the excavated record or the network of relationships which once existed between places now represented by lithic scatters and those where clusters of pits and other buried remains are known. What is needed, above all else, is a way of integrating and thinking through these different types of evidence, whilst at the same time appreciating they may have varied greatly, depending on local circumstance, regional tradition, and chronological change (see Bradley 2003; Cooney 1997; Pollard 2000). It is hoped that the following discussion, by identifying some basic themes in the results of widespaced fieldwalking at Thornborough (5.2) and the intensive investigation of four of its known lithic scatters of 'high', 'medium' and 'low' density (5.3), will contribute to the creation of such a 'framework of understand-

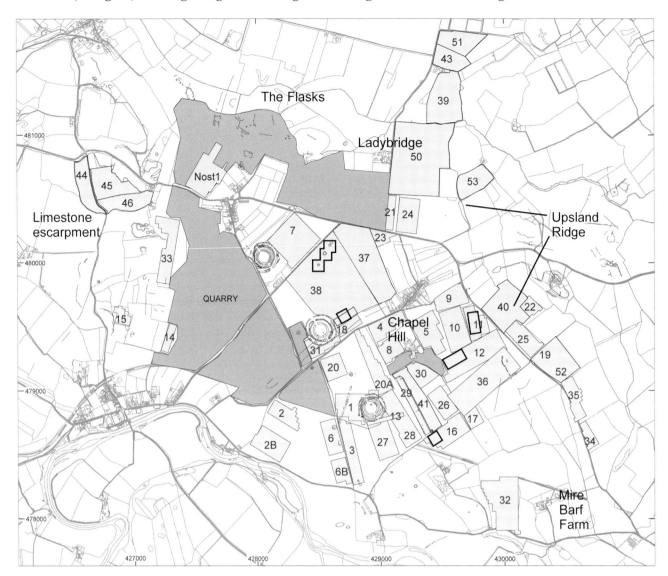

Fig 5.1 Widespaced fieldwalking and the investigation of selected scatters of lithics with place-names used in Chapter 5. © Crown Copyright / database right 2013. An Ordnance Survey / EDINA supplied service

ing'. The available evidence – consisting of 1746 worked lithics from fieldwalking and test-pitting, along with a further 755 pieces from excavation – certainly paints a vivid picture of how this 'sacred landscape' developed over a period of nearly three millennia (5.4 and 5.5), and, despite significant weaknesses, allows fine-grained insights into the experiences of worshippers.

5.2 Widespaced fieldwalking *by Jan Harding and Benjamin Johnson*

5.2.1 Introduction

The investigation of the Thornborough landscape focused intensively on the river terraces and their immediate hinterland (Fig 5.1). Widespaced walking was employed by both the VMNLP and ALSF Project across the majority of the ploughed fields of the study area to identify major lithic variations in and around the monuments. They were walked on the basis of

what was currently available and no attempt was made to sample systematically the different topographic zones described in 2.5 and depicted in Figure 2.8. The resulting evidence enabled the landscape to be divided broadly according to the varying density, chronology, and type of surface lithics. The level of information was then complemented, during the ALSF Project, by the use of geophysical prospection, total collection, and test-pitting at five selected 'low', 'medium', and 'high' density lithic scatters (5.3). Despite failing to discover buried Neolithic or Bronze Age features, these detailed investigations offer insights into the use and occupation of specific locales and the condition and potential of ploughzone archaeology.

Forty-nine fields (and subdivisions of some fields) were subject to widespaced fieldwalking, numbered 1–53 in the order they were walked, of which five were selected for total collection. This work was supplemented by the walking of 'Nost 1' on the Nosterfield Quarry site, an area now destroyed by mineral extraction. A total of 306 hectares was walked across the study area, including most of the plateau, Chapel Hill, Ladybridge, and the Upsland ridge to the east (Fig 5.1). The lower river terrace, limestone ridge to the west, and area around Mire Barf Farm witnessed more limited fieldwalking. A walking distance of 15m was employed, providing 13.3% coverage as each walker was asked to inspect the ground 1m either side of them, representing a compromise between the need to collect from as much of the landscape as possible and the likelihood of scatter detection. This walking interval was considered sufficient to locate all but the most tightly clustered Neolithic and earlier Bronze Age scatters (Ford 1987b, 127; Shennan 1985, 10–11), an assumption confirmed by the intensive investigation of the five selected scatters (5.3.2). In an attempt to eliminate any bias caused by different individual recovery rates, one in four transects was rewalked; those selected were often transects completed by the most inexperienced walkers. Different methods for recording findspots were employed. For areas walked in the late summer and early autumn of 1994 to 1998 by the VMNLP (fields 1–36), each transect was divided into 30m stints with a unique letter, and finds then bagged into these collection units. A far quicker and more accurate procedure was adopted by the ALSF Project (fields 37–53) in the late summer of 2003: the three-dimensional location of each find was recorded by the use of a Geotronics Geodimeter Total Station and data processed using Landscape Survey Systems version 8.2 and Autodesk Land Development Desktop. This data was referenced to the OS National Grid using a common survey network. The collection strategy in Nost 1 was different again. Walked in 1996, the first of these two methods was used during widespaced collection, but five of the 15m by 30m collection units then underwent total collection. Unfortunately, these were bagged with the finds from widespaced collection, making it impossible to distinguish one from the other. Hence, Nost 1 is not statistically compared with other scatters.

The collection from widespaced fieldwalking consists of 1132 pieces of worked flint and chert, with another 264 from Nost 1. They are fully described in D3. The distribution of the material varies greatly across the study area (Table 5.1; Fig 5.2), but there is an overwhelming tendency for density to be directly proportional to proximity to the three henges, with fewer flints in areas nearest the monuments. Table 5.1 converts lithic numbers into 'real' or absolute populations for each field, although adjusted density counts can be misleading, the results of widespaced fieldwalking not necessarily having a direct numerical relationship to the unsampled part of any field. It is a multi-period collection, ranging from the Mesolithic to the later Bronze Age, but with an emphasis on the later Neolithic. An unexpectedly high Mesolithic component is present. The assemblage can be described as domestic in nature, rather than industrial, being very deficient in elements such as cores, primary flakes, and core

rejuvenation flakes. The overall state of the material is poor or moderate, but it is possible to identify pieces disturbed more recently by the plough. The fieldwalking recovery rate can generally be considered quite high since many of the lithics were tiny. However, the walking conditions were far from ideal in fields 3, 8, 13–19, 24–5, 29, 39, 50, and 53, largely due to the ploughsoil being unweathered when collection was undertaken; this may have affected the total number of lithics recovered.

A very small amount of non-lithic material was found (D4.1.3). It was dominated by pieces of rustic ceramic earthenware, mostly roof tile, but perhaps with some brick or field drain, of 19th- or early 20th-century date. There were also two pieces of earthenware vessels, probably of 19th-century date, a slightly earlier fragment of glass bottle, and a single sherd of 4th-century AD Romano-British pottery. The tiny amount of ceramic material is intriguing and the complete absence of medieval pottery contrasts with the assemblage from the inner ditch excavation at the southern henge (4.6.3). It suggests that rubbish was disposed of other than through field manuring and that if fairs were held across this landscape they were confined to the henges (see 4.6.4).

5.2.2   *Lithic distribution and raw material use*

Lithic distribution varies greatly across the study area (Fig 5.2), the density ranging from 0–41 lithics per hectare, with an average of 4.7 (Table 5.1). With the exception of Nost 1, excluded for reasons cited above, the largest and most concentrated scatter is immediately to the east of Chapel Hill in fields 10, 11, and 12 with densities of 9.9, 41 and 12 lithics per hectare respectively. The numbers of worked flint and chert fall away on all sides of these fields, albeit with localised concentrations in fields 22 (10.3 lithics per hectare), 16 (10.2 lithics per hectare), and 8 (8.7 lithics per hectare). Other concentrations are focused at Ladybridge in field 21 (21.1 lithics per hectare), presumably associated with the large number of pits excavated in the south-east corner of the Nosterfield Quarry (Dickson and Hopkinson 2011, fig 53), field 2B (13.5 lithics per hectare), and field 32 (12 lithics per hectare). It is difficult to judge the extent of each of these concentrations, but the areas fieldwalked to the north and east of both fields 21 and 2B suggest they were much more spatially restricted than that by Chapel Hill. Very much smaller quantities of lithics were found elsewhere, including immediately to the east, south, and west of the southern henge (fields 1, 2, 3, 27, 28) and across the limestone ridge to the west of the study area (fields 14, 15, 33, and 44–46). The smallest lithic collections were from the middle and upper gravel terraces, or plateau, on which the three henges are located. Fields 7, 18, 20, 20A, 31, 37, and 38 produced 0–2.1 flints per hectare, the only exception being field 31A, in the vicinity

Table 5.1 Lithic numbers and density from widespaced surface collection

Field number	Total	% of assemblage*	Density per ha	Adjusted density per ha**	Retouched density per ha	Core density per ha
1	10	0.9	3.2	24.2	0.6	–
2	25	2.2	7.6	56.9	1.5	0.3
2B	69	6.1	13.5	101.4	2.2	1.6
3	12	1	2.2	16.1	0.5	0.2
4	11	1	2.8	21.2	1	–
5	35	3.1	6.1	46.1	1.2	–
6	7	0.6	1.9	14.2	0.5	–
6B	3	0.3	1.1	8.3	0.7	–
7	11	1	1.1	8.3	0.2	0.1
8	29	2.6	8.7	66	1.2	–
9	14	1.2	4.2	31.8	1.2	0.3
10	57	5	9.9	73.7	2.2	1.6
11	153	13.5	41	310.1	7	1.6
12	105	9.3	12	89.5	1.6	0.6
13	1	0.1	1.1	8.3	–	–
14	8	0.7	5.6	42.9	1.4	–
15	2	0.2	0.4	3	–	–
16	51	4.5	10.2	76.5	1.4	0.2
17	4	0.3	1.9	14.3	–	–
18	7	0.6	2.1	15.9	–	–
19	5	0.4	2.5	18.8	–	–
20	3	0.3	0.9	6.8	0.3	–
20A	0	–	–	–	–	–
21	36	3.2	21.1	158.8	4.1	1.2
22	13	1.2	10.3	75	2.3	0.8
23	3	0.3	1.7	12.5	–	–
24	20	1.8	2.6	19.5	0.4	0.1
25	11	1	2.5	18.8	0.5	–
26	10	0.9	2.8	20.8	0.3	–
27	23	2	5	37.5	0.9	0.2
28	14	1.2	2.5	18.8	0.2	0.2
29	7	0.6	2.9	21.9	–	–
30	21	1.9	6.8	50.8	1	0.6
31	3	0.3	1.4	10.7	0.5	–
31A	8	0.7	6.3	46.2	0.8	–
32	113	10	12	90.2	2.2	1.1
33	16	1.4	6.7	50	1.7	1.3
34	3	0.3	1.8	13.2	–	–
35	4	0.4	1.2	9.1	–	–
36	39	3.5	3.2	24	0.7	0.2
37	4	0.4	0.3	2.3	–	0.2
38	51	4.5	1.9	14.3	0.2	0.1
39	0	–	–	–	–	–
40	17	1.5	2	15	–	0.1
41	12	1	2.3	17.3	0.6	0.2
43	0	–	–	–	–	–
44	16	1.4	3.5	26.1	0.9	–
45	21	1.9	3.5	26.3	0.7	0.2
46	15	1.3	3.3	25	0.4	–
50	15	1.3	0.6	4.5	0.1	0.1
51	5	0.4	0.8	6	0.2	–
52	7	0.6	1.5	11.2	0.2	0.2
53	3	0.3	0.7	5.2	0.5	–
Nost 1	264	***	***	***	***	***
AVERAGES	**21.4**	**–**	**4.7**	**35.6**	**0.8**	**0.3**

Percentages have been rounded up/down 1 decimal place
* = total lithics from the field expressed as a percentage of the whole assemblage
** = The adjusted density figure is achieved by multiplying the actual number recovered by 7.5 and then dividing by the size of the walked area
*** = Excluded from statistical comparison and from the averages

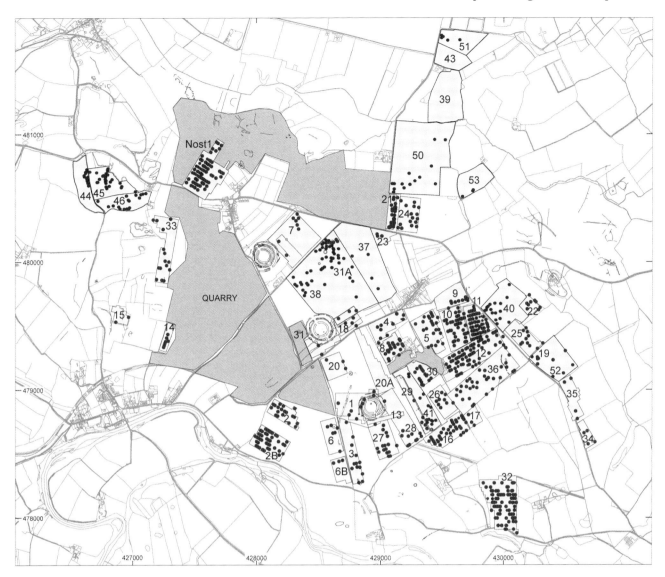

Fig 5.2 *Lithic distribution from widespaced fieldwalking. © Crown Copyright / database right 2013. An Ordnance Survey / EDINA supplied service*

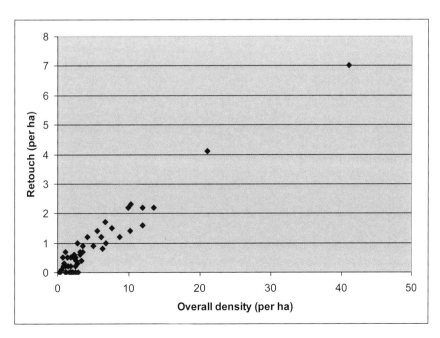

Fig 5.3 *Relationship between overall density and retouch density from widespaced fieldwalking (excluding Nost 1)*

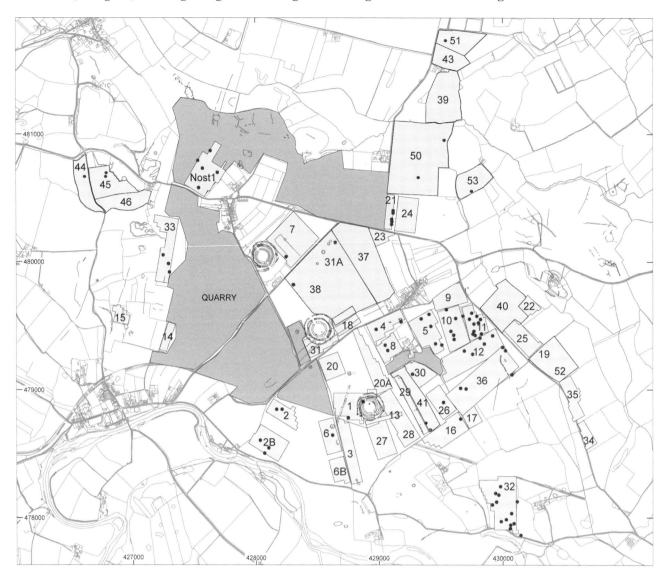

Fig 5.4   Distribution of scrapers from widespaced fieldwalking. © Crown Copyright / database right 2013. An Ordnance Survey / EDINA supplied service

of the Three Hills Barrow Group, with a density of 6.3 flints per hectare. This large area produced only 0.7% of the total lithic assemblage.

Fieldwalked areas within 500m of both the northern and central henges produced relatively small numbers of lithics with an average density of fewer than 2.1 flints per hectare, and whilst those fields immediately to the south of the southern henge were more productive, density was still low or average for the collection, varying between 0 and 5 flints per hectare (Fig 5.2). Lithic numbers increase at around 500m from the nearest henge to 1.1–8.7 flints per hectare, except to the north-east of the central site (fields 23, 37, and 38), which again produced very low densities. The largest increase in numbers, however, is in a band between 750m and 1250m from all three henges, including the concentrations at Ladybridge, near Chapel Hill, and Mire Barf Farm. It is difficult to explore the inter-relationship of these three high-density areas given the gaps in fieldwalking coverage caused by pasture and the village at Thornborough, but it is possible they were part of a continuous

expanse of occupation stretching around the eastern side of the complex. The likelihood of a similar pattern of occupation to the west of the complex is suggested by the fieldwalking results from the northern half of the limestone ridge, and indeed, immediately to the north of Nosterfield, where fieldwalking prior to quarrying produced a large number of lithics (Fig 5.2, Nost 1). From around 1250m the distribution of lithics falls off markedly – with fields 34, 35, 39, 43, and 51 producing little or no flint – to the extent that an outer edge of occupation can be identified on the till ridges to the north of Ladybridge and south-east of Chapel Hill.

The occurrence of tools in the ploughsoil generally mirrors the overall distribution, the higher the lithic density the greater the incidence of retouched pieces (Fig 5.3; see also Table 5.1). The highest density by far, in terms of total lithics and also retouched items (7 per hectare), is to the east of Chapel Hill in field 11. The density of retouched pieces falls away rapidly in the adjacent fields 10 and 12, especially in the latter (2.2 and 1.6 per hectare respectively). These

Fig 5.5   Distribution of cores from widespaced fieldwalking. © Crown Copyright/database right 2013. An Ordnance Survey/EDINA supplied service

figures are lower than for field 21 (4.1 per hectare), but broadly equivalent to other high-density fields (see Table 5.1) such as field 22 (2.3 per hectare), field 32 (2.2 per hectare), field 2B (2.2 per hectare), and field 33 (1.7 per hectare). The collection from widespaced fieldwalking in field 16, adjacent to the triple-ditched round barrow, also possessed a relatively high density of retouch (1.4 per hectare). The major concentrations are all generally associated with a higher density of scrapers (Fig 5.4), irregular knapping debris, and cores (Fig 5.5), but interestingly, scrapers both outnumber cores and are more densely distributed in fields 11 and 32, while the reverse is the case in fields 2B and 10, suggesting more knapping in the latter two areas. Fields 12 and 21 are different again, the density of cores and scrapers exactly the same, whilst very small numbers of each occur in field 16. As with overall distribution, there is a fall off in the density of retouched pieces away from Chapel Hill, and to the north and south-west of Ladybridge. The same is true for the Upsland ridge, although the three

pieces from field 22, including a single-piece sickle fragment, could conceivably be the edge of a largely undiscovered cluster.

Despite unworked gravel flint being recovered from the study area, most of the artefacts are made of non-local material. The collection from widespaced fieldwalking was overwhelmingly derived from till sources (Table D3.8), and nearly all diagnostic implement types are, unsurprisingly, manufactured from these materials (Table D3.11). It represents 70.8% of the total, but more across the lower river terrace (Fig 5.6). Till flint is characteristic of glacial clay deposits, and most would be from the coast some 80km to the east since the local Devensian tills in the Vale of Mowbray are of northern or north-western origin (Aitkinhead *et al* 2002, fig 33), which contain little or no flint. The greys and browns which predominate amongst the Thornborough material are the most frequent flint colours of the coastal tills, especially at Flamborough Head, where more brightly coloured flints, some of high knapping quality, are relatively rare

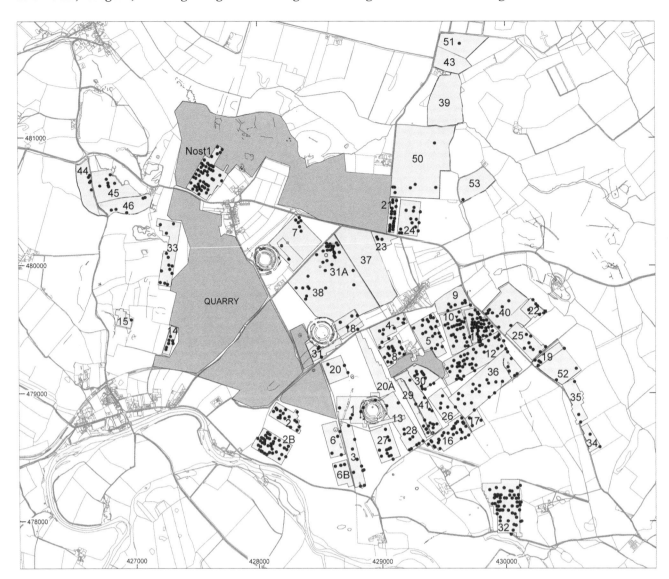

Fig 5.6   Distribution of till flint from widespaced fieldwalking. © Crown Copyright / database right 2013. An Ordnance Survey / EDINA supplied service

(Brooks 1989, 57; Henson 1985; Durden 1995, 410). Till material that may subsequently have been buried, rolled, or in some other way incorporated into a fluviatile environment, such as a stream bed, was also present, amounting to 15.3% of the total from widespaced walking (Table D3.8; Fig 5.7). This till/gravel material is particularly well represented in the collections from fields 10–12 near Chapel Hill, field 32 at Mire Barf Farm, and field 38 next to the central henge. Gravel flint was much rarer, at only 2.2% of the collection (Table D3.8), and was not used at all for the manufacture of implements. It is usually rare in the boulder clay deposits of north-east Yorkshire, but would nonetheless have been widely available at Thornborough given the extent of the alluvio-fluviatile terraces across the study area and elsewhere in the Yorkshire vales. Perhaps it was only used when no other sources were to hand.

There are very small quantities of chalk flint (with clusters in fields 2B, 38, 44, and 50) and one piece of high-quality beach flint (Table D3.8; Fig 5.8). Almost certainly some of this material comes from the veins in the upper chalk of the Yorkshire Wolds, which is normally of poor flaking quality (Brooks 1989, 57; Manby 1979, 71). The one piece of fine-quality beach flint was probably from the lower chalk, originally eroded from a cliff exposure, and a few dark grey to black pieces with thick, unrolled cortex, are of flint which conceivably could have come from the chalk of East Anglia or farther south, although the heterogeneity of the flints in the till makes it difficult to be sure of this. A relatively high proportion of implements were manufactured from chalk flint, there being three scrapers from fields 50 and 53, a serrated edged blade from field 44, two miscellaneous retouched flakes from fields 2B and 44, and a single notched blade from field 2B. Chert was also used rarely and unevenly (Table D3.8; Fig 5.9). It represents only 6% of the total and the raw material was absent from nearly a third of the walked areas, being especially under-represented

Fig 5.7   Distribution of till/gavel and gravel flint from widespaced fieldwalking. © Crown Copyright/ database right 2013. An Ordnance Survey/EDINA supplied service

around Chapel Hill and along the Upsland ridge. Three different types of chert were readily identifiable, although all were probably collected from local gravels, having been carried by the Rivers Ure and Swale, or their tributaries, from Carboniferous deposits to the north and west. Despite experimental knapping by Peter Makey which show it to have poor flaking properties, chert was actually used for the manufacture of thirteen blades and bladelets, an edge-retouched flake, three scrapers, a notched flake, and a microlith. In general, chert may have been used because it provided size: where weights have been recorded, complete chert artefacts have a mean weight of just under 7g, compared to just over 4g for complete flint ones.

Spatial variations in the use of raw materials are more apparent when colour alone is considered (Table 5.2). Greys, especially olive-greys, predominate in the majority of fields, where they often constitute over 70% of the total. There are, however, notable exceptions, best illustrated by the concen-

tration in fields 11 and 12 (Fig 5.10), where greater quantities of brownish, reddish, and brownish-yellow material were present, representing the greater use of till/gravel flint and unusual coastal sources. Some of the more common colours from these two fields were yellowish-red, brownish-yellow, olive, dusky red, and reddish-brown, their range and distribution demonstrating the complexity of these scatters. The brownish-yellow material is concentrated across the central-southern part of field 11 and the northern end of field 12, whilst the brownish and reddish material has a wider, but largely spatially discrete, distribution. Each of these fields has almost identical proportions of different coloured flint (Table 5.2), suggesting they were the product of similar practices, a pattern which is extended, albeit with lesser amounts of material, by red and brown flint in fields 25, 40, and 52, located immediately to the east on Upsland ridge. Brown, red, and brownish-yellow material is also relatively well-represented elsewhere: in the second largest collection

Table 5.2 Lithic colour from widespaced fieldwalking

Field	Greys & olive-grey		Reds & browns		Brownish-yellow		Black	
	No	%	No	%	No	%	No	%
1	8	100	–	–	–	–	–	–
2	20	80	1	4	–	–	–	–
2B	58	84.1	1	1.4	–	–	1	1.5
3	7	58.3	2	16.7	–	–	–	–
4	8	72.7	–	–	1	9.1	–	–
5	25	71.4	2	5.7	2	5.7	3	8.6
6	5	83.3	–	–	–	–	2	28.6
6B	3	100	–	–	–	–	–	–
7	9	81.8	–	–	–	–	–	–
8	20	69	3	10.3	2	6.9	2	6.9
9	10	71.4	3	21.4	1	7.1	–	–
10	40	70.2	12	21.1	2	3.5	3	5.7
11	37	24.2	68	44.4	41	26.8	2	1.3
12	22	21	46	44	30	28.6	1	1
13	1	100	–	–	–	–	–	–
14	5	62.5	–	–	–	–	1	25
15	1	50	–	–	–	–	–	–
16	39	76.4	6	11.8	2	3.9	5	9.8
17	1	25	1	25	–	–	2	50
18	5	71.4	2	28.6	–	–	–	–
19	5	100	–	–	–	–	–	–
20	3	100	–	–	–	–	–	–
21	34	94.4	–	–	–	–	–	–
22	10	77	1	7.7	–	–	2	15.4
23	3	100	–	–	–	–	–	–
24	18	90	1	5	–	–	1	5
25	4	36.4	5	45.6	–	–	–	–
26	7	70	–	–	2	20	1	10
27	10	43.5	2	8.7	–	–	1	4.3
28	11	78.6	–	–	–	–	2	14
29	6	85.7	–	–	–	–	1	14.2
30	15	71.4	1	4.7	–	–	5	23.8
31	3	100	–	–	–	–	–	–
31a	7	87.5	–	–	–	–	–	–
32	71	62.8	31	27.4	11	9.7	–	–
33	14	87.5	1	6.25	–	–	–	–
34	3	100	–	–	–	–	–	–
35	3	75	1	25	–	–	1	25
36	29	74.4	3	7.7	3	7.7	–	–
37	4	100	–	–	–	–	–	–
38	29	62.7	12	23.5	–	–	–	–
40	5	29.4	9	53	–	–	–	–
41	4	33.3	4	33.3	–	–	–	–
44	2	12.5	8	50	–	–	–	–
45	6	28.6	5	23.8	–	–	1	4.8
46	7	46.7	7	46.7	–	–	1	6.7
50	8	53.3	4	26.7	–	–	–	–
51	2	40	1	20	–	–	–	–
52	2	28.6	4	57.1	–	–	–	–
53	1	33.3	2	66.7	–	–	–	–
Nost 1	204	76.4	17	6.4	9	3.4	1	0.4
TOTALS*	**650**	**57.4%**	**249**	**22%**	**97**	**8.6%**	**38**	**3.4%**

% are for colour within each individual field
Identification for fields 1–36 by Peter Makey / identification for fields 37–53 by Frances Healy
*** = % is the average number of lithics per field (excluding Nost 1)

Fig 5.8   Distribution of other flint sources from widespaced fieldwalking. © Crown Copyright / database right 2013. An Ordnance Survey / EDINA supplied service

from the study area, in field 32 at Mire Barf Farm, although outnumbered by olive-grey flint; along the limestone escarpment in fields 44, 45, and 46, where it amounts to nearly half of the collected lithics; and to the north-east of the study area, in fields 50 and 53. Elsewhere these flint colours are more infrequent, although field 38, immediately to the east of the central henge, produced twelve worked pieces of brownish flint. Even rarer is black-coloured material, the vast majority of which is chert, its densest concentration occurring on the southern side of Chapel Hill in fields 16 and 30, suggesting perhaps the exploitation of a nearby palaeochannel (5.3.3). Only a small number of black flint and chert pieces were found in fields 11 and 12, suggesting it was largely part of a different pattern of deposition.

The procurement of raw material clearly changed between the Mesolithic and Bronze Age (Fig 5.11). Generally, grey and olive-grey till flint is pre-eminent throughout the entire period, collectively representing over 60% of the flint and chert with known chronological affinities from any one period, and most readily used during the Mesolithic and earlier Neolithic when it represented 79% of the total. There is a trend during the Neolithic and earlier Bronze Age for collections to include an increasing proportion of olive-grey till flint. This could indicate the growing significance of certain coastal sources in eastern Yorkshire, especially since it is matched by lessening amounts of black chert and local brown gravel flint. There is also an increase in the relative proportions of brownish-yellow, orange, and red-coloured material during the later Neolithic and early Bronze Age, and at a more detailed level, this represents not only an increase in the use of coloured flint but also an accompanying increase in colour variation. Colours now used, but rare or non-existent in earlier periods, were yellowish-red, brownish-yellow, yellowish-brown, reddish-brown, and dusky red. Their increasing quantities are especially evident in fields 11 and 12, where they represent over two-thirds of the collected lithics.

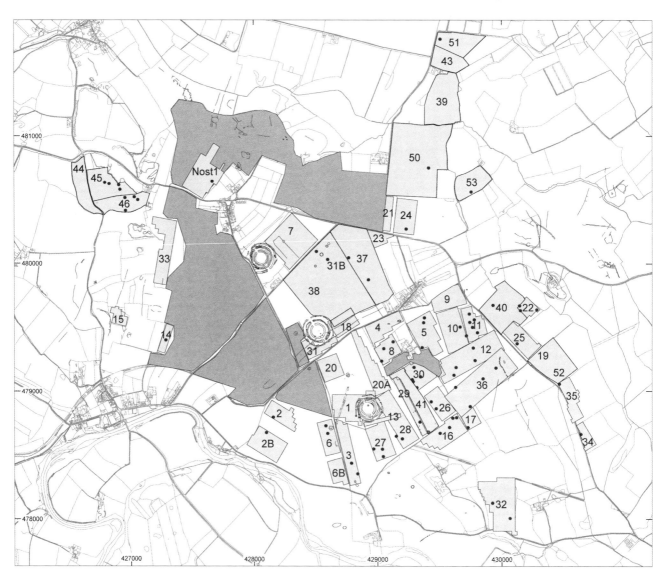

Fig 5.9   Distribution of chert from widespaced fieldwalking. © Crown Copyright / database right 2013. An Ordnance Survey / EDINA supplied service

Such variation certainly matches the suggestion that later Neolithic assemblages became specialised and possessed more emblematic roles (Bradley 1984, 48–67; Bradley 1990, 68–71; Pierpoint 1980; Thorpe and Richards 1984, 70–9), and, if this was the case at Thornborough, the scatter immediately to the east of Chapel Hill could have been perceived and used in different ways to elsewhere. In this regard, it may be informative that the admittedly much smaller cluster of flints in field 21 to the north, including material with a later Neolithic or earlier Bronze Age affinity, produced no brownish-yellow, orange, or red flint.

Despite these fluctuations in lithic supply, or what can be understood as changing priorities in deliberate selection, one trend remains consistent irrespective of chronology. The overall size of the artefacts at Thornborough is small, reflecting their till and gravel sources, so that if the entire reduction sequence had taken place across the study area, there would be a high frequency of cortical or partly cortical flakes. However, the

reverse is the case, the overwhelming majority of complete flakes and flake tools having either no or no more than 25% dorsal cortex (Tables D3.18–19), irrespective of location, suggesting that the early stages of core reduction were generally conducted elsewhere, presumably closer to the flint sources. A few complete nodules were brought to the area, indicated by the nine primary reduction flakes present in the assemblage; five of these were from field 16. Of those fields which produced more than a handful of lithics, there are relatively high numbers of at least partly cortical flakes and tools in fields 8, 9, 10, and 11, on and around Chapel Hill, and in fields 16 and 38, but in each instance they constitute less than one-fifth of the total from the field (Tables D3.18–19).

To a certain extent the distribution of cores relates directly to collection size (Table 5.1; Figs 5.5 and 5.12), with the highest core densities in fields 2B, 10, and 11, each with 1.6 per hectare from widespaced walking. Fields 21, 32, and 33 also produced a relatively high number of cores, but elsewhere in

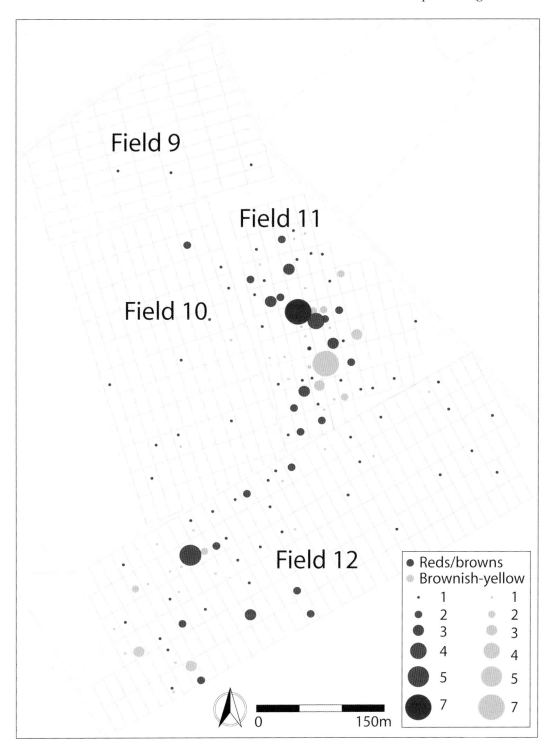

Fig 5.10   Lithic colour from widespaced fieldwalking to the east of Chapel Hill (fields 9–12). © Crown Copyright / database right 2013. An Ordnance Survey / EDINA supplied service

the study area they are either absent or occur in much lower numbers. The types of cores associated with each of the clusters are noticeably different to one another (Table D3.25–26). Nost 1 and field 32 produced over half of the assemblage's single-platform flake cores, a variety completely missing from fields 2B, 10, and 11. By contrast, multiple-platform cores, keeled flake cores, and Levallois cores predominate in fields 2B, 10, and 11; the first two types are also known in Nost 1, but Levallois cores are found only in fields 10 and 11, and multiple-

platform cores only in fields 2B and 11. One can only speculate as to whether these differences reflect chronological changes in the foci of manufacture or are the product of distinctive knapping activities.

5.2.3   Chronological and occupational variability

Overall lithic distribution is, of course, made up of discrete, overlapping, or superimposed scatters

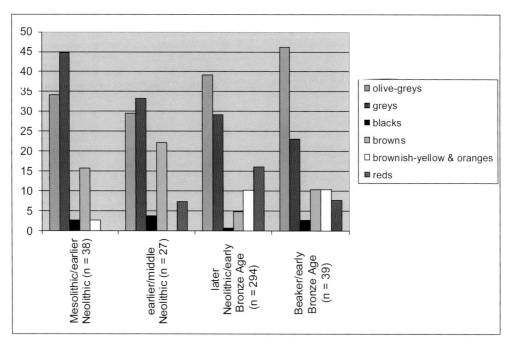

Fig 5.11   Colour of worked flint and chert with chronological affinities (excluding Nost 1)

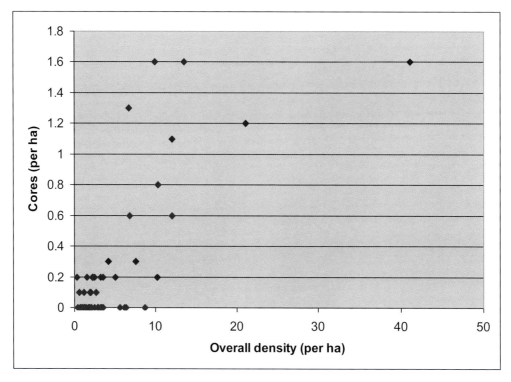

Fig 5.12   Relationship between overall density and cores from widespaced fieldwalking (excluding Nost 1)

formed during different archaeological periods. Fortunately, the concentrations of worked flint and chert in the Thornborough ploughsoil are quite sharply defined against a discontinuous and generally low-density 'background' scatter, suggesting areas of recurrent activity separated by others where only occasional tasks were undertaken. This is certainly evident in field 2B where two adjacent 15m transects produced six flints each, whilst those

surrounding produced one, two, or in one case three, worked pieces (Fig 5.13). It is also possible to define in part the edge of the study area's largest and densest concentration, stretching across fields 9, 10, 11, and 12 (Fig 5.14). It resulted from multi-period deposition, yet possesses clear edges to its north and south, in fields 9 and 12 respectively. More dispersed and lower-density concentrations, whose spatial extents are less apparent, can be seen in fields 21

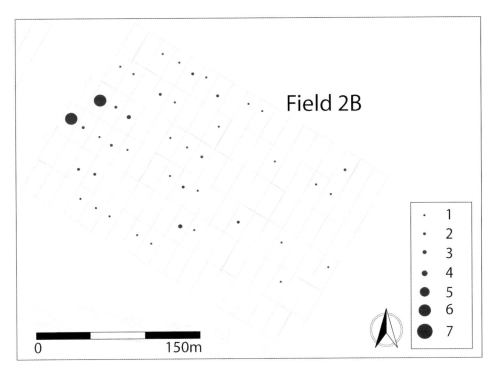

Fig 5.13   Lithic distribution from widespaced fieldwalking in field 2B. © Crown Copyright/database right 2013. An Ordnance Survey/EDINA supplied service

and 32 (Figs 5.15 and 5.16 respectively). Both seem to consist of partially overlapping scatters, each 30–45m across, which are likely to extend outside of the walked field, and between which there are either blank areas or areas with very small amounts of worked flint and chert. These differences hint at distinctive patterning in the use of different locations.

Chronological variability is likely to have played an important role in the development of these patterns. The Mesolithic is indicated by the discovery of certain diagnostic tool types and some of the general characteristics of flint working during this period (Figs 5.17 and 5.18), although earlier Neolithic knapping produced very similar traits, making it difficult to distinguish between lithics from the two eras. An early date may also be indicated by the presence of heavy patination, even if this is anything but an exacting criterion (D3.3). The single most noticeable Mesolithic collection is in field 27 (Fig 5.17), on the lower river terrace immediately to the south of the southern henge. Here a total of thirteen pieces, including a microburin, were heavily patinated, and the early date of these pieces is supported by the relatively high incidence of feather terminations (Table D3.15) and punctiform or linear butts (Table D3.12). The absence of later material makes the scatter clearly identifiable, despite the material being spread throughout much of the field. There are also two possibly Mesolithic pieces, including a rejuvenated opposed platform micro-blade core, immediately to the east, in the southern half of field 28, and another seven possibly Mesolithic pieces, including a burin and a bladelet, directly opposite in field 16. The material in these three fields is close

to the early lithic cluster identified at the triple-ditched round barrow and what could have been a nearby river channel (4.2.3). Widespaced walking also discovered two more possible foci of Mesolithic or earlier Neolithic activity, both again being near to water: in field 2B was a microburin, a tanged or shouldered blade, a bladelet, and a notched blade; and field 32 produced five pieces possibly of this date, including three scrapers and a burin spall. The occurrence of a range of Mesolithic artefacts in the southern half of the study area suggests small-scale, temporary occupation near to the River Ure and along what may have been one of its tributary streams. This activity most likely post-dates the early Mesolithic.

Similar evidence was found elsewhere. The most extensive concentration of what may be Mesolithic flintwork was on and around Chapel Hill. Fields 8 and 30, next to one another on its gently sloping western side, produced ten possibly Mesolithic pieces, including a microburin, two bladelets and a blade, a single-platform blade core, and a rod microlith. This material was dispersed across each field. Comparable amounts of material were collected further eastwards, on the other side of Chapel Hill, including: a bladelet and blade from the northern end of field 5; a micro-bladelet core and a fragmentary rod microlith found close to one another in field 10; a bladelet, blade, and exhausted blade core from field 11; and a bladelet, long scraper, and two blade cores, one of which was a rejuvenated single-platform core, from two distinct spots in field 12. These surface finds suggest an uneven distribution of early material very similar to that

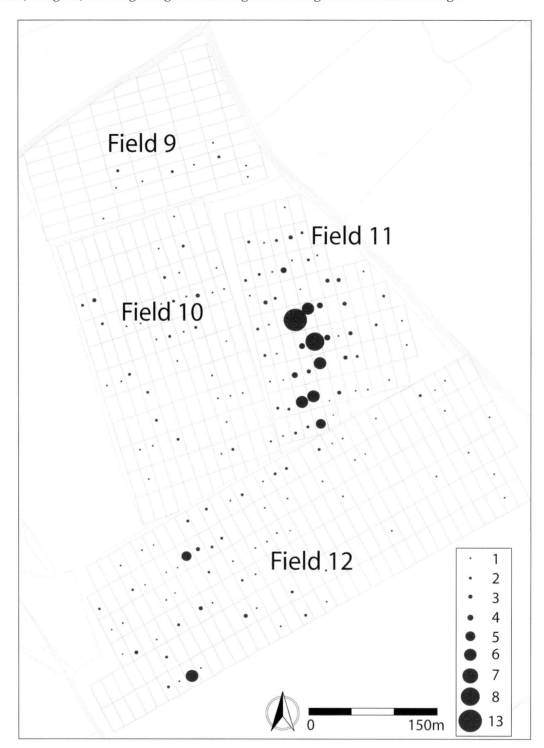

Fig 5.14 Lithic distribution from widespaced fieldwalking to the east of Chapel Hill (fields 9–12). © Crown Copyright / database right 2013. An Ordnance Survey / EDINA supplied service

across the lower terrace, this zone contrasting with the lesser quantities of Mesolithic or earlier Neolithic lithics from other parts of the study area. The remainder of the plateau produced only three bladelets, a single-platform blade core, and a bilaterally retouched microlith, all from fields 7, 24, 38, and 50, although the discovery in Nost 1 of two definite microliths, two more possible specimens, and two blade cores, along with a large number of other possibly Mesolithic pieces, hints at an activity

hotspot on its northern edge. Finally, two serrated pieces, a blade, two single-platform pyramidal flake cores, and a core rejuvenation flake from an opposed platform blade core were found along the limestone escarpment in fields 14, 33, and 44–6. These variations in quantity suggest that the entire landscape was not utilised in the same way during the earlier periods, as does the distribution of some individual lithic types. Scrapers, cores, and core rejuvenation flakes indicate isolated incidences of short-term

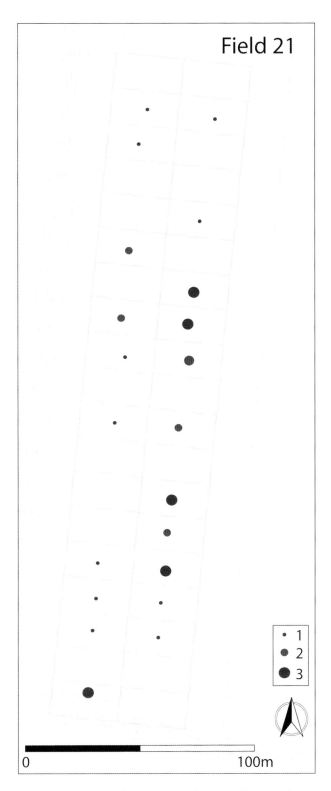

Field 21

· 1
● 2
● 3

0   100m

Fig 5.15   Lithic distribution from widespaced fieldwalking in field 21. © Crown Copyright / database right 2013. An Ordnance Survey / EDINA supplied service

occupation and knapping across much of the study area, but the isolated occurrence of microliths in fields 50 and 6B, and serrated pieces in fields 44 and 45, suggest task-specific activity towards the fringes of this landscape.

The problems of identifying earlier and middle Neolithic surface scatters – the latter defined here as broadly spanning the second half of the 4th millennium BC and the first few centuries of the 3rd millennium BC and often associated with Peterborough Ware – have been discussed by, among others, Gardiner (1991) and Healy (1988, 112). If they are under-represented generally, Thornborough is unlikely to be an exception. However, the 4th millennium did see the introduction of diagnostic forms such as leaf-shaped arrowheads, ground or polished axeheads, and sometimes elongated flake scrapers, while during the middle Neolithic, chisel arrowheads appeared (Green 1980; Manby 1975). The period is also characterised by continued blade production from prepared cores, sometimes resulting in larger blades and blade-like flakes than were produced in the later Mesolithic. The distribution of these types at Thornborough is informative (Figs 5.19 and 5.20). As with the Mesolithic, the period is most likely characterised by its broadly dispersed and light lithic distribution, and some blade-based elements from the fields with Mesolithic material may have been generated well into the 4th millennium during the reuse of previously utilised locations. On and around Chapel Hill, some possibly earlier or middle Neolithic material occurs largely in areas unassociated with Mesolithic flintwork (Fig 5.21), suggesting the emergence of new patterns of land use during the 4th millennium. Three quite large blades clustered together in the southern half of field 10 are at least 30m away from Mesolithic material, and immediately across the field boundary in field 12, a bladelet and a particularly large blade fragment were found 60m or more from what is probably the nearest Mesolithic flint. In field 11 a large blade and leaf-shaped arrowhead were unassociated with earlier flintwork. Hence, the eastern slope of Chapel Hill may have witnessed increasing occupation now spread into adjoining areas, but usually sited away from the debris of earlier visits.

There appears to have been significant change in the organisation of Thornborough's landscape during the later Neolithic. A lower proportion of blades, new retouched items like oblique arrowheads, more extensively retouched scrapers, and the use of Levallois or keeled cores are all characteristics of Grooved Ware assemblages (Green 1980; Healey 1984; Manby 1974). At Thornborough, material possibly of this date (Figs 5.22 and 5.23) is largely absent from most of the lower river terrace and the plateau, only appearing at their fringes away from the immediate vicinity of the three henges. They may represent the inner edge of what appears to be a dense, and maybe even continuous, spread of material 0.5km to 1km across, running around the north, east, south-east, and south-west of the plateau, its outer edge bounded by the lower ground of The Flasks, and the little-used Upsland and limestone ridges, to the north, east, and west respectively. Material from field 32 suggests its continuation southwards. If a dichotomy between the plateau and its surround-

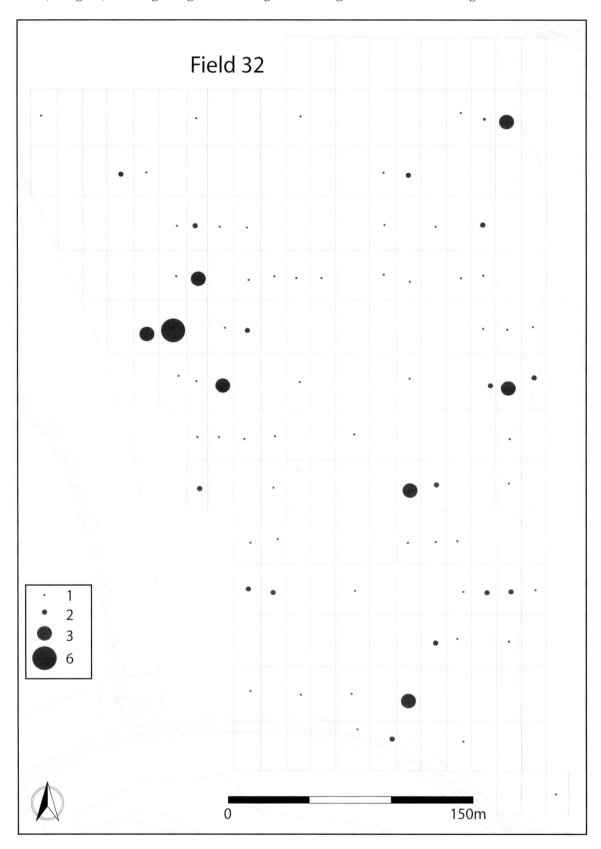

Fig 5.16   Lithic distribution from widespaced fieldwalking in field 32. © Crown Copyright / database right 2013. An Ordnance Survey / EDINA supplied service

ing areas had indeed become a key principle in the landscape's organisation then it mirrors developments across the Stonehenge Environs, where for some distance around the henges of Durrington Walls and Woodhenge there is an almost complete absence of worked flint (Richards 1990, fig 158, 270). Such a disparity runs counter to the broader tendency noted elsewhere for later Neolithic settlement to become more widely and evenly spread across a landscape (Holgate 1988, fig 6.15; Wad-

Fig 5.17 Distribution of Mesolithic lithics from widespaced fieldwalking. © Crown Copyright / database right 2013. An Ordnance Survey / EDINA supplied service

dington 1999, 79), highlighting how occupation in and around major monument complexes may have been atypical of what was going on elsewhere in the landscape.

Later Neolithic scatters are larger and denser than those of earlier periods. This is especially so to the east of Chapel Hill, where material from this period is found across much of fields 10 and 11 (Fig 5.21). Its distribution is loosely clustered into a number of separate foci, each differing in terms of the most commonly used raw materials and their colour (Tables 5.2, D3.8). The most densely distributed of these is in field 11, at the top of a knoll and immediately downslope to the south, east, and north. It is here that we see very few pieces of grey or olive-grey till flint, but conversely, the greatest concentration of coloured (reds, browns, brownish-yellow) till flint (Fig 5.10). Whilst the reds and browns are spread

across much of the field, the use of brownish-yellow material occurs largely in its southern half, and is only rarely found in the same collection unit as other coloured flint. Material is far less dense immediately to the west in field 10, although it does contain a high proportion of cores. There is an abrupt end to the distribution of later Neolithic lithics to the north in field 9, and the same is evident in the eastern half of field 12 (Fig 5.21), marking the cluster's southern extent. Fields further to the east along the Upsland ridge produced few lithics of this period (Fig 5.22), and certainly no cores or retouched pieces. The western half of field 12, by contrast, contains a dispersed scatter of material whose distribution appears largely distinct from the scatters upslope in fields 10 and 11. The spatial separation of red or brown flintwork and brownish-yellow flintwork is again evident, raising the possibility of func-

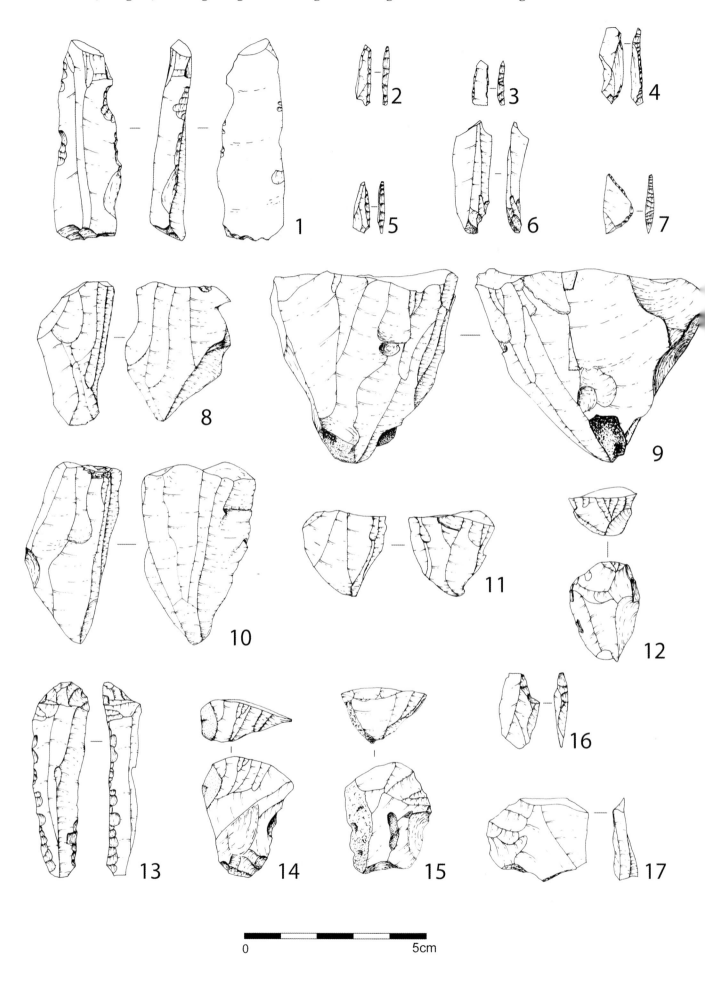

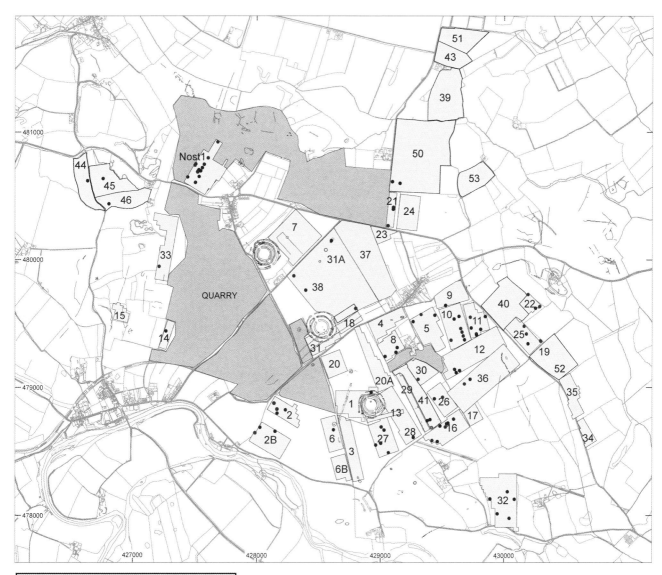

Fig 5.19 Distribution of earlier and middle Neolithic lithics from widespaced fieldwalking. © Crown Copyright/database right 2013. An Ordnance Survey/EDINA supplied service

tional or chronological variation in the scatter's development.

Later Neolithic scatters show a discernible tendency for the increased presence of cores, scrapers, or other retouched tools the higher the overall lithic density. What may be indicated is the more intensive use of the landscape, and within this general lithic spread other major foci of later Neolithic flintwork can be found in fields 2B, 21, 32,

and Nost 1 (Fig 5.22). It is impossible to ascertain their full extent from the current evidence, but the density of material falls away sharply to the east and north of field 2B. It is likely that the cluster in field 21 was originally part of a spread of material which continued to the west on the other side of the road into Nosterfield Quarry, where excavations revealed at least 30 pits associated with Grooved Ware (Dickson and Hopkinson 2011, 96–101; see

Fig 5.18 (opposite) *Selected Mesolithic and earlier Neolithic lithics from widespaced fieldwalking: 1, field 16, burin; 2, Nost 1, bilaterally retouched microlith; 3, Nost 1, edge-blunted point microlith; 4, field 6B, microlith; 5, field 8, blunted point microlith; 6, field 10, microlith fragment; 7, field 11, scalene triangle microlith; 8, field 10, blade core; 9, field 12, single-platform blade core; 10, field 30, single-platform blade core; 11, field 33, single-platform flake core; 12, field 2B, 'button' end scraper; 13, field 12, long side end scraper; 14, field 21, I2 asymmetrical end scraper; 15, field 32, end keeled scraper; 16, field 8, microburin; 17, field 25, core rejuvenation flake*

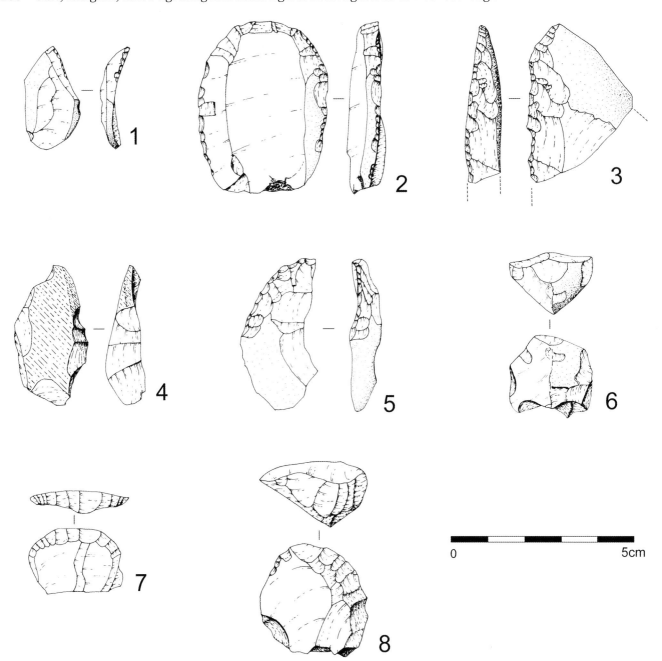

Fig 5.20   Selected earlier and middle Neolithic lithics from widespaced fieldwalking: 1, field 5, side and end scraper; 2, field 36, extended end scraper; 3, field 22, single-piece sickle fragment; 4, field 32, polished flake (possibly from axe); 5, field 32, fragment from possible extended end scraper; 6, field 32, core on fabricator fragment; 7, field 21, possible flake knife; 8, Nost 1, multi-platform flake core / scraper

also 5.5), and even perhaps as far west as Nost 1, where fieldwalking found two scrapers, four cores (including two keeled non-discoidal flake cores), and a core rejuvenation flake of possibly later Neolithic date. Unfortunately, the area between field 21 and Nost 1 was not fieldwalked during the watching-brief at the quarry, so it is impossible to complete a more detailed comparison. To the south and east of Ladybridge, in fields 24 and 50, the density of material again drops away sharply. The cluster most similar to the scatters to the east of Chapel Hill was in field 32 on the southern edge of the study area, although the density of material was far lower than in field 11 (Table 5.1). Unlike fields 2B and 21 there is a high incidence of red, brown, and brownish-yellow till flint in field 32 (Table 5.2), and ten possibly later Neolithic cores, along with two scrapers and two miscellaneous retouched pieces, attest to the intensity of activity here. There are few cores, core rejuvenation flakes, or scrapers of this date away from fields 2B, 9–12, 21, Nost 1, and 32, and of those that do occur, the majority are from fields adjoining the high-density scatters. The exceptions are a scraper in field 31A, three cores in fields 7, 28, and

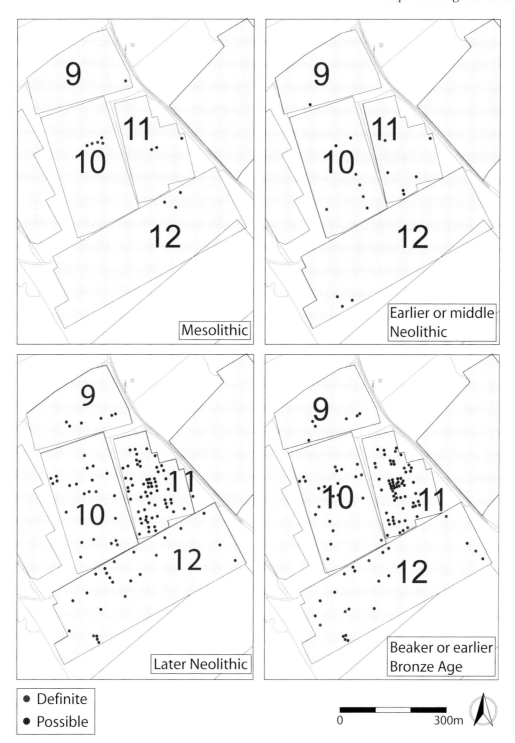

Fig 5.21 *Chronological development of Chapel Hill.* © *Crown Copyright/database right 2013. An Ordnance Survey/EDINA supplied service*

30, and three core rejuvenation flakes in fields 8 and 16. These other areas also produced an oblique arrowhead, two borers, a denticulate, thirteen miscellaneous retouched flakes, a notched flake, and a serrated piece.

These patterns were to continue into the latter half of the 3rd millennium and beyond (Fig 5.24). Telling later Neolithic and earlier Bronze Age apart, and identifying middle or later Bronze Age flintwork, is anything but straightforward,

but Beaker-associated diagnostics – most notably barbed-and-tanged arrowheads and 'button' or 'thumbnail' scrapers (Fig 5.25) – are common in certain parts of the study area. Like the later Neolithic material, it is distributed away from the monuments with a few outlying pieces of this date on the limestone and Upsland ridges to the west and east of the study area. A particular concentration of Beaker or other earlier Bronze Age material occurs on and around Chapel Hill in fields 10, 11,

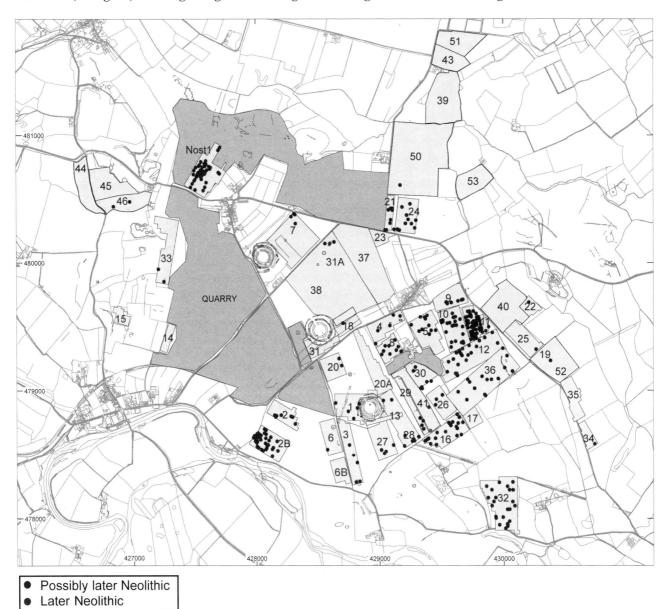

Fig 5.22   Distribution of later Neolithic lithics from widespaced fieldwalking. © Crown Copyright/database right 2013. An Ordnance Survey/EDINA supplied service

and 12, where there is a tendency for these pieces to be more closely clustered than the later Neolithic flintwork, and in more cases than not, unassociated with later Neolithic flint (Fig 5.21). The same can also be concluded for the three other definite clusters of material of this date, in fields 2B, 32, and Nost 1. Given this evidence, the notion of continuity may not adequately describe final Neolithic/earlier Bronze Age activity, and within individual scatters there may also be the deliberate exploitation of specific areas where little later Neolithic material had been deposited. Diagnostic Beaker material is rare elsewhere in the study area, including in field 21, and the small number of Beaker-associated pits from the adjacent area of excavation (Dickson and Hopkinson 2011, 129–35) confirms that this part of the study area had indeed now lost its former significance. Three barbed-and-tanged arrowheads

were discovered, two in Nost 1, the other in field 12; this artefact type is equally rare across the Stonehenge Environs and Cranborne Chase (Barrett *et al* 1991, 110–11; Richards 1990, 274). A triangular arrowhead was found in field 32.

Only a few pieces of what may be post-Beaker flintwork are known and those that do occur are largely located off the plateau (Fig 5.24). There is little evidence that fields 8–12 continued in importance, the area producing no middle or later Bronze Age material. Lithics of this period are often largely unrecognisable, but the possible abandonment of what had previously been a key area of activity is certainly paralleled across the Stonehenge Environs, its impressive round barrow cemeteries and contemporary lithic scatters concentrating across the western part of the landscape in contrast to the henge-associated eastern zone

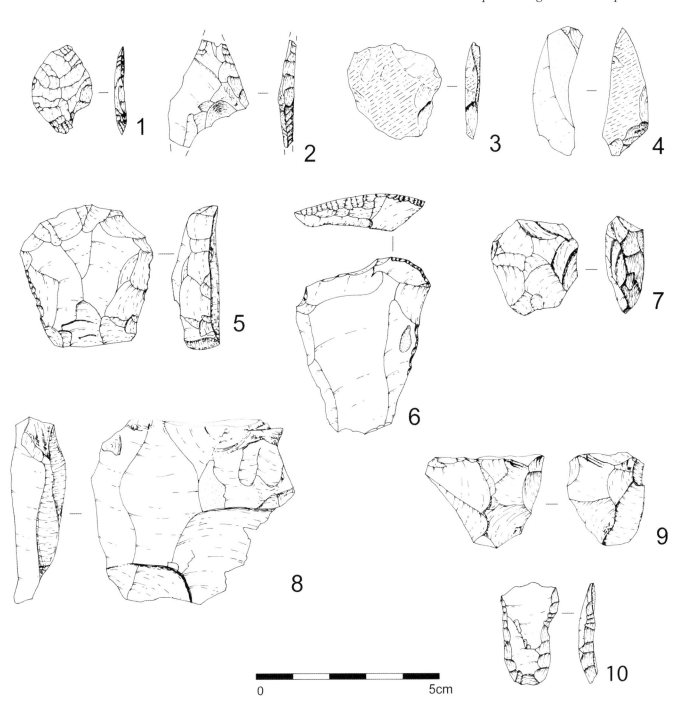

Fig 5.23 Selected later Neolithic lithics from widespaced fieldwalking: 1, field 3, leaf-shaped arrowhead (Class 4Bi); 2, field 11, PTD [Petit-Tranchet Derivative] Class H (oblique) arrowhead; 3, field 10, partially polished axe/adze flake fragment; 4, field 27, partially polished axe/adze flake; 5, field 12, double side and end scraper; 6, field 32, side and end scraper; 7, field 10, exhausted discoidal core; 8, field 21, possible single-platform flake core; 9, field 32, single-platform flake core; 10, field 22, PTD Class B (chisel) arrowhead

(Richards 1990, 271–5). Fields 5, 36, and 40, which partly surround Chapel Hill, produced a crude flake scraper, a Janus flake, and a rough multi-platform flake core, all possibly of Bronze Age date on technological grounds. Elsewhere, there is a scraper formed by exceptionally large and steep removals from field 53, and a coarse denticulate from 46. It is difficult to interpret this small collection, but it is

likely, given the possibly late date of many of Thornborough's round barrows (4.9), and the discovery of a large ditched rectilinear enclosure or enclosed field of possible later Bronze Age date in the Nosterfield Quarry (Dickson and Hopkinson 2011, 143), that some of this landscape now entered into a new phase of land use, with localised occupation occurring only around the fringes of the plateau.

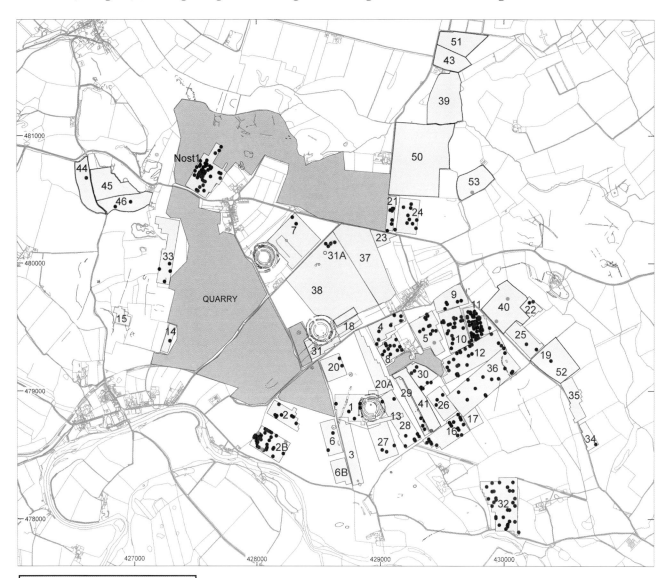

Fig 5.24 Distribution of Beaker and Bronze Age lithics from widespaced fieldwalking. © Crown Copyright / database right 2013. An Ordnance Survey / EDINA supplied service

*Fig 5.25 (*opposite*)   Selected Beaker lithics from widespaced fieldwalking: 1, field 12, barbed-and-tanged arrowhead (Class Sutton bi); 2, Nost 1, barbed-and-tanged arrowhead (Class Sutton b); 3, Nost 1, barbed-and-tanged arrowhead; 4, field 10, disc Levallois core (often associated with All-Over-Corded Beakers); 5, field 10, discoidal keeled Levallois core; 6, field 2, side scraper; 7, field 2B, double side scraper; 8, field 8, convex end thumb scraper (heavily burnt); 9, field 10, extended end thumb scraper; 10, field 11, side end scraper; 11, field 11, side end thumb scraper; 12, field 12, side end thumb scraper; 13, field 32, double end and side scraper; 14, field 32, side and end thumb scraper; 15, field 32, end thumb scraper; 16, Nost 1, side scraper; 17, Nost 1, double end disc scraper*

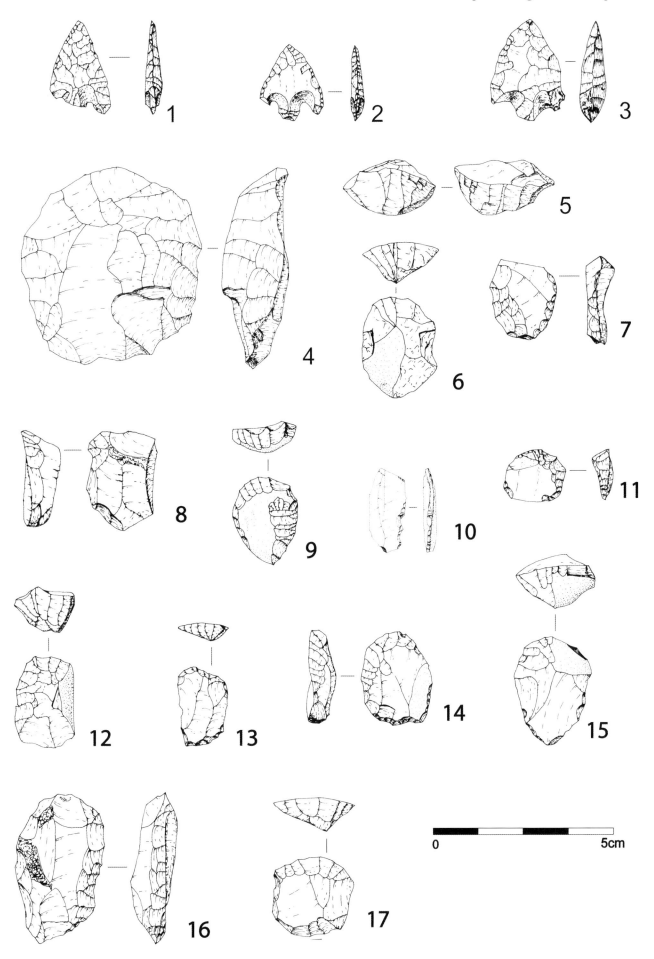

5.3   Geophysical prospection, total collection, and test-pitting

by Jan Harding and Benjamin Johnson

5.3.1   Introduction

The next stage of investigating the wider Thornborough landscape, devised and implemented as part of the ALSF Project, focused on the systematic and intensive examination of five specific locations (Fig 5.1; see D2), chosen on the basis of the results from widespaced fieldwalking. As already mentioned, these were allocated their own 'field' numbers, but will be known here by the original field in which they were located, with the exception of the work in field 38, which will be referred to as the 'Three Hills Barrow Group', given its association with these monuments. The detailed examination of surface scatters by total collection, and the exploration of any underlying archaeology by geophysical prospection and test-pitting, aimed to explore the characteristics of these scatters further, offer insights into the relationship between the ploughsoil and sub-surface, and establish the condition and archaeological potential of any buried archaeology (see D2.1). The test-pits would be expanded to expose the full extent of any discrete cultural features, enabling them to be excavated fully. In reality, only two features were actually discovered, and neither was of definite prehistoric date: the investigations in field 12 revealed a linear ditch, or what is likely to be a field boundary (D2.3), and another boundary, probably of medieval date, was found in field 18 (D2.5).

The large lithic concentration to the east of Chapel Hill was densest in field 11, the number of worked pieces per hectare above both the mean and median for the study area (Table 5.1). Here a low ridge of till rises 1.5m above the surrounding area, and it was across the southern limit of this ridge that the follow-up fieldwork occurred (Fig 5.30). The majority of the previously collected material from field 11 was either of later Neolithic or earlier Bronze Age date. Fields 12 and 16 were chosen for different reasons. Both are characterised by a lithic density well below that of field 11, but higher than elsewhere with the exception of fields 2B, 21, and 32, all of which were unavailable for further study (Table 5.1). Field 12 lies on the southern fringes of the field 11 scatter, and it was hoped that further work in the northwest of this largely flat field (Fig 5.26) would help characterise the extent and nature of activity east of Chapel Hill. The western half of field 16, located on the upper gravels opposite the triple-ditched round barrow (Fig 5.27), offered a contrast with the till. Here the field slopes very gently from north to south across an old palaeochannel. The presence of a sizeable Mesolithic and earlier Neolithic lithic collection from the site of the monument (4.2) suggests the location's importance to those who occupied the Thornborough landscape. By contrast, field 18, immediately to the east of the central henge (Fig

5.33), was selected because its lithic density is below the mean (Table 5.1), and crucially, appears to be a place where worked flint and chert was not deposited during the later Neolithic and earlier Bronze Age. Its ground surface slopes very slightly downward from north to south at its southern end, but is flat to the north. Only four worked lithics had been discovered by widespaced walking, and its further investigation would establish whether this reflected a genuine lack of archaeological activity in the immediate vicinity of the monument complex. The Three Hills Barrow Group was also selected for study since geophysical prospection had already been undertaken there (Fig 5.28), but its monuments prevented the digging of test-pits.

Magnetometry was undertaken across 90m by 90m of each scatter, the exception being field 16, an unplanned addition to the fieldwork programme where no geophysical prospection was completed. Geophysical prospection at the Three Hills Barrow Group covered an area nearly three times larger (Fig 3.25). The results at the scatters were patchy and inconclusive; no further mention is made of them here, but they are fully described in D2. The total collection of all lithic material was then undertaken across the same area, although in fields 11 and 12 it was subsequently extended to 90m by 180m. Each walker was assigned a 2m transect, thereby providing complete surface coverage. Finally, nine 2m by 1m test-pits were dug 10m apart across a 30m by 30m grid, their siting determined by the results of both geophysical prospection and total lithic collection. In a number of instances these test-pits were enlarged and further pits dug, including two 5m by 5m in field 11. The results of total collection and test-pitting, including 350 pieces of worked flint and chert, allow us to go some way towards creating a biography for the selected scatters. With such an exercise, post-depositional factors are as important as their original deposition, and consequently, the following discussion starts by examining the processes responsible for the creation and recovery of this ploughsoil evidence. Attention will then turn to their chronology and the practices responsible for their creation. The lithic material itself is fully described in D3.

5.3.2   Lithic scatters and post-depositional factors

The lithic recognition and recovery rate during total collection was very much lower than in previous widespaced fieldwalking (Table 5.3). The results from field 11 are the best example of this. Widespaced collection across the part of the field selected for the follow-up investigation recovered 94 lithics from about 13% of the ploughsoil's surface. This implies a projected total collection recovery rate of 440 lithics per hectare from the same area, but in fact only 97 pieces were found, giving a density of just 60.6 per hectare. Put another way, what was found represents only 14% of the expected number of lithics and

Table 5.3 Lithic densities at the high-, medium-, and low-density scatters

Site	Area of scatter (ha)	Number from widespaced fieldwalking	Lithics per ha*	Number [and density per ha] from total collection	Expected lithics per 2m by 1m test-pit**	Lithic average per 2m by 1m test-pit
'high' density (field 11)	1.6	94	440.6	97 [60.6]	52.3–54.6	11.3
'medium' density (field 12)	1.6	31	145.3	6 [3.8]	1.3–1.4	1
'medium' density (field 16)	0.8	19	178.1	22 [27.5]	5.7–6.0	1.9
'low' density (field 18)	0.8	1	9.4	7 [7.5]	1.5–1.6	0.9
Three Hills Barrow Group***	2.4	8	47.3	139 [57.9]	–	–

* = Adjusted × 7.5 to 100%
** = Based on flint numbers from total collection and assuming that 3–7% of a field's population on surface of ploughsoil (Boismier 1997, 130). Adjusted according to the ratio between the area walked and the average volume of the test-pits in each of the fields
*** = Widespaced fieldwalking was undertaken at the Three Hills Barrow Group during both the VMNLP (field 31A) and the ALSF Project (field 38). The number of lithics and the calculated density is based on the results from field 31A

a similarly dramatic reduction in density was also evident in fields 12 and 16, where the total finds were just 2.6% and 15.4% of what was expected. The proportion was very much higher for field 18, where the results represented 93% of the estimated population, and for the Three Hills Barrow Group, where the results exceeded expectation. The significant under-representation of lithics was unexpected and may have been exacerbated by contributing factors. In each instance, total collection had to be undertaken almost immediately after ploughing, leaving no time for the surface to weather. This would at least partly explain the lower discovery rates in fields 11 and 12, where the original widespaced walking was completed in better conditions. It would not, however, explain the lower discovery rates in fields 16 and 18, for here the widespaced walking was also completed shortly after ploughing. Another possible factor is the lower discovery rate of students undertaking the total collection when compared to previous years, although the large collection from the Three Hills Barrow Group, collected by the same students, suggests otherwise. It should be noted that a different and more experienced group of students was used for field 18. These variations, unidentified until fieldwork was completed, highlight the value of rewalking areas of total collection. The failure to do so was a regrettable oversight.

The possible significance of the student recovery rate may be explored further by examining the test-pit results, which similarly represent only a fraction of what could be reasonably expected given the numbers from total collection. In a detailed review of modern tillage processes, Boismier (1997, 25, 29, 34, 130) concluded, using data from experiments and simulation, that 3–7% of a ploughsoil's artefact population tends to be represented on the surface. The fraction, which is optimistic when compared to most other experiments (see Clark and Schofield 1991; Waddington 1999, 94), but nonetheless confirmed by

other recent work (Edmonds *et al* 1999, 60), appears to remain steady after just ten ploughing events at about 5% of the parent population. Accordingly, it can be employed to calculate a hypothetical population for each test-pit (Table 5.3). By doing so it again becomes evident that only a proportion, this time of between 21% and 77%, was actually discovered, the highest fraction found in field 12. This may suggest that the low discovery rate of students in the 2003 field season was a key factor in the shortfall in lithic numbers, yet the contents of each test-pit were completely sieved, students were encouraged to keep everything, and three experienced Site Assistants were usually on hand. Accounting for these shortfalls is therefore anything but straightforward.

It is also difficult to use the results of total collection and test-pitting, which were completed across relatively small areas, to assess the decision to use a 15m walking distance for widespaced collection. Putting aside the results from field 12, which seem seriously unrepresentative, the most tightly clustered flint scatters are in fields 16 and 18 (Figs 5.27 and 5.33 respectively), and in each instance it is likely that widespaced walking along a 15m transect would have led to the recovery of at least one worked piece. Of course, the discovery of nothing more than a single piece would result in these scatters being regarded as general background lithic 'noise', but then as clusters go those in fields 16 and 18 are exceptionally limited in both number and distribution (see Clark and Schofield 1991, 101–2). This, along with some of the consistent characteristics of scatters (eg the increasing proportion of retouch the larger the size of the collection), the discovery by widespaced walking of small pieces like microliths, and the general correlations between the results of widespaced fieldwalking and the follow-up investigations (5.3.3), all suggest that the fieldwork has indeed resulted in a fairly accurate representation of Thornborough's ploughsoil. There is, of course, considerable room for improvement in both the quantity and quality of the evidence, but it is nonetheless believed that the collected lithics allow us to speak with some confidence about the chronology and use of this landscape.

Other variables are clearly having an impact on Thornborough's ploughsoil scatters. It is known that the constitution and distribution of surface material becomes less representative of parent populations as tillage continues. The process of degradation can, within a period of no more than 25–50 years, replace the signature of the original scatter with a spurious tillage-induced pattern (Boismier 1997, 233). It is difficult to ascertain the extent of this transformation at Thornborough, although one indicator may be the relatively high number of tools located by widespaced walking and total collection. Artefact size is one of the primary determinants of whether an object type has a greater chance of occurrence on the surface than elsewhere in the ploughsoil, and large size classes, which include many finished tools or cores, are often better represented in the surface assemblage immediately after the commencement of tillage. Through time, however, these differences tend to decrease as objects become more mixed throughout the ploughsoil and 'equilibrium' occurs in their surface appearance after ten of so ploughing events (*ibid*, 29). At three of the four intensively studied fields the assemblages from total collection produced a higher percentage of retouched items than the collections from test-pitting (Table D3.7), the difference being greatest in fields 11 and 12 where the proportion of finished tools also exceeded that from earlier widespaced walking. One possibility is that the distribution of retouched pieces is still to reach equilibrium in the ploughsoil of this area. The scatters here can perhaps be described as being in what Boismier (*ibid*, 239–40) calls an 'intermediate' state, where they have been subjected to a high degree of rearrangement but nonetheless retain important elements of their original characteristics. This is further borne out by the rather suggestive distribution in field 11 (see below). In field 16, by contrast, the proportion of retouched pieces discovered by widespaced walking exceeds that discovered by later total collection, suggesting that equilibrium had already been reached, thereby reflecting the greater impact of tillage. Unfortunately, the small number of cores discovered by total collection and test-pitting makes a comparison meaningless.

The significant impact of tillage is illustrated by another facet of the available lithic collection. The results of widespaced fieldwalking suggest higher breakage rates amongst those fields walked in 2003 than those walked earlier (D3.3), perhaps demonstrating the increasing rate of attrition caused by more recent episodes of ploughing. The condition of the lithic assemblage from total collection and test-pitting confirms this interpretation. The percentages of incomplete pieces from the earlier widespaced fieldwalking in fields 11, 12, 16, and 18 were 42%, 49%, 44% and 17% respectively, the low figure in the last

of these fields further suggesting the higher levels of preservation in areas around the central henge known to have been used for out-field grazing during the medieval period (2.2). These figures contrast with the much higher proportions of broken lithics from total collection and test-pitting: 73% from field 11, 67% from fields 12 and 18, and 79% from field 16. Overall, these statistics demonstrate a marked rise in plough-damage over recent years, and suggest that the vast majority of lithics now existing in the ploughsoil have already become broken. Whether or not artefacts are broken, their margins are often so plough-damaged as to obscure any original retouch, and indeed, this may sometimes have been completely removed. The rapid degradation of this resource has obvious implications for the long-term management and research of this landscape, yet remains an understudied aspect of conservation and preservation.

5.3.3   *Lithic deposition and use*

Only six worked pieces were recovered by total collection in field 12, all towards the northern edge of the 1.6 hectares walked, and test-pitting produced just ten lithics across an area where total collection had failed to find anything (Fig 5.26). As already mentioned, these lithic numbers compare unfavourably with the 47 pieces from widespaced walking across the same area, and four of the test-pits were empty. The largest collection, from TP7, was of only three worked pieces, the other test-pits producing either one or two lithics. In total, the follow-up investigations discovered ten flakes, one core, two scrapers, two irregular waste pieces, and a fragment of retouched material. The results of widespaced walking had suggested the use of the field's north-west corner from the Mesolithic through to the earlier Bronze Age, producing a double-sided long end scraper of later Mesolithic or earlier Neolithic date, a nosed scraper which may be of later Mesolithic or later Neolithic date, and a Beaker barbed-and-tanged arrowhead, but there were no diagnostic finds from the follow-up investigations. However, the relatively high incidence of feather terminations (Table D3.17), along with the careful preparation of striking platforms as shown by punctiform and linear butts (Table D3.14), may suggest a large proportion of Mesolithic and earlier Neolithic material.

The excavations at the triple-ditched round barrow highlighted the importance of the southern extremity of the plateau to earlier Neolithic communities (4.2). The follow-up fieldwork in field 16 was located immediately to the south of the monument, across what may have been a watercourse at the time of the monument's construction (Fig 5.27). The largely ploughed-out palaeochannel was identified as a shallow silty sand deposit with a large number of cobbles in TP4, TP7, TP8, and TP9, suggesting it is curving in a south-easterly direction. Twenty-two lithics were recovered by total collection from an area of 0.8ha, most in the northern half of the area walked,

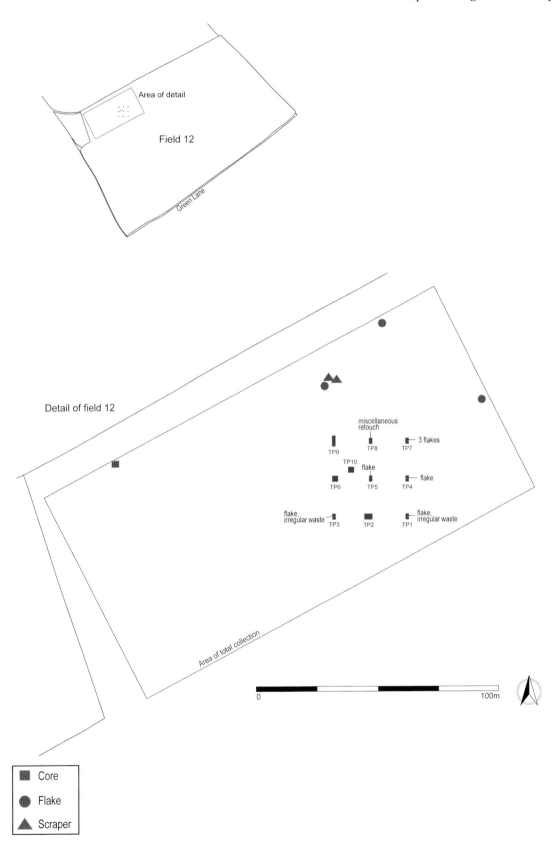

Fig 5.26 Total collection and test-pitting in field 12

their distribution corresponding very closely with the results from widespaced collection. They appear to form three discrete spreads, possibly orientated north-west to south-east, and the test-pitting, which produced seventeen lithics, confirmed the spatial extent of the middle scatter, with the three most westerly units producing just two worked pieces. The largest number was from TP4, with six, the others producing one, two, or three pieces. The overall distribution of lithics is therefore consistent with the

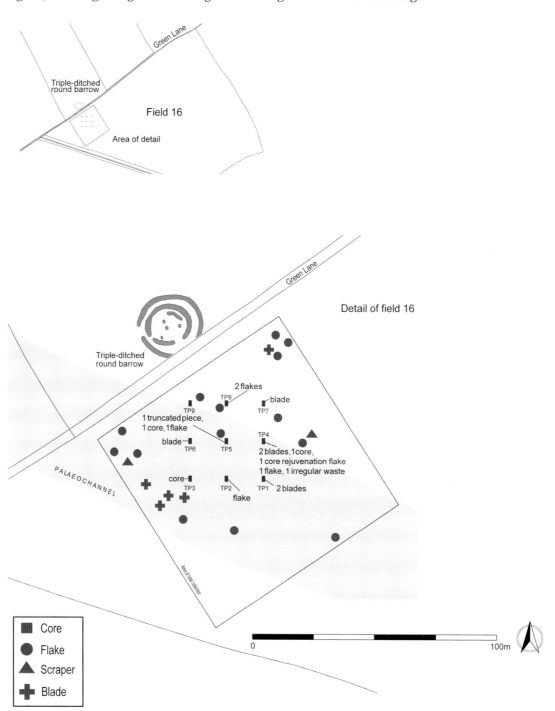

Fig 5.27   Total collection and test-pitting in field 16, showing cropmark of palaeochannel

likely course of the palaeochannel. The total lithic collection from the follow-up fieldwork consisted of: nineteen flakes and eleven blades, one of which was a bladelet; three cores, of which two are complete opposed platform pieces of Mesolithic date, along with a core rejuvenation flake; and two scrapers, including a probable 'thumbnail' of Mesolithic or earlier Bronze Age date, and the distal fragment of a possible serrated blade of Mesolithic or Neolithic date (Table D3.7). The presence of a relatively high proportion of early material is broadly in keeping with the previous discussion of landscape use.

Unlike elsewhere, earlier stages of knapping are

indicated in field 16 by at least 27% of the lithics from widespaced walking and 44% from the follow-up fieldwork being at least partly corticated (Tables D3.18–19 and D3.23–24). That the nearby watercourse may have provided a ready supply of eroded flint, which was then knapped on site, is certainly suggested by 33% of the material from the total collection and test-pitting being of till/gravel flint (Table D3.10), in excess of the results from widespaced walking, and a relatively high percentage for the study area as a whole. A core and nine partly cortical flakes were of this material. The knapping of local sources may also be indicated by the three gravel

Fig 5.28   Total collection at the Three Hills Barrow Group. © Crown Copyright/database right 2013. An Ordnance Survey/EDINA supplied service

pieces and four chert pieces with cortex. Despite this, the till provided more material than other sources and was also worked at this location. Two of the cores, and the core rejuvenation flake, were of this material, as were thirteen secondary flakes or blades. Lithic material from the excavation of the triple-ditched round barrow, which also included a relatively high proportion of corticated material (Tables D3.20 and D3.22), suggests intensive, but probably sporadic and short-term, Mesolithic and earlier Neolithic occupation in this area. The evidence from the triple-ditched round barrow and surface collection from its surrounding field indicate that the focus of activity was actually across the southern edge of field 41, the area investigated in field 16 being on its periphery. This could explain the absence of features in the test-pits, although it is equally as likely they were missed

by such a small sample, or never existed in the first place.

A total of 139 lithics were found at the Three Hills Barrow Group during total collection (Table D3.7). The material is distributed along this ridge, and especially its northern half, with notable clustering around the centremost barrow (see Figs 3.25 and 5.28). The collection consisted of 70 flakes, 32 blades, including five Mesolithic bladelets, a core rejuvenation flake from a blade core, eight pieces of irregular waste, and eleven flint cores, consisting of two complete opposed blade cores of Mesolithic date, two other blade cores, two multi-platform flake cores, and two discoidal flake cores. There was also a microlith fragment and two complete flake knives, along with the fragments of another three (eg Fig 5.29, 1–3), three unclassifiable scrapers (eg Fig 5.29, 4) and a 'thumbnail' scraper of

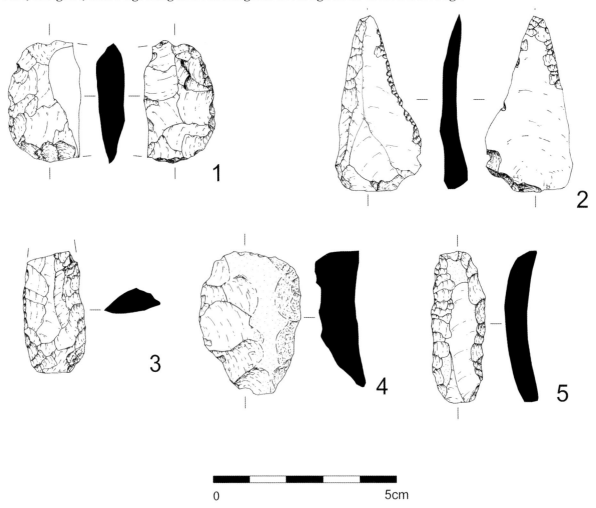

Fig 5.29   Selected lithics from total collection at Three Hills Barrow Group: 1, bifacially flaked knife; 2, bifacially flaked knife with a facetted butt; 3, scale-flaked plano-convex knife; 4, scraper with steep, step-flaked distal end; 5, fabricator

Beaker date, three 'fabricators' (eg Fig 5.29, 5), and three miscellaneous retouched flakes. The relatively high percentage of blades suggests the early use of this location and the microlith, bladelets, and opposed platform blade cores attest to a Mesolithic component in the material. 'Fabricators' had a long currency, towards the end of which they were among the few finished flint artefact types to recur in flint industries of the full Bronze Age (Ford *et al* 1984); they also occur in early Bronze Age burials (Clarke 1970, 448, where they are called 'strike-a-lights'; Longworth 1984, 68). Given that only two other specimens were found across the study area, in fields 9 and 32, they may relate to activity connected with the barrows, whether or not they derived from burials. The same holds for four of the five flake knives. One is a regularly formed fragment with all-over bifacial retouch (Fig 5.29, 1). The remaining four are all different, but elide into a wide class of straight-edged retouched flakes, some pointed (Fig 5.29, 2) and some scale-flaked, which, at their most elaborate, resemble plano-convex knives (Fig 5.29, 3), and like them, occur in early Bronze Age contexts, as in barrows at Rudston and Hutton Buscel in Yorkshire or Ovingham in Northumberland (Kinnes and Longworth 1985, cat nos 67, 153,

214). Early Bronze Age knapping at Three Hills may account for the relatively high proportions of plain (ie unprepared) flake butts (Table D3.14) and of hinge and step terminations (Table D3.17). The majority of lithics belonging to two distinct periods, one predating the monumentalisation of the plateau, the other broadly contemporary with the construction of Bronze Age round barrows, exactly matches the collection found here during excavation (4.8).

A total of 142 worked lithics were recovered from total collection and test-pitting in field 11 (Table D3.7). The 97 pieces from the 1.6ha of total collection were spread in three broad bands running approximately north-west to south-east (Fig 5.30). Their distribution closely mirrors the results from widespaced walking, and given that these bands are on approximately the same axis as the field's eastern boundary, they are perhaps the result of tillage spreading what were originally at least three spatially defined clusters. It has been calculated that the horizontal movement of objects ranges from an initial displacement of around 1.5m to between 2.16m and 6.77m after 96 ploughing events, depending on slope gradient, and that horizontal displacement is cumulative and directional through time, with the distance an object

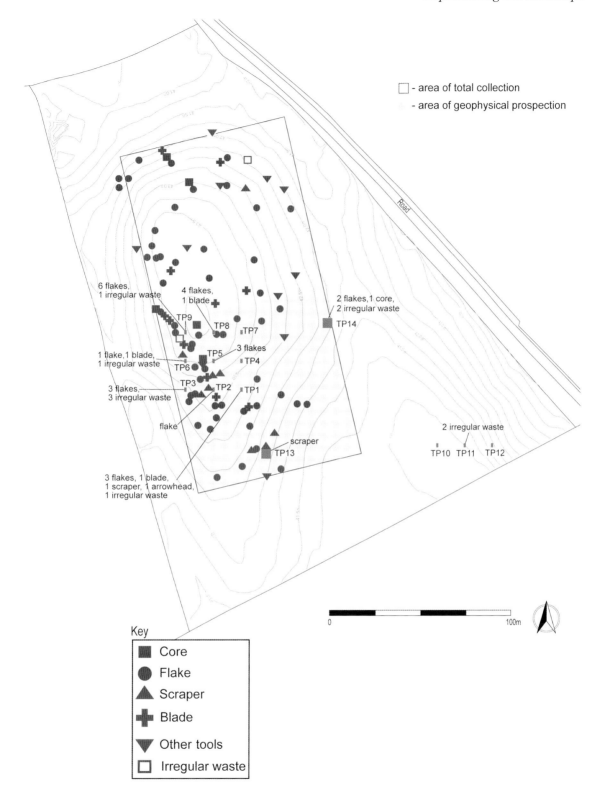

Fig 5.30 Total collection and test-pitting in field 11; test-pit numbers were unrecorded for five lithics.
© *Crown Copyright / database right 2013. An Ordnance Survey / EDINA supplied service*

moves increasing as the number of tillage events rises (Boismier 1997, 35, 163, 178–83). These actions significantly increase the area of an original scatter, although smaller pieces like trimming flakes, chips, and spalls tend to remain in situ (Edmonds *et al* 1999, 50). Given these factors, it seems probable that two of the lithic clusters were located near the top of the knoll, on its western side above the 43m OD contour.

The spatial derivation of the most northerly and least dense of these three bands is more problematic, but its concentration between the 42m and 43m OD contours suggests a marginally less elevated location than the other two scatters, overlooking a small basin, now filled by a pond, in the north-west corner of the field. These patterns are largely confirmed by the distribution of material in the test-pits, although the

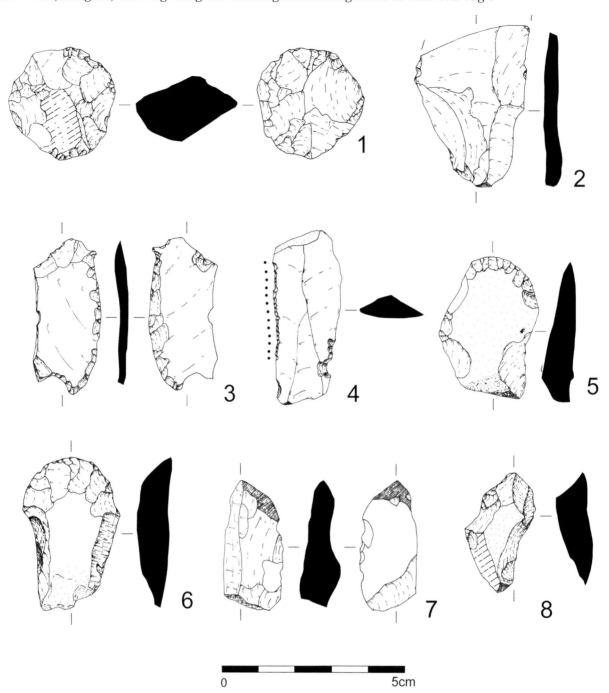

Fig 5.31   Selected lithics from total collection and test-pitting in field 11: 1, unstruck Levallois core; 2, Levallois-like flake with facetted butt and broken distal end; 3, chisel arrowhead fragment; 4, serrated blade with broken butt; 5, scale-flaked knife possibly made on flint from the southern chalk; 6, scraper; 7, fragment from edge-ground axehead or possibly a discoidal knife; 8, denticulate

fact that the largest amount is in TP1 could suggest that the most southerly of the three bands actually represents the dispersal of two previous scatters. The upper slope on the eastern side of the rise may have been less intensively used.

The flint from total collection consisted of 52 flakes, eleven blades, nine scrapers (eg Fig 5.31, 6), five of which, including a complete scale-flaked Beaker 'thumbnail' form and a complete nosed scraper, are later Neolithic or earlier Bronze Age, and four cores, at least two of which, both of till flint, are of middle or later Neolithic Levallois form (eg Fig 5.31, 1). Also

recovered were: a distal fragment of a probably early Mesolithic microlith; three serrated pieces on blade-like blanks of Mesolithic or Neolithic date (Fig 5.31, 4), two of which retain a high gloss along the serrated edge from cutting silica-rich material; a fragment of a Neolithic flint axe or a discoidal knife with a bifacially ground edge (Fig 5.31, 7); a bifacially flaked fragment of a chisel or oblique arrowhead of middle to later Neolithic date (Fig 5.31, 3); a complete denticulate of later Neolithic or Bronze Age date (Fig 5.31, 8); and a complete scale-flaked early Bronze Age knife (Fig 5.31, 5). Forty-five lithics were recovered from test-pits. Whilst seven worked pieces were found in both TP1 and TP9, the others located on the ridge-top contained only 1–3 lithics each. Two 5m by 5m test-pits, TP13 and TP14, produced surprisingly few lithics, and TP10–12, located downslope in the south-east corner of the field, just two pieces of irregular waste. The small collection from all the test-pits includes 25 flakes, two scrapers, three blades, one core, one core rejuvenation flake, and a bifacially flaked piriform leaf-shaped arrowhead, missing only its tip, of earlier Neolithic date. The material from both the test-pits and total collection reinforces many of the conclusions from widespaced fieldwalking. Unlike the other fields selected for further investigation, there is little evidence for a Mesolithic or earlier Neolithic component here and even the three serrated pieces on blade-like blanks are of a form which consistently occurs in association with Peterborough Ware and Grooved Ware (Manby 1974; 1975).

The almost complete absence of pieces which can be dated earlier than the later Neolithic/earlier Bronze Age – just 2% of the definite diagnostic pieces – suggests the field was used only very occasionally prior to the 3rd millennium BC. The overwhelming majority of the collection from both widespaced walking and the subsequent fieldwork can be seen as a homogeneous later Neolithic industry. A distinctive technology is represented by the two Levallois cores, one unstruck and the other worked to exhaustion, two Levallois flakes (eg Fig 5.31, 2), and faceting on other flake butts. This was the technique used in the middle and later Neolithic to produce blanks for transverse arrowheads and possibly even discoidal knives (Durden 1994, 158, 304; Healy 1984, 12; Makey 1996, 61–2), and a possible fragmentary example of the former is present in the scatter. The technique is notably represented at the till flint sources on Flamborough Head (Durden 1995, 410–11), as well as being more widely employed (Manby 1974, 83). The importation of a different, perhaps carefully selected, raw material seems to have been bound up with this new technology, with over half the pieces being of reddish-brown, red, or brown flint, in contrast to less than an eighth of the pieces from the other scatters, with chert virtually absent (Table D3.10). Items include the oblique arrowhead, a Levallois core and flake, and the possible discoidal knife fragment (Fig 5.31, 7), a form also made on Flamborough Head. The majority of this material is most likely from the tills, although a significant element, coloured yellowish-red, probably originates from till/gravel sources. At least some of this material was worked on the site, on the evidence of two probable retouch chips and one probable core platform chip, the latter a by-product of Levallois flaking. Higher frequencies of non-cortical flakes (Tables D3.23–24), however, indicate that much more of the material was brought here in a decorticated state. With the exception of the 'thumbnail' scraper, most tools were made on the largest available flakes, and one red flint scraper

fragment, when complete, would have been on a flake far larger than any in the collection, suggesting it was imported as a finished implement.

There are other distinctive characteristics of the lithic collection from field 11. Total collection and test-pitting produced the lowest number of cores from any of the intensively studied areas, representing just 4% of the collection (Table D3.7), a proportion which tallies with the results of widespaced fieldwalking (Table D3.5). At least six of these are of later Neolithic or earlier Bronze Age date, but given the amount of fieldwork undertaken here, this total compares unfavourably with the other broadly contemporary high-density scatters in fields 10 and 32. The lithics are also set apart from other collections by the high proportion of retouched forms, the majority of which are, as mentioned, of likely later Neolithic or earlier Bronze Age date. Widespaced fieldwalking had already discovered more retouched items here than anywhere else in the study area, representing 17% of the total collected, with a density of 7 per hectare (Table 5.1 and D3.5). Their proportion from total collection and test-pitting was similarly high, representing just over 16% of the total, with a density of 12.3 per hectare (Table D3.7). The presence of these finished tools, their manufacture on imported and brightly coloured flint which is rare elsewhere, and the evidence for Levallois flaking, all suggest the distinctive role of this location for the production or finishing of particular objects. Field 11 may therefore have possessed its own unique function, akin perhaps to sites on Flamborough Head, where specialised knapping was undertaken alongside more mundane lithic production and consumption (see 5.5). The presence of less-distinctive flake cores and scrapers certainly attests to the latter, and the overall distribution of material suggests that the knapping of cores, including the Levallois specimens, occurred across the field's northern half, with scrapers largely found across its southern half (Fig 5.32). Curiously, core rejuvenation flakes were found away from the cores. There may have been similar activity immediately along the eastern edge of field 10, where there were two further Levallois cores (Fig 5.32), one of brownish-yellow till/gravel flint and the other of black till flint. One can only speculate whether the colour differences between the Levallois material on either side of the hedgerow separating fields 10 and 11 were of any significance.

Was this area, with by far the highest lithic density from across the study area, unassociated with structural features like those discovered on the nearby Nosterfield Quarry, and further afield, on Marton-le-Moor (Dickson and Hopkinson 2011; Tavener 1996)? It is impossible to be certain if surviving features were missed by the excavation units, or indeed, whether they have been completely destroyed by ploughing. The topsoil in this area is certainly shallower than elsewhere across the Thornborough landscape, if only by a few centimetres, and the absence of subsoil, present at other excavations, suggests a general trend of

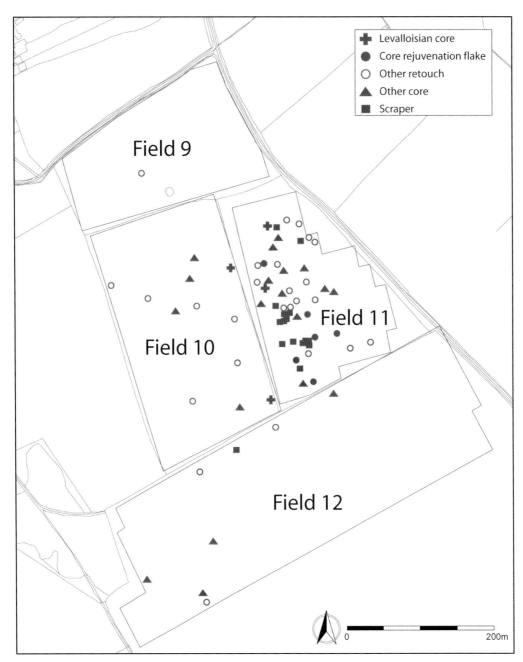

Fig 5.32   Distribution of likely later Neolithic and early Bronze Age lithics on Chapel Hill. © Crown Copyright / database right 2013. An Ordnance Survey / EDINA supplied service

soil removal from the ridge top and its redeposition downslope. Such a process would, over many years, slowly but surely destroy buried archaeological features. Despite this, it is difficult to imagine features being cut into the heavy drift geology of till which mantles Chapel Hill, and the excavation of the test-pits certainly proved a challenge. It may therefore be more likely that the remains in field 11 were simply discarded on the land surface, and indeed, elsewhere in Britain there is every indication this practice became especially popular in the later Neolithic (eg Edmonds *et al* 1999, 49–50, 60; Entwistle and Richards 1987; Richards 1990, 158–71; French and Pryor 2005, 94–8, 165; Healy 1987; 1988). An informative parallel may be King Barrow Ridge in the Stonehenge Environs, similarly located

near to a major group of henges. Here surface collection, geophysical and geochemical prospection, and small-scale excavation identified an extensive later Neolithic surface assemblage, containing a high proportion of tools, and twenty pits of later 4th- and early 3rd-millennium date (Richards 1990, 109–23). The location of the pits failed to correlate with the distribution of surface material, being adjacent to the densest lithic material instead. They were, however, always within an area of enhanced soil phosphate (Entwistle and Richards 1987, 32). It was suggested that these features had been used for waste disposal, an activity probably undertaken on the periphery of any settlement occupied for more than a single season (*ibid*, 19–20; Holgate 1988, 35–6; Schofield 1991, 4), but that this practice was

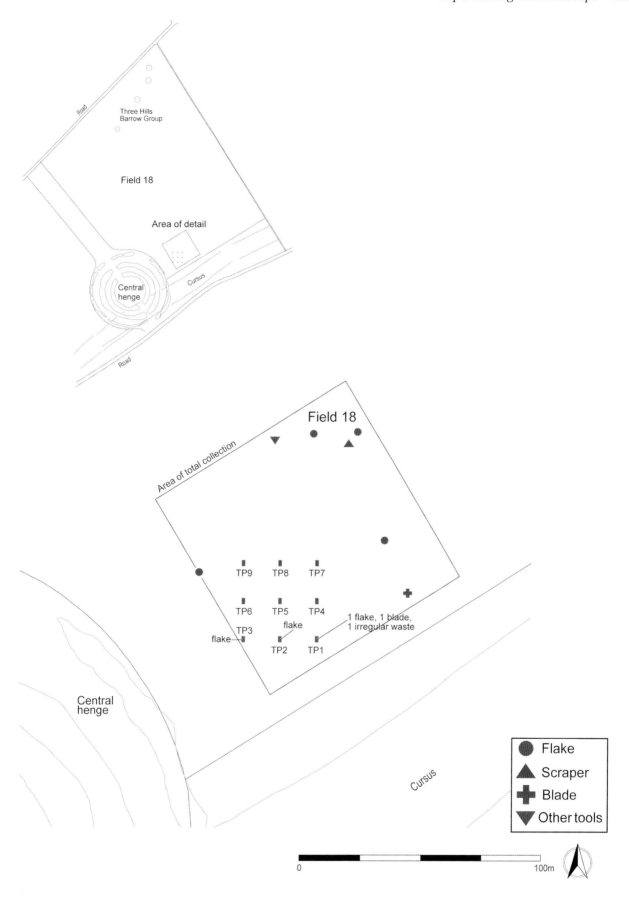

Fig 5.33 Total collection and test-pitting in field 18. © Crown Copyright / database right 2013. An Ordnance Survey / EDINA supplied service

superseded at some point in the later Neolithic by a shift towards the middening of refuse over the disued pits. Similarly, the lithic scatters in field 11 may be all that remain of three middens, or what is more accurately termed refuse dumps (Needham and Spence 1997), created just below the western and southern crest of the ridge where activity was focused.

The results from field 18 also correspond with the general model of later Neolithic activity being focused away from the henges. Unsurprisingly, its lithic collection was small (Table D3.7; Fig 5.33). Seven worked pieces were recovered by total collection from an area of 0.8ha, all but one in the north-east and south-east corners of the area walked. There were four flakes, one blade, a scraper fragment, and significantly, a fragment possibly from a ground flint axe made of white Wolds flint. A similarly small number of lithics were found in the southern row of test-pits. There were three flakes, a blade, and a piece of irregular waste although two further flakes, a core rejuvenation flake, and a fragment probably from a Mesolithic truncated blade with abrupt retouch on its distal end and right-hand side were subsequently collected from around the spoil heaps of these two test-pits. It is possible, nonetheless, that medieval land use could be masking, or have destroyed, evidence of prehistoric activity. The southern and central line of test-pits had 0.47–0.49m and 0.22–0.28m of subsoil respectively, but it was completely missing in the three northern units of excavation. The reason for this variation in stratigraphy is unclear, but geophysical prospection had discovered the probable remnants of ridge and furrow (D2.5.1), and a possible medieval field boundary in TP7 (D2.5.3). The variation in subsoil depth may therefore be medieval in origin, possibly the result of different agricultural practices, such as those presumably practised in infield and outfield systems on Thornborough Common. The test-pits in field 18 could offer a rare, if partial, insight into the impact of medieval agriculture.

5.3.4   *Conclusion*

This chapter has so far been largely concerned with the lithic evidence from Thornborough's ploughsoil, but if such evidence is 'useful in adding dots to maps' the real question is whether it is 'useful in contributing to the bigger picture' (Schofield 1993, 90) of occupation and land use. There is reason to be optimistic. The focused nature of the widespaced fieldwalking, along with the results from total collection and test-pitting, illustrate quite sharply defined lithic clusters set against a generally continuous low-density 'background' scatter. Areas of recurrent activity seem to be separated from others by the remains of occasional tasks like hunting or the opportunistic knapping of gravel pebbles encountered in broken ground. The investigations in field 12, field 16, and to a lesser extent, at the

Three Hills Barrow Group, confirm these were favoured locations from early in the development of the landscape, and widespaced walking elsewhere has produced a relatively large component of later Mesolithic and earlier Neolithic material. Lithics of this period form discrete low-density scatters which, in the case of the area around Chapel Hill, are masked by the larger and denser scatters of later periods. This is not to say that Fields 12 and 16 were unused during the later Neolithic and Bronze Age, although the only diagnostic pieces of these later periods was a barbed-and-tanged arrowhead, but that any later activity was very much peripheral to the denser scatters immediately to the north in fields 10 and 11. The follow-up fieldwork conducted in the latter confirms the area's special status. It is but one glimpse into the complex and fragmented landscapes of the 3rd millennium.

There is, of course, considerable room for improvement, and what has already been noted about the potential impact of modern ploughing highlights the urgency of these tasks. There are noticeable gaps across the study area where little or no fieldwork has been completed. Lithic distribution maps, and no doubt the bigger picture, would benefit greatly from surface collection and test-pitting to the southeast, around Mire Barf Farm, where the results from field 32 are currently unconnected to the betterstudied areas to the north, or along the limestone escarpment, a potentially important location with its extensive views over the monument complex and distant landscapes. It would also be worthwhile sampling more of those areas where lithics become rarer or disappear completely, such as along the Ladybridge and Upsland ridges. Other themes for future study would include the intensive investigation and comparison of other known high-density scatters and their post-depositional survival. This is especially a priority in fields 2B, 21, and 32, each of which may have originated from very different activities, and it would undoubtedly be of value to return to the east of Chapel Hill and consider field 10 and those parts of field 11 where no follow-up fieldwork was conducted. Conversely, the relationship between medieval agriculture and the low-density scatters near the henges offers an opportunity to explore what is an often overlooked factor.

5.4   The landscape of the Mesolithic and earlier to middle Neolithic

The lithics from both the lower river terrace and plateau are predominantly Mesolithic and earlier or middle Neolithic in character, notwithstanding a later Neolithic or earlier Bronze Age element at Three Hills and in field 2B. The most recognisable early finds are the microliths, and when diagnostic they are mainly small geometric forms of later Mesolithic type, although a few potentially earlier types are also present. Known Mesolithic sites in the region cluster in the Pennines and on the Wolds,

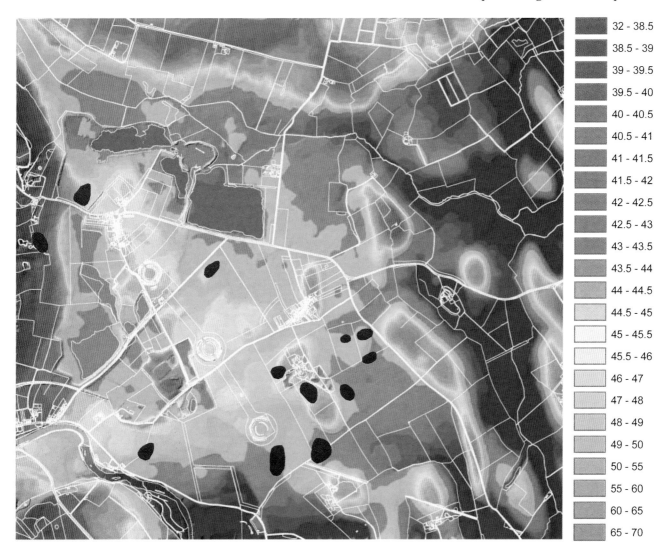

■	32 - 38.5
■	38.5 - 39
■	39 - 39.5
■	39.5 - 40
■	40 - 40.5
■	40.5 - 41
■	41 - 41.5
■	41.5 - 42
■	42 - 42.5
■	42.5 - 43
■	43 - 43.5
■	43.5 - 44
■	44 - 44.5
■	44.5 - 45
□	45 - 45.5
□	45.5 - 46
□	46 - 47
□	47 - 48
□	48 - 49
□	49 - 50
■	50 - 55
■	55 - 60
■	60 - 65
■	65 - 70

Fig 5.34   Hypothetical foci of known Mesolithic activity shown as shaded areas. The landform model is courtesy of English Heritage and Michael Clowes / Trevor Pearson

although these apparent foci may result from a concatenation of biases (Spikins 1999, 15–22). A chain of sites along the Ure-Swale confluence (Bridgland *et al* 2011, 212–13; Laurie 2003, 230–6; Spikins 1999, fig 2.3; Spikins 2002, fig 69) suggest rivers and their valleys may have been important as arteries of communication and for their plant, animal, and fish resources, and it has been argued that lowland sites served as base 'camps' for geographically extensive 'home ranges' (Mellars 1976), in this instance stretching from the Pennines to the Yorkshire Wolds. Yet there is a dearth of evidence for their existence in this region (Spikins 1999, 69–70, chapter 6), and Thornborough, whilst extensively used, is no exception, its Mesolithic material characterised by a low incidence of scrapers and cores. The uppermost edges of the lower river terrace, the plateau, and parts of Chapel Hill along with areas immediately to the east, appear to have been repeatedly visited (Fig 5.34), but probably only for very short periods of time, and the distribution of microliths suggests task-specific activity like hunting was also

undertaken here (Myers 1987). The distribution of material, including fourteen microliths found during excavations at the Nosterfield Quarry (Dickson 2011, tables 39, 44, 46–7), extends to the edge of the marshy area at The Flasks (see Bridgland *et al* 2011, 103–5, 109–10; Dickson and Hopkinson 2011, 31–2) and across the northern end of the limestone escarpment. As in other periods, those using Thornborough's landscape commonly employed flint from eastern Yorkshire, contradicting the view that local material was used more or less exclusively during the later Mesolithic (see Spikins 1999, 10). It is impossible to say if this suggests extensive 'home ranges' or exchange.

The evidence reveals a more detailed picture of particular areas being preferred to others (Fig 5.34). It seems that the lowest ground, most notably on the river terrace and to the south-west of Chapel Hill, was avoided by Mesolithic communities. One obvious explanation is that this was wetter, and the Ure was very likely closer to the southern extent of the plateau and associated with an extensive riparian wetland

(3.2). In fact, occupation may have concentrated on immediately flanking dryland, which was also presumably on the edges of the fairly dense woodland extending across much of the plateau (see Bridgland *et al* 2011, 254; Dickson and Hopkinson 2011, 31–2). More fieldwork is needed, but this preference may be illustrated by the concentration of Mesolithic material to the south of the southern henge, in what appears to be a relatively dense area of activity, and in Field 2B to the south-west of the study area. It is even more apparent across the eastern half of the landscape. The latter includes Mesolithic material at and around the later triple-ditched round barrow (4.2.2), clustered on a slight gravel hummock close to what could have been a watercourse, which itself appears to have been exploited for its ready supply of eroded flint; and the lithics to the east of Chapel Hill, which are distributed either on or close to the base of the ridge, near to what three test-pits at the southern edge of field 11 suggest was another watercourse (D2.2.3). Elsewhere in the study area there appears to have been a preference for slightly more elevated locations, and in some instances Mesolithic groups could be making use of wind-induced clearings. Mesolithic lithics were found on the western and southern slopes of Chapel Hill, in fields 8 and 30 respectively, and especially at the more intensively studied Three Hills (see also 4.8.2), where it is unclear if the palaeochannels which almost completely surround three sides were active or not during the later Mesolithic. Residual material from the double pit alignment similarly indicates activity on a gravel ridge (4.7.2). Finally, there is a cluster of Mesolithic material in field 33, on the eastern slopes of the limestone escarpment, and in Nost 1, not far from The Flask wetland and immediately to the south-west of what excavations in the quarry discovered to be four sinkholes with 'Late Mesolithic/Early Neolithic' lithics (Dickson and Hopkinson 2011, 36–7). Unsurprisingly, then, Mesolithic groups were occupying the very habitats which ensured good camping ground, a nearby water source, and the close availability of both wetland and forest resources. The lightly scattered findspots dotted elsewhere across the plateau and in immediately adjacent areas presumably attest to the task-specific use of resources.

Similar patterns of activity could have continued into the 4th millennium (Fig 5.35), and nationally, this widely recognised pattern has been taken to indicate the enduring significance of seasonal mobility to occupation and land use (Edmonds 1987, 169–73). Relatively high frequencies of blades in fields 2/2B, and in fields 16 and 41 at and around the triple-ditched round barrow (Tables D3.5 and D3.7), indicate that the lower terrace edge and the drier ground flanking the lowland to the east were still an attraction, even if the area immediately to the south of the southern henge was now little used. It seems probable that the creation of this 'founder monument', and its repeated building and use for the deposition of the dead (4.9), led to changes in the role of this previously occupied area, the low gravel ridge now taking on a meaning very different to other parts of the landscape. The monument would certainly have been impressive in its final stages, and was perhaps visible from the lower terrace and southern parts of the plateau. Continuity could also be demonstrated to the east of Chapel Hill, the distribution of its surface lithics very similar to that for the preceding Mesolithic. Across this entire area there seems to have been a low level of earlier or middle Neolithic material, the most salient elements being two leaf-shaped arrowheads from field 11.

The plateau saw striking reorganisation in the 4th millennium. As already argued, the building of the cursus can be seen as an attempt to create a greater level of order and alignment (4.9), formally demarcating a corridor or pathway across what previous excavations of this monument have demonstrated to be a deciduous forest environment (Thomas 1955, 432; Vatcher 1960, 171). From this point of view, its course along a narrow neck of land 1.5–2km wide may be suggestive, perhaps mirroring the Springfield cursus in Essex, which 'might have run across the neck of an area of dry land surrounded on three sides by floodwater' (Brown 1997, 90). Bounded to the north by extensive marsh, and to the south and south-west by the River Ure, its tributary streams, and associated riparian wetlands, the monument must have changed the way in which people moved around and experienced this landscape. Similarly, the neck of land was bounded to the east by Chapel Hill, whose north-west slope, overlooking the plateau, was now no longer used, and by the ridge at Ladybridge and the slight rise on which the modern village of Thornborough is located. To the west, the limestone escarpment forms another natural boundary, offering a vantage point with extensive views, and again the admittedly limited evidence suggests abandonment. Hence, the monument was given prominence by local topography, creating a deeply symbolic and layered medium for all 4th-millennium activity. Indeed, these relationships could have additional symbolic overtones. The location of its western and eastern terminals – respectively on a marked bend in the Ure after its descent from the Pennines and possibly under the modern village of Thornborough (3.3.1) with extensive east-facing views across the Vale of Mowbray and towards the Hambleton Hills – drew together spatially the differing parts of people's homeworlds in a way which was surely poignant to the monument's users (see Chapter 6).

This reorientation in the plateau's significance was perhaps matched by greater activity across its northern and eastern fringes. Whilst neither the collections from the east of Chapel Hill or from Nost 1 indicate the increased use of these fields, both were close to what could be new areas of activity. Upsland ridge failed to produce any Mesolithic lithics, yet a chisel arrowhead from field 22 and a single-piece sickle fragment from field 25 are compatible with use in the 4th or 3rd millennium BC. To the north

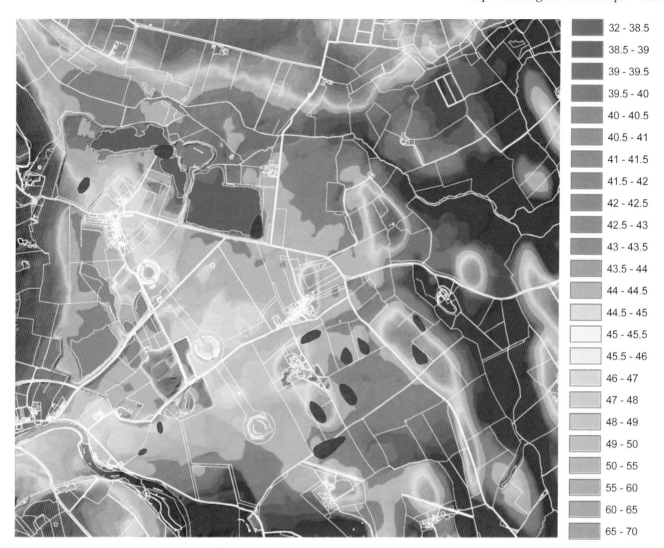

▬	32 - 38.5
▬	38.5 - 39
▬	39 - 39.5
▬	39.5 - 40
▬	40 - 40.5
▬	40.5 - 41
▬	41 - 41.5
▬	41.5 - 42
▬	42 - 42.5
▬	42.5 - 43
▬	43 - 43.5
▬	43.5 - 44
▬	44 - 44.5
▬	44.5 - 45
▬	45 - 45.5
▬	45.5 - 46
▬	46 - 47
▬	47 - 48
▬	48 - 49
▬	49 - 50
▬	50 - 55
▬	55 - 60
▬	60 - 65
▬	65 - 70

Fig 5.35   Hypothetical foci of known earlier Neolithic and middle Neolithic activity, shown as shaded areas, including excavated evidence in Nosterfield Quarry (Dickson and Hopkinson 2011). The landform model is courtesy of English Heritage and Michael Clowes/Trevor Pearson

of the study area the excavation of fifteen pits containing either earlier or middle Neolithic pottery around Flask Lane and to the south-east at Ladybridge Farm suggest broader transformations across Nosterfield Quarry (Dickson and Hopkinson 2011, 71–85, 198–9). It is difficult to judge whether either of these areas had been used in the Mesolithic given the failure to complete surface collection here, but the later activity may represent the uptake of new land. It appears to have focused on the low gravel ridges which extend into the wetland, and, whilst these spurs of drier land have produced relatively limited occupation evidence, much could have been lost in the ploughsoil. Certainly the discovery on the Flask Lane spur of a short curvilinear section of rapidly backfilled ditch, with Grimston Ware in its secondary deposits, hints at what may have once existed here (*ibid*, 74, figs 55–6).

Understanding the 4th-millennium occupation of this landscape is problematic. There is no suggestion of extensive farming, and the small quantity of charred cereal grains from some of the excavated pits at Nosterfield Quarry are not a reliable indicator that cereal cultivation was taking place here (Dickson and Hopkinson 2011, 80). Neither does the lithic evidence indicate that mobility had become less important or that people were visiting in much larger numbers. The excavated 4th-millennium features from Nosterfield Quarry produced only three scrapers and no cores (*ibid*, 79). There may have been a pattern of occupation akin to Holgate's (1988, 132, fig 8.2) model for the Thames Basin whereby there was a base camp or residential area from which trips were made to other surrounding sites to carry out specific tasks, but if so these camps were only occupied for short periods of time and by small groups. It seems more likely that major residential areas existed beyond the Thornborough landscape, groups only visiting here either as part of a shifting cycle of agriculture and foraging (see Pollard 1999; 2000; Whittle 1997b, 21–2), or perhaps more likely, during important social occasions, such as to undertake funerary practice and ancestral commemoration at the triple-ditched round barrow in the first half of the 4th millennium. Yet the location of any base camps is far from clear, and indeed, the distribution of 4th-millennium monuments could even suggest that settlement was focused a considerable distance away. The triple-ditched round barrow is a rare example of a burial site from across the Yorkshire vales, the only other being a long barrow at Giant's Grave to the east of the River Swale, and possibly also at Ferrybridge and surrounding areas far to the south (Roberts 2005, 197). By contrast, large numbers of 4th-millennium burial monuments are known from eastern Yorkshire (Manby *et al* 2003), and if ancestral sites like these tethered what were largely mobile patterns of settlement then this suggests the low-lying vales were either sparsely populated, or were one part of more extensive 'homeworlds' incorporating large swathes of Yorkshire.

Questions remain about the extent to which the reorganisation of this landscape during the 4th millennium was connected to shifting settlement patterns. As in other parts of Britain, where the building of cursuses coincides with increasing occupation material or the more regular digging and filling of pits (eg Barrett *et al* 1991, 31, fig 2.4; Richards 1990, 266, fig 157), it is possible that the Thornborough landscape was now fragmenting into different zones, with occupation focusing away from monuments which were still only visited on certain social occasions. This is certainly apparent around the giant cursus complex at Rudston, in eastern Yorkshire, where pits with Peterborough Ware outnumber those with Carinated Bowls and are generally located away from the monuments (Harding 1999, fig 3.2). If mobility continued to be important to groups using Thornborough, then perhaps people avoided camping across its plateau, suggesting a complex pattern of land use, occupation, and commemoration. A contrast may have been created between ancestral places, including areas of everyday activity littered with the vestiges of past camps and with the triple-ditched round barrow, and the freshly created ceremonial foci fashioned with great effort from the untouched forest at the heart of the landscape. This difference between the old and the new could be essential to understanding the narratives now unfolding here. Cursuses have been seen as commemorating previously important pathways (most notably, Johnston 1999), yet at Thornborough there is nothing to suggest the plateau ever served such a role. Topography, forest cover, and lithic distribution indicate other axes of movement, and indeed, the woodland surrounding the monument ensured it was largely hidden from view, even to those moving along the elevated limestone escarpment. The priority could have been the intimate physicality of interacting with the monument, and not its appreciation from afar by people living across an increasingly cleared and presumably more densely populated landscape.

5.5   The later Neolithic and Bronze Age landscape

During the 3rd millennium the plateau ceased to be occupied as it was progressively monumentalised. The distribution of later Neolithic and earlier Bronze Age lithics largely avoids the plateau, and indeed the lower terrace, being found instead towards its fringes at distances of 350–850m from the nearest henge (Fig 5.36). There could have been a band of material extending around a central area where new acts of communal monument building, which both reiterate and subvert the earlier cursus (4.9), were practised, but where everyday activity was unusual or even prohibited. It is best seen to the east of the study area, between Chapel Hill and Upsland, where the lithics were spread over an area as much as 800m across. A lower density of later Neolithic or earlier Bronze Age material was found to the south-west of the study area, on the spur of higher ground flanking the lower terrace, and to the north-east at Ladybridge. There are, of course, significant swathes of the existing Thornborough landscape still to benefit from surface collection, but the quantities of lithics from both Mire Barf Farm and Nost 1 intimate that this band encircled much of the complex, perhaps only being absent to the west, where the limestone escarpment, itself a striking natural boundary to the monumentalised plateau, was less suitable for occupation. There was certainly a substantial increase in the intensity of activity. Later Neolithic and earlier Bronze Age scatters are larger and denser than those of earlier periods, and this shift in the scale of activity is best seen in Nosterfield Quarry, where excavations found no fewer than 38 Grooved Ware-associated pits or tree-throws, dated to 2800–2200 cal BC, more than double the number from the 4th millennium (Dickson and Hopkinson 2011, 38, 96–101). Whilst they are in the same areas as earlier features, with most on the Ladybridge Farm spur, they nonetheless represent a marked increase in the use of the plateau's northern extent.

The potential complexity of these scatters is most immediately apparent east of Chapel Hill where the majority of diagnostically later Neolithic material was found. Here a spatially discrete scatter, concentrated in field 10 and on the knoll and surrounding slopes of field 11, comes to an abrupt end in field 9 and across the eastern half of field 12. The high proportion of retouched forms, especially scrapers, suggests settlement, but other aspects of the collection – the use of coloured flint, its Levallois cores and flakes, and the high incidence of faceted butts – highlight more sophisticated knapping, including the manufacture of blanks for transverse arrowheads, best evidenced near the tills of Flamborough Head on the East Riding coastline (see Durden 1994; 1995). Even an exceptionally high frequency of feather terminations, with correspondingly low frequencies of hinge and step terminations, is similar to the proportions observed close to the

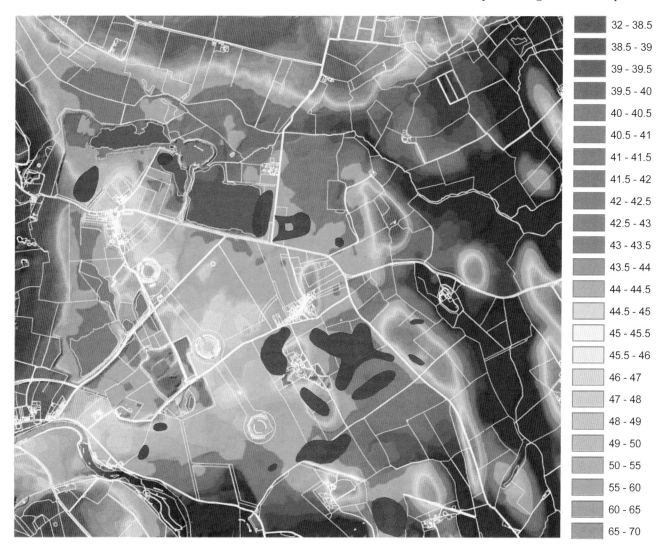

▓	32 - 38.5
▓	38.5 - 39
▓	39 - 39.5
▓	39.5 - 40
▓	40 - 40.5
▓	40.5 - 41
▓	41 - 41.5
▓	41.5 - 42
▓	42 - 42.5
▓	42.5 - 43
▓	43 - 43.5
▓	43.5 - 44
▓	44 - 44.5
▓	44.5 - 45
▓	45 - 45.5
▓	45.5 - 46
▓	46 - 47
▓	47 - 48
▓	48 - 49
▓	49 - 50
▓	50 - 55
▓	55 - 60
▓	60 - 65
▓	65 - 70

Fig 5.36   Hypothetical foci of known later Neolithic and earlier Bronze Age activity, shown as shaded areas, including excavated evidence in Nosterfield Quarry (Dickson and Hopkinson 2011). The landform model is courtesy of English Heritage and Michael Clowes / Trevor Pearson

procurement site on Flamborough Head, and interpreted as reflecting particular knapping expertise (Durden 1995, 428, fig 15). The material to the east of Chapel Hill is therefore typical of a new type of scatter which consists of 'multi-product debitage ... from the manufacture of a variety of implements and/or the blanks for them, combined with unspecialised knapping to meet the day-to-day needs of those working there' (Healy 1991, 35; see also Durden 1994, 313–16; 1995, 422–7). That specialised knapping was taking place alongside other activities, including more mundane lithic production and consumption, could suggest that the making of the objects was being directly controlled by groups, or even that there were now dedicated, highly skilled knappers (see Durden 1994, 318–30; 1995, 431). It also indicates the creation of more complex places around the plateau. It is possible to discern these differing knapping activities spatially across the scatter. Evidence for Levallois working is found in the north-west quadrant of field 11, but also over the hedgerow, along the eastern edge of field 10. The

latter area did not benefit from total collection or test-pitting, yet the distribution of material, along with the extremely high percentage of feather terminations, suggests this may have been the real focus of specialised knapping. Further evidence is provided by two discoidal cores from field 10 which may be unfinished or rejected Levallois specimens. By contrast, the distribution of scrapers and other retouched items suggest settlement focused on the central and south-west parts of field 11.

The chronological relationship of this material to the monument complex is not easily determined. Levallois flaking, the arrowheads for which it provided the blanks, and the use of coloured flint all occurred during the currency of both Peterborough Ware and Grooved Ware on the evidence of pits from the Yorkshire Wolds (Manby 1974, 11–70; 1975, 33–45; Makey 1996), and in industrial contexts on Flamborough Head (Moore 1964; Manby 1975, 45–47; Makey 1996, 70–6). The overall aspect of the Chapel Hill collection, however, seems closer to Grooved Ware-associated industries than to Peterborough Ware-associated ones. This assessment is based on the low level of blade production, the diversity of retouched forms, and the presence of an oblique arrowhead. It is, however, to some extent an intuitive judgement, constrained by the consideration that Peterborough Ware-associated industries from a wide range of contexts and locations are only beginning to be published in any number. If the guess is correct, the scatter is likely to relate to the construction and use of the henges. Transverse arrowheads are found widely throughout the British Isles and it has been suggested they were part of an inter-regional 'prestige goods economy' which developed during this period (Bradley 1982, 34ff). Their frequency suggests otherwise, but they may nonetheless have played a special emblematic role, communicating and sustaining ideas about the identities of people (Edmonds 1995, 98–102; Edmonds and Thomas 1987, 194). The oblique form in particular, which may have been later in date than chisel arrowheads, is known to have a close association with henge monuments (Green 1980, 109, tables V.1 and V.3; Richards 1990, 228). Chapel Hill may therefore highlight the explicit link that developed during the later Neolithic between ceremonial enclosures and the circulation of objects whose value was truly inter-regional. This is not the first time that henges have been connected with the control and circulation of artefacts (eg Bradley 1984, 48–67; Edmonds 1995, 127–8), but it is a rare instance of where evidence exists, within a short walk of these monuments, to justify the link. That preferentially selected coloured flint from the coastal tills was being used, its brightness contrasting with the darker and duller colours of other material, highlights the close relationship which must now have developed between Thornborough and the westward movement of Yorkshire flint.

If there was a more-or-less continuous band of occupation surrounding Thornborough's plateau, this is not to say that it was similarly dense or consistent throughout. Intensity varied as did what was practised. Currently there is little evidence for anywhere else sharing the distinctive roles of fields 10 and 11. Most comparable was the flint cluster in field 32, where there was a similarly wide range of coloured material, but no evidence for specialised knapping. Other clusters contrast more markedly. The scatter in fields 2/2B is of predominantly later Neolithic/earlier Bronze Age aspect and the number of cores shows that knapping was clearly undertaken here. The relatively high number of hinge and step fractures, however, highlights how the standard was very much lower than that practised near to Chapel Hill. Given this, it is unsurprising that grey or olive-grey till flint dominates. There is also the lithic cluster in field 21, which, along with the structural evidence for occupation across the Ladybridge Farm spur of the Nosterfield Quarry, may suggest the area's general importance during the later Neolithic. Again, there is no brightly coloured flint, the excavated pits producing only

a very small amount of reddish-brown or honey-coloured flint (Dickson 2011, 292), and the available evidence indicates its use for only temporary occupation (Dickson and Hopkinson 2011, 99–100). Whilst these pits may have been used purposefully to bury a partial representation of material generated during settlement (*ibid*, 201–2), it is also perfectly feasible that what we are seeing here is all that now survives of scattered short-lived and flimsy structures like tents, windbreaks, or even the stake- and turf-walled buildings known to date to the later Neolithic (see Barclay 2003, 80; Darvill 1996, 93, fig 6.10). As such, it may have contrasted markedly with other locations, like Chapel Hill, and indeed Nost 1, where activity seems to have resulted in the deposition of material only across the land surface, possibly creating middens. Their existence to the east of Chapel Hill has already been suggested, and they may have also been present on the Flask Lane spur of the quarry, where spreads of silty material with both lithics and different types of Neolithic pottery were found in shallow undulations in the natural subsoil (Dickson and Hopkinson 2011, 202).

If these variations hint at the bringing together or spatial integration of different tasks across a single landscape, then this could have resulted in a layered and complex regionalisation of space as people, places, and things were segregated and distinguished in close juxtaposition. Elsewhere, this is indicative of altogether new settlement patterns. Later Neolithic surface scatters are sometimes of such size and density that they must have resulted from the more regular occupancy of a specific place. In the Thames Basin they were usually 500m or more in diameter (Holgate 1988, 116), and in Cranborne Chase and the Stonehenge Environs they extend across as much as 28 hectares and 50 hectares respectively (Barrett *et al* 1991, 60; Richards 1990, 270). Test-pitting at Honey Hill, Cambridgeshire, found an average density of 81 flints per 10m^2, and it was a similar story at nearby Soham 9, with an estimated flint population in excess of 370,000 pieces (Edmonds *et al* 1999, 49–50, 60). Scatters like these could be connected to an increased sedentism during the later Neolithic, the result of the first permanently or semi-permanently occupied settlements (Holgate 1988, 135); or as is perhaps more likely, the continued but periodic use of a specific area over an extensive timespan (Edmonds 1987, 174; 1995, 82; Edmonds *et al* 1999, 75). Yet the much smaller lithics numbers for Thornborough makes this unlikely here, and whilst this could result from the scarcity of raw materials, the characteristics of the worked flint and chert, including the material from the excavated Nosterfield pits, suggest that people were only visiting this landscape for very short periods, as in previous millennia. This is supported by the Nosterfield pits producing only a single charred cereal seed (Dickson and Hopkinson 2011, 100) and the lack of other palaeoenvironmental data from the quarry for large-scale food production (Bridgland *et al* 2011, 262). What is less clear is whether these visits were connected to a broader pattern of mobility incorporating many different landscapes, or whether a visit to Thornborough was a special journey for communities with settled 'homeworlds' elsewhere.

The organisation and use of this landscape seems to have depended in large part on the relationship between the monumentalised plateau and its occupied fringes, a connectivity partly captured by the two oft-repeated terms of 'ritual landscape' and 'sacred geography'. Despite their interpretive shortcomings, they still possess unexplored potential. Originally coined to describe the clustering of impressive monuments across the Wessex chalkland (Thorpe 1984, 58; Thorpe and Richards 1984, 75, 77), they paint a vivid picture of ceremonial areas set aside from secular activity. An extensive programme of fieldwalking, geophysics, and excavation around Stonehenge's landscape led Julian Richards (1984; 1990, 267–70) to distinguish between the east and west of the study area, with henges, Grooved Ware pottery, polished stone axes, and an exceptional series of pit deposits occurring across the former, in a so-called 'Durrington Zone'. A similar interpretive theme was developed by another large-scale project, at Cranborne Chase in neighbouring Dorset. Here investigations identified an almost continuous dense scatter of later Neolithic flints across the higher ground, characterised by a wide range of tool types, whilst roughly 4km away, around the monuments, there were small scatters with lower numbers of tools, but higher numbers of elaborate and polished objects, and the cluster of special pit deposits at Firtree Field (Barrett *et al* 1991, 59–66, 75). Curiously though, since the publication of these reports, there has been little discussion as to what these patterns mean for our general understanding of later Neolithic cycles of land use and occupation or, significantly, their similarities and differences with other large-scale monument complexes, such as that at Stenness and Brodgar on the Orcadian Mainland (Richards 2005). Whether scatters nearer the monuments were the product of social elites or resulted from the get-together of worshippers for very specific occasions remain largely unexplored questions, as do the implications for the decline, or otherwise, of mobility during the 3rd millennium BC.

At Thornborough the striking distinction between the distribution of monuments and other activity poses fundamental questions about landscape perception. It could, of course, demonstrate a distinction between the sacred and profane, or ritual and domestic, but to argue for two clearly defined zones which manifested a distinction between opposing aspects of social practice and knowledge is to assume too rigid a difference. Such an interpretation would not only grossly simplify ritual, by considering it as a self-contained activity only undertaken across distinct spatial realms at specific times, but also marginalise its drama and meaning by placing it outside the context within which it was

conceptualised and seen to function (Lewis 1980, 15; Goody 1961, 155–6; Sayer 1982, 498; see also Barrett *et al* 1991, 83–4; Brück 1999, 54–5, 60–3). In reality, ritual is more complex and spatially undefined, as was appreciated for the Stonehenge landscape, where it was suggested that 'ceremonial monuments and activities played a significant role within a wider domestic context' (Richards 1990, 270). It can, within any given society, be represented by a wide range of practices, symbolic nuances, and physical arenas (Humphrey and Laidlaw 1994, 71). Ritual is therefore better understood as a quality of certain actions whose intrinsic characteristics exist to varying degrees according to the intention and motivation of those undertaking the acts (*ibid*, 3, 73, 88–9; Lewis 1980, 20–1). In this sense, the distribution of monuments and surface material at Thornborough suggest that the activities associated with the plateau may have been highly ritualised or, to put it more explicitly, consciously involved rule-bound, prescribed, repetitive, and archetypal references to cosmology (see Bell 1992, 91–2; Bloch 1974, 56–7, 64–5, 77; Douglas 1966, 63–4, 69; Goody 1961, 158; Humphrey and Laidlaw 1994, chapter 4; Lewis 1980, 7, 10–12, 19, 29, 34–5). It would accordingly be the ritualised form of these social practices, and not any intrinsic opposition between practical and discursive action or knowledge, which served to distinguish this 'sacred landscape' (see Bell 1992, 74).

Emphasising the character of social practice, instead of an abstract series of conceptual divisions, helps embed the lived human body in Thornborough's landscape. If highly ritualised activity created spatial distinction then this is a process inextricably embedded within sensual experience (see Bell 1992, chapter 5; Bourdieu 1977; Lakoff 1987; Munn 1996, 452–4) and the 'double mediation' implicit to accessing sacredness (1.3). It involved a passage from areas for making, eating, talking, and sleeping, perhaps surrounded by either open woodland or remaining dense woodland (Bridgland *et al* 2011, 94–9, 112), to the 'excluded space' of the plateau, which by the later Neolithic may have been largely covered by open grassland or scrubland (see Thomas 1955, 432; Bridgland *et al* 2011, 262; Dickson and Hopkinson 2011, 199). A sense of moving across a threshold, induced by changes in topography and vegetation, would find meaning as the view of the monument complex opened up before worshippers. As they traversed the plateau the familiar world of everyday action would pass beyond sensual reach as the impressive profile of the monuments increasingly dominated attention. Activity may now have assumed more 'ritual commitment' as people surrendered to the plateau's strangeness. The next threshold would be the monumental earthworks themselves, and upon entering the sacred world of the enclosed 'deep space' movement and action surely became highly structured and expressive. The large banks animated the adoption of this ritualised behaviour by totally blocking off the outside

Fig 5.37   Looking westwards from the knoll in field 11 showing the approximate position of the southern and central henges behind Chapel Hill. The northern henge is immediately to the right of the photograph (August 2003)

landscape with the exception of the view through the entranceways (4.9). Perception was now firmly fixed on the interiors of these sites and the sacred knowledge to which individuals were exposed. As emotionally charged and visually impressive symbols they transformed experience, and the presence of the surrounding 'excluded space' suggests that their influence extended outwards across the landscape, like a weakening gravitational field (see Munn 1996, 453–4; Tambiah 1976, 112). Yet there was a reciprocal relationship between these different zones, for the 'excluded space' enhanced the power of the monuments, quite literally making room for the mental transcendence or 'double mediation' of worshippers. Hence, the significance of the henges, and the beliefs they represented, were contrasted with the world of the everyday (see Hirsch 1995, 4; also Hubert 1994, 11). They can be imagined as standing apart, as relatively separate and detached, though never conceptually disconnected from the populations they served.

It may even be possible to discern some of the routeways by which these different parts of the landscape were navigated. The earlier cursus could, of course, have created an east–west axis for movement, and indeed, a scatter of later Neolithic or earlier Bronze Age material has been found nearby, on the north and north-east sides of Chapel Hill (Fig 5.36). There may, then, have been a pathway between the monumentalised plateau and the extensively used area to the east of Chapel Hill; if so, the experience of people on this short journey may have been neatly choreographed by topography. As viewed from the knoll in field 11, where the majority of lithics can be found, all but the very top of the northern henge bank would have been blocked by Chapel Hill (Fig 5.37), in contrast to the pits dug across Ladybridge, which potentially enjoyed views to all three henges. Yet as you move off this knoll, into areas where fewer or no worked material is found, at least one of the henges could have been seen. The impact of woodland can only be guessed at, but these patterns of visibility seem too neat to be anything but deliberate. Descending sharply off this knoll in a north-westerly direction takes you towards a narrow gap between Chapel Hill and the

Fig 5.38   Looking westwards from field 11 to the plateau. The most direct route to the plateau is between the ridges at the centre of the photograph. The limestone escarpment is visible behind this gap (August 2003)

ridge upon which the village of Thornborough is located – or what could have been a formal entrance-way to the plateau and its monuments (Fig 5.38). In contrast to the view through this gap, there is only limited visibility to the north-east, east, and south-east. It is then just a short journey to the central henge. What is therefore suggested is a highly orchestrated control of experience, which was also very natural, the symbolism of the place originating in the landscape itself and the spirits or gods responsible for its creation.

The henges create another obvious routeway through the landscape, worshippers being channelled north to south through the northern henge or south to north through the southern henge. A number of features to the north-west of the northern henge would directly indicate the former direction if they proved contemporary with the this henge. A single row of seven pits is known through excavation and cropmark evidence to run for 30m from the north-west section of the northern henge's outer ditch on the same axis as the henges (Fig 5.39), and at least some of these may have held timber uprights (3.3.2). Aerial photography shows it ending midway in the adjacent field, but excavations in the Nosterfield Quarry, about 0.5km to the north-west, discovered a double pit alignment as much as 27m wide (4.7.3) whose easternmost row is on the same alignment as the feature nearer the henge (Fig 5.39). It is impossible to say whether these pit rows, either side of Nosterfield village, were actually part of the same feature, but one large circular infilled depression has been recorded between the two in a villager's garden (Dick Lonsdale, pers comm; Fig 5.39). A connection is therefore possible, and, whilst the excavated pits are all undated, their close association with the henges – and the later Neolithic/early Bronze Age scatter discovered in Nost 1 (Fig 5.39) – raises the possibility that people's movement into or out of the northern henge was framed by architecture. If so, this was surely an impressive feature, for the pits in Nosterfield Quarry were large in size, with at least

six holding posts on average 0.47m across and over 4m tall (calculated using a pit depth to above ground ratio of 1:3 or 1:4; Dickson and Hopkinson 2011, table 11, 121). Far less is known about the equally intriguing cropmark of two concentric semi-circular ditches running immediately inside the northern causeway of the henge (Fig 3.18; 3.3.2), but this too may have been part of an attempt to choreograph experience, or was perhaps added at a later date to close down access.

Formal access to and from the northern henge again suggests a monumentalised plateau separated from other parts of the landscape. The regionalisation of space may also be demonstrated by another feature discovered during excavations in the Nosterfield Quarry. A single pit alignment, currently undated but with a single broken polished flint axe from the fills of one of its pits, was found running along a gravel spur from the marshy area of The Flasks, then showing as a cropmark heading south-west towards the northern henge (Fig 5.39; Dickson and Hopkinson 2011, 101–5, 200). It may even be connected to a cropmark which appears to show two irregular rows of pits (Fig 5.39; see also 3.3.4). There is nothing to indicate that these features once formed a solid boundary, and the excavated portion of the pit alignment appears to have been built in sections starting nearer the henge. Yet if the alignment was broadly contemporary with the enclosures it probably affected movement, creating a symbolic border or threshold across the northern edge of the monumentalised plateau. The incorporation of the axe in one of the last three pits nearest the adjacent wetland is of interest given that four complete polished stone axes have been found as stray finds elsewhere on The Flasks, three originating from Cumbria, the fourth from Cornwall. This area may therefore have been explicitly linked to their deposition, an association that was possibly older than the 3rd millennium BC: four refitted flakes from an almost complete polished stone axe of probable Cumbrian origin, along with a flake from

Fig 5.39   Pit alignments near the northern henge; the single pit alignment is shown as a solid line. The shaded area displays the lithic concentration in Nost 1. The landform model is courtesy of English Heritage and Michael Clowes / Trevor Pearson

the reworking of another, came from two Carinated Bowl-associated pits on the Flask Lane and Ladybridge Farm gravel spurs respectively, along with a retouched blade of volcanic tuff from a Peterborough Ware-associated pit in the latter area (Rowe 1998, 4–5, fig 9; Dickson and Hopkinson 2011, 79, 85, appendix 2). Hence, the axe from the single pit alignment was part of a tradition of deposition which, whilst not exclusive to the area immediately

north of the complex – a complete flint axe has also been found at either the central or southern henge (Thomas 1963), with possible flakes from two others discovered in fields 11 and 38 – was nevertheless focused on it. That this involved highly ritualised acts is highlighted by the four refitted flakes coming from an axehead that may have been pre-heated and deliberately shattered (Dickson 2011, 276–7). One interpretation is that the pit alignment was

Fig 5.40   Looking south towards the central henge in August 2003

a dramatic if perhaps short-lived attempt to rein-scribe this area's distinctiveness from the plateau beyond, and it is even plausible that whilst The Flasks witnessed the use and deposition of axes of volcanic tuff, the monuments were associated only with flint axes.

The choreography of worship may be evident elsewhere. Straight movement between the northern and central henges crosses shallow depressions and narrow ridges (Fig 5.40; D1.2.3), just beyond which geophysical prospection found six or seven pairs of anomalies with a central gap, an adjoining circular feature, and a linear anomaly running into the northern entrance of the central henge (3.3.2). Their layout is highly suggestive and may indicate a complex arrangement of pits, posts, and fences. Similar features were not known on the flatter ground between the central and southern henges, but walking this alignment makes one appreciate how the landscape changes: the view northwards from outside the southern henge slopes gently upwards, although curiously, the converse is not apparent, whilst the landscape falls away to the east, and more especially to the west on to the lower river terrace. By contrast, the largely lower-lying landscape to the south is blocked by the monument, yet it is here, at a distance of about 1.1km from the southern henge, that we may find the southern boundary to this landscape. Aerial photography shows the cropmark of a single pit row, which, like the excavated alignment in Nosterfield Quarry mentioned above, runs south-west to north-east at right angles to the henge axis (Fig 3.4, x; 3.3.4). It is impossible to say if this is contemporary with the henges or, like other single pit alignments excavated in the quarry, of later date (Dickson and Hopkinson 2011, 156–64). Its layout suggests a rela-tionship with the monuments, yet it lies on terrace deposits which may be significantly later than the complex. Further investigation is required of all these possible associations, but if at least some were meaningful to those worshipping here, they hint at a complex layering of space. There is a real sense that successive generations of monument builders explored this place fully and thought carefully about the meaning of its changing appearance before digging its earth, mounding the spoil, and erecting timbers. Little may have been left to chance in an attempt to maximise religiosity.

Regarding the monumentalised plateau as lifted

out of everyday existence does not necessarily mean that only religious worship occurred there. Actually building the henges may have meant people living and working here for periods of time, and this could be one interpretation of the camps created at Ladybridge, next to a marshy area perhaps linked to some fundamental religious beliefs (see Chapter 6). It could also explain the small amounts of later Neolithic lithics found even closer to the henges, such as the small collection redeposited into the double pit alignment (4.7.2), and activity like the preparation of gypsum in the specially dug pits 0.4km south-east of the southern henge (4.3.2). Nevertheless, it appears as though the monument's use during worship was little associated with the production and discard of portable material culture. Irrespective of their chronology, the earlier work by Nicholas Thomas (1955, 438) found just six worked lithics, more recent excavations resulting in a further 37 from the southern henge (4.6.2 and 4.6.3), mostly from the plough-disturbed horizon and, remarkably, none from the outer ditch of the central henge (4.5.2). Similarly striking is the fact that only two tiny sherds of Neolithic date have been found from all these henge excavations (4.6.2; *ibid*, 437). What is indicated is an almost pathological obsession with keeping these sites clear of everyday debris, which fits neatly with the absence of contemporary scatters from their hinterland. It appears that social tradition enforced levels of cleanliness at the henges, and, as with historical ceremonial centres recorded elsewhere, this may have gone some way to ensure the ritual purity of the monuments (see Douglas 1966, chapters 1–2; Hubert 1994, 16; Silverman 1994, 10, 13).

Ascertaining the extent to which these patterns continued into the earlier Bronze Age is tricky, yet uncertainties about the dating of the henges (4.9) makes this an especially important question. A substantial Beaker industry is difficult to distinguish, the most representative of the tools, the small 'thumbnail' scraper, being scarce and scattered, amounting to a little less than 20% of all scrapers. There are also only three barbed-and-tanged arrowheads, two of which were from Nost 1. Caveats aside, the occurrence of this material in fields 2B and 32, to the south of the study area, in fields 4, 8, 11, and 12 on and around Chapel Hill, and in Nost 1 to the north of the plateau suggests the same general areas continued to be favoured (Fig 5.36), reflecting a national pattern of mixed later Neolithic/earlier Bronze Age lithic scatters (Gardiner 1984, 37; Bradley and Holgate 1984, 114). Changes did occur, for the evidence from Nost 1 and from the north and north-east sides of Chapel Hill indicates new areas around the edges of existing scatters may have been populated, whilst the small number of Beaker-associated features at Nosterfield Quarry (Dickson and Hopkinson 2011, 126, 129–35, 215) suggest Ladybridge was now abandoned or used differently. Despite this, it does not appear that the users of 'Beaker' lithics organised their landscape in fundamentally different ways. Indeed, it is perfectly feasible

the henges were built and used by the same people, perhaps explaining the absence of Beaker-associated burials or round barrows from this landscape (4.9). The relatively late start of this funerary tradition is certainly confirmed by the results of surface collection at the Three Hills Barrow Group. Much of the scatter found here is likely to relate to the barrows, and, if so, the fabricators and knives, along with the dearth of Beaker-associated material, accord with the content of the mounds themselves (5.3.3).

The distribution of round barrows also echoes earlier patterns. It is impossible to determine exactly how many were built at Thornborough or their exact chronology, although they were all probably erected in the first half of the 2nd millennium. There may conceivably have been as many as twenty clustered around the axis of the henges, with most sited across the plateau (3.3.3), and those closest to these earlier enclosures were not only the largest, but also perhaps the first built (4.9). They therefore seem to have been deliberately located to assert or reinscribe older patterns of association and the well-trodden pathways between and around the henges. If the plateau remained largely cleared, their siting on its slightly more elevated parts would have made them visible to anyone approaching from Chapel Hill, the knoll at Thornborough, or the northern end of the Upsland ridge. They could even have been visible from the limestone escarpment. The linear barrow cemetery at Three Hills may have been especially striking, and its location to the east of the henges, broadly mirroring the north-east to south-west alignment of the single pit row noted above, must have been part of a complex genealogical narrative now being written across the plateau. It would have certainly offered an impressive façade to anyone approaching from the areas to the east of Chapel Hill, and intriguingly, produced a proportionally large amount of chalk flint (Tables D3.8–3.10), and a few non-chalk flints with chalky or gypsum encrustations on cortex or in cavities, suggesting its association with especially exotic materials. Collectively, these barrows, and their associations with earlier earthworks, must have been central to the experience of those using the plateau, the remains of earlier generations being drawn upon, and therefore sanctifying this newer tradition of burial and mound building. Given this, it seems inconceivable that the giant henges themselves did not continue to play some role in the routines and ceremonial practice of the barrow builders. All this evidence contrasts with the Stonehenge Environs, where impressive round barrow cemeteries and contemporary lithic scatters concentrate across the western part of the landscape, suggesting that the previously monumentalised 'Durrington Zone' was now almost totally abandoned (Richards 1990, 271–5). Instead, it further highlights the significance of continuity between the later Neolithic and early Bronze Age (see also eg Brück 1999; Gibson 2004; Harding 2003, chapter 5).

The evidence may also suggest that the plateau continued to be a place for the ancestral dead in following centuries. The expedient, hard-hammer lithic industry of the full Bronze Age is found at Thornborough in very low quantities. This scarcity and the fact that the only other stray finds of Bronze Age date – a middle Bronze Age palstave and a later Bronze Age socketed spearhead found on the Upsland ridge (Peter Almack, pers comm) – are also from the fringes of the study area support the idea that the plateau continued to hold special meaning. Indeed, the inhumation burial and small cremation cemetery excavated in Nosterfield Quarry demonstrates that funerary practice continued at least along its northern edge throughout the middle Bronze Age (4.9). Whilst the construction of a large ditched rectilinear enclosure perhaps late in the 2nd millennium BC or early in the 1st millennium BC (Dickson and Hopkinson 2011, 143, fig 114, 217), associated with broadly contemporary evidence from elsewhere in Nosterfield Quarry for clearance and a rise in cereal pollen (Bridgland *et al* 2011, 94–106, 112, 263–4; Dickson and Hopkinson 2011, 126), suggests the development of an intensively farmed landscape, it is far from clear if this extended further across the study area. The possibly late date of the double pit alignment, connecting two round barrows and the lower terrace with the plateau, indicates the continuing commemoration of the dead and the orchestration of both movement and interaction during such events. It is even conceivable that the plateau was being inscribed in some way. Aerial photographs demonstrate a number of single pit rows, and a large oval enclosure (3.3.4), beyond its eastern edge, with another pit row to the south nearer the river (see above). These features could conceivably have been an attempt during the Bronze Age to separate the still sacred plateau from a surrounding agricultural landscape. If so, they demonstrate a remarkable longevity of meaning.

6   Pathways to purity

6.1   Introduction

The previous chapter contends that throughout the Mesolithic, Neolithic, and even perhaps the Bronze Age people were visiting Thornborough, probably for only short periods of time, instead of settling there permanently. If this is correct, it is important to consider whether these visitors originated from elsewhere in the Ure-Swale Interfluve and adjacent landscapes, or alternatively, travelled from areas further afield like eastern Yorkshire. Addressing this issue is essential if we wish to understand the role, significance, and symbolism of Thornborough's monuments. If people were living nearby, with communal monuments serving as 'central places' to social polities (see 1.2), it becomes necessary to explain why there was such a multiplication of effort during at least the later Neolithic: monuments may conspicuously reverse the 'principle of least effort' (see 1.3), but the building of no fewer than six almost identical henges within 12km of each other – three at Thornborough, and others at Nunwick, Hutton Moor, and Cana Barn – suggests that more complex processes were at work. And if Thornborough lay beyond people's 'homeworlds' it is necessary to explain why monuments were built there in the first place and why people went to the trouble of travelling to this landscape. The final chapter will explore these issues, firstly by reconsidering Thornborough's location and its possible role in regional exchange systems during the Neolithic. It will be suggested that, along with other nearby monuments, it acted as a regional 'hub' for distant populations and the circulation of polished stone axes and Yorkshire flint. The specific religious beliefs with which it was associated are also considered. It will be argued that Thornborough, and the Ure-Swale Interfluve more generally, was a renowned cult centre, most of those gathering there, at least during the later Neolithic, coming specifically to worship at a place of pilgrimage. The chapter will end by exploring the implications of this interpretation for our understanding of 3rd-millennium BC society.

6.2   Rivers, routes, and exchange

There is every reason to consider the Thornborough monument complex as conspicuously located. Built alongside the River Ure, it lies within a bounded landscape physiographically discrete from areas immediately to the west and the east (3.2). Its distinctiveness would have been very apparent to those prehistoric travellers crossing the Rivers Swale or Ure, or coming from the Pennines to the west, before moving on to the narrow shelf of land where the monuments are found (Fig 6.1). To them, Thornborough's juxtaposition – or liminality – between the uplands to the west and the lowlands to the east and south must have been all too obvious. At the same time, the complex appears well connected to surrounding landscapes. This shelf of land comprises a narrow band of Magnesian Limestone and marl running from Nottingham to the River Tees which has been used historically as a natural north–south routeway connecting the English Midlands and northern England. It was probably used in the same way in the Neolithic, taking the traveller along a course which avoids the more arduous Pennines to the west and the densely wooded flood plains of the vales to the east (Brennand *et al* 2007, 390; Vyner 2000, 103). The nearby River Ure offered connections in different directions. Flowing through Wensleydale, a wide-bottomed valley dissecting the Pennines, it bends sharply southwards near to Thornborough, and eastwards again not far from Boroughbridge, before emptying into the River Ouse, the major waterway draining the Pennines and low-lying vales into the Humber Estuary (Fig 6.2). This could potentially be a major east–west axis which connected the Pennines, their easterly low-lying vales, and the more distant coastal plain, with ease of access to the bordering Hambleton Hills, Howardian Hills, and Yorkshire Wolds.

Thornborough's conspicuous location provides a context for its monuments. The riverine setting of cursuses has been linked to the role of waterways in socio-political interaction and the symbolic connotations of the monuments themselves (Barclay and Hey 1999; Brophy 2000a; 2000b; *pace* Loveday 2006, 133–6). Similarly, it is argued that the largest henges are often in close proximity to watercourses because they participated in lines of communication and movement, and particularly those long-distance networks concerned with the exchange of polished stone axes (Bradley 1984, 55; 1993, 109–10; Bradley and Edmonds 1993, 52–3). They may have even been socially neutral locations or 'staging points' where people met to trade information, resources, and objects from distant sources (Bradley and Edmonds 1993, 198; Loveday 1998, 27; Manby 1979, 76–7). The connection between both types of monument on the one hand, and movement and exchange on the other, seems especially pertinent at Thornborough given its location on or close to what may have been a major routeway for the movement of Group VI polished stone axes, originally from the central Lake District, but found in especially large numbers across the Yorkshire Wolds and areas immediately south of the Humber Estuary (Bradley and Edmonds

Fig 6.1   Looking south-west over the shelf of Permian rock on which the monuments are located. The Thornborough complex lies on the right of the photograph. Image reproduced courtesy of Dick Lonsdale

1993, 162, fig 9.8; Clough and Cummins 1988, map 6; Manby *et al* 2003, 47, 49). These widely circulated objects could have followed a number of routes across the Cumbrian mountains and the central Pennines to reach eastern Yorkshire (Fig 6.3), including via Keswick to the Eden Valley and the Stainmore Gap, along what is often regarded as the most logical

pathway (Bradley and Edmonds 1993, 198; Lynch 2005; Manby 1965; 1979). However, the quickest route from the principal centre of axe production at Great Langdale is likely to have been south-east to Kendal, along Garsdale until the River Ure is reached, and then by following its course, through Wensleydale and directly onwards to Thornbor-

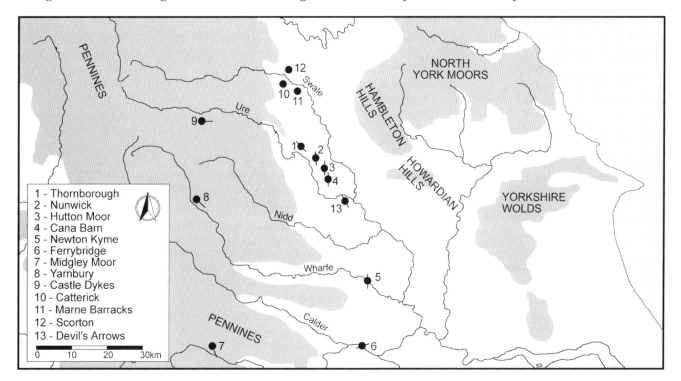

Fig 6.2   Monuments of central and western Yorkshire. The axial lines show the alignment of henges and the orientation of the Devil's Arrows stone row

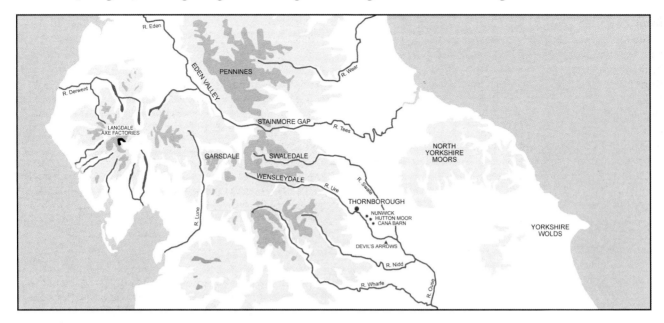

Fig 6.3   Thornborough and trans-Pennine exchange

ough – and indeed, Cumbrian axes have been found around Thornborough and to the east beyond the River Swale (5.5; Harding and Johnson 2003, fig 5; 17–18; Lynch 2005, fig 4.3; Manby 1979, figs 6, 8, and 9). Hence, the Thornborough complex, and its neighbouring henges, appear 'strategically placed for access' (Manby 1979, 76).

Flint likely moved along the same routes in the opposite direction. Till material, originating in eastern Yorkshire, was used by communities as far afield as eastern Cumbria (Cherry and Cherry 1987; 2002; Lynch 2005) and northern Northumberland (Waddington 1999, 155), and may have been exchanged for the axes. Given this, it is of interest that perhaps as much as 80% of the flint from Thornborough was from coastal tills some 80km to the east, from what is believed to be the principal Yorkshire flint source (Henson 1985; Manby *et al* 2003, 72), with comparable amounts possibly found at Nosterfield (Rowe 1998, 1; 2004, 1; Dickson 2011, 292). Both Peter Makey and Frances Healy have recorded a substantial proportion of this material as being in various shades of grey, counter to several descriptions of the till flint from Flamborough Head, the most extensively investigated source, as being predominantly brown or black, with smaller quantities of other colours (Manby 1974, 83; Manby 1979, 71; Henson 1985, 6; Durden 1995, 410). Indeed, a distinction may have been drawn across the Yorkshire Wolds between the brown flint commonly placed in Neolithic pits in this area (Manby 1974, 11–76; 1975, 26–47), based on the evidence of a heap of ten tested, beach-derived nodules above a hearth associated with plain Neolithic Bowl pottery at West Reservoir Field site 5 on Rudston Wold (Manby 1975, 34–38), and the grey and largely worked material found to have been predominantly placed in other recently excavated Neolithic features on Rudston Wold (Makey 1996, 63). This material appears to have been transported there in a largely

unworked state. The exact source or sources of the Thornborough grey flint remains in question – it may perhaps have been obtained from other tills, farther north along the coast – but its circulation and use was in some way distinctive. Similarly, the preferential use at Thornborough of brightly coloured till flint for the manufacture of transverse arrowheads suggests another more specialised system drawing upon a different source. Complex choices were clearly being made about the role of resources as part of long-distance networks of movement, contact, and exchange.

The organisation of the circulation of raw materials can be discerned from other characteristics of the lithic assemblage. Durden's (1994; 1995) study of South Landing and North Dale – the former site, on Flamborough Head, where raw material was collected and received preliminary working, the other, just 8km inland, where the later stages of knapping were undertaken – demonstrated significant differences in the two groups of debitage. Over even this distance, the site away from the source was distinguished by, *inter alia,* a higher proportion of retouched forms, a higher proportion of non-cortical flakes, a predominance of one specialised core type, smaller core size, more frequent platform preparation, and a lower incidence of hinge and step terminations (Durden 1995, figs 13–15). Some of these characteristics reflect the predominance of the later stages of the reduction sequence; others reflect the production of particularly fine retouched forms, including quadrangular discoidal knives and ripple-flaked oblique arrowheads. There was a greater incidence of the later stages of the reduction sequence at Thornborough, regardless of period, flint type, or location, when compared to South Landing and North Dale. Complete flint flakes without cortex reach frequencies of 60–70%, in contrast to values of 40–50% for the two sites from the East Riding. Weights of complete flint cores peak at 10–35g at Thornborough instead of the 60–85g and 35–60g for the other collections, and the disparity visible between the size of the final removals from the cores and that of the large flakes, blades, and flake tools is representative of the collection as a whole. Retouched forms amount to nearly 13% of the total, in contrast to less than 5% and less than 10% at South Landing and North Dale respectively. These characteristics are consistent with the maximisation of raw material which had been transported over some distance and had already been to some extent decorticated, indicating that many of those spending short periods of time at Thornborough were not only largely dependent on eastern Yorkshire for a supply of flint, but could also have spent time there. People consistently travelling long distances, possibly in part using the rivers as navigable arteries in much the same way that they did in later periods (Moorhouse 2003, fig 53; *pace* Bridgland *et al* 2011, 218), may therefore account for the widespread distribution of Yorkshire till flint.

The scarcity of lithic assemblages from elsewhere in the Ure-Swale Interfluve, and across the larger Vale of Mowbray, makes it difficult to know if these characteristics are typical for the area, or whether more permanently occupied sites ever existed there. Excavations about 11km to the south-east at Marton-le-Moor discovered a largely later Neolithic assemblage in association with a cluster of pits and post alignments (Tavener 1996; Makey nd a). Over 92% was of till flint, there were remarkably few retouched pieces, and a complete absence of primary flakes, again indicating temporary occupation. The small size of both cores and related debitage suggest that raw material was at a premium here. Excavations at Catterick, about 20km to the north (Fig 6.2, 10), produced a small multi-period lithic assemblage from the general area of a large chambered cairn assumed to be of later Neolithic/early Bronze Age date; primary reduction had clearly been undertaken elsewhere (Brooks 2003, 35). Meanwhile, at nearby Marne Barracks (Fig 6.2, 11), a collection largely of chert from the later Neolithic palisaded enclosure is of late Mesolithic/early Neolithic date (Hale *et al* 2009, 275), suggesting that the monument itself was, like Thornborough, kept clear of material residues. Watching briefs or excavations elsewhere in Catterick and in the quarries to the north of the river near the Scorton cursus (Fig 6.2, 12) produced few worked lithics, the largest assemblages, of 56 and 10 pieces from Hollow Banks Quarry and Bridge Road respectively, again largely being of till flint from tertiary stages of lithic reduction (Speed 2003a; 2003b, 2004; 2008a; 2008b; 2010; in preparation). The evidence suggests that the low-lying part of the Ure-Swale Interfluve, from Catterick in the north to Borough-bridge in the south, was only episodically used during the Neolithic and earlier Bronze Age by communities who spent the rest of the year elsewhere, and indeed, there is nothing to suggest extensive deforestation and farming across the area until the Bronze Age

(Bridgland *et al* 2011, 258–64). By contrast, the large quantity of lithics, barrows, and cairns from eastern Yorkshire (5.4.2; Manby 1974; 1975; Manby *et al* 2003; Vyner 2007, 76) are testament to its relatively high population in the 4th and 3rd millennium BC.

If this is correct, then the monumental landscapes of the Ure-Swale Interfluve bordered the western fringes of people's homeworlds, suggesting that its cursuses and henges, presumably built during their visits, were clustered in the sorts of liminal locations where exchange and interaction could occur freely. The cursuses at Thornborough and Scorton, with similar central banks or platforms (4.5.3) and less than 21km apart, were closely associated with the Rivers Ure and Swale respectively (Fig 6.2, 1, 12), which, along with the Ouse, are the region's great natural features. At Thornborough, the earthwork stretched along a narrow spur of flat, densely wooded land bounded by wetland which seems to have been little used. That it was built across a landscape with few or no ancestral places (4.9) makes it ideal for the creation of supra-local relations implicit to long-distance movement, communication, and exchange. The very experience of discovering new places, clearing trees, and moulding an earthwork focused people on the novelty of what they were doing together, and the cursus physically expressed principles of long-distance interaction and relations, its east–west orientation reflecting the key axis of movement, possibly with views over the River Ure to the west and the more distant Hambleton Hills to the east (5.4). Perhaps, then, its building marked an escalation in cross-Pennine exchange, constructed by peoples from different areas who came together at the boundaries of their homeworlds to celebrate new friends, alliances, and resources. This could certainly explain why the only other definite cursuses from Yorkshire are far to the east, across the Wolds at Rudston. This unparalleled cluster of five sites straddles the Gypsey Race watercourse close to the source of the coastal till flint and on a probable routeway connecting the chalklands with the plain to the south (Manby *et al* 2003, fig 17), again suggesting an association with establishing and negotiating supra-local identity and contact.

Later monuments may demonstrate similar concerns. The six almost identical henges along the Ure (Fig 6.2,1–4; Fig 6.4, A–F) are associated to the north with the probable henge 'ringwork' at Catterick (Fig 6.2, 10; MacLeod 2002, 40–3; Moloney *et al* 2003; see also Bradley 2007, fig 3.22) and the nearby Marne Barracks palisaded enclosure (Fig 6.2, 11; Hale *et al* 2009); and to the south, with the row of four or possibly five giant standing stones of the Devil's Arrows at Boroughbridge (Fig 6.2, 13), described as 'one of the most astonishing megalithic settings in Western Europe' (Burl 1991, 1). Further south, and very close to the Rivers Wharfe and Aire, lie the henges of Newton Kyme and Ferrybridge respectively (Fig 6.2, 5, 6), both also possessing at least two encircling earthworks and comparable in size to the sites in the Ure-Swale Interfluve (Fig 6.4,

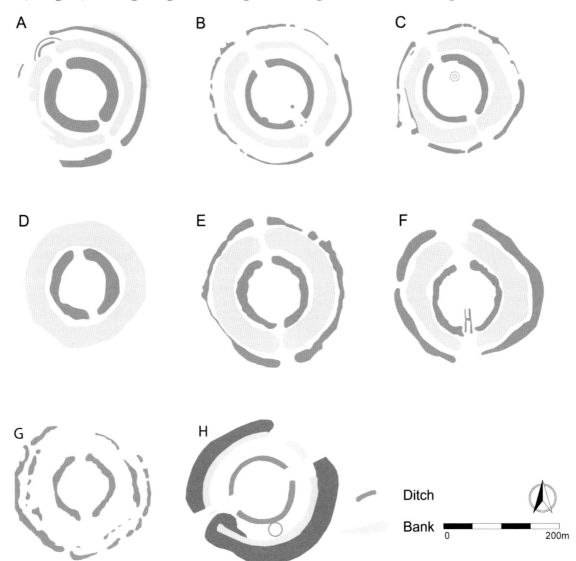

*Fig 6.4 Yorkshire's double-entranced henges: A, northern Thornborough; B, central Thornborough;
C, southern Thornborough; D, Nunwick; E, Hutton Moor; F, Cana Barn; G, Newton Kyme; H, Ferrybridge
(A–F are original transcriptions from aerial photographs; G after Harding and Lee 1987, 311; H after Roberts
et al 2005, fig 135)*

G, H). Despite uncertainties about the dates of these sites and their chronological relationship to each other, they may well have been built during the same epoch, for similar reasons, and in carefully planned locations. These large earthworks occur on or very close to the shelf of Permian rock where the region's rivers enter the lowland (Manby *et al* 2003, 97, 109), their distribution standing out against Yorkshire's other known henges, all smaller sites from the dales and eastern Yorkshire (see 1.2). Their siting has been taken by Blaise Vyner (2007; see also Bridgland *et al* 2011, 218–19) as marking out a 'Great North Route' running north to south through the river-strewn lowlands separating the hills of eastern Yorkshire and the coast beyond from the Pennine uplands and north-west England. They are certainly located 'close to the lowest readily fordable points on each of the rivers' (Vyner 2007, 75) – and near, therefore, to key Roman centres and the headports of the Middle

Ages (Moorhouse 2003, fig 53) – at distances which further the suspicion they were planned and built together. The Thornborough complex, the Devil's Arrows, Newton Kyme, and Ferrybridge are 17km, 23km, and 22km from each other as the crow flies, similar to the 21km between the earlier Thornborough and Scorton cursuses. They could be no more than a day's walk from each other, making them ideally placed to act as 'staging points' for any travelling and trading along this 'Great North Route'.

A link with movement and exchange could account for their aligned double-entrances (Fig 6.4). In a discussion of British henges with this characteristic, Roy Loveday (1998) noted a general correlation between orientation and the course of nearby Roman roads, including a link between the Yorkshire enclosures and Dere Street. He concluded that double-entrance henges were literally strung out along routeways with their entrances both physically and symbolically sending the traveller along the course of their journey; this fits neatly with the above. The north-west to south-east or north to south alignment of the henges at Thornborough, Nunwick, Hutton Moor, and Cana Barn all loosely reproduce the course of the River Ure (Fig 6.2; see also Richards 1996, 330), which, as already suggested, marks people's approximate direction of travel. Next on this postulated routeway are the Devil's Arrows, aligned north-north-west to south-south-east on the southern bank of the Ure (Burl 1991, fig 1), and Newton Kyme, near the River Wharfe, which has a similar alignment. Both are orientated across the river, and may therefore be associated with crossing-points. They also broadly point towards each other, highlighting the possible symbolism being written out along this routeway. The north-east to south-west alignment of Ferry-bridge is different again, yet can also be understood in terms of routeways, for if it marked the end of a 'Great North Route' it was redirecting people either eastwards along the River Aire, and then perhaps to the Humber Estuary, or westwards across the Pennines following the course of the Aire and the Calder. If these monuments both physically and symbolically 'signposted' a routeway down the eastern side of the Pennines, then its extensions across the Pennines to the west could be indicated by the smaller upland enclosures of Midgley Moor, Yarnbury, and Castle Dykes (Fig 6.2, 7, 8, 9), all three of which are likely to be henges (Dymond 1965; Harding and Lee 1987, 307, 317; Howcroft 2011, 88, fig. 4). Sited on the opposite side of the rivers to the larger enclosures downstream, their single entrances either point towards or mirror the course of these waterways.

The large earthen monuments of Yorkshire may therefore have been closely linked with movement, communication, and exchange, the scale of the henges indicating large numbers of travellers and presumably a rise in the intensity of cross-Pennine exchange. They brought into being, articulated, and represented new types of affiliations and relationships held together by shared interests and strong social bonds, acting as nodes in a system which connected the population centres of the east with peoples to the west of the Pennines, in areas like the upper Eden valley and its adjoining limestone upland, where lithic scatters, axe finds, and Neolithic burial monuments suggest a sizable community (Bradley and Edmonds 1993, fig 7.4–7.5, 150–1, 158, 160–2, 196–7; Cherry and Cherry 1987; Masters 1984). These enclosures may also have been the destination of people 'travelling long distances on the eastern side of the Pennines to visit monument complexes where these axes might be acquired' (Vyner 2007, 73). Geographic and demographic liminality seem closely connected to their role, and a commonality of purpose may explain the shared design of these cursuses and henges (see Loveday 1998, 31; Harding in press). If the Thornborough complex was well placed to attract travellers then the diversity of lithic raw materials found here may reflect its strategic location; it certainly exceeded the range from nearby Marton-le-Moor (Tavener 1996;

Makey nd a) and sites further afield like those at Rudston (Manby 1974, 83; 1975), with the very small collections from Catterick (Brooks 2003, 35) and Ferrybridge (Brooks 2005, 143), both probably located on the same routeway, being similarly diverse. Whilst the majority of the assemblage was of coastal till flint from eastern Yorkshire, there are also small quantities of worked lithics from local gravel sources, the boulder clays of Yorkshire, and the chalklands of the Yorkshire Wolds (D3.2). There are even a few pieces of chalkland flint most likely originating in East Anglia or even further south. This diversity, most evident for the later Neolithic (5.2.2), could reflect the ebb and flow of exchange systems, yet could also indicate the geographical origin of the complex's visitors: Thornborough could be bringing together people from many different social networks.

6.3   Water, gypsum, and the sky

Yet there must have been more to Thornborough than just routeways and exchange. Clearly, this was a place of religious worship during the Neolithic, and whilst gatherings of this nature would go hand-in-hand with the circulation of objects, goods, and people, these factors cannot explain its poignancy and symbolism, and anyway, the need for strategically placed meeting-places or monumental 'signposts' was surely exceeded by the building of three henges, suggesting more primordial forces were at work. So what was it that motivated people to build these giant earthworks next to each other, and erect more nearby, at Nunwick, Hutton Moor, and Cana Barn? At least part of the answer must lie with this landscape's natural physicality, for it surely created parameters and opportunities for cultural expression. It is therefore worth asking what it is about *this* landscape which could have generated monument building on such a scale. Popular religious centres with the largest temples are often in places which in some way appear atypical or unique, these unusual features used to suspend disbelief, encourage bewilderment, and therefore complete the 'double mediation' necessary if people are to negotiate sacredness successfully (1.3). Whether these features be spectacular rock formations, mountains, caves, springs, or waterfalls, they are often regarded as what Mircea Eliade described as 'hierophanies' – instances of the sacred world breaking into the lived world and revealing itself to believers (Eliade 1959, 21; 1963, 6) – which ensure the proper attitude on the part of the beholder. Thus, in what ways would Thornborough's landscape have been distinctive or different to its visitors, and could its physicality have been an intrinsic part of its symbolism, attracting people and monument building on such a scale?

The often steep-sided River Ure, flanked by extensive wetland (3.2), is one of the landscape's most obvious characteristics (Fig 6.5), in historic times forming part of the boundary between the North and

Fig 6.5   The River Ure near to the Thornborough monument complex

West Ridings of Yorkshire. Undoubtedly a source of sustenance and life, those following or crossing it, presumably at known fords, must have also been aware of the river's temperamental power and inherent danger. Building monuments close to these crossing-points would not only ensure the latter's visibility to strangers, but could also constitute acts of religious supplication and ritual appeasement, even if their builders were wisely cautious, placing them safely away on adjacent dryland (Fig 6.6; Vyner 2007, 74). The involvement of water in people's experiences is demonstrated in other ways. Place names indicate that wetlands were once widespread across the interfluve and traces of pools and mires are still to be seen (Moorhouse 2004, 30–1). Intermittent larger expanses of wetland may once have been prevalent (Fig 6.6), probably restricting movement across the interfluve. The Devil's Arrows monument was probably flanked by mires either side of the Ure (Bridgland *et al* 2011, fig 1.5), whilst to the north of Thornborough the peat deposits of Snape Mires once extended for many kilometres, along with Langwith and The Flasks forming a permeable but tricky boundary to the interfluve's monumental landscapes (3.2). If so, then movement northwards was along two principal corridors, one to the east which runs parallel to the River Swale and leads to the cluster of monuments around Catterick (see Hale *et al* 2009; Moloney *et al* 2003), the other along the Lower Magnesian Limestone scarp and onwards to Wensleydale. Springs are numerous across Snape Mires (Powell *et al* 1992, 80–1), and well represented elsewhere, especially around the fringes of the monumentalised landscapes (Fig 6.6). Some may have had closer and more deliberate relationships with the henges: 2.4km north-west of the Thornborough complex is St Michael's Well, near the alignment formed by its henges and Nunwick to the south; and exactly the same distance to the north-west of the Hutton Moor henge, and close to its alignment with Cana Barn, is Hallikeld Springs. It is impossible to know if either was important during prehistory, but springs were presumably primary foci of many early paths and tracks (Loveday 1998, 31).

Water, one of nature's most powerful phenomena, was therefore intricately woven into the very fabric of the interfluve landscape. At Thornborough the importance of this relationship may go back to when the triple-ditched round barrow, the complex's 'founder monument', was built next to a watercourse (5.4); it was then recreated through the nearby con-

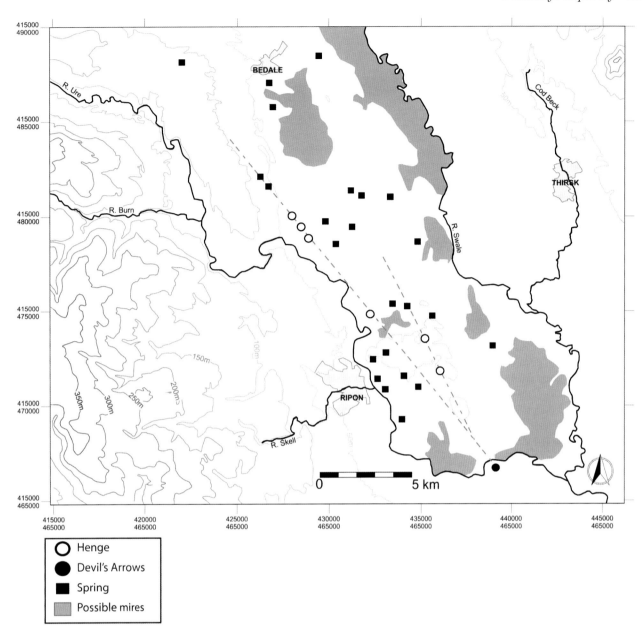

Fig 6.6   The low-lying Ure-Swale Interfluve showing the alignments of henges relative to the Devils' Arrows. The distribution of possible mires is based on historic place-name evidence and the extent of lake sediments as shown in Bridgland et al 2011, fig 1.5. The location of springs is taken from OS 1:25,000 Sheets SE27/37, SE26/36 and SE28/38. © Crown Copyright/database right 2013. An Ordnance Survey/EDINA supplied service

struction of a cursus, and renewed again by henges dedicated to the 'very ancient tradition of the Sacred river' and an associated 'archetypal creation rite' (A C Thomas 1955, 445). If water was closely associated with spirits and sacredness, and the springs with an underworld, this could have been good reason for repeatedly returning to this location. Just as today, water from special places may have been especially significant to travellers. There is surely little doubt that water possessed spiritual connotations, for elsewhere it was the context for many deliberate acts of deposition during the Neolithic, like the large number of stone and flint axes from the River Thames (Bradley 1990, 57ff). It is impossible to say whether similar finds exist in the

Ure – whose name, suggestively, derives from the Celtic 'isura' meaning 'holy one' (Ekwall 1928, 427) – but four specimens, including three from Cumbria, have been found from the edge of the area of intermittent woodland and marsh immediately to the north of Thornborough (Fig 6.7; 5.5). As objects of exchange they may have been appropriate 'gifts to the gods', and their deposition even accompanied by human bone (see Bradley and Gordon 1988, 508; Harding and Healy 2007, 113–17, 227). However, evidence of this is lacking across both the Ure-Swale Interfluve and further afield in the Yorkshire vales, where human remains are extremely rare until the 2nd millennium BC. If at least some of the dead did find a watery grave here, either as intact bodies or in

Fig 6.7   Three polished stone axes from The Flasks

Fig 6.8   Gypsum collapse at Hutton Conyers (British Geological Survey P223243). The water-filled hollow in the foreground was 3m across and 1.5m deep when this photograph was taken in 1983; behind it is another much larger hollow. Image CP13/042 British Geological Survey © NERC. All rights reserved

part as ancestral relics or scattered burnt remains, it would be understandable given the probable associations of rivers, springs, and bogs with concepts like transformation and the journey (Bradley 2000a; Fowler and Cummings 2003, 10; Richards 1996, 316–17). Evidence from elsewhere includes the possible exposure of the dead on a partly submerged later Neolithic riverside structure at Raunds in Northamptonshire (Harding *et al* 2007, 227).

The henges themselves may have been intertwined with the afterlife. It has been argued that Durrington Walls, far to the south on the chalklands of Wiltshire, was associated with the newly dead, who would then have journeyed along the nearby River Avon to Stonehenge, where they entered the world of the ancestors (Parker Pearson and Ramilisonina 1998; see also Pitts 2000, 258ff). If correct, the symbolism and use of this sacred landscape drew most readily on its link to funerary practice and the transformative potential of the river. There was certainly a large number of cremations within the Aubrey Holes of Stonehenge I (Parker Pearson *et al* 2009), and smaller deposits of both burnt and unburnt bone have been found elsewhere, within and around other henges (Harding 2003, 114–15), including, most notably, in the ditches of four hengiforms clustered near the Big Rings henge at the Dorchester-on-Thames complex in Oxfordshire (Atkinson *et al* 1951; Whittle *et al* 1992, 153–8). Whilst no comparable enclosures are known from Thornborough, and they are perhaps unlikely ever to have existed (see below), there are eight possible hengiforms at Ferrybridge (Roberts and Richardson 2005, 200). The latter have not been excavated fully, but one has produced cremated remains dating to the 3rd and early 2nd millennium, and a nearby timber circle is associated with similar remains of 4th- and late 3rd- or early 2nd-millennium date (Wheelhouse 2005, 35, 41). This evidence indicates that at least one of Yorkshire's henges was probably associated with smaller monuments explicitly connected to death, and it is perfectly feasible that activity like

the scattering of burnt ashes was conducted within the larger arenas of the double-ditched henges. If rivers were intrinsically associated with the journey into the afterlife, then it is possible that the proper treatment of human remains, or at least of their representative relics, in a sacred place beyond people's homeworlds was an important motivation for making the journey to this sacred landscape. Water, the afterlife, and henges could be closely woven together in a narrative which stretched across large swathes of the interfluve.

One of the area's other natural characteristics – its abundant deposits of gypsum – adds to the landscape's distinctiveness. This soft white calcium sulphate occurs in a 3km wide band of Permian rock which extends from Catterick to south of Doncaster, and it was upon this very geology that the Thornborough and Nunwick henges were built (3.2). Gypsum would have had a striking impact on some of the interfluve landscape. Underground its dissolution forms caves which then collapse inwards creating the area's many subsidence hollows or sinkholes (Fig 6.8), with at least 30 appearing since they were first recorded in the 1800s (Cooper 1986; Powell *et al* 1992, 15–18, 94–5). Their formation was certainly occurring in prehistory (Cooper 1986, 131; see also 2000), and two of the large number of sinkholes discovered during excavations at the Nosterfield Quarry produced later Mesolithic or earlier Neolithic lithics, whilst another two may have been used to orientate the double pit alignment of possible

Neolithic date (Dickson and Hopkinson 2011, 36–7, 199; see also 24, 58, 60ff). The sudden creation of what are often very large steep-sided shafts is frightening even today; such events have engulfed large trees, brought down a row of modern garages, and caused convulsions 'which shook almost every house' in Ripon (Cooper 1986, 127). Their impact during prehistory must have been deeply unsettling: as if the underworld was swallowing up the domain of the living in an act of supernatural power. Even if the events themselves went unwitnessed by Neolithic travellers, the resulting subsidence hollows were surely noticed, and could have been considered points of access between two planes of existence. Whether this invoked fear, celebration, or both, can only be guessed at, but it was surely justification for ritual appeasement or commemoration. Hence, it again appears there was good reason for building monuments here, and all six henges cluster around the northern and eastern edges of the most subsidence-prone part of the Gypsum Belt, between Ripon and North Stainley to the west of the river (Powell *et al* 1992, 16, fig 4). One parallel may be the 'swallets', or natural solution hollows in limestone, found alongside the Priddy Circles, four henge-related enclosures of probable 3rd-millennium date, which, whilst far to the south-west in Somerset, are the only other earthen monuments of this date aligned in a row (Bradley 2000a, 88, fig. 25; Harding and Lee 1987, 263–8; Lewis 2000; Lewis and Mullin 2010).

The potential impact of these subsidence hollows is all the more apparent when we consider that gypsum was valued by the monument builders at Thornborough. It was deliberately incorporated into a small pit containing human bone at the centre of the triple-ditched round barrow in use in the earlier Neolithic (4.2.2), and there seems little doubt it lined the bottom of the central grave at the early Bronze Age Centre Hill round barrow (Fig 2.3; 4.3.3). It may even have been added to the fabrics of Grimston Ware, Grooved Ware, and middle Bronze Age pottery found at the Nosterfield Quarry (Vyner 2011, 237, 240, 250–1, 253, 264). However, it is the henges which attest most vividly to the potential significance of gypsum. The earlier excavations at the central enclosure found 'wherever a layer of gravel occurred in the make up of the bank, it showed an accretion of a white substance having the colour and consistency of cotton wool' (Thomas 1955, 433). Analysis demonstrated it was likely to be gypsum which 'once lay on the surface of the bank, as originally constructed, and has, during the elapsed centuries, been completely dissolved by rain, washed deeper into the soil and recrystallised among the loose stones' (see Cornwall 1955, 442; see also 1953). Evidence from the other two henges supports this interpretation. Gypsum was found in redeposited bank material during the excavations of the southern henge, yet was absent from elsewhere across the trench (4.6.3), and animal burrows and tree-throws at the northern henge show it coating disturbed stones from the bank, often on only one of their sides, but not elsewhere at the monument. It is therefore likely that all three henge banks had been at least partially covered in this material, and indeed, it may have first been prepared into a suitable medium at the cluster of admittedly undated pits found near the southern henge (4.3.3). This must have been a time-consuming exercise, especially since large quantities of gypsum would first have to be quarried and transported, presumably from places like Ripon Parks, about 4km downstream to the west of the river, where it is known to have been exposed by the Ure (Powell *et al* 1992, 13). The endeavour surely highlights the value placed on the substance: through its use the henges would have presented a striking contrast with their surrounding landscape, invoking alterity amongst people approaching and moving within the earthworks.

Gypsum's properties may help us better understand its value. Neolithic people placed special importance on certain substances, with some, like quartz and chalk, often being deliberately incorporated into funerary contexts, and perhaps symbolically connected to regeneration and death (Bradley 2000b; Fowler and Cummings 2003, 6–8; Ruggles 1999, 98, 124, 155). Gypsum could have had similar connotations. Its use at Thornborough in two funerary monuments as much as 2000 years apart is certainly suggestive. Gypsum's brilliant whiteness is reminiscent of weathered bone, and its rapid solubility, both below and above ground, may have added to this association with life-cycles. Indeed, could it be that gypsum and bone were regarded as the same, with people quite literally being born from an underworld to which they returned upon death? If so, the application of gypsum to the henges not only inverted the universe by bringing the underworld to the domain of the living, but was also a profound act of commemoration, creating a strong bond between people, their ancestors, and their earthworks. By startling or even shocking worshippers in such a way the 'double mediation' essential to religiosity became possible. Hence, a belief that humanity was somehow dependent on, or made out of, the underworld's very fabric could explain its use at the henges, and if such a view was widely held, could account for the range of deposits known to have been specially placed in caves, windypits, the 'swallets' mentioned earlier, and other types of natural shafts (Lewis 2000). A connection between white substances and the underworld is demonstrated by the apparent fertility or regenerative 'symbols' made of chalk and often found at 4th- and 3rd-millennium enclosures across Wessex (Gillings *et al* 2008, 223).

These beliefs may have been closely embedded in people's seasonal cycles. As argued, many of those using Thornborough's monuments could have spent much of their time across the Yorkshire Wolds, and consequently been fully aware of the similarities between its underlying chalk geology and the colour and texture of gypsum. Indeed, they might not have distinguished between the two, seeing both as the innards of a continuous underworld. However, these two distant areas being seen in such a way – as, quite literally, a land united by its pure white rock – does not mean they were held in the same regard. Their contrasting topographies highlight how people's experiences of each would have differed, but it was perhaps the availability of water and its relationship with the underworld – two sacred elements of life – which most determined attitudes. To the west, the abundance of water and gypsum's exposure were closely connected, gypsum's soluble nature accounting for why collapses occur especially during very wet seasons when the sinkholes themselves rapidly fill with water (Cooper 1986). While we today understand the geological reasons for this, Neolithic peoples could have taken it as a measure of a landscape's inherent spirituality. It was here that different elements of the universe coalesced or violently cohabited. By contrast, the Wolds saw less annual rainfall and more modest watercourses, and if this was taken to indicate that the area was less charged by sacredness – perhaps with exceptions like Rudston and its link to water (Loveday in press) – then the same logic would explain why the less soluble chalk could only be reached by digging into the ground. It too was the underworld, but its separation from the world of the living was more secure, making the Wolds a spiritually safer land. These relationships could be appreciated only by those travelling between and experiencing both landscapes, and in this way people's beliefs were repeatedly brought alive by their seasonal cycles, and vice versa. Journeying was essential to understanding the world.

If water, gypsum, the underworld, and even life and death themselves were physically and symbolically entwined across the interfluve, then Thornborough's landscape was not just geographically liminal, but was also metaphorically liminal or otherworldly, with the enclosures themselves encapsulating this enmeshing of spiritual forces, providing arenas where the living could negotiate with the supernatural. Yet if the interfluve was a place were the strata of people's universe co-existed, then there is one further dimension to consider: the sky, or overworld, whose celestial phenomena are of almost universal concern to pre-literate non-Western beliefs (Ruggles 1997, 204–5; 1999, 83; Thorpe 1981). Certainly many of the most complex and impressive monumental centres through the ages were orientated according to observed astronomical events, the dynamics of the sun, moon, planets, and stars being invested with the supernatural and taken to symbolise essential beliefs such as cyclical return and the renewal of the world (Aveni 1997; Krupp 1997). Known archaeoastronomical orientations of British monuments suggest that the 4th and 3rd millennia were no different (Ruggles 1984; 1999; 2006), and the plateau at Thornborough afforded a wide expanse of sky for worshippers gathered there, a connectivity emphasised from within the henges, their encircling earthworks blocking all but the view above

(4.9), and seemingly lifting those in their interiors closer to this rotating supernatural domain. Hence, the overworld, like the underworld, may have been part of the very fabric of this landscape, especially if comparisons were drawn between the unnatural brilliance of the white gypsum and the stars in the night sky. Given this, were any of the monuments at Thornborough deliberately orientated towards celestial phenomena?

There are indications that they might have been. An archaeoastronomical investigation identified a number of possible correlations (Harding *et al* 2006). This was carried out using the software program SkyMap and techniques borrowed from virtual-reality modelling to create a fully negotiable digital landscape within which the relationship between the sun and stars, and the cursus, henges, and double pit alignment could be explored. The open eastern end of the cursus was aligned on the rising of Mirfax and Pollux between 3500 and 3000 BC, although it is far from clear if this was where the monument originally ended (3.3.1). Its western terminal framed the setting of seven stars during the same period, including Alnitak, Alnilam, and Mintaka, which collectively form Orion's Belt (Fig 6.9), one of the most visible and historically significant stellar constellations. This could be coincidental and therefore meaningless, yet the rising of the same three stars correlates with the alignment of two undated cropmark anomalies near the northern end of the double pit alignment (3.3.4) and the impressive triple-ditched round barrow between 3000 and 2500 BC (Fig 6.10); and it may not be just chance that the undated gypsum-associated pits cluster along the alignment close to the barrow (4.3). Results for the henges were more complex given their wide entrances and lack of obvious foresights, with no fewer than twelve and ten stars rising and setting respectively within their entrances between 3000 and 2000 BC. This includes the rise of Sirius within the southern entrance of all three henges at 3000 BC (Fig 6.11) – the brightest star in the night sky, and a star associated with Orion's Belt. Also potentially meaningful given the associations of the Dorset Cursus (Barrett *et al* 1991, 50–1), the passage graves of Newgrange and Maes Howe (Burl 1981, 251–2; Mackie 1997; Moir 1981, 223–4; O'Kelly 1982, 123–4), and Durrington Walls (Ruggles 2006), is the fact that the relatively well-preserved southern entrances of at least the northern and central henges are aligned upon the midwinter solstice sunrise during the later Neolithic (Fig 6.12). This phenomenon is linked to some of the most spectacular of monuments.

Inadequate knowledge about the chronological development and original appearance of the complex makes these results speculative, and identifying that a monument was aligned on celestial phenomena is not the same as proving it was done deliberately by the builders, or indeed, that it was integral to religious belief and practice. Yet at Thornborough there is perhaps a context for why some of

Fig 6.9 View from within the cursus of the setting of Orion's Belt at 3500 BC (A) and 3000 BC (B). Image reproduced courtesy of the University of Texas

these associations may be meaningful. Orion's Belt is a constellation which during the Neolithic rose in the direction of the Yorkshire Wolds, the final destination for numerous Cumbrian axes and possibly the homeworld from which many of Thornborough's worshippers came, before moving westward and setting behind the central Pennines where the Ure descends from Wensleydale. Its movement through the night sky would therefore surely resonate with many travelling to and from the complex, especially if we consider when in the year the constellation can be seen. It would first have become visible towards the end of summer, initially in mid-August for an

hour or so, but by mid-September for much of the night, at a time of year when the landscape had began to change. The first appearance of Orion's Belt, used in historic mythology and folklore around the world to mark or time the social calendar (Aveni 1997; Nilsson 1920; Thorpe 1981), could herald a new phase in the life-cycle of the cosmos as plants and animals became less plentiful. If this was one of the year's two 'great portals', then Orion's total disappearance from the night sky in March marks the other as the landscape, and the life it supports, starts to rejuvenate as temperatures rise (Stephen Sayers, pers comm). Of course, Neolithic commu-

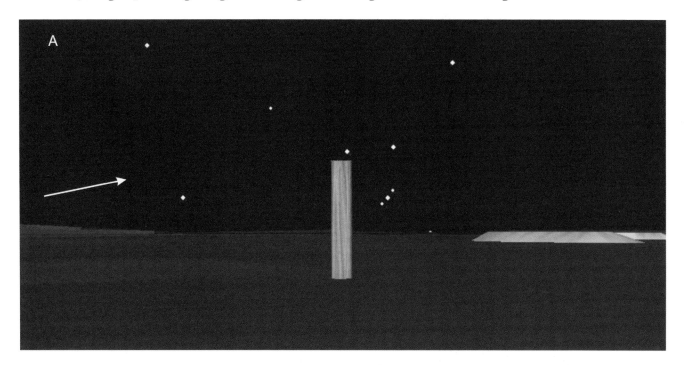

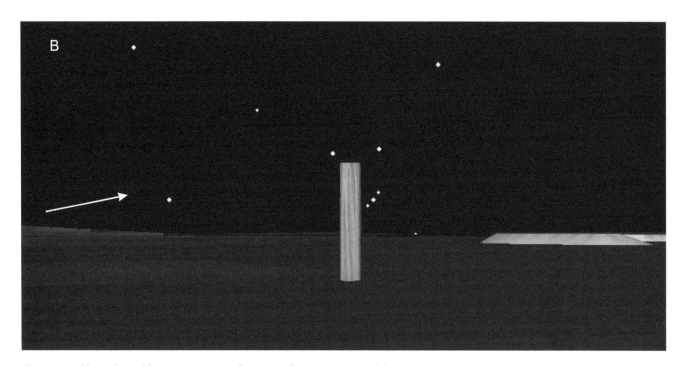

Fig 6.10   View from the two cropmark anomalies, interpreted here as originally holding large posts, of the rising of Orion's Belt at 3000 BC (A) and 2500 BC (B). The more distant triple-ditched round barrow is not shown. Image reproduced courtesy of the University of Texas

nities hardly needed a time-reckoning scheme to keep track of these seasonal transitions or make decisions about when to travel, but by linking their movements, and the transportation of goods, to this celestial phenomenon they were ensuring their lives, their landscapes, and their sky were in harmony with each other. This symbolic representation of east–west travel by Orion's Belt evoked the timelessness

and ahistorical character of the relationships which found form at the monuments, bridging the divide between the living and their ancestors, especially if the stars above, the gypsum below, and human bone were perceived as of the same substance, the first returning to the underworld as they disappear beneath the horizon. Indeed, all these elements could have been connected together in a cycle which

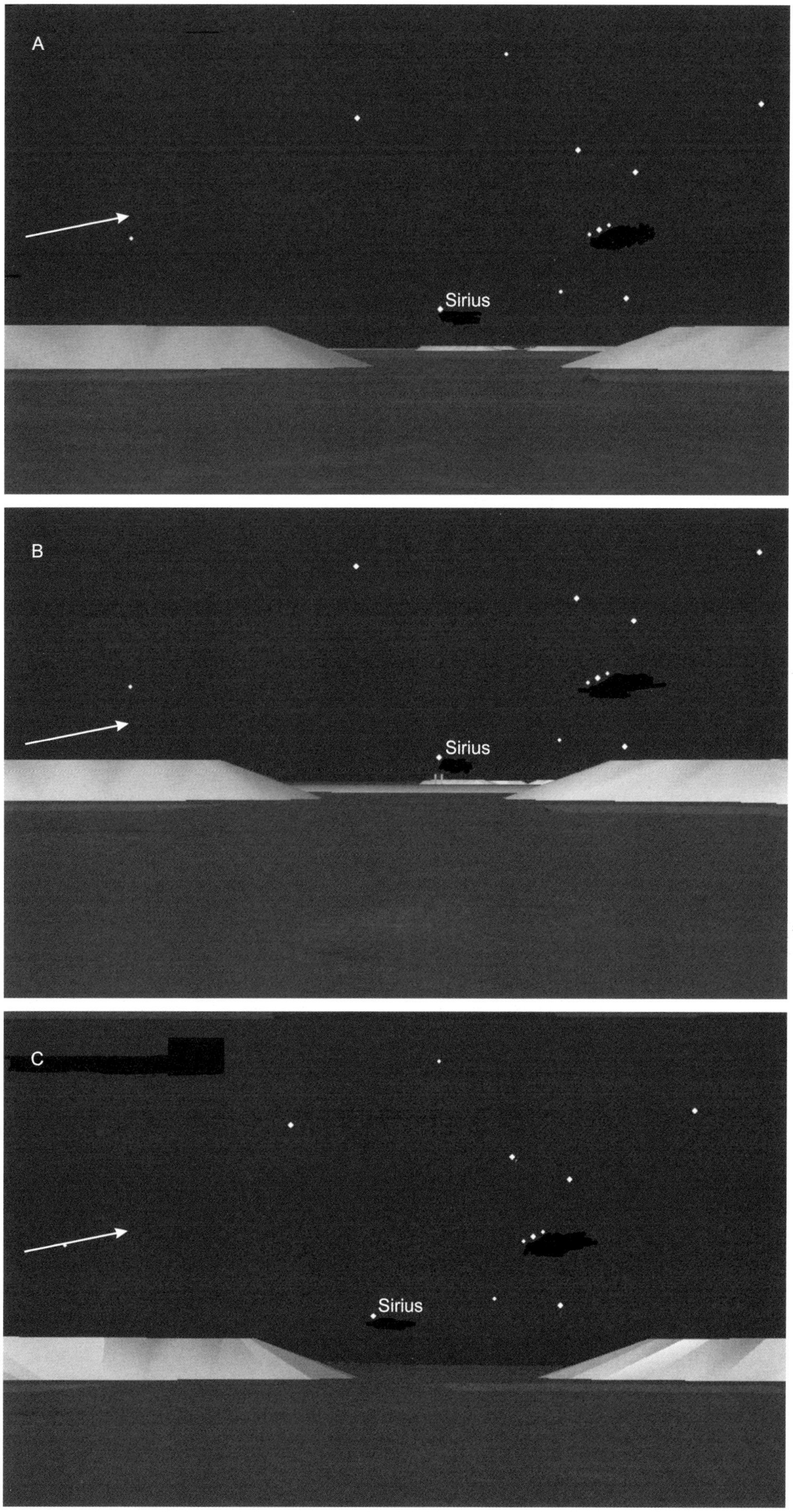

Fig 6.11   View at 3000 BC of Sirius and Orion's Belt from within the northern henge (A), the central henge (B) and the southern henge (C). Image reproduced courtesy of the University of Texas

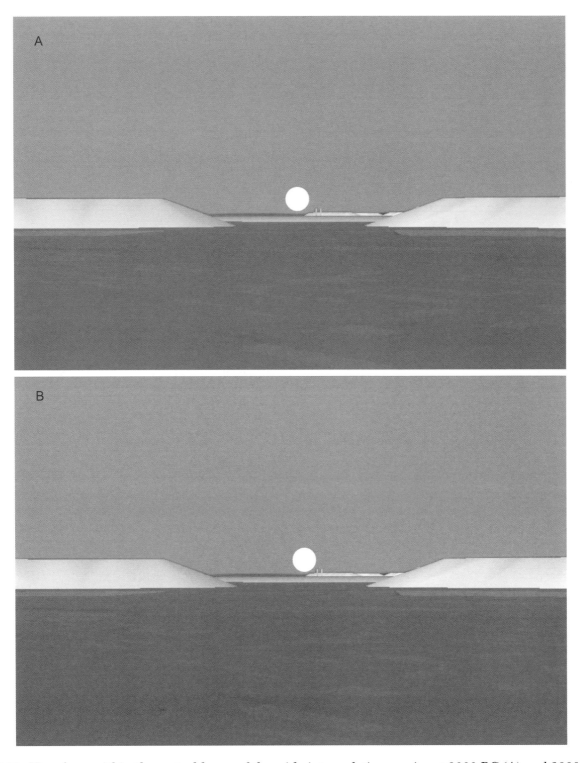

Fig 6.12   View from within the central henge of the midwinter solstice sunrise at 3000 BC (A) and 2000 BC (B). Image reproduced courtesy of the University of Texas

transcended life and death itself. Visiting Thornborough was a journey through the universe's strata, undertaken repeatedly both before and after death.

This is not to argue that its symbolism was concerned exclusively with celestial phenomena and the season's changes, for it was surely much more complex, meaning different things to different people, and different things at different points in the landscape's complex development. It does, however, demonstrate the close relationship between skyscape and life-cycles, a connection anchored by the monuments themselves. The association of the cursus with Orion's Belt is striking and may have been reproduced by Thornborough's rather distinctive and unusual development during the later Neolithic. The three marginally misaligned henges

(3.3.2) could be taken as a physical depiction of the three offset stars of Orion's Belt (Harding and Johnson 2000), but this is problematic given how the latter's alignment shifts as it moves across the night sky. It is also far from clear if all three henges were conceived, planned, and built together (4.9). Nonetheless, the central henge was very *deliberately* sited over the earlier cursus, perhaps in an attempt to draw upon and manipulate the lapsed relationship between this earlier monument and the setting of Orion's Belt, and, irrespective of the sequence and tempo of building, *three* enclosures were sited across the full extent of the plateau, at the heart of what appears to have been a highly structured landscape (5.5). It is difficult to avoid the conclusion that a carefully planned and long-term vision – or what can be more accurately described as a religious imperative – was responsible. That a single scheme of symbolic expression was adhered to across this landscape during both the middle and later Neolithic raises many issues about both the relationship between monument building and celestial phenomena, and the longevity of belief and memory here. All the same, Orion's Belt could have been interwoven into the beliefs, practices, and spiritual associations which collectively enlivened the complex and transformed it into a place of special religious poignancy. Interestingly, the constellation has also been linked to The Hurlers in Cornwall, where three stone circles are aligned upon the stars at midnight on the winter solstice (Brian Sheen, pers comm).

The potential link with the midwinter solstice in the later Neolithic may reflect a more widely celebrated religious festival which had added resonance at Thornborough. Its significance can be understood both practically and symbolically. Despite the poorer weather of the winter season, especially perilous for east–west travel in Yorkshire given its upland landscapes and swollen waterways, it is likely that many long-distance journeys, such as those connected to the exchange of polished stone axes and flint, were undertaken then. Summer was a busy period as resources like plants required harvesting and animal herds were at their largest and most demanding. Given this, people congregating at Thornborough in the depth of winter is perhaps not as surprising as it first appears. There may also have been powerful religious reasons for this. If the annual appearance and disappearance of Orion's Belt concurs with the year's 'great portals', delineating a time when people travel, then the midwinter solstice is equidistant between both, offering a neat temporal framework for people's life-cycles. This mattered because if autumn marks the beginning of the end, then midwinter 'is the time when the sun rises and sets farthest to the south', an important motivation as worshippers tried to stop the sun's movement 'southwards until it vanished, leaving the world in everlasting darkness' (Burl 1981, 87). In other words, those congregating at Thornborough and elsewhere were attempting to

stop the world falling ever deeper into the grips of winter, and, by doing so, were ensuring the gradual rejuvenation of their cosmos during the time when Orion is no longer visible. The orientation of the southern entrances could reflect this keen interest, and possibly explain why they are approximately aligned on the Nunwick henge, some 5km distant, and the Devil's Arrows at Boroughbridge (Burl 1991), creating an axis which extends for 20km if we take the springs at Well as its northern extremity (Fig 6.6). A connection with the winter solstice, and all it represented, would have legitimated these monumental 'signposts' and the direction of travel to which they allude. Such connotations enlivened the routeways which issued through and out of the earthworks, and which were travelled by worshippers coming and going to the henges. Indeed, the importance of this alignment is echoed on the other side of the Pennines where the outlying stone of Long Meg and her Daughters, the impressive stone circle in Cumbria, appears to be orientated on the sunset of the shortest day (Burl 1988, 196–7; Thom *et al* 1980, 42–3). That monuments immediately to the east and west of the Pennines were similarly linked with the ancestors, spirits, or gods of the sky, suggests the same beliefs and practices spanned this upland chain, its flanking lowlands, and the Cumbrian mountains and Yorkshire coast beyond. Many worlds were being drawn together into a single symbolic universe through shared interests and practices.

Nothing is known about what actually happened within the earthen banks and ditches of the henges. However, if these monuments were indeed built across a landscape where the hierarchical order of the cosmos – the underworld, the land, the sky – was exposed for all to see, then they were surely the 'betwixt and between': the place where communication was possible between different cosmic elements. As such, what happened within them was not concerned with symbolic representation, celebration, or control, but rather with negotiation, worshippers hoping 'The universe responds to speech and mime. It discerns the social order and intervenes to uphold it' (Douglas 1966, 89). Of course, this does not necessarily explain why it was necessary to build these circular earthworks in the first place. It could be that people believed these negotiations were best conducted within formalised arenas or that the henges were residences for spirits and gods; but other issues could have driven this vast building project. If their construction was actually an intrinsic part of the festivals conducted there, then people were uniting in communal endeavour during the wetter, colder part of the year, when there was the potential of social crisis as resources diminished and groups or families tended not to be involved in collective appropriation. It is at such times that social regeneration is most needed. By working together to build arenas within which spiritual transactions could occur, as opposed to congregating at natural places like the river bank or around known gypsum collapses, worshippers actively invoked the past by reflecting on the activities and journeys which brought people there in the first place. They also looked to the future as the fruits of their labours, the monuments themselves, became a gambit, a sort of material expression of righteousness, in their pleas for fecundity, social cohesion, and new possibilities in the next growing season. The very creation of the monuments constituted an act of meditation upon the axis of social temporality.

6.4   Cult, pilgrimage, and social identity

This account hints at some of the intentions, motivations, and strategies implicit in Thornborough's development. Undoubtedly, they were more complex, and the landscape's story more convoluted (see 4.9), than this simple narrative, and it seems probable that a wide range of tasks and activities were undertaken there, including those likely to be archaeologically invisible such as exchange itself. Its multiplicity of monuments surely meant different things to different people. Yet for all this likely complexity, it was first and foremost a landscape where the air was thick with religion. Exactly when its spiritual energy and sacredness was first realised is impossible to tell, but from early on its very physicality could have evoked people's beliefs and the powerful forces responsible for the cosmos. Highly mobile later Mesolithic visitors would have appreciated the area's supra-abundance of special natural places and strategic location, celebrating its rivers, its wetland, the gypsum collapses, and the sky above as living entities upon which life depended. However, it is with those who built the triple-ditched round barrow, and thereby became its initial 'Neolithic' occupants, that we see the first surviving example of propitiation. The fact they built and rebuilt a dedicatory monument to the dead early in the 4th millennium suggests that prehistoric communities were already attracted to this area's spirituality. Frequent visits to the site saw its mound of earth and cobbles grow to an impressive size but, imposing though this may have been, it was surpassed by the earthworks and timbers of the cursus, which, quite literally, stretched the transcendent quality of sacred architecture across the length of the plateau to encourage and accommodate many more worshippers. It too is likely to have emerged gradually, and as people increasingly journeyed over the Pennines to exchange polished stone axes and flint, it was intermittently visited by those who learnt to accept the landscape's holiness and its sanctification of the socially unfettered circulation and exchange of these materials. As practicality and religiosity interleaved, subsequent acts of monumental construction and worship were completed along the length of the cursus to appease, assuage, make peace with, or otherwise strategically negotiate with, spirits and gods.

The action of building the cursus could have been linked with a new cult or spiritual narrative which celebrated and enhanced Thornborough's unique role in east–west relations and exchange, its apparent success perhaps measured by the return of Orion's Belt to the night sky each year. Thornborough emerged as a supra-local 'cult centre' with its own beliefs, practices, and spiritual associations (see Keyes 1975; Rutkowski 1972, 24), a place of renown where different worldly elements came together to mould a 'sacred landscape'. Of course, the constellation did eventually stop setting 'within' the cursus at around 3000 BC, but if this created a crisis of belief, then the fact it was happening alongside other transformations in Britain would only help focus minds on Thornborough's religious significance. The situation could have been rescued by starting work on the henges, whose scale and planned magnificence surpassed the earlier monuments, and whose complex relationship with the past was clearly stated at the central enclosure (4.9). A rupture of belief may have been acknowledged, but disquiet and tension were turned into triumph by this monument's blatant message of spiritual renewal and socio-political reinvention. Cults create narratives which travel freely and are retold, and curiosity, self-interest, and a desire for cosmic harmony all surely added to the spread of Thornborough's reputation and popularity during the 3rd millennium. Certainly Cumbrian axes were more common across Yorkshire during the later Neolithic (Bradley and Edmonds 1993, 180ff). Unfortunately, it is impossible to say how long it continued as a cult centre since so little is known about the chronology and development of the henges, and indeed, about stone axe exchange, but there are glimpses of traditions continuing in the 2nd millennium (4.9). Further work is needed to determine when they faded, and disappeared altogether.

Understanding Thornborough as a cult centre for inter-group festivals evokes Loveday's (1998, 26) suggestion that double-entranced henges were located along, or at the end of, ritual paths or pilgrims' routeways. Others have discussed the likely role of pilgrimages in fulfilling a wide range of social, economic, and religious considerations in 3rd-millennium BC Britain (Barnatt 1998, 96; Loveday in press; Renfrew 1985, 255–6; 2000, 16–18). Whilst historic pilgrimage is unlikely to be directly analogous – Loveday (in press) argues that during the Neolithic 'out of the ordinary journeying to sacred locales' was likely to be 'calendrical and collective rather than open and individual' – it does offer potential insights. Key sites of attraction on historic pilgrim routes are places where ritual action and religious belief are most fully played out and, indeed, are sometimes considered as 'centres' of the world (Silverman 1994). It is common for pilgrims to travel to a place separated from the surrounding landscape to complete a 'quest' or seek something which lies outside the accustomed patterns of everyday life (Reader 1993a, 9–10; 1993b, 236): a place where heaven and earth intersect, where there existed the possibility of crossing over into the realm of the transcendent, and where 'pilgrims devoutly pour their hopes, prayers and aspirations' (Eade and Sallnow 1991, 6, 15). The Rivers Ure and Swale would certainly achieve this level of separation, and it is perfectly possible that crossing these sacred barriers, a potentially dangerous act which could have left an impression on the traveller, was the first step in a 'rite of passage', or process of spiritual rebirth, which involved visits to the interfluve's other monuments before arriving at Thornborough's sacred plateau. The Devil's Arrows, distinctive as they are on account of their megalithic architecture and siting to the south of the Ure near its confluence with the Swale, were perhaps a 'gateway', or, if later than the henges, a commemoration of the earlier routeway. Beyond them, movement could have been formalised, perhaps along the alignment formed by the Devil's Arrows and the henges at Nunwick and Thornborough, and indeed, the alignment of Cana Barn and Hutton Moor (Fig 6.6; Harding 2012). It is impossible to say if Thornborough was the key shrine along these routes, although being the largest complex must make it a strong contender. Nor indeed can we currently speculate about the relationship between these two different alignments or the direction in which pilgrims came. Regarding the henges as places of worship along a pilgrimage route, however, possibly built to sanctify existing places of religious significance like the nearby springs, would accord with their dense clustering within the Ure-Swale Interfluve.

It also implies that the complex's development was not necessarily anchored in the history and mythology of particular communities. Pilgrimages offer opportunities to trade and exchange objects, to make and renew friendships, to communicate information and meet sexual partners, to retell stories and reinvigorate society's core values, or to challenge them and suggest new beliefs. All these activities would have had a profoundly significant impact on the long-term socio-political developments of those families and groups worshipping there, especially if, as seems likely, the pilgrimage itself was collective rather than individual (Loveday in press). Crucially, these interactions occur within a community and moral order created *during* the pilgrimage, thereby distancing social interaction from the tensions, themes, and power structures of group relations and identities (Douglas 1966, 173; Reader 1993a, 1–10). New webs of relations and new forms of identity resulted, and the fact this was happening across such a symbolically charged landscape made them more enduring and memorable. This distinctiveness is why pilgrimage centres often develop at different tempos, or in completely different ways, to other centres of religious worship. By surpassing the specific rites of religious practice to focus on those primordial spiritual issues which affect all, their architecture assumes timeless and ahistorical qualities not seen elsewhere. They could certainly

be places where radical invention often gives way to a tradition of design with remarkable longevity, as at Thornborough. As already argued (4.9), the triple-ditched round barrow, the cursus, and the henges possess elements which were profoundly original, and through this alterity invoked the 'double mediation' necessary for effective religious worship. Yet the building of the cursus established a sacred geometry across the plateau which continued for as much as 2000 years. As a 'cult centre', this landscape was free of much of the ebb and flow which accompanies socio-political identity and history, represented elsewhere by the building of small enclosures, ring-ditches, and timber or pit circles, including at both Maxey in Cambridgeshire and Dorchester-on-Thames in Oxfordshire (Atkinson *et al* 1951; French and Pryor 2005; Loveday 1999; Pryor *et al* 1985, 59–70, 250–4; Whittle *et al* 1992), perhaps the two closest parallels to Thornborough (1.2). If these sites were built to create, represent, commemorate, and sustain local or kin-based relationships, then their apparent absence at Thornborough ensured this place's clarity of purpose (see also Gillings *et al* 2008, 214, 220). Its monuments served to impress the spirit world and worshipper alike, and by so doing, enabled a meaningful religious dialogue between both parties. In short, they were attempts to calibrate, at least in part, an otherwise disparate and uncertain world.

This association with cults and pilgrimage moves interpretation beyond seeing large monuments like those at Thornborough as the product of centralised social polities with fixed notions of identity and power (1.2), though this is not to say that the complex created a religious utopia where all were equal and life was free of worldly concerns, inequalities, or petty squabbles. 'Belonging' may have been achieved by participating in activities conducted at the monuments, including their building and upkeep by large numbers of people, rather than by any sense of territorial affiliation, but there would have been a granularity to pilgrimage and worship as differences, interests, intrigue, disagreement, and even revulsion gave rise to drama. Pilgrimage is a pragmatic act, religious activities being 'both matters for making merit for the eternal life and [a] means of gaining benefits in this world' (Stirrat 1984, 208). Neither can we assume that pilgrimage, involving large numbers of people from very different backgrounds, is unregulated worship. Thornborough may not have been 'conceived as an entity, a plan in the mind of some autocratic chief' (Barrett 1994, 13), but it could have been necessary all the same for visitors to be organised, for the purity of the monuments and their hinterland to be maintained, and all acts of worship to be orchestrated to ensure their appropriateness. Those completing this role, perhaps a 'specialised priesthood' (Renfrew 1973, 555; see also Mackie 1977, 201–11), may not have necessarily had any power of authority over those assembled, but they surely had spiritual knowledge on their side. There is the possibility, then, of a religiously empowered group overseeing activity, permanently based at Thornborough along with their extended families. They could have coordinated the labour of worshippers, thereby ensuring what got built where; they could also have been responsible for the complex's physical upkeep and the maintenance of a top-down apprehension which ensured the landscape's role as a cult centre.

Bibliography

Abramson, P, 1996 Excavations along the Caythorpe Gas Pipeline, north Humberside, *Yorkshire Archaeol J* **68**, 1–88

Abramson, P, 2003 The Neolithic and Bronze Age: a time of early agriculture. Appendix 1: Marton-le-Moor radiocarbon dates, in Manby, Moorhouse & Ottaway (eds) 2003, 114–16

Abungu, G H O, 1994 Islam on the Kenyan coast: an overview of Kenyan coastal sacred sites, in Carmichael *et al* 1994, 152–62

Addyman, P V, Coles, J M & Hartley, C E, 1964 A late Bronze Age vessel from Flaxby, *Yorkshire Archaeol J* **41**, 184–90

Adler, M A & Wilshusen, R H, 1990 Large-scale integrative facilities in tribal societies: cross-cultural and southwestern US examples, *World Archaeol* **22**(2), 133–46

Aitkenhead, N, Barclay, W J, Brandon, A, Chadwick, R A, Chisholm, J I, Cooper, A H & Johnson, E W, 2002 *British Regional Geology: the Pennines and adjacent areas* (4th edition). Nottingham: British Geological Survey

Allason-Jones, L & Miket, R F, 1984 *Catalogue of small finds from South Shields Roman fort*. Newcastle upon Tyne: Society of Antiquaries of Newcastle upon Tyne

Allen, T, Barclay, A & Lamdin-Whymark, H, 2004 Opening the wood, making the land: the study of a Neolithic landscape in the Dorney area of the Middle Thames Valley, in J Cotton & D Field (eds), *Towards a new Stone Age: aspects of the Neolithic in south-east England*, CBA Res Rep **137**. York: Council for British Archaeology, 82–98

Anderson, S, 1997 *Human skeletal remains from Long Melford, Suffolk (Site LMD115)*. Available: http://www.spoilheap.co.uk/pdfs/LMD115SK.pdf. Accessed: 14 January 2007

Århem, K, 1998 Powers of place: landscape, territory and local belonging in Northwest Amazonia, in N Lovell (ed), *Locality and Belonging*. London & New York: Routledge, 78–102

Armit, I, Murphy, E, Nelis, E & Simpson, D (eds), 2003 *Neolithic settlement in Ireland and western Britain*. Oxford: Oxbow Books

Atkins Heritage, 2005 Thornborough henges conservation plan. Unpubl public consultation draft report for North Yorkshire County Council, English Heritage & Tarmac Northern Ltd

Atkinson, R J C, 1956 *Stonehenge*. London: Hamish Hamilton

Atkinson, R J C, 1976 Lukis, Dryden and the Carnac monuments, in J V S Megaw (ed), *To illustrate the monuments*. London: Thames and Hudson

Atkinson, R J C, Piggott, C M & Sandars, N K, 1951 *Excavations at Dorchester, Oxon: first report*. Oxford: Department of Antiquities, Ashmolean Museum

Aveni, A F, 1997 *Stairways to the stars: skywatching in three great ancient cultures*. London: Cassell Publishers Ltd

Barclay, A & Bayliss, A, 1999 Cursus monuments and the radiocarbon problem, in Barclay & Harding (eds) 1999, 11–29

Barclay, A & Harding, J (eds), 1999 *Pathways and ceremonies: the cursus monuments of Britain and Ireland*, Neolithic Studies Group Sem Pap **4**. Oxford: Oxbow Books

Barclay, A & Hey, G, 1999 Cattle, cursus monuments and the river: the development of ritual and domestic landscapes in the Upper Thames Valley, in Barclay & Harding (eds) 1999, 67–76

Barclay, A, Lambrick, G, Moore, J. & Robinson, M, 2003 *Lines in the landscape: cursus monuments in the Upper Thames Valley*, Oxford Archaeol Thames Valley Landscapes Monogr **15**. Oxford: Oxford Archaeology

Barclay, G J, 1983 Sites of the third millennium bc to the first millennium ad at North Mains, Strathallan, Perthshire. *Proc Soc Antiq Scot* **113**, 122–281

Barclay, G J, 1999 Cairnpapple revisited: 1948–1998. *Proc Prehist Soc* **65**, 17–46

Barclay, G J, 2003 Neolithic settlement in the lowlands of Scotland: a preliminary survey, in Armit, Murphy, Nelis & Simpson (eds) 2003, 71–83

Barclay, G J & Maxwell, G S, 1991 Excavation of a Neolithic long mortuary enclosure within the Roman legionary fortress at Inchtuthil, Perthshire, *Proc Soc Antiq Scot* **121**, 27–44

Barclay, G J & Maxwell, G S (eds), 1998 *The Cleaven Dyke and Littleour: monuments in the Neolithic of Tayside*, Soc Antiq Scot Monogr Ser **13**. Edinburgh: Society of Antiquaries of Scotland

Barker, G, 1981 Approaches to prehistoric man in northern England, in G Barker (ed), *Prehistoric communities in northern England: essays in economic and social reconstruction*. Sheffield: University of Sheffield, 1–10

Barnatt, J, 1989 *Stone circles of Britain: taxonomic and distributional analyses and a catalogue of sites in England, Scotland and Wales*, BAR Brit Ser **215** (i & ii). Oxford: British Archaeological Reports

Barnatt, J, 1998 Monuments in the landscape: thoughts from the Peak, in A Gibson & D Simpson (eds), *Prehistoric ritual and religion: essays in honour of Aubrey Burl*. Stroud: Sutton Publishing Ltd, 92–107

Barnatt, J & Collis, J, 1996 *Barrows in the Peak District: recent research*. Sheffield: J R Collis

Barrett, J C, 1994 *Fragments from antiquity: an archaeology of social life in Britain, 2900–1200 BC*. Oxford & Cambridge: Blackwell

Barrett, J C, Bradley, R & Green, M, 1991 *Landscape, monuments and society: the prehistory of Cranborne Chase*. Cambridge: Cambridge University Press

Bayliss, A, Hedges, R, Otlet, R, Switsur, R & Walker, J, 2012 *Radiocarbon dates from samples funded by English Heritage between 1981 and 1988*. Swindon: English Heritage

Bell, C, 1992 *Ritual theory, ritual practice*. New York & Oxford: Oxford University Press

Bellamy, C V, & Le Patourel, H E J, 1970 Four medieval pottery kilns from Woodhouse Farm, Winksley, near

Ripon, W Riding of Yorkshire, *Medieval Archaeol* **20**, 104–25

Bender, B, 1998 *Stonehenge: making space*. Oxford & New York: Berg

Berg, D S, 1991 Peat from the Rushwood Estate, Nosterfield, North Yorkshire. Unpubl report

Bloch, M, 1974 Symbols, song, dance and features of articulation: is religion an extreme form of traditional authority?, *Archives Européenes de Sociologie* **15**, 55–81

Boismier, W A, 1997 *Modelling the effects of tillage processes on artefact distributions in the ploughzone: a simulation study of tillage-induced pattern formation*, BAR Brit Ser **259**. Oxford: British Archaeological Reports

Bourdieu, P, 1977 *Outline of a theory of practice*. Cambridge: Cambridge University Press

Bowie, F, 2000 *The anthropology of religion: an introduction*. Oxford: Blackwell

Bradley, R, 1982 Position and possession: assemblage variation in the British Neolithic, *Oxford J Archaeol* **1**(1), 27–38

Bradley, R, 1984 *The social foundations of prehistoric Britain: themes and variations in the archaeology of power*. London & New York: Longman

Bradley, R, 1985 *Consumption, change and the archaeological record: the archaeology of monuments and the archaeology of deliberate deposits*, Univ Edinburgh Dept Archaeol Occas Pap **13**. Edinburgh: University of Edinburgh

Bradley, R, 1987a Time regained: the creation of continuity, *J Brit Archaeol Ass* **140**, 1–17

Bradley, R, 1987b A field method for investigating the spatial structure of lithic scatters, in Brown & Edmonds (eds) 1987, 39–47

Bradley, R, 1990 *The passage of arms: an archaeological analysis of prehistoric hoards and votive deposits*. Cambridge: Cambridge University Press

Bradley, R, 1991 The evidence of earthen monuments, in Barrett, Bradley & Green 1991, 36–58

Bradley, R, 1992a The gravels and British prehistory from the Neolithic to the Early Iron Age, in Fulford & Nichols 1992, 15–22

Bradley, R, 1992b The excavation of an oval barrow beside the Abingdon causewayed enclosure, Oxfordshire, *Proc Prehist Soc* **58**, 127–42

Bradley, R, 1993 *Altering the earth: the origins of monuments in Britain and Continental Europe*, Soc Antiq Scot Monogr Ser **8** (The Rhind Lectures 1991–92). Edinburgh: Society of Antiquaries of Scotland

Bradley, R, 1998 *The significance of monuments: on the shaping of human experience in Neolithic and Bronze Age Europe*. London: Routledge

Bradley, R, 2000a *An archaeology of natural places*. London & New York: Routledge

Bradley, R, 2000b *The Good Stones: a new investigation of the Clava Cairns*, Soc Antiq Scot Monogr Ser **17**. Edinburgh: Society of Antiquaries of Scotland

Bradley, R, 2003 Neolithic expectations, in Armit, Murphy, Nelis & Simpson (eds) 2003, 218–22

Bradley, R, 2007 *The prehistory of Britain and Ireland*. Cambridge: Cambridge University Press

Bradley, R & Chambers, R, 1988 A new study of the cursus complex at Dorchester on Thames, *Oxford J Archaeol* **7**(3), 271–89

Bradley, R & Edmonds, M, 1993 *Interpreting the axe trade. Production and exchange in Neolithic Britain*. Cambridge: Cambridge University Press

Bradley, R & Gardiner, J, 1984 Introduction: closing doors and opening windows, in R Bradley & J Gardiner (eds) *Neolithic studies: a review of some current research*, BAR Brit Ser **133**. Oxford: British Archaeological Reports, 1–3

Bradley, R & Gordon, K, 1988 Human skulls from the River Thames, their dating and significance, *Antiquity* **62**, 503–9

Bradley, R & Holgate, R, 1984 The Neolithic sequence in the Upper Thames Valley, in R Bradley & J Gardiner (eds), *Neolithic studies: a review of some current research*, BAR Brit Ser **133**. Oxford: British Archaeological Reports, 107–34

Bradley, R I, 1987 Soil survey and agricultural land classification. Rushwood Estate, Nosterfield, North Yorkshire. Unpubl Report, Soil Survey and Land Research Centre, Cranfield

Brailsford, J W, 1962 *Hod Hill, Volume I: antiquities from Hod Hill in the Durden Collection*. London: Trustees of the British Museum

Braithwaite, M, 1984 Ritual and prestige in the prehistory of Wessex c.2000–1400 BC: a new dimension to the archaeological evidence, in D Miller & C Tilley (eds), *Ideology, power and prehistory*. Cambridge: Cambridge University Press, 93–110

Brennand, M, Brown, F, Howard-Davis, C & Lupton, A, 2007 Synthesis, in F Brown, C Howard-Davis, M Brennand, A Boyle, T Evans, S O'Connor, A Spence, R Heawood & A Lupton, *The archaeology of the A1(M) Darrington to Dishforth DBFO Road Scheme*, Oxford Archaeol North Lancaster Imprints **12**. Oxford: Oxford Archaeology North, 379–410

Brewster, A, 1984 *The excavation of Whitegrounds, Burythorpe*. Wintringham: John Gett

Brewster, T C M & Finney, A E, 1995 *The excavations of seven Bronze Age barrows on the moorlands of North East Yorkshire*, Yorkshire Archaeol Rep **1**. Leeds: Yorkshire Archaeological Reports

Bridgland, D, Innes, J, Long, A & Mitchell, W, 2011 *Late Quaternary landscape evolution of the Swale-Ure Washlands, North Yorkshire*. Oxford & Oakville: Oxbow Books

Brodie, N, 1994 *The Neolithic–Bronze Age transition in Britain*, BAR Brit Ser **238**. Oxford: Tempus Reparatum

Bronk Ramsey, C, 1995 Radiocarbon calibration and analysis of stratigraphy: The OxCal Program, *Radiocarbon* **37**(2), 425–30

Bronk Ramsey, C, 2010 *OxCal Program, v.4.1.7, Radiocarbon Accelerator Unit, University of Oxford, UK*. Avaliable http://c14.arch.ox.ac.uk/embed.php?File=oxcal.html. Accessed 20 December 2012

Bronk Ramsey, C, Higham, T H F, Owen, D C, Pike, A W G & Hedges, R E M, 2002 Radiocarbon dates from the Oxford AMS system: Archaeometry datelist 31, *Archaeometry* **44**(3, Supplement 1), 1–149

Brooks, I P, 1989 Debugging the system: the characterization of flint by micropalaeontology, in I Brooks & P Phillips (eds), *Breaking the Stony Silence*, BAR Brit Ser **213**. Oxford: British Archaeological Reports, 53–63

Brooks, I P, 2003 Flint and chert, in Moloney *et al* 2003, 35–6

Brooks, I P, 2005 Flint artefacts, in Roberts (ed) 2005, 143–9

Brophy, K, 2000a Wet Drybridge: a cursus in Ayrshire, in Harding & Johnston (eds) 2000, 45–56

Brophy, K, 2000b Water coincidence? Cursus monuments

and rivers, in A Ritchie (ed), *Neolithic Orkney in its European context*. Cambridge: McDonald Institute Monographs, 59–70

Brothwell, D R, 1981 *Digging up bones* (3rd edition). Oxford: Oxford University Press & Natural History, British Museum

Brown, A G & Edmonds, M R (eds), 1987 *Lithic analysis and later British prehistory: some problems and approaches*, BAR Brit Ser **162**. Oxford: British Archaeological Reports

Brown, N, 1997 A landscape of two halves: the Neolithic of the Chelmer Valley/Blackwater Estuary, Essex, in Topping (ed) 1997, 87–98

Brück, J, 1999 What's in a settlement? Domestic practice and residential mobility in Early Bronze Age southern England, in J Brück & M Goodman (eds), *Making places in the prehistoric world: themes in settlement archaeology*. London: University of London Press, 52–75

Buckley, D, Major, H & Milton, B, 1988 Excavation of a possible Neolithic long barrow or mortuary enclosure at Rivenhall, Essex, 1986, *Proc Prehist Soc* **54**, 77–91

Buckley, D G, Hedges, J D & Brown, N, 2001 Excavations at a Neolithic cursus, Springfield, Essex, 1979–85. *Proc Prehist Soc* **67**, 101–62

Burgess, C, 1995 Bronze Age settlements and domestic pottery in Northern Britain, in I Kinnes and G Varndell (eds), *'Unbaked Urns of Rudely Shape': essays on British and Irish Pottery for Ian Longworth*, Oxbow Monographs **55**. Oxford: Oxbow Books, 145–58

Burl, A, 1969 Henges: internal features and regional groups, *Archaeol J* **126**, 1–19

Burl, A, 1981 *Rites of the gods*. London: J M Dent and Sons Ltd

Burl, A, 1988 'Without sharp north …' Alexander Thom and the Great Stone Circles of Cumbria, in C. Ruggles (ed), *Records in stone: papers in memory of Alexander Thom*. Cambridge: Cambridge University Press, 175–205

Burl, A, 1991 The Devil's Arrows, Boroughbridge, North Yorkshire: the archaeology of a stone row, *Yorkshire Archaeol J* **63**, 1–24

Cameron, R A D & Redfern, M, 1976 *British Land Snails*, Synopses of the British Fauna (New Series) **6**, Linnean Society of London. London: Academic Press

Card, N, 2010 Colour, cups and tiles – recent discoveries at the Ness of Brodgar, *Past* **66**, 1–3

Carmichael, D L, Hubert, J, Reeves, B & Schanche, A (eds), 1994 *Sacred sites, sacred places*, One World Archaeol **23**. London & New York: Routledge

Case, H J, 1982 The linear ditches and southern enclosure, North Stoke, in Case & Whittle (eds) 1982, 60–71

Case, H J & Whittle, A W R (eds), 1982 *Settlement patterns in the Oxford Region: excavations at the Abingdon causewayed enclosure and other sites*, CBA Res Rep **44**. London: Council for British Archaeology

Challis, A J & Harding, D W, 1975 *Later prehistory from the Trent to the Tyne*, BAR Brit Archaeol Rep **20**. Oxford: British Archaeological Reports

Cheetham, P & Clarke, S, no date Archaeological assessment and evaluation report for Hanson Aggregates (Ripon Quarry Site). Unpubl Report by Specialist Archaeology Services at Bradford University

Cherry, J, 1978 Generalisation and the archaeology of the state, in D Green, C Haselgrove & M Spriggs (eds), *Social organisation and settlement*, BAR Int Ser **47**. Oxford: British Archaeological Reports, 411–37

Cherry, J & Cherry, P J, 1987 *Prehistoric habitation sites on the limestone uplands of eastern Cumbria*, Cumberland and Westmorland Archaeol Soc Res Series **2**. Kendal: Cumberland and Westmorland Archaeological Society

Cherry, J & Cherry, P J, 2002 Coastline and upland in Cumbrian prehistory, *Trans Cumberland and Westmorland Antiq Archaeol Soc* **II**, 1–21

Childe, V R, 1930 Operations at Skara Brae during 1929. *Proc Soc Antiq Scot* **64**, 158–91

Childe, V R, 1931 Final report on the operations at Skara Brae. *Proc Soc Antiq Scot* **65**, 27–77

Childe, V G, 1940 *Prehistoric communities of the British Isles*. London & Edinburgh: W & R Chambers

Chippindale, C, Devereux, P, Fowler, P, Jones, R & Sebastian, T, 1990 *Who owns Stonehenge?* London: Batsford

Clare, T, 1987 Towards a reappraisal of henge monuments: origins, evolution and hierarchies, *Proc Prehist Soc* **53**, 457–77

Clark, G, 1936 The timber monument at Arminghall and its affinities, *Proc Prehist Soc* **1**, 1–51

Clark, J G D, 1934 Derivative forms of the petit tranchet in Britain, *Archaeol J* **91**, 32–58

Clark, R H & Schofield, A J, 1991 By experiment and calibration: an integrated approach to archaeology of the ploughsoil, in A J Schofield (ed) *Interpreting artefact scatters: contributions to ploughzone archaeology*, Oxbow Monographs **4**. Oxford: Oxbow Books, 93–105

Clarke, D L, 1970 *Beaker pottery of Great Britain and Ireland*. Cambridge: Cambridge University Press

Cleal, R M J, Walker, K E & Montague, R, 1995 *Stonehenge in its landscape: Twentieth-Century excavations*, English Heritage Archaeological Report **10**. London: English Heritage

Clough, T H McK & Cummins, W A, 1988 *Stone axe studies volume 2: the petrology of prehistoric stone implements from the British Isles*, CBA Res Rep **67**. London: Council for British Archaeology

Coombs, D G, 1976 Callis Wold round barrow, Humberside, *Antiquity* **50**(198), 130–1

Cooney, G, 1997 Images of settlement and the landscape in the Neolithic, in Topping (ed) 1997, 23–32

Cooper, A H, 1986 Subsidence and foundering of strata caused by the dissolution of Permian gypsum in the Ripon and Bedale areas, North Yorkshire, in G M Harwood & D B Smith (eds), *The English Zechstein and related topics*, Geological Soc Special Publ **22**. Oxford, London, Edinburgh, Boston, Palo Alto & Melbourne: Geological Society, 127–39

Cooper, A H, 2000 Discussion of 'Early Holocene environments of the River Ure near Ripon, North Yorkshire, UK', *Proc Yorkshire Geological Soc* **53**(2), 155–6

Copp, A & Toop, N, 2005 Nosterfield Quarry, Nosterfield, North Yorkshire: interim report. Unpubl Report, Field Archaeology Specialists Ltd

Cornwall, I W, 1953 Thornborough (middle) rings, *Proc Prehist Soc* **19**, 144–7

Cornwall, I W, 1955 Appendix I. Thornborough Rings, *Yorkshire Archaeol J* **38**, 441–2

Cosgrove, D, 1984 *Social formation and symbolic landscape*. London: Croom Helm

Cowell, R, 2000 The Neolithic and Bronze Age in the lowlands of North West England, in Harding & Johnston (eds) 2000, 111–30

Crawford, O G S, 1927 *Leeds: British Association Excursion Handbook* **L**

Curwen, E C, 1934 Excavations in Whitehawk Neolithic Camp, Brighton, 1932–3, *Antiq J* **14**, 99–132

Curwen, E C, 1937 Excavations in Whitehawk Camp, Brighton, third season, *Sussex Archaeol Collect* **77**, 60–92

Darvill, T, 1996 Neolithic buildings in England, Wales and the Isles of Man, in T Darvill & J Thomas (eds), *Neolithic houses in Northwest Europe and beyond*, Neolithic Studies Group Sem Pap **1**. Oxford: Neolithic Studies Group, 77–111

David, A, 1998 Two assemblages of later Mesolithic microliths from Seamer Carr, North Yorkshire: fact and fantasy, in N Ashton, F Healy & P Pettitt (eds), *Stone Age Archaeology. Essays in Honour of John Wymer*, Oxbow Monogr **102**. Oxford: Oxbow Books, 196–204

Deegan, A, 2005 Thornborough Henges Air Photo Mapping Project: summary of resources and results. Unpubl West Yorkshire Archaeological Services Report 1358

Dennison, E, 1998 Thornborough North Henge, Tanfield, North Yorkshire: archaeological and ecological survey. Unpubl EDAS Report 1996/25.RO1 for English Heritage and Tanfield Lodge Estate

Dickson, A, 2011 Appendix 2: lithics, in Dickson and Hopkinson 2011, 271–310

Dickson, A & Hopkinson, G, 2011 *Holes in the landscape. Seventeen years of archaeological investigations at Nosterfield Quarry, North Yorkshire*. Available: http://www.archaeologicalplanningconsultancy.co.uk/index.php

Dillehay, T D, 1990 Mapuche ceremonial landscape, social recruitment and resource rights, *World Archaeol* **22**(2), 223–41

Douglas, M, 1966 *Purity and danger: an analysis of the concepts of pollution and taboo*. London: Routledge

Drewett, P, 1977 The excavation of a Neolithic causewayed enclosure on Offham Hill, East Sussex, 1976, *Proc Prehist Soc* **43**, 201–41

Durden, T, 1994 The production and consumption of specialised flint artefacts from the Yorkshire Wolds. Unpubl PhD Thesis, University of Reading

Durden, T, 1995 The production of specialised flintwork in the later Neolithic: a case study form the Yorkshire Wolds, *Proc Prehist Soc* **61**, 409–32

Dymond, D P, 1963 The 'henge' monument at Nunwick, near Ripon: 1961 excavation, *Yorkshire Archaeol J* **41**, 98–107

Dymond, D P, 1965 Grassington, W R (90), *Yorkshire Archaeol J* **41**, 323–4

Dymond, D P, 1966 Ritual monuments at Rudston, E. Yorkshire, England, *Proc Prehist Soc* **32**, 86–95

Eade, J & Sallnow, M J 1991 Introduction, in J Eade & M J Sallnow (eds), *Contesting the Sacred: the Anthropology of Christian Pilgrimage*. London: Routledge, 1–29

Earle, T, 1991 Property rights and the evolution of chiefdoms, in T Earle (ed), *Chiefdoms: power, economy and ideology*, School of American Research Advanced Seminar Series. Cambridge: Cambridge University Press, 71–99

Earle, T, 1997 *How chiefs come to power: the political economy in prehistory*. Stanford: Stanford University Press

Edmonds, M, 1987 Rocks and risks: problems with lithic procurement strategies, in Brown & Edmonds (eds) 1987, 155–80

Edmonds, M, 1995 *Stone tools and society*. London: Batsford

Edmonds, M & Thomas, J, 1987 The archers: an everyday story of country folk, in Brown & Edmonds (eds) 1987, 187–99

Edmonds, M, Evans, C & Gibson, D, 1999 Assembly and collection – lithic complexes in the Cambridgeshire Fenlands, *Proc Prehist Soc* **65**, 47–82

Edwards, W & Trotter, F M, 1954 *The Pennines and adjacent areas* (3rd edition). London: HMSO (British Regional Geology)

Ekwall, E, 1928 *English river-names*. Oxford: Oxford University Press

Elgee, F & Elgee, H W, 1933 *Archaeology of Yorkshire*. London: Methuen

Eliade, M, 1959 *The sacred and the profane: the nature of religion* (translated W R Trask). New York: Harcourt Brace Jovanovich

Eliade, M, 1963 *Myth and Reality* (translated W R Trask). New York: Harper Colophon Books

Ellis, C J, 2004 *A prehistoric ritual complex at Eynesbury, Cambridgeshire. Excavation of a multi-period site in the Great Ouse valley, 2000–2001*, E Anglian Archaeol Report **17**. Salisbury: Trust for Wessex Archaeology

Entwistle, R & Richards, J, 1987 The geochemical and geophysical properties of lithic scatters, in Brown & Edmonds (eds) 1987, 19–38

Eogan, G, 1986 *Knowth and the passage-tombs of Ireland*. London: Thames and Hudson

Evans, J G, 1972 *Land snails in archaeology*. London: Seminar Press Inc Ltd

Evans, J G, Limbrey, S & Cleere, H (eds), 1975 *The effect of man on the landscape: the highland zone*, CBA Res Rep **11**. London: Council for British Archaeology

Fasham, P J & Ross, J M, 1978 A Bronze Age flint industry from the barrow site in Micheldever Wood, Hampshire, *Proc Prehist Soc* **44**, 47–67

Fleming, A, 1971 Territorial patterns in Bronze Age Wessex, *Proc Prehist Soc* **37**(1), 138–66

Ford, S, 1987a The chronological and functional aspect of flint assemblages, in Brown & Edmonds (eds) 1987, 67–83

Ford, S, 1987b Flint scatters and prehistoric settlement patterns in south Oxfordshire and East Berkshire, in Brown & Edmonds (eds) 1987, 101–35

Ford, S & Pine, J, 2003 Neolithic ring ditches and Roman landscape features at Horton (1989–1996), in S Preston (ed), *Prehistoric, Roman and Saxon Sites in eastern Berkshire: excavations 1989–1997*, Thames Valley Archaeol Service Monogr **2**. Reading: Thames Valley Archaeological Service, 13–66

Ford, S, Bradley, R, Hawkes, J & Fisher, P, 1984 Flintworking in the metal age, *Oxford J Archaeol* **3**(2), 157–73

Fowler, C & Cummings, V, 2003 Places of transformation: building monuments from water and stone in the Neolithic of the Irish Sea, *J Royal Anthropological Inst* **9**, 1–20

Fox, C, 1932 *The personality of Britain: its influence on inhabitant and invader in prehistoric and early historic times*. Cardiff: National Museum of Wales

French, C & Pryor, F, 2005 *Archaeology and environment of the Etton landscape*, E Anglian Archaeol Rep **109**. Peterborough: East Anglian Archaeology & Fenland Archaeological Trust

Fulford, M & Nichols, E (eds), 1992 *Developing landscapes of lowland Britain. The archaeology of the British gravels: a review*, Soc Antiq London Occas Pap **14**. London: Society of Antiquaries of London

Gale, R (ed), 1709 *Antonini Iter Britanniarum*. London

Gardiner, J, 1984 Lithic distributions and Neolithic settlement patterns in central southern England, in R Bradley & J Gardiner (eds), Neolithic studies: a review of some current research, BAR Brit Ser **133**. Oxford: British Archaeological Reports, 15–40

Gardiner, J, 1991 The [earlier Neolithic] flint industries in the study area, in Barrett, Bradley & Green 1991, 31

Garner-Lahire, J, Spall, C & Toop, N, 2005 Ladybridge Farm, Nosterfield, North Yorkshire: archaeological evaluation. Unpubl Report, Field Archaeology Specialists Ltd

Gibson, A, 2004 Burials and beakers: seeing beneath the veneer in late Neolithic Britain, in J Czebreszuk (ed), *Similar but different: Bell Beakers in Europe*. Poznań: Adam Mickiewicz University, 173–92

Gibson, A & Bayliss, A, 2010 Recent work on the Neolithic round barrows of the upper Great Wold Valley, Yorkshire, in J Leary, T Darvill & D Field (eds), *Round Mounds and Monumentality in the British Neolithic and Beyond*, Neolithic Studies Group Sem Paper **10**. Oxford: Oxbow Books, 72–107

Gibson, A & Loveday, R, 1989 Excavations at the cursus monument of Aston Upon Trent, Derbyshire, in A Gibson (ed), *Midlands prehistory: some recent and current researches into the prehistory of Central England*, BAR Brit Ser **204**. Oxford: British Archaeological Reports, 27–50

Gibson, A M & McCormick, A, 1985 Archaeology at Grendon Quarry, Northamptonshire. Part 1: Neolithic and Bronze Age sites excavated in 1974–75, *Northamptonshire Archaeol* **20**, 23–66

Gillings, M, Pollard, J, Wheatley, D & Peterson, R, 2008 *Landscape of the megaliths. Excavation and fieldwork on the Avebury monuments, 1997–2003*. Oxford: Oxbow Books

Goody, J, 1961 Religion and ritual: the definitional problem, *Brit J Sociology* **12**, 142–64

Green, H S, 1980 *The flint arrowheads of the British Isles*, BAR Brit Ser **75**(i & ii). Oxford: British Archaeological Reports

Green, M, 2000 *A landscape revealed: 10,000 years on a chalkland farm*. Stroud: Tempus

Griffiths, M & Timms, S, 2005 An archaeological assessment of Nosterfield, Ladybridge and the Thornborough Plain. Unpubl Report. Available: www.archaeologicalplanningconsultancy.co.uk/mga/Projects/noster/speciali/mga2005p1.html

Grinsell, L V, 1976 *Folklore of prehistoric sites in Britain*. Newton Abbot: David and Charles

Hale, D, Platell, A & Millard, A, 2009 A late Neolithic palisaded enclosure at Marne Barracks, Catterick, North Yorkshire, *Proc Prehist Soc* **75**, 265–304

Hall, R A, 2003 Yorkshire AD 700–1066, in Manby, Moorhouse & Ottaway (eds) 2003, 171–80

Hall R A, 2005 Local antiquarians, Thornborough Rings, and other prehistoric monuments near Ripon, *Yorkshire Archaeol J* **77**, 1–15

Halliday, S, 1985 Unenclosed upland settlement in the east and south-east of Scotland, in Spratt & Burgess (eds) 1985, 231–51

Harding, A F, 1981 Excavations in the prehistoric ritual complex near Milfield, Northumberland, *Proc Prehist Soc* **47**, 87–135

Harding, A F & Lee, G E, 1987 *Henge monuments and related sites of Great Britain. Air photographic evidence and catalogue*, BAR Brit Ser **175**. Oxford: British Archaeological Reports

Harding, J, 1991 Using the unique as the typical: monuments and the ritual landscape, in P Garwood, D Jennings, R Skeates & J Toms (eds), Sacred and profane. Proceedings of a conference on archaeology, ritual and religion, Oxford 1989, Oxford Univ Comm Archaeol Monogr **32**. Oxford: Oxbow Books, 141–51

Harding, J, 1995 Social histories and regional perspectives in the Neolithic of lowland England, *Proc Prehist Soc* **61**, 117–36

Harding, J, 1996 Reconsidering the Neolithic round barrows of eastern Yorkshire, in P Frodsham (ed), *Neolithic studies in no-man's land. Papers on the Neolithic of Northern England from the Trent to the Tweed*, Northern Archaeology **13/14**. Newcastle: Northumberland Archaeology Group, 67–78

Harding, J, 1997a Interpreting the Neolithic: the monuments of northern England, *Oxford J Archaeol* **16**(3), 279–95

Harding J 1997b Salvage recording at Tancred Quarry, Scorton, North Yorkshire: the Scorton Cursus. Unpubl Report, Department of Archaeology, University of Newcastle

Harding, J, 1999 Pathways to new realms: cursus monuments and symbolic territories, in Barclay & Harding (eds) 1999, 30–8

Harding, J, 2000 Later Neolithic ceremonial centres, ritual and pilgrimage: the monument complex of Thornborough, North Yorkshire, in A Ritchie (ed), *Neolithic Orkney in its European Context*. Cambridge: McDonald Institute Monograph Series, University of Cambridge, 30–46

Harding, J, 2003 *Henge Monuments of the British Isles*. Stroud: Tempus

Harding, J, 2012 Conformity, routeways and religious experience – the henges of central Yorkshire, in A Gibson (ed), *Enclosing the Neolithic: recent research in Britain and Europe*, BAR Int Ser **2440**. Oxford: Archaeopress, 67–80

Harding, J & Johnson, B, 2000 The layout of the Thornborough complex, North Yorkshire: a brief appraisal. Unpubl Report, Department of Archaeology, University of Newcastle

Harding, J & Johnson, B, 2003 The Mesolithic, Neolithic and Bronze Age archaeology of the Ure-Swale catchment. Unpubl Report, Department of Archaeology, University of Newcastle

Harding, J, & Healy, F, 2007 *The Raunds Area Project: a Neolithic and Bronze Age landscape in Northamptonshire*. Swindon: English Heritage

Harding J, Healy, F & Boyle, A, 2007 The treatment of the human body, in Harding & Healy 2007, 224–38

Harding, J & Johnston, R (eds), 2000 *Northern pasts: interpretations of the later prehistory of Northern England and Southern Scotland*, BAR Brit Ser **302**. Oxford: British Archaeological Reports

Harding, J, Johnson, B & Goodrick, G, 2006 Neolithic cosmology and the monument complex of Thornborough, North Yorkshire. *Archaeoastronomy* **XX**, 28–53

Hastie, M, 2000 Assessment of soil samples from Thornborough monument complex, THP 99/VMNLP 99). Unpubl Report, Headland Archaeology Ltd, Edinburgh

Hastie, M, 2003 Assessment of samples from double ring-ditch barrow and Three Hills north barrow:

Thornborough henge project 2003. Unpubl Report, Headland Archaeology Ltd, Edinburgh

Hawkes, J & Hawkes, C, 1944 *Prehistoric Britain*. Harmondsworth: Penguin Books

Healey, E, 1984 The flint axe, in Brewster 1984

Healy, F, 1984 Lithic assemblage variation in the late third and early second millennia BC in eastern England, *Lithics* **5**, 10–18

Healy, F, 1987 Prediction or prejudice? The relationship between field survey and excavation, in Brown & Edmonds (eds) 1987, 9–18

Healy, F, 1988 *The Anglo-Saxon cemetery at Spong Hill, North Elmham, Part VI: occupation during the seventh to second millennium BC*, E Anglian Archaeol Rep **39**. Dereham: East Anglian Archaeology

Healy, F, 1991 The hunting of the floorstone, in A J Schofield (ed), *Interpreting artefact scatters: contributions to ploughzone archaeology*, Oxbow Monogr **4**. Oxford: Oxbow Books, 29–37

Heaton, T J, Blackwell, P G & Buck, C E, 2009 A Bayesian approach to the estimate of radiocarbon calibration curves: the IntCal09 methodology, *Radiocarbon* **51(4)**, 1151–64

Henson, D, 1985 The flint resources of Yorkshire and the east Midlands, *Lithics* **6**, 2–9

Hey, G, 1997 Neolithic Settlement at Yarnton, Oxfordshire, in Topping (ed) 1997, 99–112

Hirsch, E, 1995 Landscape: between place and space, in E Hirsch & M O'Hanlon (eds), *The anthropology of landscape: perspectives on place and space*. Oxford: Clarendon Press, 1–30

Hodder, I, 1990 *The domestication of Europe*. Oxford: Basil Blackwell

Hodges, H W M, 1955 The medieval pottery from Thornborough, in N Thomas 1955, 438–9

Hodges, H W M, 1957 Braces, beakers and battle-axes, *Antiquity* **31**, 142–6

Holgate, R, 1988 *Neolithic settlement of the Thames Basin*, BAR Brit Ser **194**. Oxford: British Archaeological Reports

Howard, A J & Macklin, M G, 1999 A generic geomorphological approach to archaeological interpretation and prospection in British river valleys: a guide for archaeologists investigating Holocene landscapes, *Antiquity* **73**(281), 527–41

Howard, A J, Keen, D H, Mighall, T M, Field, M H, Coope, G R, Griffiths, H I & Macklin, M G, 2000 Early Holocene environments of the River Ure near Ripon, North Yorkshire, UK, *Proc Yorkshire Geological Soc* **53**(1), 31–42

Howcroft, B, 2011 Prehistoric sites on Wadsworth and Midgley Moors, Calderdale, West Yorkshire, *Yorkshire Archaeol Soc Prehist Res Section Bull* **48**, 88–93

Hubert, J, 1994 Sacred beliefs and beliefs of sacredness, in Carmichael *et al* 1994, 9–19

Humphrey, C & Laidlaw, J, 1994 *The archetypal actions of ritual: a theory of ritual illustrated by the Jain rite of worship*. Oxford: Oxford University Press

Innes, J, no date Palynology, Core 69 from 'The Flasks'. Unpubl Report

Insoll, T, 2004a Are archaeologists afraid of gods? Some thoughts on archaeology and religion, in T Insoll (ed), *Belief in the past: the proceedings of the 2002 Manchester Conference on Archaeology and Religion*. BAR Int Ser **1212**, Oxford: British Archaeological Reports, 1–6

Insoll, T, 2004b *Archaeology, ritual, religion*. London and New York: Routledge

Jackson, D A, 1976 The excavation of Neolithic and Bronze Age sites at Aldwincle, Northants, 1967–71, *Northamptonshire Archaeol* **11**, 12–64

Janus, H, 1965 *The Young Specialist looks at land and freshwater molluscs*. London: Burke Publishing Company Ltd

Jennings, S, 1992 *Medieval pottery in the Yorkshire Museum*. York: Yorkshire Museum

Johnston, R, 1999 An empty path? Processions, memories and the Dorset Cursus, in Barclay & Harding (eds) 1999, 39–48

Jones, D, 1998 Long barrows and Neolithic elongated enclosures in Lincolnshire: an analysis of the air photographic evidence, *Proc Prehist Soc* **64**, 83–114

Jones, L, 2000a *The hermeneutics of sacred architecture: experience, interpretation, comparison. Volume One: monumental occasions. Reflections on the eventfulness of religious architecture*. Cambridge, Massachusetts: Harvard University Press

Jones, L, 2000b *The hermeneutics of sacred architecture: experience, interpretation, comparison. Volume Two: hermeneutical calisthenics. A morphology of ritual-architectural priorities*. Cambridge, Massachusetts: Harvard University Press

Jordan, D, Haddon-Reece, D & Bayliss, A, 1994 *Radiocarbon dates from samples funded by English Heritage and dated before 1981*. London: English Heritage

Kendrick, T D & Hawkes, C F C, 1932 *Archaeology in England and Wales 1914–1931*. London: Methuen & Co Ltd

Kenward, R, 1982 A Neolithic burial enclosure at New Wintles Farm, Eynesham, in Case & Whittle (eds) 1982, 51–4

Kerney, M, 1999 *Atlas of the land and freshwater molluscs of Britain and Ireland*. Colchester: Harley Books

Kerney, M P & Cameron, R A D, 1979 *A field guide to the land snails of Britain and North-West Europe*. London: William Collins Sons and Co Ltd

Keyes, C F, 1975 Buddhist pilgrimage centres and the twelve-year cycle: northern Thai moral order in space and time, *Hist Religions* **15**(1), 71–89

Kinnes, I A, 1979 *Round barrows and ring-ditches in the British Neolithic*, Brit Mus Occas Pap **7**. London: British Museum

Kinnes, I A & Longworth, I H, 1985 *Catalogue of the excavated prehistoric and Romano-British material in the Greenwell Collection*. London: British Museum

Kirch, P V, 1990 Monumental architecture and power in Polynesian chiefdoms: a comparison of Tonga and Hawaii, *World Archaeol* **22**(2), 206–21

Kirch, P V, 1991 Chiefship and competitive involution: the Marquesas Islands of eastern Polynesia, in T Earle (ed), *Chiefdoms: power, economy and ideology*, Sch American Res Advanced Sem Ser. Cambridge: Cambridge University Press, 119–45

Krupp, E C, 1997 *Skywatchers, shamans and kings: astronomy and the archaeology of power*. New York: John Wiley and Sons

Lakoff, G, 1987 *Women, fire and other dangerous things*. Chicago: University of Chicago Press

Lambek, M (ed), 2000 *A reader in the anthropology of religion*. Oxford: Blackwell

Last, J, 1999 Out of line: cursuses and monument typology in eastern England, in Barclay & Harding (eds) 1999, 86–97

Laurie, T C, 2003 Researching the prehistory of Wensleydale, Swaledale and Teesdale, in Manby, Moorhouse & Ottaway (eds) 2003, 223–54

Lewis, G, 1980 *Day of shining red: an essay on understanding ritual*. Cambridge: Cambridge University Press

Lewis, J, 2000 Upwards at 45 degrees: the use of vertical caves during the Neolithic and Early Bronze Age on Mendip, Somerset, *Cave Archaeol Palaeontology Res Archives* **2**. Available: http://www.capra.group.shef.ac.uk/2/upwards.html

Lewis, J, 2010 C1 Stanwell cursus, in J Lewis, M Leivers, L Brown, A Smith, K Cramp, L Mepham & C Phillpotts, *Landscape evolution in the middle Thames valley. Heathrow Terminal 5 excavations, Volume 2*, Framework Archaeol Monogr **3**. Oxford and Salisbury: Oxford Archaeology and Wessex Archaeology, 77–93

Lewis, J & Mullin, D, 2010 Dating the Priddy Circles, Somerset, *Past* **64**, 4–5

Lewis, J S C & Welsh, K, 2004 Perry Oaks – Neolithic inhabitation of a west London landscape, in J Cotton & D Field (eds), *Towards a new Stone Age: aspects of the Neolithic in South-East England*, CBA Res Rep **137**. York: Council for British Archaeology, 105–9

Lewis-Williams, D & Pearce, D, 2005 *Inside the Neolithic mind: consciousness, cosmos and the realm of the gods*. London: Thames and Hudson

Limbrey, S & Evans, J G (eds), 1978 *The effect of man on the landscape: the lowland zone*, CBA Res Rep **21**. London: Council for British Archaeology

Lofthouse, C A, 1993 Segmented embanked pit-alignments in the North York Moors: a survey by the Royal Commission on the Historical Monuments of England, *Proc Prehist Soc* **59**, 383–92

Long, A J, Bridgland, D R, Innes, J B, Mitchell, W A, Rutherford, M & Vyner, B, 2004 *The Swale-Ure Washlands: landscape history and human impacts*, Environmental Research Centre Publication **7**. Durham: University of Durham

Long, D J & Tipping, R, 1998 Report on the sediment stratigraphies of three shafts. Unpubl Report, Department of Environmental Science, University of Stirling

Longworth, I H, 1984 *Collared urns of the Bronze Age in Great Britain and Ireland*. Cambridge: Cambridge University Press

Longworth, I H, Ellison, A & Rigby, V, 1988 *Excavations at Grimes Graves, Norfolk 1972–1976. Fascicule 2: The Neolithic, Bronze Age and Later Pottery*. London: British Museum Press

Loveday, R, 1985 Cursus and related monuments of the British Isles. Unpubl PhD Thesis, Leicester University

Loveday, R, 1989 The Barford ritual complex: further excavations (1972) and a regional perspective, in A Gibson (ed), *Midlands prehistory: some recent and current researches into the prehistory of central England*, BAR Brit Ser **204**. Oxford: British Archaeological Reports, 51–84

Loveday, R, 1998 Double entrance henges – routes to the past?, in A Gibson & D Simpson (eds), *Essays in honour of Aubrey Burl: prehistoric ritual and religion*. Stroud: Sutton Publishing, 14–31

Loveday, R, 1999 Dorchester-on-Thames – ritual complex or ritual landscape?, in Barclay & Harding (eds) 1999, 49–66

Loveday, R, 2003 Appendix. Charlecote 71: an evaluation in the light of recent evidence, *Birmingham Warwickshire Archaeol Soc Trans* **107**, 30–9

Loveday, R, 2006 *Inscribed across the landscape: the cursus enigma*. Stroud: Tempus

Loveday, R, in press. Religious routine and pilgrimage in the British Isles, in C Fowler, J Harding & D Hofmann (eds), *The Oxford Handbook of Neolithic Europe*. Oxford: Oxford University Press

Loveday, R & Petchey, M, 1982 Oblong ditches: a discussion and some new evidence, *Aerial Archaeol* **8**, 17–24

Lukis, W C, 1870a On some Anglo-Saxon graves on Howe Hill, near Carthorpe, *Yorkshire Archaeol Topographical J* **1**, 175–81

Lukis, W C, 1870b On the flint implements and tumuli of the neighbourhood of Wath, *Yorkshire Archaeol Topographical J* **1**, 116–26

Lynch, H, 2005 A study of cross Pennine exchange during the Neolithic. Unpubl PhD Thesis, Newcastle University

Macinnes, L & Wickham-Jones, C R, 1992 *All natural things: archaeology and the Green Debate*, Oxbow Monogr **21**. Oxford: Oxbow Books

Mackie, E W, 1977 *Science and society in prehistoric Britain*. London: Elek

Mackie, E W, 1997 Maeshowe and the winter solstice: ceremonial aspects of the Orkney Grooved Ware culture, *Antiquity* **71**, 338–59

Macklin, M G, Taylor, M P, Hudson-Edwards, K A & Howard, A J, 2000 Holocene environmental change in the Yorkshire Ouse basin and its influence on river dynamics and sediment fluxes to the coastal zone, in I Shennan & J Andrews (eds), *Holocene land-ocean interaction and environmental change around the North Sea*, Geological Soc London Special Publ **166**. London: Geological Society of London, 87–96

MacLeod, D, 2002 Cropmarks in the A1 corridor between Catterick and Brompton-on-Swale, in P R Wilson *Cataractonium: Roman Catterick and its hinterland excavations and research, 1958–1997. Part 1*, CBA Res Rep **128**, York: Council for British Archaeology, 36–45

Makey, P, 1996 The flint, in Abramson 1996, 54–64

Makey, P, 1997 Flint report: Pits Plantation, Rudston. Unpubl Report

Makey, P, no date a The flint from Marton-le-Moor. Unpubl Report

Makey, P, no date b Rudston arrowheads. Unpubl dissertation, Sheffield University

Mainman, A J, 1997 The pottery, in M Whyman, Excavations in Deanery Gardens and Low St Agnesgate, Ripon, North Yorkshire, *Yorkshire Archaeol J* **69**, 129–45

Malim, T, 1999 Cursuses and related monuments of the Cambridgeshire Ouse, in Barclay & Harding (eds) 1999, 77–85

Manby, T G, 1965 The distribution of rough-out, 'Cumbrian' and related stone axes of Lake District origin in Northern England. *Trans Cumberland Westmorland Antiq Archaeol Soc* **LXV**, 1–38

Manby, T G, 1974 *Grooved Ware sites in the north of England*, BAR Brit Ser **9**. Oxford: British Archaeological Reports

Manby, T G, 1975 Neolithic occupation sites on the Yorkshire Wolds, *Yorkshire Archaeol J* **47**, 23–59

Manby, T G, 1976 Excavation of the Kilham Long Barrow, East Riding of Yorkshire, *Proc Prehist Soc* **42**, 111–59

Manby, T G 1979 Typology, materials, and distribution of flint and stone axes in Yorkshire, in T H McK Clough & W A Cummins (eds), *Stone Axe Studies*, CBA Res

Rep **67**. London: Council for British Archaeology, 65–81

Manby, T G, 1980 Excavation of barrows at Grindale and Boynton, East Yorkshire, 1972, *Yorkshire Archaeol J* **52**, 19–47

Manby, T G, 1986 The Bronze Age in western Yorkshire, in Manby & Turnbull (eds) 1986, 55–126

Manby, T G, 1988a The Neolithic in eastern Yorkshire, in T G Manby (ed), *Archaeology in eastern Yorkshire: essays in honour of T C M Brewster*. Sheffield: Department of Archaeology and Prehistory, University of Sheffield, 35–88

Manby, T G, 1988b *Thwing: excavation and fieldwork in east Yorkshire 1987*, Yorkshire Archaeological Society Prehistory Research Section

Manby, T G, 1996 Prehistoric pottery: Marton-le-Moor and Roecliffe. Unpubl Report for Northern Archaeological Associates, Barnard Castle

Manby, T G, forthcoming *Excavation of a later Bronze Age Settlement at Paddock Hill, Thwing, East Yorkshire*

Manby, T G & Turnbull, P (eds), 1986 *Archaeology in the Pennines: studies in honour of Arthur Raistrick*, BAR Brit Ser **158**. Oxford: British Archaeological Reports

Manby, T G, King, A & Vyner, B, 2003 The Neolithic and Bronze Age: a time of early agriculture, in Manby, Moorhouse & Ottaway (eds) 2003, 35–113

Manby, T G, Moorhouse, S & Ottaway, P (eds), 2003 *The archaeology of Yorkshire: an assessment at the beginning of the 21st century*, Yorkshire Archaeol Soc Occasional Paper **3**. Leeds: Yorkshire Archaeological Society

Masters, L, 1984 The Neolithic long cairns of Cumbria and Northumberland, in R Miket & C Burgess (eds), *Between and beyond the walls*. Edinburgh: John Donald, 52–73

Mayes, P, Atherden, M, Manchester, K & Manby, T G, 1986 A beaker burial at West Tanfield, North Yorkshire, *Yorkshire Archaeol J* **58**, 1–4

Mays, S, de la Rua, C & Molleson, T, 1995. Molar crown height as a means of evaluating existing dental wear scales for estimating age at death in human skeletal remains, *J Archaeol Sci* **22**, 659–70

McCarthy, M, 2000 Prehistoric settlement in northern Cumbria, in Harding & Johnston (eds) 2000, 131–40

McInnes, I J, 1964 A class II henge in the East Riding of Yorkshire, *Antiquity* **38**, 218–19

McKern, T W & Stewart, T D, 1957 *Skeletal age changes in young American males,* Technical Report **EP-45**, Headquarters Quartermaster Research and Development Command. Natick: Quartermaster Research and Development Centre, US Army

McKinley, J I, 2004 Compiling a skeletal inventory: disarticulated and co-mingled remains, in M Brickley & J I McKinley (eds), *Guidelines to the Standards for Recording Human Remains*, IFA Paper No **7**, 14–17

Mellars, P A, 1976 Fire ecology, animal populations and man: a study of some ecological relationships in prehistory, *Proc Prehist Soc* **42**, 15–45

Mellars, P & Dark, P, 1998 *Star Carr in context: new archaeological and palaeoecological investigations at the early Mesolithic Site of Star Carr, Yorkshire*. Cambridge: McDonald Institute Monographs

Miket, R, 1976 The evidence for Neolithic activity in the Milfield Basin, Northumberland, in C Burgess & R Miket (eds), *Settlement and economy in the third and second millennia BC*, BAR Brit Ser **33**. Oxford: British Archaeological Reports, 113–42

Miket, R, 1981 Pit alignments in the Milfield Basin, and the excavation of Ewart 1, *Proc Prehist Soc* **47**, 137–46

Miket, R, 1985 Ritual enclosures at Whitton Hill, Northumberland, Proc Prehist Soc **51**, 137–48

Moir, G, 1981 Some archaeological and astronomical objections to scientific astronomy in British prehistory, in C Ruggles & A Whittle (eds), *Astronomy and society in Britain during the period 4000–1500 BC*, BAR Brit Ser **88**. Oxford: British Archaeological Reports, 221–42

Moloney, C, Holbrey, R, Wheelhouse, P & Roberts, I, 2003 *Catterick Racecourse, North Yorkshire. The reuse and adaptation of a monument from prehistoric to Anglian times*, Archaeological Services (WYAS) Publ **4**. Wakefield: Archaeological Services (WYAS)

Moore, J W, 1950 Mesolithic sites in the neighbourhood of Flixton, north-east Yorkshire, *Proc Prehist Soc* **16**, 101–8

Moore, J W, 1964 Excavation at Beacon Hill, Flamborough Head, *Yorkshire Archaeol J* **41**, 191–202

Moores, A, no date Vale of Mowbray Neolithic Landscape Project: palynological assessment report. Unpubl Report, Newcastle University

Moorhouse, S, 2003 Medieval Yorkshire: a rural landscape for the future, in Manby, Moorhouse & Ottaway (eds) 2003, 181–214

Moorhouse, S, 2004 Thornborough henges: a landscape through time, *Medieval Yorkshire* **33**, 19–33

Muir, R, 1997 *The Yorkshire countryside: a landscape history*. Edinburgh: Keele University Press

Mumah, M M, 1994 Sacred sites in the Bamenda Grasslands of Cameroon: a study of sacred sites in the Nso' Fondom, in Carmichael *et al* 1994, 99–114

Munn, N D, 1996 Excluded spaces: the figure in the Australian Aboriginal landscape, *Critical Inquiry* **22**, 446–65

Mutoro, H W, 1994 The Mijikenda kaya as a sacred site, in Carmichael *et al* 1994, 132–9

Myers, A, 1987 All shot to pieces? Inter-assemblage variability, lithic analysis and Mesolithic assemblage 'types': some preliminary suggestions, in Brown & Edmonds (eds) 1987, 137–54

Needham, S, 1996 Chronology and periodisation in the British Bronze Age, *Acta Archaeologica* **67**, 121–40

Needham, S & Spence, T, 1997 Refuse and the formation of middens, *Antiquity* **71**(271), 77–90

Nilsson, M P, 1920 *Primitive time-reckoning: a study in the origins and first development of the art of counting time among the primitive and early culture peoples*. Lund: C W K Gleerup

Noble, G, 2009 Forteviot, *Current Archaeol* **231**, 12–9

Oeschger, H, Siegenthaler, U, Schotterer, U, Gugelmann, A, 1975 A box diffusion model to study the carbon dioxide exchange in nature, *Tellus* **27**(2), 168–92

O'Kelly, M, 1982 *Newgrange: archaeology, art and legend*. London: Thames and Hudson

Olwig, K R, 1984 *Nature's ideological landscape*. London: Allen & Unwin

Oswald, A, Dyer, C & Barber, M, 2001 *The creation of monuments: Neolithic causewayed enclosures in the British Isles*. Swindon: English Heritage

Parker Pearson, M & Ramilisonina, 1998 Stonehenge for the ancestors: the stones pass on the message, *Antiquity* **72**(276), 308–26

Parker Pearson, M, Chamberlain, A, Jay, M, Marshall, P, Pollard, J, Richards, C, Thomas, J, Tilley, C & Welham,

K, 2009 Who was buried at Stonehenge, *Antiquity* **83**(319), 23–39

Pennant, T, 1804 *A tour from Alston-Moor to Harrowgate, and Brimham Crags*. London: John Scott

Peters, F, 2000 Two traditions of Bronze Age burial in the Stonehenge landscape, *Oxford J Archaeol* **19**(4), 343–58

Pierpoint, S, 1980 *Social patterns in Yorkshire prehistory 3500–750 BC*, BAR Brit Ser **74**. Oxford: British Archaeological Reports

Piggott, S, 1948 The excavations at Cairnpapple Hill, West Lothian, 1947–48, *Proc Soc Antiq Scot* **82**, 68–123

Piggott, S, 1950 *William Stukeley: an Eighteenth-Century antiquary*. Oxford: Clarendon Press

Piggott, S, 1954 *The Neolithic cultures of the British Isles* (1st edition). Cambridge: The University Press

Piggott, S, 1962 *The West Kennet long barrow*. London: HMSO

Piggott, S, 1970 *The Neolithic cultures of the British Isles* (2nd edition). Cambridge: Cambridge University Press

Piggott, S & Piggott, C M, 1939 Stone and earth circles in Dorset, *Antiquity* **13**, 138–58

Pitts, M, 2000 *Hengeworld*. London: Century

Pollard, J, 1999 'These places have their moments': thoughts on settlement practices in the British Neolithic, in J Brück & M Goodman (eds), *Making places in the prehistoric world: themes in settlement archaeology*. London: UCL Press, 76–93

Pollard, J, 2000 Neolithic occupational practices and social ecologies from Rinyo to Clacton, in A Ritchie (ed), *Neolithic Orkney in its European context*. Cambridge: McDonald Institute Monographs, University of Cambridge, 363–70

Powell, J H, Cooper, A H & Benfield, A C, 1992 *Geology of the country around Thirsk*, Memoir for 1:50,000 Geological Sheet 52. London: HMSO

Powlesland, D, 1986 Excavations at Heslerton, North Yorkshire 1978–82, *Archaeol J* **143**, 53–173

Powlesland, D, 2003 The Heslerton Parish Project: 20 years of archaeological research in the Vale of Pickering, in Manby, Moorhouse & Ottaway (eds) 2003, 275–91

Pryor, F, French, C, Crowther, D, Gurney, D, Simpson, G & Taylor, M, 1985 *The Fenland Project, No. 1: archaeology and environment in the Lower Welland Valley*, E Anglian Archaeol **27**. Cambridge: East Anglian Archaeology

Radimilahy, C, 1994 Sacred sites in Madagascar, in Carmichael *et al* 1994, 82–8

Raistrick, A, 1929 The Bronze Age in West Yorkshire, *Yorkshire Archaeol J* **29**, 354–65

RCHM(E), 1960 *A matter of time*. London: HMSO

Reader, I, 1993a Introduction, in I Reader & T Walter (eds), *Pilgrimage in popular culture*. London: Macmillan Press Ltd, 1–26

Reader, I, 1993b Conclusion, in I Reader & T Walter (eds), *Pilgrimage in popular culture*. London: Macmillan Press Ltd, 220–46

Reimer, P J, Baillie, M G L, Bard, E, Bayliss, A, Beck, J W, Blackwell, P G, Bronk Ramsey, C, Buck, C E, Burr, G S, Edwards, R L, Friedrich, M, Grootes, P M, Guilderson, T P, Hajdas, I, Heaton, T J, Hogg, A G, Hughen, K A, Kaiser, K F, Kromer, B, McCormac, F G, Manning, S W, Reimer, R W, Richards, D A, Southon, J R, Talamo, S, Turney, C S M, van der Plicht, J & Weyhenmeyer, C E, 2009 IntCal09 and Marine09 radiocarbon age calibration curves, 0–50,000 years cal BP, *Radiocarbon* **51**(4), 1111–50

Renfrew, C, 1973 Monuments, mobilization and social organization in Neolithic Wessex, in C Renfrew (ed), *The explanation of cultural change*. London: Gerald Duckworth, 539–58

Renfrew, C, 1977 Space, time and polity, in J Friedman and M J Rowlands (eds), *The evolution of social systems*. London: Duckworth, 89–112

Renfrew, C, 1979 *Investigations in Orkney*, Rep Res Comm Soc Antiq London **XXXVIII**. London: Society of Antiquities of London

Renfrew, C, 1985 *The prehistory of Orkney*. Edinburgh: Edinburgh University Press

Renfrew, C, 1994 The archaeology of religion, in C Renfrew & E Zubrow (eds), *The Ancient Mind, New Direction in Archaeology*. Cambridge: Cambridge University Press, 47–54

Renfrew, C, 2000 The auld hoose spaeks: society and life in Stone Age Orkney, in A Ritchie (ed), *Neolithic Orkney in its European context*. Cambridge: McDonald Institute Monographs, 1–20

Richards, C, 1996 Henges and water: towards an elemental understanding of monumentality and landscape in late Neolithic Britain, *J Material Culture* **1**(3), 313–26

Richards, C, 2004 A choreography of construction: monuments, mobilization and social organization in Neolithic Orkney, in J Cherry, C Scarre & S Shennan (eds), *Explaining social change: studies in honour of Colin Renfrew*. Cambridge: McDonald Institute Monographs, University of Cambridge, 103–13

Richards, C (ed), 2005 *Dwelling among the monuments: the Neolithic village of Barnhouse, Maeshowe Passage Grave and surrounding monuments at Stenness, Orkney*. Cambridge: McDonald Institute Monographs, University of Cambridge

Richards, J, 1984 The development of the Neolithic landscape in the environs of Stonehenge, in R Bradley & J Gardiner (eds), *Neolithic studies: a review of some current research*, BAR Brit Ser **133**. Oxford: British Archaeological Reports, 177–88

Richards, J, 1990 *The Stonehenge Environs Project*, English Heritage Archaeol Rep **16**. London: English Heritage

Richards, Janet, 1999 Conceptual landscapes in the Egyptian Nile Valley, in W Ashmore & A B Knapp (eds), *Archaeologies of landscape: contemporary perspectives*. Oxford: Blackwell, 83–100

Riha, E, 1979 Die *Römischen fibeln aus Augst und Kaiseraugst*. Augst: Forschungen in Augst Band

Riley, D N, 1988 Air survey of Neolithic sites on the Yorkshire, in T G Manby (ed), *Archaeology in eastern Yorkshire*. Sheffield: Department of Archaeology and Prehistory, University of Sheffield, 89–93

Riley, H, 1990 The scraper assemblages and petit tranchet derivative arrowheads, in Richards 1990, 225–8

Roberts, I (ed), 2005 *Ferrybridge henge: the ritual landscape*. Leeds: Archaeological Services (WYAS)

Roberts, I & Richardson, J, 2005 Discussion and synthesis, in Roberts (ed) 2005, Part Five

Roberts, I, with Stead I M, Rush, P, Sitch, B J, McHugh, M & Milles, A, 2005 Appendix 1: excavation of the henge bank and ditches, 1991: a summary report, in Roberts (ed) 2005, 223–35

Roe, A, 2003 Draft desk based assessment. Unpubl Report, Field Archaeology Specialists

Romney, P (ed), 1984 The Diary of Charles Fothergill 1805. *An itinerary to York, Flamborough and the North-Western Dales of Yorkshire*. Leeds: Yorkshire Archaeological Society

Roughley, C, Sherratt, A & Shell, C, 2002 Past records, new views: Carnac 1830–2000, *Antiquity* **76**(291), 218–23

Rowe, P, 1998 Flint report – Nosterfield 1991, 1994–1996. Unpubl Report for Blaise Vyner, Heritage and Arts

Rowe, P, 1999 Report on the flint assemblage, 1998 season. Unpubl Report

Rowe, P, 2004 Flint report, 1999–2003, 1998. Unpubl Report

Ruggles, C, 1984 *Megalithic astronomy: a new archaeological and statistical study of 300 western Scottish sites*, BAR Brit Ser **123**. Oxford: British Archaeological Report

Ruggles, C, 1997 Astronomy and Stonehenge, in B Cunliffe & C Renfrew (eds), *Science and Stonehenge*. Oxford: British Academy, 203–30

Ruggles, C, 1999 *Astronomy in prehistoric Britain and Ireland*. New Haven & London: Yale University Press

Ruggles, C, 2006 Interpreting solstitial alignments in late Neolithic Wessex, *Archaeoastronomy* **XX**, 1–27

Rutherford M, no date Nosterfield – The Flasks: Shake Hole 1. Unpubl Report

Rutkowski, B, 1972 *Cult places in the Aegean world* (translated by K Kozłowska). Wrocław: Zakład Narodowy

St Joseph, J K, 1977 Aerial reconnaissance: recent results, 43, *Antiquity* **51**, 143–5

St Joseph, J K, 1980 Aerial reconnaissance: recent results, 50, *Antiquity* **54**, 132–5

Saville, A, 1973 A reconsideration of the prehistoric flint assemblage from Bourne Pool, Aldridge, Staffs, *Trans South Staffordshire Archaeol and Hist Soc* **14**, 6–28

Sayer, R A, 1982 Misconceptions of space in social thought, *Trans Inst Brit Geographers* **7**, 494–503

Schofield, A J, 1987 Putting lithics to the test: non-site analysis and the Neolithic settlement of southern England, *Oxford J Archaeol* **6**(3), 269–86

Schofield, A J, 1991 Interpreting artefact scatters: an introduction, in A J Schofield (ed), *Interpreting artefact scatters: contributions to ploughzone archaeology*, Oxford Monogr **4**. Oxford: Oxbow Books, 3–8

Schofield, A J, 1993 Looking back with regret, looking forward with optimism: making more of surface lithic scatters, in N Aston & A David (eds), *Stories in stone*, Lithic Studies Soc Occas Pap **4**. Oxford: Lithics Studies Society, 90–8

Scott, J G, 1992 Mortuary structures and megaliths, in N Sharples and A Sheridan (eds), *Vessels for the Ancestors*. Edinburgh: Edinburgh University Press, 104–19

Scull, C J & Harding, A F, 1990 Two early medieval cemeteries at Milfield, Northumberland, *Durham Archaeol J* **6**, 1–29

Shennan, S, 1985 *Experiments in the collection and analysis of archaeological survey data: the East Hampshire Survey*. Sheffield: Department of Archaeology and Prehistory, University of Sheffield

Silverman, H, 1994 The archaeological identification of an ancient Peruvian pilgrimage center, *World Archaeol* **26**(1), 1–18

Slade, C F, 1963–64 A late Neolithic site at Sonning, Berkshire, *Berkshire Archaeol J* **61**, 4–19

Smith, I F, 1965 *Windmill Hill and Avebury: excavations by Alexander Keiller 1925–1939*. Oxford: Clarendon Press

Smith, M, 2006 Bones chewed by canids as evidence for human excarnation: a British case study, *Antiquity* **80** (309), 671–85

Snape, M E, 1993 *Roman brooches from north Britain: a classification and a catalogue of brooches from sites on the Stanegate*, BAR Brit Ser **23**. Oxford: British Archaeological Report

Speed, G, 2003a Tancred Quarry, Scorton, North Yorkshire: archaeological watching brief. Unpubl Report, Northern Archaeological Associates **03/137**

Speed, G, 2003b Bridge Road, Brompton on Swale, North Yorkshire: archaeological post-excavation assessment. Unpubl Report, Northern Archaeological Associates **03/141**

Speed, G, 2004 Tancred Quarry Scorton, North Yorkshire: Phase 2 archaeological watching brief. Unpubl Report, Northern Archaeological Associates **04/110**

Speed, G, 2008a Scorton Quarry, North Yorkshire, Area 1A: archaeological monitoring and excavation post–excavation assessment report. Unpubl Report, Northern Archaeological Associates **08/39**

Speed, G, 2008b Scorton Quarry (Areas 2 and 4B), North Yorkshire: programme of archaeological investigation report. Unpubl Report, Northern Archaeological Associates **08/89**

Speed, G, 2010 Scorton Quarry, North Yorkshire. Area 3(1) archaeological excavation and watching brief: post-excavation assessment report. Unpubl Report, Northern Archaeological Associates **10/29**

Speed, G, in prep *Excavations at Hollow Banks Quarry, Scorton, North Yorkshire. Volume 1*

Spikins, P, 1999 *Mesolithic northern England: environment, population and settlement*, BAR Brit Ser **283**. Oxford: British Archaeological Reports

Spikins, P, 2002 *Prehistoric people of the Pennines. Reconstructing the lifestyles of Mesolithic hunter-gatherers on Marsden Moor*. Leeds: West Yorkshire Archaeology Service

Spratt, D A, 1982 *Prehistoric and Roman archaeology of North-East Yorkshire*, BAR Brit Ser **104**. Oxford: British Archaeological Reports

Spratt, D A (ed), 1993 *Prehistoric and Roman Archaeology of North-East Yorkshire*, CBA Res Rep **104**. York: Council for British Archaeology

Spratt, D & Burgess, C, 1985 *Upland settlement in Britain: the second millennium BC and after*, BAR Brit Ser **143**. Oxford: British Archaeological Reports

Startin, D W A, 1982 The labour force involved in constructing the (Abingdon) causewayed enclosure, The labour force involved in constructing the [North Stoke] monuments, The labour force required in constructing ring-ditches XXIX, 1 and XXIX, 3 (at Stanton Harcourt) & Prehistoric earthmoving, in Case & Whittle (eds) 1982, 49–50, 74–5, 87, 143–55

Stirrat, R L, 1984 Sacred models, *Man* **19**(2), 199–215

Stoertz, C, 1997 *Ancient landscapes of the Yorkshire Wolds: aerial photographic transcription and analysis*. Swindon: Royal Commission on the Historic Monuments of England

Strickland, H J & Bunnett, R J A, no date Thornborough Circle Excavation Fund. Unpubl note to members of Yorkshire Archaeological Society

Stuart-Macadam, P, 1989 Nutritional Deficiency Disease: A survey of Scurvy, Rickets and Iron Deficiency Anaemia, in M Y Işcan & K A R Kennedy (eds), *Reconstruction of life from the skeleton*. New York: Alan Liss, 201–22

Stuiver, M & Braziunas, T F, 1993 Modeling atmospheric 14C influences and 14C ages of marine samples to 10,000 BC, *Radiocarbon* **35(1)**, 137–89

Stuiver, M, Reimer, P J, Bard, E, Beck, J W, Burr, G S, Hughen, K A, Kromer, B, McCormac, G, van der Plicht, J, Spurk, M, 1998 IntCal98 radiocarbon age calibration, 24,000–0 cal BP, *Radiocarbon* **40**(3), 1041–83

Sullivan, L E, 2000 Monumental works and eventful occasions, Foreword to Jones 2000a, xi–xxi

Talma, A S & Vogel, J C, 1993 A simplified approach to calibrating 14C dates, *Radiocarbon* **35(2),** 317–22

Tambiah, S J, 1976 *World conqueror and world renouncer: a study of Buddhism and polity in Thailand against a historical background*. Cambridge: Cambridge University Press

Tavener, N, 1996 Evidence of Neolithic activity near Marton-le-Moor, North Yorkshire, in P Frodsham (ed), *Neolithic studies in no-man's land. Papers on the Neolithic of northern England from the Trent to the Tweed*, Northern Archaeology **13/14**. Newcastle: Northumberland Archaeology Group, 183–8

Thom, A, Thom, A S & Burl, A, 1980 *Megalithic rings*, BAR Brit Ser **81**. Oxford: British Archaeological Reports

Thomas, A C, 1955 The folklore of the Thornborough henge monuments, in N Thomas 1955, 443–5

Thomas, J, 1993 The politics of vision and the archaeologies of landscape, in B Bender (ed), *Landscape: politics and perspectives*. Providence & Oxford: Berg, 19–48

Thomas, J, 1996 *Time, culture and identity: an interpretive archaeology*. London: Routledge

Thomas, J (eds), 2007 *Place and memory: excavations at the Pict's Knowe, Holywood and Holm Farm, Dumfries and Galloway, 1994–8*. Oxford: Oxbow Books

Thomas, J, Marshall, P, Pearson, M P, Pollard, J, Richards, C, Tilley, C & Welham, K, 2009 The date of the Greater Stonehenge Cursus, *Antiquity* **83**(319), 40–53

Thomas, N, 1955 The Thornborough Circles, near Ripon, North Riding, *Yorkshire Archaeol J* **38**, 425–46

Thomas, N, 1963 Notes on archaeological finds, *Yorkshire Archaeol J* **161**, 14–5

Thomas, N, 1976 *A guide to prehistoric England* (2nd edition). London: Book Club Associates

Thorpe, I J, 1981 Ethnoastronomy: its patterns and archaeological implications, in C Ruggles & A Whittle (eds), *Astronomy and society in Britain during the period 4000–1500 BC*, BAR Brit Ser **88**. Oxford: British Archaeological Reports, 275–88

Thorpe, I J, 1984 Ritual, power and ideology: a reconstruction of earlier Neolithic rituals in Wessex, in Bradley & Gardiner (eds) 1984, 41–60

Thorpe, I J & Richards, C, 1984 The decline of ritual authority and the introduction of Beakers into Britain, in Bradley & Gardiner (eds) 1984, 67–84

Thurnam, J, 1867 On the Leaf-Shaped Type of Flint Arrow-head, and its Connection with long Barrows, *Proc Soc Antiquaries, New series* **76**, 81–106

Tilley, C, 1994 *A phenomenology of landscape: places, paths and monuments*. Oxford/Providence: Berg

Tipping, R, 2000 C14 Dating for sediments from F44, F45, F46 and Find 14. Unpubl Report, Department of Environmental Science, University of Stirling

Topping, P, 1982 Excavation at the cursus at Scorton, North Yorkshire 1978, *Yorkshire Archaeol J* **54**, 7–20

Topping, P, 1992 The Penrith henges: a survey by the Royal Commission on the Historical Monuments of England, *Proc Prehist Soc* **58**, 249–64

Topping, P (ed), 1997 *Neolithic Landscapes*, Neolithic Studies Group Sem Pap **2**. Oxford: Neolithic Studies Group

Tratman, E K, 1967 The Priddy Circles, Mendip, Somerset. Henges monuments, *Proc Spelaeological Soc* **11**(2), 97–121

Trigger, B G, 1990 Monumental architecture: a thermodynamic explanation of symbolic behaviour, *World Archaeol* **22**(2), 119–132

van der Guchte, M, 1999 The Inca cognition of landscape: archaeology, ethnohistory, and the aesthetic of alterity, in W Ashmore & A B Knapp (eds), *Archaeologies of landscape: contemporary perspectives*. Oxford: Blackwell, 149–68

Vatcher, F, 1960 Thornborough Cursus, Yorks, *Yorkshire Archaeol J* **158**, 425–45

Vatcher, F, 1961 The excavation of the long mortuary enclosure on Normanton Down, Wilts, *Proc Prehist Soc* **27**, 160–73

Vyner, B, 1995 The brides of place: cross-ridge boundaries reviewed, in B Vyner (ed), *Moorland monuments: studies in the archaeology of north-east Yorkshire in honour of Raymond Hays and Don Spratt*, CBA Res Rep **101**. York: Council for British Archaeology, 16–30

Vyner, B, 2000 Lost horizons: the location of activity in the later Neolithic and early Bronze Age in north-east England, in Harding & Johnston (eds) 2000, 101–10

Vyner, B, 2003a Pottery, in Moloney *et al* 2003, 30–5

Vyner, B, 2003b Report on prehistoric pottery from excavations adjacent to Ferrybridge henge, West Yorkshire. Unpubl report for West Yorkshire Archaeology Service

Vyner, B, 2005 Early prehistoric pottery, in Roberts (ed) 2005, 127–30

Vyner, B, 2007 A Great North Route in Neolithic and Bronze Age Yorkshire: the evidence of landscape and monuments, *Landscapes* **1**, 69–84

Vyner, B, 2009 Pottery from fieldwalking and excavation, in R Daniels, The deserted medieval village of High Worsall, North Yorkshire, *Durham Archaeol J* **18**, 82–5

Vyner, B, 2011 Appendix 1: ceramics. Neolithic pottery, in Dickson and Hopkinson 2011, 237–69. Available: http://www.archaeologicalplanningconsultancy.co.uk/index.php

Vyner, B, forthcoming Report on prehistoric pottery from excavations on the A1, North Yorkshire (A1D2B), in P G Johnson (ed), *The Archaeology of the A1: Dishforth to Barton*

Waddington, C, 1997 A review of 'pit alignments' and a tentative interpretation of the Milfield complex, *Durham Archaeol J* **13**, 21–33

Waddington, C, 1999 *A landscape archaeological study of the Mesolithic-Neolithic in the Milfield Basin, Northumberland*, BAR Brit Ser **291**. Oxford: British Archaeological Reports

Waddington, C, 2001 Breaking out of the morphological straightjacket: early Neolithic enclosures in northern Britain, *Durham Archaeol J* **16**, 1–14

Wainwright, G J, 1979 *Mount Pleasant, Dorset: excavations 1970–71*, Rep Res Comm Soc Antiq London **XXXVII**. Dorking: Society of Antiquaries of London

Walker, A J, Young, A W & Otlet, R L, 1991 Harwell radiocarbon measurements X, *Radiocarbon* **33**, 87–113

Wandibba, S, 1994 Bukusu sacred sites, in Carmichael *et al* 1994, 115–20

Waterman, D M, 1951 Quernhow: a food vessel barrow in Yorkshire, *Antiq J* **XXXI**, 1–24

Watson, A, 2001 The sounds of transformation: acoustics, monuments and ritual in the British Neolithic, in N Price (ed), *The archaeology of shamanism*. London & New York: Routledge, 178–92

Wheelhouse, P, 2005 The Ritual Monuments, in Roberts (ed) 2005, 21–49

White, R, 1997 *The Yorkshire Dales: Landscapes through time*. London: English Heritage

White, T D & Folkens, P A, 2000 *Human Osteology* (2nd edition). London: Academic Trust

Whittle, A, 1997a *Sacred mound, holy rings: Silbury Hill and the West Kennet palisade enclosures. A later Neolithic complex in North Wiltshire*, Oxbow Monogr **74** & Cardiff Studies in Archaeology. Oxford: Oxbow Books

Whittle, A, 1997b Moving on and moving around: Neolithic settlement mobility, in Topping (ed) 1997, 15–22

Whittle, A & Pollard, J, 1999 The harmony of symbols: wider meanings, in A Whittle, J Pollard & C Grigson, *The harmony of symbols: the Windmill Hill causewayed enclosure*. Oxford: Oxbow Books, chapter 18

Whittle, A, Atkinson R J C, Chambers, R & Thomas, N, 1992 Excavations in the Neolithic and the Bronze Age complex at Dorchester-on-Thames, Oxfordshire, 1947–1952 and 1981, *Proc Prehist Soc* **58**, 143–202

Whittle, A, Barclay, A, Bayliss, A, McFadyen, L, Schulting, R & Wysocki, M, 2007 Building for the dead: events, processes and changing worldviews from the thirty-eighth to the thirty-fourth centuries cal. BC in southern Britain, in A Bayliss & A Whittle (eds), *Histories of the dead: building chronologies for five southern British long barrows*, Supplement of Cambridge Archaeol J **17**(1), 123–47

Williams, H, 1998 Monuments and the past in early Anglo-Saxon England, *World Archaeol* **30**(1), 90–108

Young, R, 1987 *Lithics and subsistence in north-eastern England*, BAR Brit Ser **161**. Oxford: British Archaeological Reports

Index

Entries in bold refer to the Figures